Behavior Modification Procedure

Behavior Modification Procedure
A Sourcebook

Edited by Edwin J. Thomas

Routledge
Taylor & Francis Group
LONDON AND NEW YORK

First published 1974 by Transaction Publishers

Published 2017 by Routledge
2 Park Square, Milton Park, Abingdon, Oxon OX14 4RN
711 Third Avenue, New York, NY 10017, USA

First issued in hardback 2017

Routledge is an imprint of the Taylor & Francis Group, an informa business

Library of Congress Catalog Number: 2007026107

Library of Congress Cataloging-in-Publication Data

Behavior modification procedure : a sourcebook / Edwin J. Thomas, editor.
p. cm.
Originally published: Chicago : Aldine Pub. Co., 1974.
Includes bibliographical references and index.
ISBN 978-0-202-36171-0
1. Behavior modification. I. Thomas, Edwin J. (Edwin John), 1927-

BF637.B4T47 2007
153.8'5—dc22

2007026107

ISBN 13: 978-1-138-51933-6 (hbk)
ISBN 13: 978-0-202-36171-0 (pbk)

Contents

Contributors

R. A. Aitchison
Ventura County Mental Health Department, Oxnard, California.
K. Eileen Allen
University of Washington.
Sidney W. Bijou
University of Illinois.
John J. Boren
American University.
Robert C. Branch
University of Washington.
William H. Butterfield
Washington University.
Robert D. Carter
University of Michigan.
Joseph R. Cautela
Boston College.
Arthur D. Colman
University of California, Berkeley.
William H. Cormier
University of Tennessee.
Marie Erickson
Retired, formerly with Bell County Health Center Pineville, Kentucky.
Eileen D. Gambrill
University of California, Berkeley.
Larry A. Gaupp
U. S. Army Hospital, Seoul, Korea.
Judy Kopp Green
Kansas City Regional Council for Higher Education.
Florence R. Harris
Retired, formerly with University of Wasington.
Cornelius J. Holland
University of Windsor.
James M. Johnston
Georgia State University.
Margaret S. Johnston
North Seattle Community College.
Robert Kastenbaum
Wayne State University.
Anton Kris
Private practitioner, Brookline, Massachusetts.
Edward S. Kubany
University of Hawaii.
Frank J. Landy
Pennsylvania State University.
Peter J. Lang
University of Wisconsin, Madison.
Harry Lawrence
University of Michigan.

Paul Lehrer
Rutgers University.
Robert M. Liebert
State University of New York.
Daniel L. Logan,
University of Texas.
Perry London
University of Southern California.
William R. Morrow
University of Wisconsin.
Kevin O'Flaherty
University of Michigan.
Robert F. Peterson
University of Nevada.
Spencer A. Rathus
Montclair State College, New Jersey.
Sheldon D. Rose
University of Wisconsin.
Lawrence Schiff
Tufts University.
Barbara B. Sloggett
University of Hawaii.
Michael D. Spiegler
University of Texas, Austin.
Stephen I. Sulzbacher
University of Washington.
Martin Sundel
University of Louisville, Kentucky.
Edwin J. Thomas
University of Michigan.
Robert G. Wahler
University of Tennessee.
Claude L. Walter
University of Michigan.
Joseph Wolpe
Temple University.

I

Introduction

Behavior modification has grown tremendously since the late 1950s and early 1960s when the field was taking form and gaining momentum. There is now an immense literature, an increasingly impressive body of knowledge, and numerous professionals and paraprofessionals who employ behavioral methods in clinics, social agencies, homes, schools, and institutions. The promise, rhetoric, and apologia characteristic of many of the earlier writings on behavior modification have been superseded by the more enduring contributions of disciplined practice, demonstration projects, evaluative research, and applied behavior analysis. Behavior modification can not yet be considered a mature field but it has at least survived the early years when its reception by the professional community was for the most part considerably less than cordial.

At present there are at least three identifiable components of behavior modification knowledge. These are the foundation principles, techniques of assessment, and methods of modification. Whereas the foundation principles consist largely of scientific knowledge based upon scientific inquiry such as research on operant and respondent conditioning, the techniques of assessment and modification constitute the technology of behavior modification and derive from a variety of more practical sources. The technology is of course essential to behavioral practice. No matter how much one knows about the results of evaluative studies, demonstrations, and basic research of the field, he cannot practice behavior modification successfully without a strong background in the techniques of assessment and modification.

Although knowledge is clearly being generated in all of the component areas of behavior modification, the developments of each component area have been uneven and have occurred at different rates. For example, some of the foundation principles, such as those of classical and operant conditioning, were the earliest to emerge. It was later that specialized techniques of modification, such as systematic desensitization, aversion conditioning, and systems of token exchange, were developed and applied. Techniques of assessment and of clinical, case, and program management lagged behind other areas and have only recently begun to be elaborated. It is this last area that deserves accelerated development and constitutes the principal focus of this book.

With its emphasis on procedure, this book covers a variety of technological subjects relevant to behavioral assessment and case and program management. Included here are general- and special-purpose practitioner guidelines for assessment and modification that are applicable to diverse clientele who may display any of a variety of behavioral difficulties. The volume also treats techniques of obtaining information (e.g., interviewing guidelines and styles, checklists and schedules, observation, and electromechanical devices); storing information (e.g., recording systems); processing information (e.g., rate transformations); displaying information (e.g., graphing formats); and some of the ways practitioner behavior should be guided by data collected in practice.

This book presumes that the reader already knows something about behavior modification. Specifically, the volume will serve its objectives best if the reader is familiar with the main behavioral principles, the techniques of assessment and modification, and has had or is beginning behavioral practice. For individuals with this background, the book may be employed as a sourcebook in routine clinical practice, innovative clinical practice, practice combined with research, and in selected areas of behavior modification research. The book may also be used as a text on procedure for those who have the requisite background.

The first selection is "The End of Ideology in Behavior Modification," by Perry London. This article is an appropriate introductory selection because it emphasizes the importance of technology and procedure at this point in the history of the field. The central thesis is that it is time for behavior modification to build a domain, to develop operational procedures, and to sharpen its techniques and equipment. For example, London asserts the following: "I am saying that theory has worn itself out in behavior modification and that technology, especially of treatment, should now be the primary focus, perhaps, in the long range, even for serving scientific purposes." London has written a strongly worded and provocative piece. The reader may or may not agree with London's points that the early stages of the development of behavior modification involve mainly the political enterprise of using theory as rhetoric for purposes of ideology, that there actually aren't very many principles of behavior modification anyway, that in any case there is more ideology than theory, that behavior modification is basically a technology, and that what passes for theory in behavior modification has been largely metaphor and paradigm. In any event, if London is correct, the field of behavior modification is about to embark upon a new era, one in which technology and procedure will be the order of the day.

1

PERRY LONDON

The End of Ideology in Behavior Modification

When little "behavior modifiers" sit at their professional daddies' knees and ask, "Where did I come from?" they are usually told a story about the "principles of learning" that spawned them, the evil clinicians who left them to perish on a hillside, and the kindly shepherd doctors who found them, raised them as their own, and eventually restored them to their rightful position as the benefactors of behavior. When they grow up, confer their own benefits, and spawn their own little behavior modifiers, they became disabused of the myth. But not entirely—there remains, at the very least, a tradition of deferring to the principles of learning as the ultimate source of all good modifications and a parallel ritual of knocking psychoanalysts, Rogerians, existentialists, and general psychiatrists who have not yet mastered or endorsed the jargon of respondents, operants, and reinforcements.

Like most myths, this tale has been based on some true events and has proved useful for the promotion of behavioristic patriotism and for extending the frontiers of experimentation and the clinical and technical growth of the field. And it makes a good story. But enough is enough. The borders are secure now, the settlers are thriving, the dark untrammeled forests are trammeled and cut down, the stumps blown, the fields plowed. It is time now to build this domain, not defend it.

Building it requires three things: first, abandoning strife with other modalities and developing peaceful commerce to see what they have to offer and exchange; second, examining the constructs that underlie modifying operations and that give clues for the design of new ones; and finally, devoting ourselves to "criterion validity," that is, to building treatment methods that

From *The American Psychologist,* Vol. 27, No. 10, October 1972, pp. 913–920.

work. The entire field has been moving in these directions during the past few years, but only partly I think, as a result of the intelligent pressures of people making these recommendations. The shift results also from technological changes in related disciplines and from attitude changes in the entire society that supports them. New equipment brings new possibilities for use and a new social readiness to use it, and the speed with which it gets advertised and talked about pushes advances in practice that no theory is likely to keep up with. This article argues that it is probably just as well.

For public purposes, behavior modifiers of the 1960s usually described their activities as logically inevitable corollaries of theorems or principles of learning and of ongoing discoveries about how they applied to disordered human behavior. Actually, there were only about three principles that they ever referred to, all of which can be reduced to one or one and a half principles—namely, that learning depends on the connections in time, space, and attention between what you do and what happens to you subsequently (Franks, 1969; Lazarus, 1971). In addition, the special application to human behavior was predicated less on ongoing scientific discoveries about learning or about people than on the idea that human neuroses are probably about the same as animal neuroses (Wolpe, 1958). The critical principles of learning involved had all been spelled out rather elaborately between 1898 and 1938, and the business about animal neuroses was posited by Pavlov in the same period. During that period, in fact, Pavlov, Watson, Jones, Mowrer, and Guthrie pretty much spelled out all of the major behavior therapy methods that became popular for treating people since 1958, with the possible exception of desensitization and operant behavior shaping (London, 1964). And they are exceptions only because the former is not derived from the usual learning principles, and cannot be, and because the latter is something everybody knew about anyhow but never applied ingeniously until Skinner laboriously spelled out its monumental implications.

Evolution of Behavior Modification

The early growth of behavior modification as a professional specialty was largely polemical and political, not theoretical, and most of its scientific hoopla evolved to serve the polemical needs of the people who made it up—not all of it, however, and not only polemical needs.

The study of learning for behavior therapists, in fact, was always more for the purpose of metapor, paradigm, and analogy than for strict guidance about how to operate or about what it all means. Whatever value theory may have for dictating laboratory procedures, therapeutic operations have been essentially seat-of-the-pants affairs, and still are, because they address immediate practical problems that require solutions in fact, not in principle. The disregarding of principles to see what really works, in this connection, reflects the intelligence and scientific good sense of therapists. The search for principles to explain what works, on the other hand, reflects their integrity and their anxiety—integrity because only fools would accept their own results without question, anxiety because therapists seek principles as much to increase their confidence as to reduce their ignorance. People also look for principles to help fight intellectual battles. Conventional therapies could be assaulted for their ineffectiveness, but the basis for offering new ones had to be more than complaints about the old ones. And in the case of behavior modification, it had to be more than a simplistic appeal to "what works." Of all popular therapies, psychoanalysis in particular was based on a pretentious, respectable, and smart *theory*. It could not be challenged with less than a theory.

Learning theory was an obvious choice: first, because there is a history of suggested therapeutic applications of learning principles, from Thorndike and Pavlov through Mowrer and Guthrie; and second, because the heart of any *psycho*therapy is changing people's behavior without changing their body structure or gross functions—which means, in plain language, teaching them and getting them to learn.

Even so, the evolution of behavior modification did not go so neatly. It could not make much use of learning theory, except for the broadest principles of learning, because most of the principles either do not yet have any really systematic application to disorders, or because they are much more in dispute than naive students realize.

The polemics actually used attacked evident flaws in psychoanalytic and other psychiatric formulations, sometimes also getting a little professional jealousy of psychologists for doctors into the act. Their main points were (*a*) an attack on "the medical model"; (*b*) the insistence that the origins of disorder were in *learning* instead of biochemical or genetic events; (*c*) the proposition that effective therapeutics should treat symptoms instead of their causes, that is, that disorders are identical with their symptoms; and finally, (*d*) the demand that even the name of the game should be changed from psychotherapy to behavior therapy, so no one thinks we are mentalistic or unscientific, as other therapies obviously are (sic).

This description is not exaggerated at all. Eysenck's (1959) tabulation of "the more important differences between Freudian Psychotherapy and Behavior Therapy," for instance, says that Freudian therapy is "based on inconsistent theory never properly formulated in postulate form," while behavior therapy is "based on consistent, properly formulated theory leading to testable deductions." Similarly, Freudian practice is "derived from clinical observations made without necessary control, observation or experiment," while behavior therapy is "derived from experimental studies specifically designed to test basic theory and deductions made therefrom [p. 67]." Franks (1969) is kinder than Eysenck, but even he says, a decade later, "for most behavior therapists, the preferred sequence of events is from experimental observation to clinical practice. This may be contrasted with the approach of traditional psychotherapists, in which the sequence is often reversed [p. 3]."

These arguments are not entirely pointless, but they are not entirely apropos of anything either, except who is smart and who will get the last word. What makes them largely irrelevant is that explanatory concepts are only necessary to explain what is going on—and until you know that, you do not need a theory, at least not much of one. Such theory, at this point in this enterprise, has to be stretched to fit facts rather than tailored to them. And it is damaging in the long run because people may start believing it and making up nonsense to plead silly cases that confuse everybody and enlighten no one. Enormous time and space have been wasted in pious debates on irrelevant aspects of most of the popular polemic issues of psychotherapy.

Discussions of "the medical model," for instance, often contrast "learning theory" approaches to "psychodynamic" approaches. There is a real question about the relative utility of *organic* versus *dynamic* perspectives on some behavior disorders, but all learning theory formulations are, in fact, dynamic ones. Also, there are many medical models, and the general attack on "the" medical model is only applicable to the *infectious disease* model, and only usable against psychoanalysis by lamely borrowing against Freud's (1961) unfortunate statement about putting demonology inside people's heads. Medical *epidemiological* models should have some appeal to Skinnerians, in fact, with their emphasis on environmental determinants of disorder, just as psychological models of habit formation are good for understanding the course of some developmental or degenerative medical conditions like heart disease.

The controversy about (learned versus structural) origins of disorder is mostly pointless because it is mostly irrelevant to treatment. The behaviorist attack commonly assumes that a genetic or biochemical view of etiology is bad because if disorder is learned, then treatment must be a learning process. This is nonsense. Etiology and treatment have no logical connection in either direction. Anxiety, for example, may be the result of prior experience, but can be alleviated chemically: or it may be aroused by essentially chemical circumstances (like fatigue plus mild arousal to danger), but can be soothed physically or verbally (Davison, 1968).

The only treatment question of relevance is that of the functional relationship between the problem and its solution. The process is what matters and nothing else.

The biggest polemic, of course, about treating symptoms versus causes has occurred largely because of the uncertain danger of symptom return or symptom substitution. Everywhere, much confusion has occurred, mostly because of confusion about the "medical model"—in this instance, about the exact meaning of symptom. If symptom means trouble, surely it should be treated. If not, maybe not. The polemic has been around the question of symptoms as "the main trouble"; this is because of the widespread belief, largely from psychoanalysis, in symptom return or substitution. (Buchwald and Young [1969] point out, incidentally, that some analysts, such as Fenichel and, later, Alexander, thought that symptoms should be treated directly.)

The real issue, in any case, is the consequence of the treatment for the person's condition—or his life. Sometimes too, the issue is prophylactic or preventive rather than ameliorative. This becomes clear by comparing the infectious disease and chronic ailment models in medicine. Behavior disorders are more like chronic ailments, where medical treatment generally aims at the symptoms only. The control of diabetes, on the other hand, is not treatment of symptoms, but their prevention. Is the shaping of behavior likewise? For changing the table manners of psychotics' ward behavior, maybe not; for molding children's manners, maybe so. The same question may be addressed to assertive training or to aversion training. Is teaching someone to talk back to his mother-in-law "reducing his anxiety" or preventing it from happening? Is teaching a homosexual man to attend to women when aroused and to feel repugnance for sex with men relieving his symptom or preventing a disorder (which does not exist legally until he "goes for" the man), teaching a habit pattern or unteaching one, changing a life style, altering a phenomenological field, shifting ego boundaries, redirecting id impulses or superego functions, or cathexis? And if he "feels" different or thinks about it differently, is it still behavior therapy?

These are silly questions. The change in the homosexual is all those things, depending on how you want to talk about them. Understanding the process is what matters, not belaboring the different styles of talking about it. The only important question about systematic treatment is that of the simultaneous relevance of the treatment technique to the person's manifest trouble and to the rest of his life.

Sometimes it accounts for both at once—as when he is suicidal. Sometimes it accounts for the rest of his life but not for the symptom—which is the behavior modifier's claim against insight types' preoccupation with motivation. Sometimes it accounts for only the manifest trouble—which is the insight therapists' accusation against behavior modifiers, based on the specious presumption that everything in a person's life is integral to it.

All of these polemics were not so much meaningless as overdone. The assault on psychoanalysts and existentialists was too extreme; the scientific claims on learning were too grandiose (Buchwald and Young, 1969; Franks, 1969). Changing from psychotherapy to behavior therapy may have been useful for people brought up on mind-body dualism, but for those of us who always thought the mind hung around the brain and that behavior meant "what happened," the distinction was graceless and gratuitous.

When you eliminate the polemics and politics and gratuities, however, what remains of theory to define the field and to tell you what it is about? Not a whole lot. The definition of the field either becomes very inclusive

(Lazarus, 1971; Marks, 1971; Marston, 1970; Paul, 1969; Skinner, 1971) of very narrow (Eysenck, 1960; Skinner, 1963; Wolpe, 1968). This probably makes no serious difference to anything. As Kuhn (1962) said, "Can a definition tell a man whether he is a scientist or not [p. 160]?"

But what about theory? If behavior modification lacks theory, then is it not reduced to a technology rather than a science? Yes it is, and I believe that is what it should be, just as medicine is technology rather than science.

There is some dispute in the field about this point. The sides are well represented by Lazarus, who agrees with my view, and Franks, who does not. Lazarus (1971) said, in his latest book:

> The emphasis of the volume is upon techniques rather than upon theories. . . . Methods of therapy are often effective for reasons which are at variance with the views of their inventors or discoverers. Technical eclecticism (Lazarus, 1967) does not imply a random melange of techniques taken haphazardly out of the air. It is an approach which urges therapists to experiment with empirically useful methods instead of using their theories as a priori predictors of what will and will not succeed in therapy (Eysenck, 1957, p. 271). The rationale behind the methods described in this book is predicated upon London's (1964) observation that: "However interesting, plausible, and appealing a theory may be, it is techniques, not theories, that are actually used on people. Study of the effect of psychotherapy, therefore, is always the study of the effectiveness of techniques" [p. 33].

Franks (1969) argued, to the contrary:

> It would seem to be highly desirable for the therapist to aspire to be a scientist even if this goal were difficult to realize. To function as a scientist, it is necessary to espouse some theoretical framework. For reasons too obvious to detail here, this is true of the behavioral therapist. . . . How the behavior therapist practices (including his choice of technique, his approach to the problems of general strategy, and his specific relationships with his patient) thus depending both upon his explicit theoretical orientation and upon his implicit philosophical and cultural milieu [p. 21].

The argument that behavior modification should view itself as technology rather than as science is not meant to denigrate the importance of theory, either scientifically or heuristically. Scientifically, theory is valuable because it directs the systematic search for new information by interpreting and integrating what is already known. Heuristically, theory is valuable because it lays our biases out in the open and, by explicating them, makes it easier for us to disavow them when they are found to be inadequate.

The question with respect to behavior modification is twofold: First, is current theory very good (scientifically) in this case? Second, is any theory very useful for the current development of this field at this time? I think the answer to both questions is no.

In reality, behavior therapists never did have so much a theory as an "ideology"; in my own paraphrase of Bell (1960) and Tomkins (1964), "Ideology does not mean just ideas, but ideas to be acted on . . . [London, 1969]." What behavior therapists called theory actually served as bases for commitment or a rallying point for talking about disorder and treatment in a certain way and, more important, about acting on it within particular sets of limited operations, that is, technical limits. In this case, the commitment is to the *functional analysis of problems.* And it is for this reason that the domain incorporated within the legitimate purview of the field becomes broader and broader and the polemics milder and milder—as it is recognized that even Rogerians and humanists and psychoanalysts may analyze some things functionally and act on them accordingly.

What results from the increasing functional analysis of problems is an increasing number of plausible methods for coping with them—until the proliferation of methods is tested and found to work, no theory is really very necessary to explain *why* they work. For practitioners, none may be needed even then, if they work well. In any case, theory will largely grow from practice (Lazarus and Davison, 1971) and practice from instrumentation, in the broadest sense; this will happen to behavior modification just like it did to psychoanalysis, but with two generations' more experience, the results, hopefully, will be more scientific.

The status of theory comes largely from the belief that technique develops out of theory, that is, that science underlies engineering. But this is only partly true even among very "hard" sciences, less so among "soft" sciences, like the social and behavioral sciences, and not at all true for many endeavors where the existence of the technological capacity and the practical need is what produces the technical application and, indeed, what "nourishes" much of the theoretical development itself (Oppenheimer, 1956).

This does not mean that the alternative to rude theory is rude empiricism; rather, it suggests a close-to-the-situation functional analysis instead of a premature and precocious search for general principles from which to get overextended, or for a professional ideology to which to be committed. Such a development seems to be proceeding now, with practitioners using the techniques of behavior modification but declining the identity (Paul, 1969b), and scholars recommending heterodoxies like "technical electicism" without shame (Lazarus, 1971). The rest of the article spells out what this development means, so we will see clearly what we are doing, with the view to doing it better.

By deducing the intellectual condition of behavior modification from the technology it uses, there seem to be two kinds of conceptual schemes which characterize it. Borrowing from Price's (1971) book, *Abnormal Psychology: Perspectives in Conflict,* in turn derived from Kuhn's (1962) *Structure of Scientific Revolutions,* these are first, *metaphors* or analogies, and second, *paradigms* or models.

In the conventional classification of how much we seem to know what we are talking about in science, these concepts fit the lower end of the scale of certainty whose upper rungs are called "theories" and "laws." A scientific law, in other words, is an idea that seems absolutely to comprehend all of the facts it talks about; a theory is one that hopes to do so, but is not so compellingly known to do so. The activities involved in behavior modification are a good distance below both those points on the same continuum. A few are paradigms or models, that is, ideas that seem to explain a group of facts pretty precisely; most are metaphors or analogies, that is, ideas that look like they might fit a group of facts, where there is no clear evidence that they really do.

In general, the treatment methods derived from speculations about conditioning studies of animals are metaphorical or analogous, especially desensitization and implosion, or flooding. In general, the treatment methods that fall under the heading of education or training or, in jargon, of instrumental learning are paradigmatic or exemplary, including modeling, shaping, and possibly aversion techniques.

The difference between the metaphoric and the paradigmatic treatments is not how well they work, but only in how well their workings are understood. This, in turn, reduces to how much of the mechanics involved can be predicted or explained with what degree of precision, which reduces still further to how many of the details are visible or can be inferred with different degrees of correlation. For practical purposes, the difference is simply one of the extent to which you can see what is going on enough to figure out how variations in your approach will affect it. The more you can peer intellectually into the "black box," in other words, and the prediction proves correct, the more you are dealing with a paradigm rather than a metaphor. A paradigm, in other words, is an attempt to construct a direct model or example of how something works. A metaphor is a more oblique comparison, in which the flaws in the analogy are obvious, but the similarities are still big enough to allow us to ask whether the comparison might "work."

Desensitization is only a metaphor or analogy to conditioning: first, because it involves a specific cognitive process (the use of language) that classical conditioning does not; second, because it involves a mechanism of sequential imagination that can only be guessed at from conditioning studies; and third, because it is subject to a variety of successful variations that could not be predicted from the situations from which the metaphor was derived in the first place. Finally, desensitization does the same thing that implosion or flooding does, though it appears to be an opposite method.

Implosion is a better analogy than desensitization because Stampfl's original experiment (London, 1964) seems to parallel both Mowrer's (1950) theoretical statement, Solomon, Kamin, and Wynne's (1953), and Black's (1958) animal experiments more closely than Wolpe fits Masserman's cats or Pavlov's dogs. Also, implosion technique does predict all of its own variants—including Watson, Gaind, and Marks' (1971) finding that practice helps to extinguish phobic reactions and that using real objects instead of imagination as fearful stimuli also is helpful—but it is metaphorical nonetheless because it is between people, and because it is administered in social situations where the pressure *not* to escape is obviously coming from the thoughts that the patient has about the situation, not from physical restraints on his action.

Shaping is more exemplary or paradigmatic than conditioning treatments because it presumes less, in the first place, on the black box—modeling, likewise. Stated differently, both shaping and modeling methods can aim for precision in establishing the conditions that will work the desired effects without having to worry much about what is going on in the person that makes them work. *Aversion* treatment is more paradigmatic than metaphoric because its critical stimulus is not cognitive; that is, it hurts the patient physically. Giving a person an electric shock is much more like shocking a dog than telling scary stories to a person is like blowing air up a rat's behind; ergo, it is more paradigmatic than metaphoric.

Neither metaphors nor paradigms are scientific theories by some distance, but both of them are useful intellectual tools. *Metaphor* and *analogy* are good heuristically—they help to turn images into thoughts and inchoate hunches into articulate propositions. *Paradigms* are more literally useful—they model to scale what you need to do, or give a mathematical formula into which you can put specific quanta.

Notice, however, that none of this has anything to do with whether anything works for any practical problem. Desensitization may be a poor deduction from conditioning, but it is a fine treatment for phobias. Behavior shaping may be an excellent paradigm for getting autistic children to hug people, but it does not teach them syntactical speech.

Whatever scientific concern people have about the intellectual status of the field, at this point in the development of this enterprise, none of this material is yet very important to practitioners, and it is barely important to clinical research. What *is* important, at this juncture, is the development of systematic practice and of a technology to sustain it. My thesis is that, in the long run, scientific understanding will derive from them.

The practitioner tries to figure out what will work, for the most part, and then, if he is scientifically inclined, looks for a way to rationalize it if it does. The technologist devises machinery to support him. This is not a bad idea, even if it doesn't add up to test-tube-pure, white-coat science. Systematic desensitization is a good example of this process because, by "working" in the first place, it has given rise to technological refinements of itself that also work and that still leave the reasons unexplained. In the long run, this must force better and better logical and experimental confrontations with the reasons for the phenomenon—which success alone would not have done.

New equipment, new drugs, new gimmickry and gadgetry should now be the basis for systematically developing new methods of behavior modification and for streamlining the established techniques with controlled experimental testing. Instead of looking for new principles, or justifying worn-out ones, we should look for new applications: What could we do to treat such-and-such if we had such-and-such machinery? What would be required to build it? To test it? And then, finally, to determine what it means?

The critical point is that *good technology always undermines bad theory.* "Bad" is not meant to be pejorative here; it means metaphoric. Precise technology reveals the empirical error in metaphoric reasoning and in the operations that result from it. So Lang's (1969a, 1969b) on-line computer removes the therapist from the desensitization process; Quirk's (1970) machine removes the imagining and the relevance of the phobic subject matter; and Wolpin's (Jacobs and Wolpin, 1971; Wolpin, 1969; Wolpin and Raines, 1966) removes the need for hypnosis, for the fear hierarchy, and, indeed, for relaxation. Since the method still works, the need for explanation becomes more and more apparent (Davison, 1969), as does the inadequacy of the very plausible metaphor that launched Wolpe (1958) on the whole business.

Technology promises, in fact, more and more to turn metaphor to paradigm, if not paradigm to theory, by going directly into the black box and doing funny things to it and, increasingly, by bringing the black box out into the open where we can see more and more what has been happening in it. For the former, I refer to drug research and to the work in progress on electrical stimulation of the brain (Cohen, 1969; Delgado, 1969; London, 1969). These activities undercut specious distinctions between learned and unlearned patterns, either by manipulating the patterns out of hand or by potentiating learning so effectively that the issue of its importance disappears.

Bringing the black box out into the open is one of the main results likely to accrue from *biofeedback* research, and it is probably the best illustration one can find of technology feeding science with one hand as it enhances practice with the other. All of the biofeedback methods work on a single principle, whether they teach people to ring buzzers from a switch in their heads or to alter their blood pressure or heartbeat or skin resistance by monitoring lights and gauges. The principle is finding a means of accurately externally recording some internal process, then of projecting that record into the person's consciousness so that he can literally see or hear what his blood vessels or brain waves or heart muscles are doing. Then let him learn to manipulate his conscious sensory experience in whatever way people learn to do anything consciously—something about which we really know next to nothing.

The clinical value of biofeedback methods remains to be seen and will certainly not be what alpha-machine hucksters seem to wish—instant cool for overheated psyches. Its clinical utility is not yet the point, only its technological sophistication and the scientific potential that comes from that.

To turn the point around, I am saying that theory has worn itself out in behavior modification and that technology, essentially of treatment, should now be a primary focus, perhaps, in the long range, even for serving scientific purposes. What began with the Mowrers' quilted pad in 1938 is extending now into therapeutic on-line computers, electric potty chairs, electronic skin braille, and an almost self-generating brace of valuable hardware for therapeutic purposes. A summary of much of it has appeared in a book by Robert and Ralph Schwitzgebel (1973) entitled *Psychotechnology.*

But the proper development that I am suggesting is not limited to hardware and is not self-generating, but reaches to the systematic exploration of all kinds of therapeutic things without inhibition or concern as to whether they fit ostensible *principles* of learning, or reinforcement, or whatever, but with a singular focus on whether they fit the *facts* of human experience. No one has been more forthright or resourceful in this connection than Lazarus (1971), whose latest work, *Behavior Therapy and Beyond,* goes into such things as imagery exercises for depression; thought control, straight out, for whatever it works for; hypnosis for all kinds of things; exaggerated role taking à la the late George Kelly; differential relaxation; covert sensitization for aversive imaging; and Masters and Johnson's penis squeezing for premature ejaculation. It would take a genius or a madman to shelter this whole array of techniques under the intellectual umbrella of conditioning, or learning, or any other single psychological theory. It would take a fool to want to. The first issue, scientifically as well as clinically, is the factual one—Do they work? On whom? When? The how and why come later.

With the era of polemics virtually ended, and Skinner (1971) citing Freud over and over again in his latest work, and the American Psychoanalytic Association at a recent convention casually incorporating behavior modification into its discourses on psychotherapy, the political utility of learning theory, so called for the definition of the field, is ended. It was never really theory anyhow, as we used it, but ideology for professional purposes and mostly metaphor for clinical ones. It is time now, I think, for the remedial branch of this business to stop worrying about its scientific pretensions, in the theoretical sense, as long as it keeps its functional nose clean, and to devise a kind of engineering subsidiary, or more precisely, a systems analysis approach to its own operations. We have gotten about as much mileage as we are going to out of old principles, even correct ones, but we have barely begun to work the new technology.

NOTE

1. Oppenheimer (1956) distinguished analogy from metaphor because the "structural similarity" of analogous events implies more precision in their comparison than is ordinarily true of metaphoric comparisons. I am putting them together here, however, to distinguish them both from paradigm.

References

Bell, D. *End of ideology: Exhaustion of political ideas in the fifties*. Glencoe, Ill.: Free Press, 1960.

Black, A. H. The extinction of avoidance responses under curare. *Journal of Comparative and Physiological Psychology*, 1958, *51*, 519–524.

Buchwald, A. M., and Young, R. D. Some comments on the foundations of behavior therapy. In C. M. Franks (Ed.), *Behavior therapy: Appraisal and status*. New York: McGraw-Hill, 1969.

Cohen, S. I. Neurobiological considerations for behavior therapy. In C. M. Franks (Ed.), *Behavior therapy: Appraisal and status*. New York: McGraw-Hill, 1969.

Davison, G. C. Systematic desensitization as a counter-conditioning process. *Journal of Abnormal Psychology*, 1968, *73*, 91–99.

Davison, G. C. A procedural critique of "desensitization and the experimental reduction of threat." *Journal of Abnormal Psychology*, 1969, *74*, 86–87.

Delgado, J. M. R. *Physical control of the mind*. New York: Harper and Row, 1969.

Eysenck, H. J. Learning theory and behavior therapy. *Journal of Mental Science*, 1959, *105*, 61–75.

Eysenck, H. J. (Ed.) *Behavior therapy and neuroses*. London: Pergamon Press, 1960.

Franks, C. M. *Behavior therapy: Appraisal and status*. New York: McGraw-Hill, 1969.

Freud, S. *The standard edition of the complete psychological works of Sigmund Freud*. London: Hogarth Press, 1961.

Jacobs, A. and Wolpin, M. A second look at systematic desensitization. In *Psychology of private events*. New York: Academic Press, 1971.

Kuhn, T. S. *The structure of scientific revolutions*. Chicago: University of Chicago Press, 1962.

Lang, P. J. The mechanics of desensitization and the laboratory study of human fear. In C. M. Franks (Ed.), *Behavior therapy*. New York: McGraw-Hill, 1969. (a)

Lang, P. J. The on-line computer in behavior therapy research. *American Psychologist*, 1969, *24*, 236–239. (b)

Lazarus, A. A. *Behavior therapy and beyond*. New York: McGraw-Hill, 1971.

Lazarus, A. A. and Davison, G. C. Clinical innovation in research and practice. In A. E. Bergin and S. L. Garfield (Eds.), *Handbook of psychotherapy and behavior change*. New York: Wiley, 1971.

London, P. *The modes and morals of psychotherapy*. New York: Holt, Rinehart and Winston, 1964.

London, P. *Behavior control*. New York: Harper and Row, 1969.

Marks, I. M. The future of the psychotherapies. *British Journal of Psychiatry*, 1971, *118*, 69–73.

Marston, A. Parables for behavior therapists. Address given to Southern California Behavior Modification Conference, Los Angeles, October 1970.

Mower, O. H. *Learning theory and personality dynamics*. New York: Ronald Press, 1950.

Oppenheimer, R. Analogy in science. *American Psychologist*, 1956, *11*, 127–135.

Paul, G. L. Behavior modification research: Design and tactics. In C. M. Franks

(Ed.), *Behavior therapy: Appraisal and status.* New York: McGraw-Hill, 1969. (a)

PAUL, G. L. Outcome of systematic desensitization: II. Controlled investigations of individual treatment, technique variations and current status. In C. M. Franks (Ed.), *Behavior therapy.* New York: McGraw-Hill, 1969. (b)

PRICE, R. *Abnormal psychology: Positions in perspective.* New York: Holt, Rinehart and Winston, in press.

QUIRK, D. A. *Stimulus conditioned autonomic response suppression: A behavioral therapy.* Toronto: University of Toronto, Clarke Institute of Psychiatry, 1970.

SCHWITZGEBEL, R. L., and SCHWITZGEBEL, R. K. *Psychotechnology.* New York: Holt, Rinehart and Winston, 1973.

SKINNER, B. F. Behaviorism at fifty. *Science,* 1963, *140,* 951–958.

SKINNER, B. F. *Beyond freedom and dignity.* New York: Knopf, 1971.

SOLOMON, R. L., KAMIN, L. J., and WYNNE, L. C. Traumatic avoidance learning: The outcomes of several extinction procedures with dogs. *Journal of Abnormal and Social Psychology,* 1953, *48,* 291–302.

TOMKINS, S. The psychology of knowledge. Invited address to Division 8 presented at the meeting of the American Psychological Association, Los Angeles, September 7, 1964.

WATSON, J. P., GAIND, R., and MARKS, I. M. Prolonged exposure: A rapid treatment for phobias. *British Medical Journal,* 1971, *1,* 13–15.

WOLPE, J. *Psychotherapy by reciprocal inhibition.* Stanford: Stanford University Press, 1958.

WOLPIN, M. Guided imagining to reduce avoidance behavior. *Psychotherapy: Theory, Research and Practice,* 1969, *6,* 122–124.

WOLPIN, M., and RAINES, J. Visual imagery, expected roles and extinction as possible factors in reducing fear and avoidance behavior. *Behavior Research and Therapy,* 1966, *4,* 25–37.

II

General Procedural Guidelines

Guidelines for Practice with Individuals and Families

The procedural guidelines presented in this section represent an endeavor to specify the generic activities of the behavior modifier involved in assessment and modification. These guidelines consist mainly of recommended, step-wise practice activities, such as contract formulation, specification, baselining, determination of possible controlling conditions, and monitoring. These activities are intended to assist the behavior modifier in collecting information and in making decisions about modification. The guidelines constitute an essential type of information for practice which are less abstract and general than the principles of learning and behavior therapy, on the one hand, and more widely applicable than the very specialized techniques of assessment and modification, on the other. The guidelines may be employed with a wide variety of problems and clientele in open-service settings, such as those found in outpatient clinics, family agencies, mental health clinics, child guidance clinics, and community mental health centers. Most of the steps of these procedures may also be adapted to work with individuals in closed settings, such as mental hospitals and correctional facilities. It has only been in recent years that attention has been given to such guidelines, and one may anticipate that there will be increasing emphasis upon the development, explication, and refinement of such general procedures.

Despite some similarities, the procedures included here should not necessarily be thought of as equally suitable to accomplish given practice objectives. Although the many differences among these sets of guidelines can be discerned best by carefully studying them, several distinctive features are noted here. Lindsley's procedure, as reported by Green and Morrow in their article entitled "Precision Social Work: General Model and Illustrative Projects with Clients," requires the fewest number of steps. Lindsley's procedure pertains mainly to operant behavior and employs essentially operant techniques that may be implemented by paraprofessionals and parents. Much of the above also characterizes the procedures employed in the program described by Wahler and Erickson in their paper entitled "Child Behavior Therapy: A Community Program in Appalachia," except that there is a particular division of labor between the professional and the volunteer. The professional conducts the initial interview with the clients and, later, with the assistance of the volunteer, formulates and institutes a program of modification. The volunteer, on the other hand, works essentially under the supervision of the professional in carrying out home observation and following the modification plan with the clients.

The guidelines described by Gambrill, Thomas, and Carter in their "Procedure for Sociobehavioral Practice in Open Settings" involvė the most number of steps (twelve) and also specify selected recurring activities associated with assessment and modification. These more detailed guidelines should generally yield a large amount of information. Problems mainly involving respondent behavioral components, as well as operant features, may be addressed with this framework, and the planning for modification would make it possible to draw upon any behavior modification technique, not just operant techniques.

A method of field experimental research by Bijou, Peterson, Harris and Allen, entitled "Methodology for Experimental Studies of Young Children in Natural Settings," is a general operant method applicable as a practice procedure to many behavioral difficulties encountered in natural settings. The paper covers the approach of the functional analysis of behavior which includes the definition of response events, aspects of single-case design, baselining and monitoring, the initiation, temporary cessation and reinstatement of the intervention, and the interpretation of possible functional relationships. Thanks to the great impact that operant researchers have had upon behavior modification, these topics are now as much the concern of the general behavior modification practitioner as they are of the behavioral researcher.

Other procedures not included for discussion in this part should be mentioned also. The guidelines of Tharp and Wetzel (1969) are generally widely applicable. Their framework is essentially an operant one in which paraprofessional behavior analysts, with professional guidance and supervision, carry out assessment and modification in the natural environment.

Wolpe (1969) has described selected general procedures as well as those related to specific modification techniques, such as systematic desensitization. Somewhat more specialized procedures are those of Watson and Tharp (1972) on self control; Patterson (1971) on parent training and child management; Salzinger, Feldman, and Portney (1970) on parent training in operant conditioning procedures; and Browning and Stover (1971) and Schaefer and Martin (1969) on behavioral procedures applicable in closed institutions.

Attention in the selections included here has been given only to the more general procedural guidelines generic to work with many different problems. These guidelines, again, should be clearly distinguished from the numerous specialized modification procedures such as systematic desensitization, covert sensitization, aversive conditioning, and token economies.

Guidelines for Practice with Groups

The use of groups to assist in the modification of behavior has long been a promising approach for many practitioners. Much of the promise stems from studies of sociologists and psychologists, who have amply documented the capability of groups to alter member behavior, and from the belief that groups may sometimes facilitate more efficient service. The use of groups in psychotherapy and in group therapy has of course antedated the application of behavioral methods in groups. Although procedures that may be employed in groups are less developed than those applicable to individuals and families, group procedures in which behavioral methods are employed have been receiving increasing attention.

Examination of the application of behavioral methods to groups indicates that there are at least four distinguishable types of procedure. In the first the members essentially coact in response to what is generally a common set of stimuli, much as if they were members of an audience. Members do not function as modification agents for one another. The leader generally dispenses the modification stimuli, and the group serves largely as a context for the application of a modification method directed at each person individually. This is perhaps best illustrated by the use of systematic desensitization in group settings for patients with anxiety reactions. A group of individuals with a similar problem is generally taken simultaneously through the steps of a desensitization program. Thus, acrophobia, claustrophobia, and impotence have been worked with by Lazarus (1961); impotence and frigidity were addressed in another study by Lazarus (1968); spider phobias were addressed by Rachman (1965, 1966); interpersonal performance anxiety was worked on by Paul and Shannon (1966) and Paul (1968); test anxiety by Katahn et al. (1966); and snake phobia by Shannon and Wolff (1967). Group process is minimal here and the modification is largely an individual technique applied simultaneously to a group of persons.

A second type of group procedure involves the use of the leader to apply behavioral principles in order to affect group processes and dynamics—

primarily to alter the within-group behavior of interacting group members. For example, there may be the preplanned use of therapist approval and attention to affect such behaviors as member participation (Shapiro and Birk, 1967), or the therapist's use of reinforcement for intermember expressions of group cohesiveness (Liberman, 1970, 1972).

A third variety of group procedure is to employ group contingencies to modify selected behaviors that may be displayed in the group. There have been several recent studies that demonstrate the efficacy of group approaches to the classroom modification of out-of-seat and talking behavior (Barrish, Saunders, and Wolf, 1969), excessive sound intensity (Schmidt and Ulrich, 1969), and not paying attention (Packard, 1970). In these studies, a group contingency is applied for a performance requirement involving most or all individuals in the group.

The fourth type of group procedure is perhaps the most ambitious and challenging in that both the leader as well as the members are active in modification and efforts are made to change member behavior in the group as well as outside it. Although this use of groups in principle exploits more fully the capability of the group to modify behavior, special problems with the guidance and coordination of member behavior are typically encountered. Leader and member behavior must be harnessed so that the procedures they implement or mediate serve to accelerate prosocial behavior of members and do not strengthen deviant or problem behavior. The two group procedures included here are examples of this last type of group procedure.

In the selection by Rose entitled "A Behavioral Approach to the Group Treatment of Parents" the focus is on teaching parents skills of child management. In contrast, the selection by Lawrence and Sundel entitled "Behavior Modification in Adult Groups" presents guidelines to work on individual, marital, and parent-child problems of adults. In addition to providing education in behavioral methods, both procedures offer a variety of training experiences, advocate the use of behavioral assignments outside of the group, and enlist fellow group members and the leader in completing the assessment, planning for modification, and monitoring outcomes.

References

Barrish, H. H., Saunders, M., and Wolf, M. M. Good behavior game: Effects of individual contingencies for group consequences on disruptive behavior in a classroom. *Journal of Applied Behavior Analysis*, 1969, *2*, 119–124.

Browning, R. M., and Stover, D. O. *Behavior modification in child treatment: An experimental and clinical approach.* Chicago: Aldine-Atherton, 1971.

Katahn, M., Stranger, S., and Cherry, N. Group counseling and behaviour therapy with test anxious college students. *Journal of Consulting Psychology*, 1966, *30*, 544–549.

Lazarus, A. A. Group therapy of phobic disorders by systematic desensitization. *Journal of Abnormal and Social Psychology*, 1961, *63*, 504–510.

LAZARUS, A. A. Behavior therapy in groups. In G. M. Gazda (Ed.), *Basic approaches to group psychotherapy and counseling*. Springfield, Illinois: Charles C. Thomas, 1968.

LIBERMAN, R. A behavioral approach to group dynamics: 1. Reinforcement and prompting of cohesiveness in group therapy. *Behavior therapy,* 1970, *1,* 141–175.

LIBERMAN, R. Behavioral methods in group and family therapy. *Seminars in Psychiatry,* 1972, 145–156.

PACKARD, R. G. The control of "classroom attention": a group contingency for complex behavior. *Journal of Applied Behavior Analysis,* 1970, *3,* 13–28.

PATTERSON, G. R. *Families: Applications of social learning to family life*. Champaign, Ill.: Research Press, 1971.

PAUL, G. L. A two-year follow-up of systematic desensitization in therapy groups. *Journal of Abnormal Psychology,* 1968, *73,* 119–130.

PAUL, G. L. and SHANNON, D. T. Treatment of anxiety through systematic desensitization in therapy groups. *Journal of Abnormal Psychology,* 1966, *71,* 124–135.

RACHMAN, S. Studies in desensitization—I: The separate effects of relaxation and desensitization. *Behaviour Research and Therapy,* 1965, *3,* 245–252.

RACHMAN, S. Studies in desensitization—III: Speed of generalization. *Behaviour Research and Therapy,* 1966, *4,* 7–15.

SALZINGER, K., FELDMAN, R. S., and PORTNOY, S. Training parents of brain injured children in the use of operant conditioning procedures. *Behavior Therapy,* 1970, *1,* 4–33.

SCHAEFER, H. H. and MARTIN, P. L. *Behavioral Therapy*. New York: McGraw-Hill, 1969.

SCHMIDT, G. W. and ULRICH, R. E. Effects of group contingent events on classroom noise. *Journal of Applied Behavior Analysis,* 1969, *2,* 171–179.

SHANNON, D. T. and WOLFF, M. E. The effects of modeling in reduction of snake phobia by systematic desensitization. Urbana, Ill.: University of Illinois, 1967.

SHAPIRO, D. and BIRK, L. Group therapy in an experimental perspective. *International Journal of Group Therapy,* 1967, *17,* 211–224.

THARP, R. G. and WETZEL, R. J. *Behavior modification in the natural environment*. New York: Academic Press, 1969.

WATSON, W. and THARP, R. *Self-directed behavior: Self modification for personal adjustment*. Belmont, California: Brooks/Cole, 1972.

2

EILEEN D. GAMBRILL, EDWIN J. THOMAS, AND
ROBERT D. CARTER

Procedure for Sociobehavioral Practice in Open Settings

As social workers become more familiar with the principles and methods of the sociobehavioral approach, an increasing number will wish to apply these principles in practice.[1] Judging by the increasing amount of empirical research that supports this approach, there would appear to be a substantial basis for such application.[2] However, practitioners frequently encounter difficulty in their early attempts to implement behavioral methods in work with clients. In some cases this appears to be due to the combining of behavioral with other methods, often producing an incongruent blend; in other instances, misapplication may follow from insufficient knowledge of the methods and principles themselves. A more pervasive difficulty, however, is that there is presently no set of procedural guidelines to aid the worker in approaching cases from a behavioral point of view and organizing his practice activities sequentially and systematically in accordance with that view. In addition, most practitioners who try to use behavioral methods were originally trained and have had most of their experience in non-behavioral methods. Also, there are often influences inimical to behavioral practice deriving from agencies and professional groups. For example, agency policy may not favor client-worker contacts in the natural environment that often are important in the behavioral approach; or supervisors may not permit their workers to use this approach.

What follows is based on the authors' efforts to evolve a procedural guide within which sociobehavioral knowledge can be applied to the modification of behavior in noninstitutional open-service settings.[3] The guide was formulated with explicit recognition that in open-service settings clients are

Reprinted with permission of the National Association of Social Workers, from *Social Work*, Vol. 16, No. 1 (January 1971), pp. 51–62.

free to come and go at will, highly diverse behavioral problems are presented for professional attention, and services such as the provision of legal information or material resources must often be given in addition to those activities pertaining more directly to behavioral change.

Details of the procedural steps are subject to change as more is learned about this kind of practice, but the general framework is regarded as viable in its present form. The discussion focuses primarily on the main steps of the procedure. Some limited attention is also paid to certain constant features that cut across steps and to occasions for departure from the procedure. It should be understood that in its present form the use of this guide in practice assumes familiarity with the main principles and techniques of the sociobehavioral approach.

The worker's activities are separated into procedural steps when given activities are identifiable as the predominant behavior of the worker during a specific period of client contact. As will become evident, steps can be expected to overlap and even merge on occasion. In general, however, the division of major activities into twelve steps seems appropriate for most cases.

STEP 1. INVENTORY OF PROBLEM AREAS

Objective. To obtain the spectrum of presenting problems as seen by the client and worker.

Rationale. To provide the client and worker with an early profile of problem areas so that each can discern priorities and arrive at some basis for deciding which problem to address first.

Operation. The worker obtains the client's descriptions of presenting problems and as the interview proceeds he lists the more conspicuous problems he discerns. At this time there is ordinarily little attempt to specify details of the form of the behaviors or their situational context or history. If this type of information emerges, it is noted, but the focus is on getting an idea of the spectrum of the problem areas.

STEP 2. PROBLEM SELECTION AND CONTRACT

Objective. To reach a verbal or written agreement with the client concerning which one of the problem areas needs the most immediate attention.

Rationale. Such an agreement between worker and client increases the likelihood of early client involvement and cooperation in the treatment effort.[4] In addition, through a mutual focusing on one problem area at a time, it is possible to maximize the efficiency and speed with which assessment is carried out and modification initiated.

Operation. The profile of problems noted by client and worker is either read out loud to the client or presented to him in a written list. The client is asked to select the problem area that is of greatest immediate concern to him. Unless the worker has compelling reasons for choosing a different problem area, the client is told that the one he has selected will be addressed first. If the worker believes that another problem area is preferable, the client is so informed and an explanation is provided. If the client concurs, then the worker's selection prevails. If, however, the client disagrees, the worker and client negotiate still another alternative. If client and worker cannot agree on a problem area, subsequent steps are not pursued.

Step 3. Commitment to Cooperate

Objective. To obtain the client's agreement to cooperate fully in the activities associated with assessment and modification.

Rationale. Commitment to full cooperation tends to enhance the likelihood of compliance with the regimen of assessment and modification.[5] Compliance is regarded as necessary (although not sufficient) for successful modification. One important feature of the regimen is that of maintaining contact with clients, whether in the agency, home, or elsewhere. Accessibility to clients is necessary to achieve change, and in open-service settings, where clients come voluntarily, commitment to cooperate with the regimen must include an agreement to have regular appointments with the worker. This should serve to reduce the likelihood of premature termination.

Operation. The remaining steps of the procedure are briefly previewed for the client, with emphasis placed on the importance of obtaining full, accurate information during assessment, of the client's cooperating with what may be requested of him during the modification program, and of maintaining regular contact at the appointed times. Then the client is asked if he agrees to cooperate fully in the ways indicated. If he does not agree and if further discussion fails to resolve the issue, subsequent procedural steps are not initiated.

Step 4. Specification of Target Behaviors

Objective. To denote the specific behaviors of the client and relevant others associated with him that constitute the essential elements of the selected problem area.

Rationale. An effort is made to determine the exact behavioral referents of the labels used by the client and others in describing the problem, as well as to discover desirable behaviors that may be incompatible with the undesirable behaviors. Client labels are not regarded as adequate in and of themselves, since the same label (e.g., "nervousness") can have diverse behavioral referents from client to client. It is necessary to go beyond the labels and specify what behaviors are controlling the use of these labels by the client.

Operation. Samples of problem behavior and desirable alternatives are sought. Thus examples are collected in the interview, reports of others obtained when needed, and, when possible, the behavior itself is observed by the worker as it occurs in the natural environment.

Step 5. Baseline of Target Behaviors

Objective. To obtain a preintervention estimate of the frequency, magnitude, or duration of the specified problem behaviors. This should be quantitatively expressed and carefully measured for a suitable period prior to intervention.

Rationale. Baseline information provides the worker and client with a concrete, quantitative basis for judging the severity or seriousness of the problem. As a baseline, the data offer one important standard against which the success of the intervention may subsequently be assessed.[6] At a more general level baselines and the monitoring of changes that follow intervention provide the worker with essential feedback for determining the most effective modification techniques for specific problem behaviors.

Operation. A prebaseline estimate of the frequency, magnitude, or duration of problem behavior is obtained. This is generally in the form of a report by the client.

Information for the baseline period may consist of records kept by the client or others (including the worker) or those obtained by such devices as tape recorders or special monitoring devices.[7] When possible, records should be checked for their reliability. If records are kept by clients or their family members, the recording should be made as simple, accurate, systematic, and unobtrusive as possible.

Some baselines can be obtained in a relatively short period, provided that the problem behaviors occur frequently (e.g., stuttering). Other less frequent behaviors, such as some drinking patterns or sexual practices, might require a considerably longer period for adequate baselining. Needless to say, infrequent behaviors that require immediate crisis intervention are not ordinarily subject to baselining, at least initially.

The results of the baseline may disclose that the problem behavior does not merit intervention. Some behaviors, if too infrequent or brief in occurrence or too weak in intensity would be judged by the client or worker to be too trivial for intervention. If the problem behaviors are found to be sufficiently intense, frequent, or of long enough duration to justify intervention, then subsequent steps are embarked on.[8] It is important to note that Step 4 may be combined with this step and that Step 6 is often best accomplished with baselining.

Step 6. Identification of Probable Controlling Conditions

Objective. To isolate the stimuli that precede and follow the problem behavior and serve to control its occurrence.

Rationale. The behavioral approach emphasizes the significance for controlling behavior of discriminative and eliciting stimuli that immediately precede behavior and reinforcing or punishing stimuli that immediately follow it. Of course, developmental factors are not denied, nor are existing behavioral repertoires. But it is the current controlling conditions, evident in the stimuli directly preceding or following behavior, that either maintain problem behavior or, by some deficit in their operation, fail to sustain desirable behavior.

For respondent behavior, such as sexual arousal or anxiety, the controlling conditions are generally the previously neutral stimuli that have acquired the ability to elicit the involuntary behavior. For operant behavior, such as talking, most thinking, and all the more obvious motor reactions of the skeletal-muscular system, the controlling conditions are the reinforcing or punishing stimuli that follow and the discriminative stimuli that occasion the emission of such so-called voluntary behavior.

The central assumption concerning assessment is that the controlling conditions for problem behavior must be determined empirically. Problem behaviors may be identical in form but have different controlling conditions; likewise those that are different in form may have similar or identical controlling conditions. It is important to identify the maintaining conditions for problem behavior since this knowledge affects the selection and use of a modification technique.

Operation. Specific information is obtained concerning what happens before, during, and after the emission of problem behavior. For example, if client self-reports concerning states of depression are to be relied on, the client can be supplied with a form on which he can record the time, behaviors, and events that occur just before, during, and after each period of depression. If this step is combined with Steps 4 and 5, the form would also make it possible for the client to note the specific behaviors that are associated with his depression.

The methods of obtaining information are the same as those referred to in Step 5, and the same criteria for method selection would apply. Here, as elsewhere, accurate and reliable data are required for the successful execution of procedural steps.

Step 7. Assessment of Environmental Resources

Objective. To determine what environmental resources may be used in the modification of behavior.

Rationale. Without access to the controlling stimuli in the client's environment, the worker will not be able to effect those stimulus changes that would reduce the problem behavior or accelerate desirable prosocial alternatives. Determination of environmental resources typically requires an assessment of (1) available mediators, such as parents, siblings, or peers who may function as auxiliary helping agents, (2) available reinforcers and possibly punishers for use with both clients and mediators, and (3) available stimulus contexts in which specific interventions may be used.

Operation. It is not infrequent at this point that the requisite information is known to the worker and no additional inquiry is necessary. When there is some doubt concerning environmental resources, however, there are several aspects of the assessment procedure that should be considered.

1. With reference to potential mediators, it is often necessary to interview various family members and others to see who might be willing to coperate and who would have the ability to alter stimulus conditions so as to bring about desired changes in client behavior.

2. With respect to potential reinforcers for a client, it is often sufficient merely to determine in which activities the client engages in his free time. There is now considerable evidence to indicate that behaviors that occur with a high frequency may be used to reinforce behaviors that occur less frequently.[9] A less reliable but nonetheless useful method of obtaining information concerning possible reinforcers is to ask people what they like and want to do.[10]

3. Analogous methods may be used for discerning possible punishers in those situations in which they might be of some value in the modification program. In such cases, information may be obtained by asking what the client finds aversive and tends to avoid.

Step 8. Specification of Behavioral Objectives

Objective. To specify the behavioral objectives of the modification plan.

Rationale. To intervene planfully, the worker must specify what the terminal behavioral repertoire of the client should consist of relevant to the problem area and the stimulus conditions under which its components are to occur. It is also usually necessary to specify a series of successive approximations to the desired terminal behavioral repertoire. Achieving the intermediate and terminal repertoire necessitates specification of the behaviors the client should be helped to acquire, strengthen, maintain, weaken, or eliminate. Thus, behaviors must be specified as to their form; the frequency, intensity, or duration with which they are to occur; and the stimulus context in which they are to take place.

Operation. Baseline and assessment information will have revealed the specific responses that occur either in surfeit or deficit. Problematic responses that occur in surfeit suggest objectives that call for a reduction or elimination of these behaviors. Desirable behaviors that occur in deficit suggest objectives that emphasize acquisition, strengthening, or maintenance. (More will be said of this later.) Assessment of environmental resources will generally reveal which objectives are potentially feasible.

Step 9. Formulation of a Modification Plan

Objective. To select an appropriate behavioral modification role for the worker and the modification techniques to use in achieving the behavioral objectives.

Rationale. In addition to specifying intermediate and terminal behaviors, the worker must also select a behavioral modification role (e.g., instigation or direct intervention) and the appropriate modification techniques to use with that role.[11]

Instigation consists of the worker's specific behaviors during the interview, which are designed to influence the client's or mediator's behaviors in the natural environment. It may be used to alter environmental conditions that both precede and follow behavior (see Homme *et al.*, 1968). An instigation generally consists of an instruction to carry out a certain behavior in a given stimulus situation in the outside environment. It is expected that the assigned behavior will serve to decrease problem behavior and accelerate the development of alternate desirable behaviors.

Direct intervention involves the worker's activity in the immediate situation and is intended to have a direct impact on the client or mediator. Although it might be used in the interview if the behavior to be modified is or can be evoked there (e.g., marital arguing), it is more commonly used for target behavior that occurs in the external natural environment while the worker is present and actively involved in modification efforts. For example, the worker, while present in the home, may reinforce selected parental behaviors.

After the worker selects an appropriate modification role, he must select appropriate behavioral modification techniques.[12] Most techniques may be implemented by instigation or direct intervention. They are used to alter a maintaining condition for problem behavior, to accelerate a desirable behavior alternative, or both.

Operation. When formulating a modification plan, the worker first reviews all the information obtained in prior steps, particularly that which pertains to the problem area. When direct intervention is not possible, instigation may be productively used. However, certain criteria are felt to be important to the successful implementation of instigation as the modification role of choice. They are as follows:

1. The client or mediator must correctly discriminate the behavior he is to carry out and the appropriate stimulus context for its emission.
2. The behavior to be carried out must be present in the person's repertoire.
3. Stimulus conditions under which this behavior is to be carried out must be available in the environment. An important component of these stimulus conditions is a cue that controls the emission of the appropriate behavior; otherwise, the person may "forget" to engage in the behavior.

4. The worker must have sufficient ability to influence the client so that the assigned behavior is likely to be carried out.

Direct intervention is generally preferable to instigation because the modification of behavior does not depend, as it does in instigation, on the intervening step of the client or mediator carrying out an instigated behavior. In direct intervention there is direct impact on controlling conditions in the client's life situation.

Criteria for Technique Selection

The worker also is concerned with selecting the most suitable technique. There are several classes of criteria that narrow the range of relevant techniques.[13] The first involves the main area of behavior—operant, respondent, or a combination of the two—into which the behavioral difficulty predominantly falls. The so-called operant techniques (e.g., positive reinforcement, negative reinforcement, extinction, differential reinforcement, response-shaping, and punishment) are generally applicable to behavioral difficulties involving primarily operant behavior. If the behavioral problem falls conspicuously into the area of respondent behavior, respondent techniques such as classical conditioning, systematic desensitization, and flooding may be most relevant.[14] Certain more complex techniques may be applied to problems involving both operant and respondent behavior. Among these are stimulus-shaping ("fading"), verbal instructions, behavioral rehearsal (role-playing), rule-making, model presentation, and position-structuring.

Another class of selection criteria relates to the behavioral objectives of intervention. Some techniques apply mainly to acquisition, others to strengthening and maintenance, and still others to weakening and eliminating behavior. For example, behaviors that occur in deficit call for techniques that will strengthen them. If the deficit responses are not even in the client's repertoire, they must be established; techniques pertaining to response acquisition are applicable for this purpose.

Still another class of criteria concerns the effectiveness of alternative techniques for handling the same behavioral problems. For example, for most of the techniques pertaining to operant behavior, there is considerable evidence that when appropriately used, they have a high probability of being successful. Also, when given a choice, techniques to accelerate desirable behavioral alternatives are preferable to techniques that serve merely to decelerate undesirable behaviors (see, for example, Franks 1967 and Ferster, 1958). For example, in the illustration referred to previously, a contract was made with a 23-year-old female client to reduce her crying spells and periods of depression. One portion of the modification plan involved an instigation for the woman to work because it was found that behavior at work interfered with her crying and depression. In this instance, working not only served to reduce the undesirable behavior but also provided remuneration that helped both her and her husband pay off their debts. Other activities, such as reading, cleaning the apartment, and the like, were also found to be incompatible with crying and depression. Thus a structured activity program was instituted to accelerate behaviors incompatible with the problem behaviors. (See Figure 2.1 for the effects.)

When possible, the most efficient techniques in terms of time and effort should be chosen. Also, techniques having greater feasibility for implementation would be preferred over those more difficult to execute.

Step 10. Implementation of Modification Plan

Objective. To modify or maintain behavior with respect to the modification objectives and the contract made with the client.

Rationale. To focus the worker's modification efforts and abide by the ethics of voluntarism and choice on the part of the client, intervention is restricted to the area of the contracted problem. By engaging in intervention only after the completion of assessment, the worker is prevented from intervening before he knows precisely what the problem behaviors are, their seriousness by his own standards, and the feasibility and appropriateness of his proposed intervention.

Operation. The interventions are carried out according to plan and no other interventions are engaged in without returning to appropriate earlier steps. If the plan cannot be carried out as formulated, the worker tries to find the reason for this and then acts accordingly.

Step 11. Monitoring Outcomes

Objective. To obtain information concerning the effectiveness of intervention.

Rationale. Feedback to the worker concerning the effectiveness of intervention serves to control both the client's and worker's behavior in several ways.[15] Monitoring outcomes enables the worker to ascertain whether the modification effort has been successful and in the long run provides crucial information concerning the efficacy of various techniques. Based on such information, he can not only modify his interventions in the situation at hand, but can also alter his approach to intervention for subsequent occasions and ultimately contribute to the growth of concrete information so that knowledge of modification can be made genuinely cumulative.

Operation. By means of the data-gathering techniques discussed in Steps 5 and 6, the intervention outcomes are monitored during the period when the intervention is first introduced as well as through follow-up. Changes that occur in the problem behavior and prosocial alternatives are of greatest interest and, in addition, when the worker engages in instigation, it is generally desirable to keep records concerning the emission of these assigned

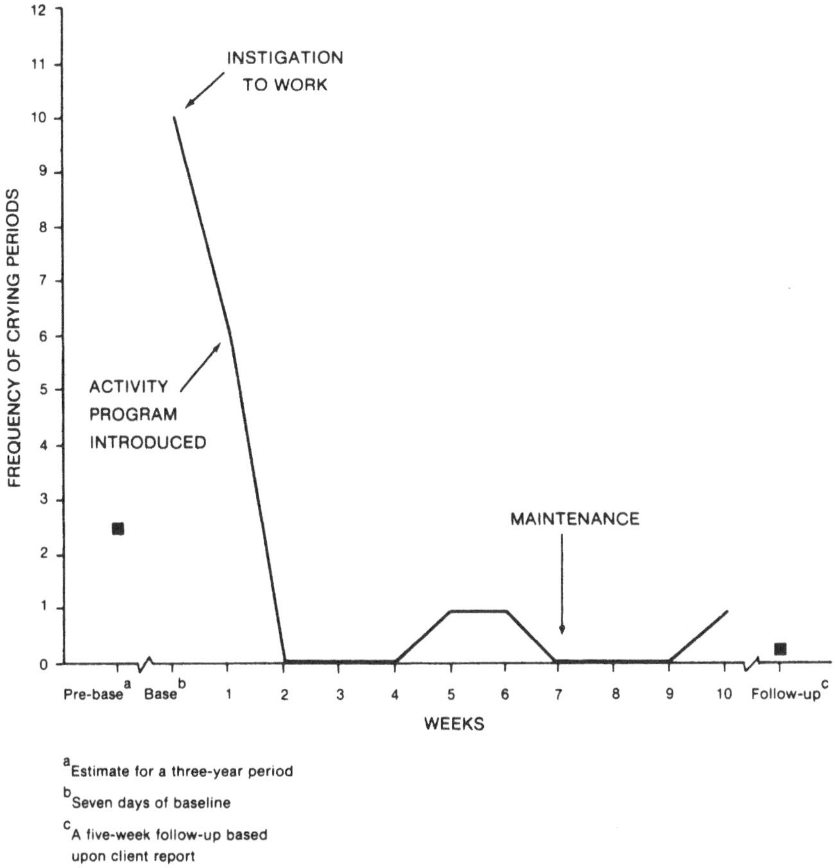

FIGURE 2.1 *Periods of crying per week*

behaviors as well. If compliance with instigation is inadequate, there is no basis for expecting that desired behavioral changes will occur. If the desired terminal behaviors occur after the intervention plan has been introduced, the worker may then proceed to the following step. However, if these behaviors do not occur following intervention, the worker must try to determine the reason why and, if necessary, return to the appropriate earlier step.

STEP 12. MAINTENANCE OF CHANGE

Objective. To achieve the maintenance and stabilization of the desired terminal behaviors for which intervention was undertaken.

Rationale. Following successful intervention, a program of maintenance and stabilization may be required to insure that the desired terminal behaviors are maintained at an appropriate level after service is terminated. Plans for maintenance should be directed toward establishing those conditions that will enable the desired terminal behaviors to persist in the natural environment independent of the worker's influence.

Operation. This step may not be required in many cases, owing to the fact that when desirable behavior changes are produced by intervention, they are often maintained by reinforcers naturally available in the environment. Relatives, friends, and others may have found the client's problem behavior aversive and may reinforce desirable behavioral changes. This may also prove true for mediators whose own altered behavior helped promote desirable client change in the first place.

In other cases a special maintenance plan may be called for. Unfortunately, the field has devoted little attention to developing maintenance techniques. In general, however, two approaches that seem viable are mediator control and client self-control. Establishing mediator control over client behavior involves gaining the cooperation of auxiliary helpers in the same way as is done when mediators are used during the intervention proper. Special attention may have to be given to making sure that sufficient reinforcers are available in the environment to sustain the mediators' behavior.

Client self-control follows from the idea that clients can be trained to manage their own behavior through self-manipulation of environmental factors that control the behavior.[16] Instigation would probably be most effective in such training.

Recurring Activities

Each of the twelve steps discussed in this paper is in sequence and entails a primary concentration on one activity. Other important activities may occur within any given step and often across steps as well. Although secondary when compared with the procedural steps, the recurring activities are nevertheless essential to successful sociobehavioral practice.

Demeanor to clients. One aspect of what is often referred to as relationship should be maintained more or less continuously. That is, respect, courtesy, and civility should always be shown to clients.

Maintenance of contact with clients. Premature termination is common in most open settings. To offset this, the present procedure calls for active, assertive efforts by the worker to enhance client accessibility. In general, it is not assumed that maintaining contact is primarily the client's responsibility, and worker initiative in establishing and arranging contacts is regarded as appropriate and necessary.

Client socialization. Initial socialization of clients includes provision of an overview of and rationale for the steps to be followed in the procedure. In addition, the client is informed of what his principal responsibilities are likely to be throughout the procedure. Subsequently, additional socialization is carried out in relation to each step. In all cases, socialization is presumed to enhance compliance to the requisites of the procedure and to facilitate successful modification.

Reinforcement of appropriate client behavior. Through such means as praise and approval the client is positively reinforced promptly for all behaviors relating to compliance with the procedure and for any other contributions he makes to the intervention process. Progress in the reduction of the problem or the acceleration of desirable alternative behaviors is strongly reinforced.

Feedback. Information obtained in relation to the outcomes of each procedural operation is shared with the client and others when relevant and appropriate. The intent is to evoke and sustain client awareness of, commitment to, and involvement in the modification regimen. There is evidence that feedback can itself serve to facilitate behavioral modification.

There are several other recurring activities. Some of them include maintaining a viable contract with the client at all times, reaffirming client commitment to cooperate (especially when there have been indications of noncooperation), and cuing and prompting to control conversation in the interview, to provide reminders of appointments, and to increase the likelihood of complying with other aspects of the procedure.

Departure from Steps

In most instances it has been found best to adhere scrupulously to the steps of the procedure and to progress systematically through them for each problem area for which a contract has been made. However, there are legitimate occasions when departures from the ordered steps may be anticipated.

Omission of steps. Some of the steps associated with assessment may have to be omitted in extreme situations that involve crisis and the need for immediate intervention. The recovery of such steps might be possible at some later point, but they are freely sacrificed when the situation demands.

It is not unusual to find that clients demonstrate a positive surveillance effect as a result of early phases of the procedure (especially during baselining) in that marked improvements in problem behavior occur before the worker engages in the intervention proper. When this occurs, much or all of assessment and intervention may be bypassed and Step 12—maintenance of change—may be embarked on immediately.

Temporary interruption of steps. Occasions for temporary interruption of the procedure are represented by crises that emerge subsequent to the onset of service; needs for auxiliary services such as medical, legal, or financial aid; and points of indecision or disagreement between client and worker that require negotiation and resolution before the procedure can be resumed.

Recycling through earlier steps. The worker may have to return to earlier steps in the procedure when, among other reasons, an additional problem area is contracted, there has been some failure in intervention, the assessment has been inadequate, there has been lack of compliance with the regimen, or mediators have been found to be unreliable.

Occasions to stop. There are at least three major occasions for the cessation of service oriented toward behavioral modification or stabilization. One of these is failure to reach a mutually satisfactory agreement concerning the problem area to be addressed. Another is the client's or mediator's irremediable noncompliance with the requisites of the procedure. Still another failure is the failure of the modification plan to be effective because, in the worker's judgment, there are overriding countervailing influences in the environment that he feels unable to overcome.

Conclusion

The twelve-step procedure described in this paper serves to guide worker behavior systematically in relation to the activities of problem selection, assessment, and modification while also giving suitable attention to crises and special needs for auxiliary services. It makes possible a clear-cut objective to be pursued jointly by the client and the worker acting in an aboveboard contractual relationship. It seems appropriate to the handling of diverse problem behaviors and client situations commonly encountered in open settings.

Contrary to the authors' own earlier misgivings and those of their colleagues oriented toward more conventional approaches to practice, it has been found that practice activity can be directed to one problem area at a time, even while others must temporarily be set aside, and that instead of feeling constrained or unduly limited, both client and worker derive reinforcement from the focus and structure the procedure affords. In this regard, it has been observed that as positive changes occur in the target problem, improvements in other noncontracted problem areas occur as well (see Patterson *et al.*, 1967). Moreover, so far no evidence has been found of any concomitant negative changes that would merit the term "symptom substitution."[17] Areas for continuing work on the procedure involve further refinement and specification of its component activities, how workers may be trained in its use, and its utility and efficacy in various open welfare settings.

Notes

1. The project on which this chapter is based was facilitated by a grant from the Social and Rehabilitation Administration, U. S. Department of Health, Education, and Welfare (grant SRS-CRD 425–8–286), Edwin J. Thomas, principal investigator. The procedures described in this paper were developed as one portion of the authors' research project, located in Family Service of Ypsilanti, Ypsilanti, Michigan. The

authors wish to acknowledge the administrative assistance of Gareld Williams, Jesse Woodring, Mrs. Roni Newman, and Mrs. Joellen Ahlgren. For literature on the basic principles and techniques of the sociobehavioral approach, see Thomas (1967, 1968), Bandura (1969), Schaefer and Martin (1969), and Ayllon and Azrin (1968).

2. Much relevant research has been reported in four journals devoted to behavioral modification: *Behaviour Research and Therapy, Journal of Applied Behavior Analysis, Behavior Therapy,* and *Behavior Therapy and Experimental Psychiatry.* Also note such studies as Paul (1966).

3. For an earlier report on this portion of the project, conducted at Family Service of Ypsilanti, Michigan, as well as other aspects of the research, see Thomas, Gambrill, and Carter (1969).

4. See Sulzer (1962). For a review of small-group research dealing with the effects of contracts on cooperative interdependence, see Burnstein (1969).

5. For research evidence dealing with the effects of commitment on behavior, see Schachter and Hall (1952), Deutsch and Gerard (1955), Gerard (1965), and Greenwald (1965).

6. Baselining turns each case so treated into a before-after experiment. This basic design allows for more sophisticated extensions, such as reversal and then reinstatement of intervention, and thereby affords substantial improvement over the usual methods of causal inference in case studies. For further details, see Bijou *et al.* (1969) and Campbell (1969).

7. For examples of such devices see Schwitzgebel (1968).

8. An example of one way of presenting prebaseline and baseline data is given in Figure 2.1. The reader will note that for the periods of involuntary crying, a baseline period of ten days was deemed adequate.

9. For a discussion of the so-called Premack Principle, see Premack (1965).

10. The use of verbal reports for discovering reinforcers is discussed by Ayllon and Azrin (1968: 67–72).

11. The labels "instigation" and "direct intervention" designating types of intervention were suggested by Kanfer and Phillips (1966). Although there are other behavioral modification roles (e.g., teacher, adviser), the authors believe that instigation and direct intervention are presently the most important.

12. For an overview of these techniques, see Thomas (1968).

13. These criteria are discussed in more detail in Thomas (1971).

14. It should be noted, however, that recent data indicate that operant methods may be effectively utilized to change respondent as well as operant behavior. See, for example, Agras, Leitenberg, and Barlow (1968). Also, operant components of methods falling predominantly within the respondent realm have been identified as critical to the effectiveness of the overall procedure. See, for example, Leitenberg, Agras, Barlow, and Olivau (1969).

15. Feedback tends to sharpen the performer's discriminations and in general to increase the likelihood that performance will correspond more closely to a behavioral criterion. Relevant studies and reviews include the following: Howell and Emanuel (1968), Locke, Cartledge, and Koeppel (1968), and Aiken and Lau (1967).

16. For a behavioral discussion of self-control, see Skinner (1953).

17. Behaviorally oriented studies have as yet uncovered no evidence of so-called symptom substitution. For a recent example, see Baker (1969).

References

Agras, W. Stewart, Leitenberg, Harold, and Barlow, David H. Social reinforcement in the modification of agoraphobia. *Archives of General Psychiatry,* 1968, *19,* 423–427.

Aiken, Edwin G., and Lau, Alan W. Response prompting and response confirmation: A review of recent literature. *Psychological Bulletin,* 1967, *68,* 330–341.

Ayllon, Teodoro, and Azrin, Nathan. *The token economy: A motivational system for therapy and rehabilitation.* New York: Appleton-Century-Crofts, 1968.

BAKER, BRUCE L. Symptom treatment and symptom substitution in enuresis. *Journal of Abnormal Psychology,* 1969, *74,* 42–49.

BANDURA, ALBERT. *Principles of behavior modification.* New York: Holt, Rinehart and Winston, 1969.

BIJOU, S., *et al.* Methodology for experimental studies of young children in natural settings. *Psychological Record,* 1969, *19,* 177–210.

BURNSTEIN, EUGENE. Interpersonal strategies as determinants of behavioral interdependence. In Judson Mills (Ed.), *Experimental social psychology.* New York: Macmillan, 1969.

CAMPBELL, DONALD T. Reforms as experiments. *American Psychologist,* 1969, *24,* 409–430.

DEUTSCH, MORTON, and GERARD, HAROLD B. A study of normative and informational social influences upon individual judgment. *Journal of Abnormal and Social Psychology,* 1955, *51,* 629–636.

FERSTER, C. B. Reinforcement and punishment in the control of human behavior by social agencies. *Psychiatric Research Reports,* 1958, *10,* 101–118.

FRANKS, CYRIL M. Reflections upon the treatment of sexual disorders by the behavioral clinician: An historical comparison with the treatment of the alcoholic. *Journal of Sex Research,* 1967, *3,* 212–222.

GERARD, HAROLD B. Deviation, conformity, and commitment. In Ivan D. Steiner and Martin Fishbein (Eds.), *Current studies in social psychology.* New York: Holt, Rinehart and Winston, 1965.

GREENWALD, ANTHONY G. Effects of prior commitment on behavior change after a persuasive communication. *Public Opinion Quarterly,* 1965, *29,* 595–601.

HOMME, LLOYD, *et al.* What behavioral engineering is. *Psychological Record,* 1968, *18,* 425–434.

HOWELL, WILLIAM C., and EMANUEL, JOSEPH T. Information feedback, instructions, and incentives in the guidance of human choice behavior. *Journal of Experimental Psychology,* 1968, *78,* 410–416.

KANFER, FREDERICK H., and PHILLIPS, JEANNE S. Behavior therapy: A panacea for all ills or a passing fancy? *Archives of General Psychiatry,* 1966, *15,* 114–128.

LEITENBERG, HAROLD, *et al.* Contribution of selective positive reinforcement and therapeutic instructions to systematic desensitization therapy. *Journal of Abnormal Psychology,* 1969, *74,* 113–118.

LOCKE, EDWIN A., CARTLEDGE, NORMAN, and KOEPPEL, JEFFREY. Motivational effects of knowledge of results: A goal-setting phenomenon? *Psychological Bulletin,* 1968, *70,* 474–485.

PATTERSON, G. R., *et al.* Reprogramming the social environment. *Journal of Child Psychology and Psychiatry,* 1967, *8,* 181–195.

PAUL, GORDON L. *Insight vs. desensitization: An experiment in anxiety reduction.* Stanford: Stanford University Press, 1966.

PREMACK, DAVID. Reinforcement theory. In David Levine (Ed.), *Nebraska symposium on motivation.* Lincoln: University of Nebraska Press, 1965.

SCHACHTER, STANLEY, and HALL, ROBERT. Group-derived restraints and audience persuasion. *Human Relations,* 1952, *5,* 397–406.

SCHAEFER, HALMUTH H., and MARTIN, PATRICK L. *Behavioral therapy.* New York: McGraw-Hill, 1969.

SCHWITZGEBEL, ROBERT L. Survey of electromechanical devices for behavior modification. *Psychological Bulletin,* 1968, *70,* 444–459.

SKINNER, B. F. *Science and human behavior.* New York: Free Press, 1953.

SULZER, EDWARD S. Reinforcement and the therapeutic contract. *Journal of Counseling Psychology,* 1962, *9,* 271–276.

THOMAS, EDWIN J. (Ed.) *The socio-behavioral approach and applications to social work.* New York: Council on Social Work Education, 1967.

THOMAS, EDWIN J. Selected sociobehavioral techniques and principles: An approach to interpersonal helping. *Social Work,* 1968, *13,* 12–26.

THOMAS, EDWIN J. Behavioral modification in casework. In Robert W. Roberts and Robert H. Nee (Eds.), *Theories of social casework.* Chicago: University of Chicago Press, 1971.

THOMAS, EDWIN J., GAMBRILL, EILEEN, and CARTER, ROBERT D. Progress report and plans for further work: Utilization and appraisal of socio-behavioral techniques in social welfare—pilot phase. Ann Arbor: University of Michigan, mimeo, 1969.

3

ROBERT G. WAHLER
AND MARIE ERICKSON

Child Behavior Therapy: A Community Program in Appalachia

Community psychology is a currently popular concept in the "mental health" field (e.g., Sarason *et al.*, 1966). It implies the notion that the clinician should concentrate his therapeutic and prophylactic efforts on the patient's immediate and not-so-immediate environment rather than on the patient *per se*. That is, instead of following the traditional dyadic treatment model, the clinician's role should be that of an agent for change in his client's community—community, meaning the client's relatives, friends, and working associates as well as the more impersonal aspects of his social and physical surroundings. It is clear that the clinician is seen from this point of view as an expert in human ecology; a practitioner who assumes that man's behavior is an important function of his current environment.

While a number of theoretical models could be employed to implement the community psychology concept, one is of particular relevance in view of its emphasis upon human ecology. Reinforcement theory has as one of its basic tenets the assumption that the development and maintenance of behavior is a function of stimulus contingencies set by one's environment. It is argued that man behaves as he does because of differential reinforcement, provided primarily by the social attention of other people. In the case of the child, people such as his parents, his peers, his siblings, his teachers, etc. are seen as selective dispensers of social attention; in a very real sense these social agents "teach" him which aspects of his behavior will be most instrumental in obtaining approval, reassurance, affection, nearness, and other forms of their attention. From this view, then, the question of whether

Reprinted with permission of Pergamon Press, from *Behaviour Research and Therapy*, 1969, Vol. 7, No. 1, pp. 71–78.

the child develops normal or deviant behavior can be answered only through an assessment of his social community and how it interacts with him.

The above contention is an intriguing one and readily lends itself to research evaluation. Thus far, attempts to isolate naturalistic events which may support or maintain deviant child behavior have proved promising. For example, evidence is now available to show that parents may inadventently support their child's deviant behavior through their social attention to it (Wahler *et al.*, 1965). Similar studies of teacher-child interactions in preschool settings have demonstrated that teachers may also function in this capacity. That is, teachers have been found to function as powerful sources of reinforcement for child behavior such as excessive crying (Hart *et al.*, 1964), isolate play (Allen *et al.*, 1964), excessive passivity (Johnson *et al.*, 1966), regressive crawling (Harris *et al.*, 1964), and aggressive behavior (Scott *et al.*, 1967; Brown and Elliot, 1965). Finally, more recent studies have indicated that the preschool child's peer group adds a further component to these sources of control (Patterson *et al.*, 1967; Wahler, 1967).

In addition to demonstrating the roles which parents, teachers and peers may play in the maintenance of deviant child behavior, the above studies also brought to light a highly practical finding: In many cases the parents, teachers, and peers could be trained in the use of behavior modification techniques, enabling them to produce dramatic changes in the children's deviant behavior. The techniques, of course, were based on reinforcement theory and the previously discussed analyses of the adult-child interactions.

A community psychology program based on reinforcement theory has several features to recommend it as far as child therapy is concerned: (1) the previously discussed research findings support the assumption that social agents in the child's immediate community may be responsible for the maintenance of his deviant behavior; (2) reinforcement contingencies set by these social agents may often be modified, and these modifications may produce therapeutic changes in the deviant child behavior; (3) the operations involved in modifying the social reinforcement contingencies are simple, and the T requires relatively little formal training to implement them. This latter point raises the possibility of training clinically unsophisticated community members as Ts. The present program was initiated with these three points in mind.[1]

Community and Clinic Settings

Pineville, Kentucky (population, 3000) is the county seat of Bell County, and the location of the Bell County Health Center. This clinic is state supported and serves the medical and psychological needs of residents in Bell County (population 35,000) and in Harlan County (population 65,000). As far as psychological services are concerned, the Clinic represents the only source of this type in the two counties. The staff of the psychology unit is made up of one permanent member (a social worker) and one consulting member (a clinical psychologist) who visits the Clinic twice a month.

A picture of the two counties describes a rather typical cross-section of Appalachia. Poverty, unemployment, and low educational attainment are widespread among the residents, and many are dependent on social welfare for financial security. As might be expected, birth control is a serious problem among the poorer families.

Ninety-five per cent of the referrals to the psychological clinic are children. The majority of these are from the poorer families who generally bring their children in at the urging of public health nurses or public assistance workers. Presenting complaints range from retardation and autism to less serious problems such as low achievement motivation in school settings. At the present time the Clinic charges no fees for services rendered.

Program Development and Current Functioning

The senior author's very limited contact with the Clinic was instrumental in the decision to develop a community program. Not only were the senior author's consulting visits restricted to two a month, but because of travel time to and from Pineville, each visit was restricted to a period of about five hours. It seemed obvious that a clinician would find it difficult to work therapeutically with a patient, much less handle a large waiting-list of prospective patients, on such a contact basis. Therefore, it seemed advisable to consider a program which emphasized the use of non-professionals as Ts—in this case, community members who could be trained in the use of child behavior therapy techniques.

Recruitment procedures were complicated by a lack of funds to hire new clinic staff members. Since it was then apparent that staffing the program would require volunteer workers, efforts were made to obtain the cooperation of Pineville churches, the city school board, and the local mental health committee. The senior author provided these groups with mimeographed manuscripts which describe the plight of the Clinic and the proposed behavior therapy program. In addition, the manuscript stated that the educational background of the volunteers was immaterial and that they would be expected to serve no more than two hours per week.

Within a period of two months following the community group effort to recruit workers, a total of 13 volunteers were available to the Clinic. Of this number, six were public health nurses from Bell and Harlan Counties, three were public assistance workers in Bell County, and four were citizens in Pineville engaged in other occupations. In addition to these regular workers, several teachers and school counselors requested to assist the Clinic on specific cases.

Training of the workers was primarily of an in-service type. Although the authors did provide interested workers with reprints of several studies cited earlier in this paper, most of the workers did not find the material to be helpful. The following steps characterized the training and the regular functioning of the workers and the Clinic staff:

(1) When a prospective child therapy case was seen at the Clinic, the child, his immediate family, and any other people who were closely involved with the child (e.g., teachers) were interviewed by the professional Clinic staff. These interviews were aimed at obtaining descriptions of the behavior which created problems at home, at school, or elsewhere. In addition, efforts were made to determine the usual consequences of such behavior—consequences provided by the child's parents, his teachers, his peers, etc. The interviews were diagnostic in the sense that their function was to provide a list of the child's deviant behavior and a list of probable reinforcers for the behavior.

(2) A volunteer worker was then introduced to the interview data by the Clinic psychologist. Discussion of the case emphasized descriptions of those physical and verbal responses of the child which were considered deviant in his regular environment. Following this description, the clinician emphasized the notion that the behavior was probably being maintained by people in the child's environment. Then followed a brief essay on reinforcement theory, with emphasis on the concepts of reinforcement, extinction, and punishment. Finally, the clinician pointed to those social agents whom he suspected to be responsible for the maintenance of the deviant behavior; therapy for the child was described as a process of modifying the probable reinforcement contingencies currently provided by these social agents.

(3) Prior to step 3, the volunteer worker obtained at least two one-hour observations of the child's behavior within the problem setting (e.g., home or classroom). These observational procedures will be described later. Second interviews were then scheduled for those social agents who seemed to provide clear and potentially modifiable contingencies for the child's deviant behavior. The volunteer worker and the clinician conducted these interviews together. Essentially, these social agents were given descriptions of the child's deviant behavior and they were then advised that their social attention to such behavior was a likely cause of their maintenance. The social agents were then told to ignore the child's deviant behavior but to respond as usual to his other behavior patterns, especially those which seemed incompatible with the deviant behavior. In cases where the deviant behavior involved highly aggressive or oppositional actions, a punishment procedure was suggested as well. In all instances this suggested procedure involved social isolation of the child for short periods of time following his deviant behavior. It was then made clear to the social agents that the volunteer worker would make weekly visits to observe interactions between them and the child and to point out needed corrections in social contingencies.

(4) For an inexperienced volunteer worker, these interviews were con-

tinued on a twice-a-month basis until the clinician felt confident in the volunteer worker's understanding of the therapeutic process as it applied to the child. When this occurred, the clinician met only with the volunteer worker on the same time basis. Discussion centered around the child's progress and the progress of the social agents in maintaining their "therapeutic" contingencies for the child.

The following case study is cited to illustrate these procedures: Ricky (age eight) was referred to the Clinic by his school principal because of his disruptive behavior in the classroom. According to his teacher, Ricky would frequently tease the other children in a variety of ways. Following an interview with the teacher, numerous examples of Ricky's disruptive behavior were recorded; in addition, the interview revealed that the teacher's usual response to this behavior was to shout at Ricky, argue with him and at times to spank him. The teacher also admitted that her usual response to Ricky's infrequently cooperative behavior was to ignore him; she pointed out that Ricky irritated her so much of the time that she found it exceedingly difficult "to be nice to him" even when his behavior was appropriate. Since Ricky's parents were unwilling to come to the Clinic, the therapy program focused on the school setting.

The volunteer behavior T was a young public health nurse who normally visited the school on a weekly basis. This was her first behavior therapy case. She and the phychologist discussed the interview data for about thirty minutes prior to the second meeting with Ricky's teacher. During the discussion, Ricky's disruptive classroom behavior was described in detail and the psychologist emphasized the possibility that the teachers' attention (admittedly negative) could be maintaining this behavior. The psychologist pointed out that if the teacher could ignore it, however, it was evident that this procedure would be impractical in terms of maintaining any semblance of classroom routine. Therefore, a punishment technique was outlined by the psychologist. Essentially, the proposed procedure involved isolating Ricky from his peers and his teacher for short time periods following the occurrence of his disruptive behavior. The psychologist speculated that if the punishment procedure could suppress Ricky's disruptive behavior, the teacher might find it much easier to provide positive social attention following his appropriate behavior.

The second interview with Ricky's teacher included the volunteer behavior T. Prior to the interview, the psychologist urged the T to comment whenever possible on the therapeutic procedure. In beginning the interview, the psychologist reviewed Ricky's problem behavior and then briefly outlined the proposed behavior therapy program for Ricky. During the ensuing discussion of the program, Ricky's teacher offered suggestions for implementing the procedures—particularly the punishment portions. It was decided to use the teachers' lounge (a former cloakroom adjacent to the classroom) as the isolation area in the punishment program. The teacher agreed to attempt the program and to work closely with the volunteer T, who would visit the classroom twice weekly.

After the program had been in effect for two weeks, a third Clinic meeting was scheduled for the teacher and the therapist. However, since the teacher was unable to attend, only the psychologist and the T were present. According to the T's report, little change had occurred in Ricky's disruptive behavior; both she and the teacher were quite discouraged. The T's reports revealed that the teacher had used the punishment procedure for five days with little success. At the end of that time she decided "it wouldn't work" and discontinued its use.

A careful analysis of the T's classroom observations provided a possible explanation for the program's failure. Two features of her report were of interest: (1) the teacher's use of the punishment procedure was inconsistent, that is, only about 60 per cent of Ricky's disruptive episodes were followed by social isolation; (2) when she did use the procedure, it was not used promptly upon the occurrence of the disruptive behavior. Often the teacher would first warn Ricky or argue with him before ordering him to the isolation room. The T agreed to discuss these problems with the teacher and to monitor the teacher's behavior more carefully in the next two weeks.

At the next interview, both the teacher and the T were present. Both were enthusiastic about the marked improvement in Ricky. According to the report, Ricky's disruptive behavior had dropped from about twenty episodes a day to only one or two. The teacher also reported that her attitude toward Ricky had changed to the point that she could now offer genuine approval for his appropriate behavior.

The T agreed to continue her observations on a weekly basis and to meet twice a month with the psychologist to describe her experiences. Two months later, therapeutic changes in Ricky were still in evidence and his case was closed.

Program Effectiveness

The program has now been in effect for over two years and 14 volunteer workers are now actively involved in it. In all cases treated, the deviant behavior was in evidence either in the child's home or in his school. Therefore, most of the social agents were either the child's parents or his teachers, or both.

The major claims of the program's effectiveness rest on observational reports of improvement by the volunteer worker, the number of cases seen by the Clinic, and the time spent treating these cases.

Observational data were collected in the following manner: after a volunteer worker became familiar with the behavioral problems presented by her case, she was introduced to a checklist method of recording the behavior. This method, similar to one described by Zeilberger *et al.*, (1968), required the observer to make coded checks for the occurrence or non-occurrence of the problem behavior and the stimulus contingencies, within successive 20-sec intervals. For each case, the worker obtained two 1-hr observations prior to treatment and two 1-hr observations just after termination of treatment. These observations were made in the child's home or classroom or both, depending on the stimulus location of the presenting problem.

Because of time and scheduling problems, it proved possible to assess the scoring reliability of approximately half of the volunteer workers. In assessing observer reliability, observers worked in pairs; an agreement or disagreement was tallied for each 20-sec interval and the percentage of agreements for the two observers was computed for each response and stimulus class. All reliability tests showed agreement levels of 85 per cent or better; since all behavior categories were based on quite distinct physical and verbal behaviors, this kind of reliability is not particularly surprising.

It proved possible to classify the presenting problems for all cases in five general categories: (1) classroom disruptive behavior; this category included fighting with other children, shouting, and not obeying teacher instructions; (2) classroom study behavior; this category included attending (i.e., looking) to either the teacher or to the learning materials; (3) school absences; this record was obtained from teacher attendance records; (4) home disruptive behavior; this category included fighting with siblings, parents, or other people in the home, destruction of property, and not obeying parent instructions; (5) home study behavior; this category included attending to school homework materials.

Table 3.1 describes pre- and post-treatment measures of the above behavior problems over two years of the community program. As this table indicates, many of the 66 cases handled during this time were deviant in terms of more than one of the problem categories. An examination of mean differences in the problem behavior categories before and after treatment revealed significant changes in the frequencies of these behaviors; all categories displayed marked changes in the therapeutic direction. Unfortunately, because of a lack of personnel, an appropriate control group was not included to evaluate the causal influence of the treatment procedures. Thus, although the children *did* show improvement, the role of the volunteer workers in producing the improvement is not clear.

During the senior author's first year at the Clinic, he and the junior author engaged in fairly traditional techniques of diagnosis and therapy; no attempts were made to assess the effectiveness of these procedures. Table 3.2 presents a description of the number of cases seen during this initial year compared to the community program years; in addition, the same comparison is made for time between the screening of a case and its termination. As Table 3.2 indicates, the mean treatment time for the community program years was significantly shorter than that for the initial year—and a larger number of cases were seen during each program year.

TABLE 3.1 *Mean number of problem behavior episodes before and after treatment*

	Mean Variance							
	pre-treatment		*post-treatment*		*F test*	*t test*	*corrected t test*	*number of cases*
Classroom disruptive behavior	25.77	128.70	7.77	27.83	4.62*		4.03*	35
Classroom study behavior	51.68	660.22	95.12	1366.68	2.28*		10.70*	50
School absences (Days absent)	7.60	5.69	1.66	4.67	1.22	2.68*		15
Home study behavior	13.49	120.35	59.67	1075.00	8.93*		8.37*	45
Home disruptive behavior	29.87	259.10	9.88	76.40	3.39*		7.87*	52

*$P<0.05$

Although no great emphasis can be placed on the correlational improvement data, results based on the number of cases treated and on the time between screening and termination of cases must be considered compelling. There are certainly many treatment facilities in the United States which are similar to this Appalachian unit in terms of the undesirable ratio between patients and professional workers. Since it is unlikely that many of those units will obtain an adequate number of professional workers in the near future, programs emphasizing the use of indigenous non-professional work-

TABLE 3.2 *Mean number of treatment weeks per patient over 3 years*

		Weeks between screening and termination			
	number of cases	*mean*	*variance*	*F test*	*corrected t test*
Traditional treatment year (T)	17	19.00	20.88		
First community program year (C1)	31	8.63	5.08		
Second community program year (C2)	35	9.17	5.00		
T vs. C1				4.11*	8.50*
T vs. C2				4.17*	8.40*
C1 vs. C2				1.02	.01

*$P<0.05$

ers must be considered; as the present results show, a reinforcement-theory-based training program can lead to highly desirable outcomes. Thus, in terms of efficient use of the professional clinician's time, such a community program has much to recommend it.

Note

1. The authors are grateful to Ira Weinstein for his helpful suggestions in the preparation of this manuscript. Thanks are also due to Norman Teeter for his statistical analysis of the data.

References

Allen, K. E., Hart, B. M., Buell, J. S., Harris, F. R., and Wolf, M. M. (1965) Effects of social reinforcement on isolated behavior of a nursery school child. *Child Dev. 35,* 511–518.

Brown, P. and Elliot, R. (1965) Control of aggression in a nursery school class. *J. Exp. Child Psychol. 2,* 103–107.

Harris, F. R., Johnson, M. K., Kelley, C. S., and Wolf, M. M. (1964) Effects of positive social reinforcement on regressed crawling of a nursery school child. *J. Educ. Psychol. 55,* 35–41.

Harris, F. R., Wolf, M. M., and Baer, D. M. (1964) Effects of adult social reinforcement on child behavior. *Young Child. 20,* 8–17.

Hart, B. M., Allen, K. E., Buell, J. S., Harris, F. R., and Wolf, M. M. (1964) Effects of social reinforcement on operant crying. *J. Exp. Child Psychol. 1,* 145–153.

Hawkins, R. P., Peterson, R. F., Schweid, E., and Bijou, S. W. (1966) Behavior therapy in the home: amelioration of problem parent-child relations with the parent in the therapeutic role. *J. Exp. Child Psychol. 4,* 99–107.

Johnson, M. K., Kelley, C. S., Harris, F. R., and Wolf, M. M. (1966) An application of reinforcement principles to development of motor skills of a young child. In *Control of Human Behavior,* pp. 135–136. (Eds. Ulrich, R., Stachnik, T., and Mabry, J.). Scott, Foresman and Company.

Patterson, G. R., Littman, R. A., and Bricker, W. (1967) Assertive behavior in children: A step toward a theory of aggression. *Soc. Res. Child Dev. Monogr. 32,* No. 5.

Sarason, S. B., Levine, M., Goldenberg, I., Cherlin, D. L., and Bennett, E. M. (1966) *Psychology in Community Settings: Clinical, Educational, Vocational, Social Aspects.* John Wiley, New York.

Scott, P. M., Burton, R. V., and Yarrow, M. R. (1967) Social reinforcement under natural conditions. *Child Dev. 38,* 53–63.

Wahler, R. G. (1967) Child-child interactions in free field settings: some experimental analyses. *J. Exp. Child Psychol. 5,* 278–293.

Wahler, R. G., Winkel, G. H., Peterson, R. F., and Morrison, D. C. (1965). Mothers as behavior therapists for their own children. *Behav. Res. & Therapy 3,* 113–124.

Zeilberger, J., Sampen, S., and Sloane, H. (1968) Modification of a child's problem behaviours in the home with the mother as therapist. *J. App. Behav. Anal. 1,* 47–53.

4

JUDY KOPP GREEN AND
WILLIAM R. MORROW

Precision Social Work: General Model and Illustrative Projects with Clients

To facilitate individual change is one of the major tasks of social work and other helping professions. Traditional treatment methods aimed at accomplishing this task have been described only in rather general, vague terms. Criteria for assessing whether desired changes have been accomplished have likewise been vague and poorly operationalized. When traditional treatment methods have been subjected to controlled experimental evaluation of outcomes, the results have been disappointing. See, for example, Brown (1968); Meyer, Borgatta, and Jones (1965); Teuber and Powers (1953); also reviews by Briar (1966); Eysenck (1960a); Eysenck and Rachman (1965); Levitt (1957, 1963); Stuart (1969).

This paper combines three aims:

a. to describe and illustrate a relatively precise behavior modification model applied in social work practice for facilitating individual client change, accurately evaluating such change, and communicating objective data on clients' behavior and behavior change to clients themselves as well as to colleagues;

b. to describe a pedagogical experiment in which graduate social work students applied this new methodology as a field instruction assignment;

c. to suggest the applicability of "precision social work" in varied agency settings.

Thomas and his associates have introduced the behavior modification approach, based on learning principles, to the social work profession and have demonstrated its relevance for social work practice (Thomas and Goodman, 1967; Thomas, 1968; Stuart, 1967). Below a simplified, four-

Reprinted with permission of The Council on Social Work Education, from *Journal of Education for Social Work,* Fall, 1972, Vol. 8, No. 3.

step model is presented, developed by Ogden Lindsley (1967–68), for applying that approach with considerable precision.

First the behavior modification approach is briefly characterized, followed by the introduction and illustration of Lindsley's four-step model. Next a set of student projects applying the model with clients is summarized. An explanation of each step of the model is outlined in more detail and two additional case examples are presented. We conclude with comments on the values and limitations of the students' field instruction assignment, and on the utility of the model for social work education and practice.

THE BEHAVIOR MODIFICATION APPROACH

To facilitate individual change means to help individuals acquire, strengthen, maintain, or eliminate specifiable behaviors. A powerful causal principle, relevant to this task and supported by extensive experimental evidence (see, for example, Holland and Skinner, 1961; Honig, 1967; Kimball, 1961; 1967; Verhave, 1966), is that behavior is governed primarily by its environmental consequences: Behavior closely followed by reinforcing ("rewarding") consequences tends to increase in rate. A previously reinforced behavior that is consistently followed by no consequences (extinction) or by negative consequences (punishment) tends to decelerate.

In the behavior modification approach these and other behavior principles are systematically applied to alter problematic behaviors and behavior-deficits. The primary, though by no means exclusive, focus is on altering the environmental consequences of the behavior in order to change its frequency.

LINDSLEY'S SIMPLIFIED PRECISION MODEL—A CASE EXAMPLE

Lindsley's simplified model for applying these principles has four steps:

1. *pinpoint* the target behavior to be modified;
2. *record* the rate of that behavior;
3. *change consequences* of the behavior (or alter antecedent conditions preceding the behavior in such a way that consequences are indirectly changed); and
4. if the first try does not succeed, *try and try again* with revised modification procedures.

Figure 4.1 illustrates the model through a project conducted by a first-year graduate social work student assigned to a public welfare office.[1] The graph shows the rate at which "Jay," a twenty-year-old spastic, retarded man urinated in his clothes.[2] A physician had ruled out any organic basis for this behavior. Recently transferred from a state hospital to a nursing home, Jay had been referred to the local public welfare office for public assistance benefits. The nursing home director said that Jay must leave if he continued to be enuretic. He agreed, with reservation, to let the student try a program to eliminate the wetting behavior.

Conveniently, the nurses had been routinely recording the number of times Jay wet his clothes each day. (Ideally, a record should also have been obtained of Jay's then very low rate of urinating appropriately in the toilet.)

Jay's daily rate of wets was calculated in terms of a standard unit, "movements per minute," by dividing number of wets each day by number of minutes awake that day. This rate was plotted on a standardized graph form. Jay's median daily rate for a 15-day phase before modification was .0023, or twice in 840 minutes of waking time (See Figure 4.1).

Questionable punishment procedures, insisted upon by the nursing home director, were used in the first two modification phases. First, Jay was left wet for thirty minutes following each wet. Second, Jay was left in his room for the remainder of the day after he wet once. Throughout both punishment phases the median rate remained unchanged.

In a fourth phase, following consultation by the student with the junior author, and with the nursing home director's reluctant consent, Jay was given verbal praise and a piece of candy each time he urinated in the toilet. No punishment was used. Candy and praise were chosen as consequences after discussion with the nursing home personnel disclosed what Jay seemed to "go for." The procedure essentially eliminated wetting (p=.00,000,001 by Lindsley's mid-median test;[3] see Figure 4.1).

In an "after" phase (after specially arranged consequences were discontinued), the rate remained at zero except for one lapse. Presumably, approved toilet behavior and nonwetting were now maintained by natural consequences, such as social approval and the comfort of staying dry.

Summary of Student Projects with Clients

The client projects described in this paper were conducted by graduate social work students at the University of Missouri (Columbia) to fulfill a field instruction assignment in a wide variety of both inpatient and outpatient agencies. First-year students had two-day-a-week placements; second-year students, five-month full-time placements.

The assignment required each student to complete two behavior modification projects preferably with clients.[4] The assignment called for counting, recording, and graphing the rate of each target behavior throughout "before" and "during" modification phases, and successfully modifying the behavior.

The students were exposed to behavior modification principles in a first-semester theory course taught by the junior author. The specific Lindsley procedures were taught to the first-year students in that course through self-projects, and to the second-year students in an intensive one-day session.

The Lindsley model was introduced to field instructors of the first-year students in a five-session weekly seminar conducted by the senior author in

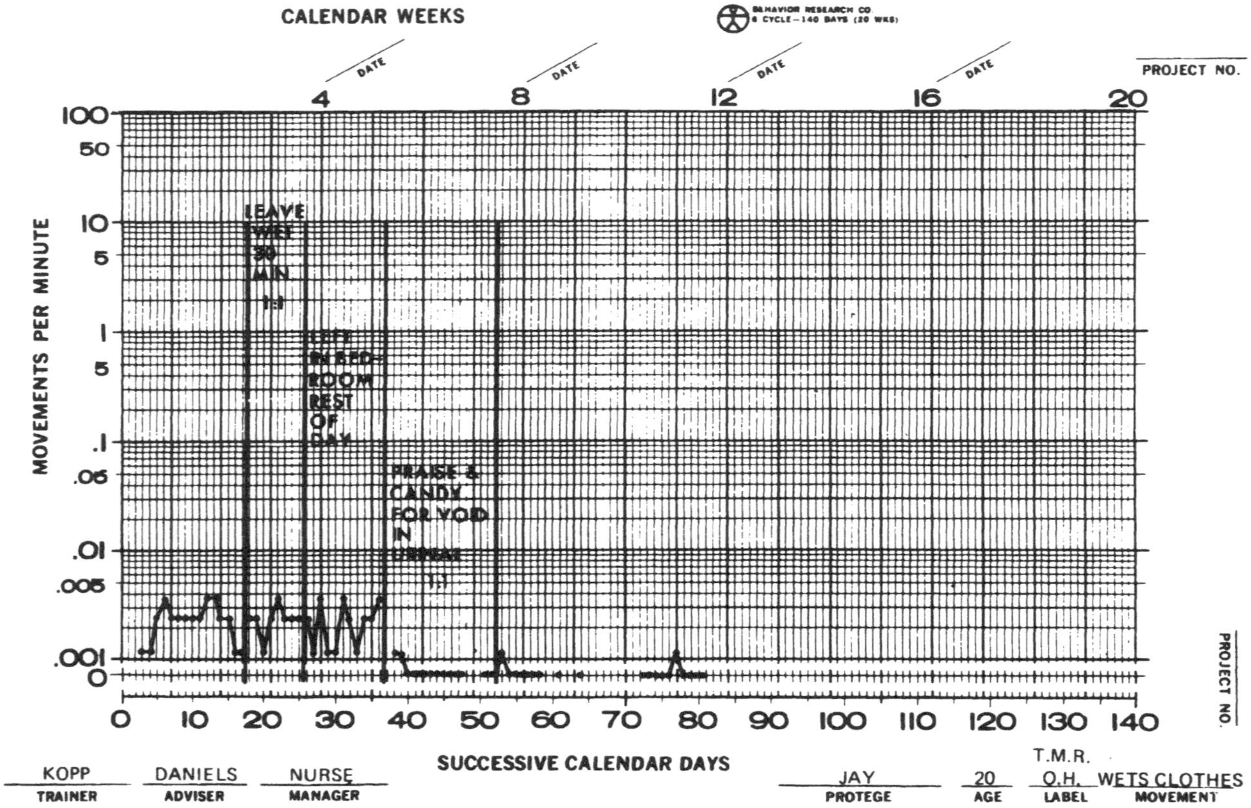

FIGURE 4.1 *Nursing home patient's rate of wetting clothes: before phase; two phases using punishment procedures; fourth phase using reward of incompatible desired behavior: and an after phase (same conditions as before phase).*

the preceding spring semester. Attendance was voluntary; three of 18 field instructors attended all five sessions, 13 attended three or more sessions, four did not attend at all. Many first- and second-year field instructors also participated in two one-day institutes that summer, in which this material was presented by a visiting speaker and by the senior author. The latter was available as a consultant to field instructors on request during the academic year; 11 first-year instructors (including three new instructors) and two second-year instructors requested consultation.

All but ten of 98 students completed the assignment on time; 67 turned in one or more projects involving clients—122 client projects in all.[5] Other projects involved behaviors of friends, relatives, co-workers, and the students themselves. The following summary applies only to *client* projects.

The person who keeps the daily behavior-record and sometimes also controls the consequences is called the manager. Projects were managed in the natural environment by agency aides, teachers, parents, spouses, or clients themselves—with the students serving as advisors, or sometimes directly by the students.

A wide variety of client behaviors were pinpointed for modification; these behaviors are categorized in Table 4.1. About three-fifths of the target behaviors involved deceleration goals; two-fifths, acceleration goals.

The median duration of projects from the first data-point (the behavior rate for one day) to the last was eight weeks for first-year students, five weeks for second-year students. Most projects included only two phases: "before" and "during" one (successful) modification procedure; 15 projects required more than one modification phase (five required three) before success was achieved. Eight projects included an "after" phase in which specially arranged consequences were discontinued so as to determine, by continued recording, whether the desired behavior rate was now maintained by naturally occurring consequences.

Most projects had 10-day "before" phases. The number of days per modification phase varied widely.

More than half of the projects yielded clearcut changes in the rate of the target behavior that were statistically significant at the .0001 level or beyond. The other projects yielded changes at more moderate significance levels.

Step 1. Pinpointing

A requirement of both scientific research and sound professional practice is that terms must be used to describe observed events in such a way that independent observers can agree as to when the events have occurred and when they have not. Otherwise error and pseudo-communication result. In the context of psychological treatment, this requirement calls for pinpointing each target behavior so that its occurrence during specific time-periods can be reliably observed and potentially counted. To this end, the

TABLE 4.1 *Problem behaviors pinpointed by graduate students*

Academic Skills	*Self-care skills*
correct words	brush teeth
homework	lipstick on
pegs in board	shaved
Attendance	soils
church	steps in dressing
school	wets
Distracting / disrupting behaviors	*Thoughts*
"crazy" noises	hate thoughts toward guards
feet on furniture	*Verbalization*
hit others	*(Except to worker)*
masturbate publicly	anti-treatment-goal comments
obey parent	argumentative responses
out of seat	complaints of illness
talk-out	criticisms to spouse
tap on desk	cuss words
various rule violations	incoherent mumbles
Interview behaviors	nags
complaints	"no's" and requests for self
complaints re: imagined illness	paranoid accusations
eye contact	tease siblings
positive verbalizations	verbalization to others
throat-clearing	*Miscellaneous*
Items in mouth	affection to wife (compliments, kisses,
cigarettes	invites to shared activities)
food	friendly acts to peers
liquor	initiates taking medication
lunch at same time daily	participates in activities
thumb	phone calls to staff
Tasks (at home or job)	receptionists' greetings
chores	shoulder spasms
items out of place	spouse doesn't answer
job tasks	steals
wash dishes	
On time	
out of bed	
to work	

behavior must be defined in terms of a definite beginning and end, that is, as a complete "movement cycle," so that the unit to be counted is clearly indicated. Thus, "typing" does not clearly pinpoint the unit to be counted; "words typed" does.

Accurate pinpointing necessitates individualizing clients, obtaining detailed information on their behavior, and replacing vague terms with precise descriptions of observed behavior. Social workers often find these tasks difficult. In a training workshop conducted by the senior author, 16 MSW social workers tried to pinpoint 117 problem behaviors of clients and workers. Of these initial attempts, 84 per cent were clearly inadequate. The most common errors were: (a) the use of vague, interpretive, mentalistic terms such as "anxious," instead of terms referring to the observed behaviors (verbal and nonverbal) that led the worker to apply the mentalistic label "anxious"; (b) the use of vague, overgeneral "trait" labels (e.g., "aggressive," "shy," "nervous") or primarily evaluative, nondescriptive labels (e.g., "immature," "psychopathic"), instead of terms referring to observed behaviors; and (c) the use of terms (e.g., "swearing") that fail to define a countable unit of behavior (e.g., a swear word uttered). The first two types of errors predominated.

In the case of problem behaviors to be eliminated, it is often useful to pinpoint—and record and modify—in addition, alternative approved behaviors to be accelerated. For example, it would have been useful to record Jay's daily rate of urinating in the toilet (as well as his rate of wetting).

Clients often desire help on more than one problem. Each problem behavior may be pinpointed, recorded, and modified—one at a time, starting with the behavior that most concerns the client or is most disruptive, or the one that seems most likely to yield an early success.

Step 2. Recording

The crucial aspect of a behavior viewed as a problem is usually its excessively high or low rate. Impressionistic estimates of behavior rates and changes in rates are imprecise and often grossly inaccurate. A continuous record of the observed daily rate of pinpointing behavior(s) before and during (preferably also after) modification procedures is essential. Such a record shows "where the client is" at all times, providing continuous feedback on the effectiveness of treatment procedures and when to revise them. Such a record replaces the guesswork of clinical impressions, which characterizes much traditional casework. To determine objectively whether the behavior rate has changed reliably from before phase to modification phase (or from modification phase to after phase), a shortcut statistical test such as the mid-median test can be used.[6]

High-rate behaviors may be counted reliably during one or more short time-samples each day; the recording periods should be at the same time of day and in similar circumstances from day to day. Enough days should be recorded in each phase to yield a reliable measure of the average daily rate for that phase. Ten days is usually adequate unless the daily rate fluctuates widely.

Economy and reliability of recording may be facilitated by using simple counters such as wrist golf scorers, keychain counters, knitting-stitch counters, or pieces of masking tape attached to the wrist on which to mark tallies.

Recording daily behavior rates on a graph yields important advantages.

The graph permits direct visual inspection of changes in behavior. Such visual evidence of change is usually rewarding and motivating for clients (including young children) as well as for therapists. Lack of change points up a need to revise modification procedures. The graph provides an objective visual focus for problem-solving discussion between client and worker, and helps to forestall aimless rambling and vague generalities.

The use of a standard rate-measure (movements per minute) and an all-purpose standardized graph saves much time (avoiding the need to prepare a new graph for each behavior) and facilitates comparisons.[7] The graph accommodates a very wide range of rates (.001 to 1,000 per minute) and up to 140 days.

Step 3. Changing Consequences

The main focus of modification procedures is usually on altering environmental consequences of the target behavior. This focus is an operational approach to the otherwise elusive problem of influencing motivation. Modification procedures may take the form of arranging for rewarding consequences to follow desired behavior, and/or arranging that unwanted behavior is consistently followed by no consequences (e.g., no attention) or by aversive consequences (presentation of aversive stimuli or removal of rewarding stimuli). In some cases (e.g., Jay's wetting), unwanted behavior may be altered most readily by rewarding an alternative desired behavior.

The consequences of behavior may also be changed indirectly. The individual may be taught new behaviors which evoke more positive consequences from the environment than did his previous repertoire. Or, situations may be rearranged so as to remove antecedent cues for unwanted behaviors and/or to augment cues for desired behavior. Or, the effectiveness of existing consequences may be altered by manipulating deprivation-satiation conditions or by rescheduling consequences (their immediacy or delay, or their intermittent vs. invariable occurrence).

Consequences must be suitable for repeated presentation, closely following occurrences of the target behavior, without sating the individual. Consequences that cannot be literally "sliced up" for such repeated presentation may be "sliced up" indirectly by use of tokens (or tallies) that are exchangeable later for the back-up consequences.

Above all, consequences must be custom-tailored to each individual. Suitable individualized positive consequences can be selected by observing what the individual does when he is free to choose activities, persons, objects, consumables, and other environmental events. Or one may ask a person who has observed the individual extensively to report this information; or the individual himself may be asked his preferences. Similarly, suitable individualized negative consequences may be discovered by observing what the individual avoids, or by asking others (including the individual himself) to report such observations. The client should usually be involved in selecting the consequence. (The proof, of course, is whether the presumed "consequence" turns out in fact to *function* as a consequence by altering the rate of the target behavior when it regularly follows that behavior.)

Additional Case Examples

A mother receiving aid-to-dependent-children assistance, when seen by a social work student, complained that her teenage daughter often left personal clothing scattered about the house.[8] The mother had repeatedly "gotten after" the girl about this, to no avail. After the "before" rate of this behavior was recorded for 16 days, a litterbox procedure was introduced (see Lindsley, 1966). Any item of clothing discovered out of place would be put in a grocery carton kept in a closet. Not until the following Sunday, when sins are forgiven, would the item be returned to its owner. To increase its perceived fairness and acceptability, the procedure was made a family affair, applicable to the mother and to her other children as well as to the girl in question. For several days the procedure had an apparent effect. Then the daughter wanted urgently to wear to a school dance a pair of slacks which had disappeared into the Sunday Box. With some difficulty, the mother held to the rule. After this incident, no more clothes were left out of place, and the rate remained at zero even after the procedure was discontinued (see Figure 4.2). The change was (marginally) significant from before phase to modification phase ($p=.05$), and from before phase to after phase ($p=.03$).

A young mother with family problems was seen by a student social worker in a public health center where the client initially came for prenatal care.[9] The client persistently voiced vague physical complaints (headaches, chest and leg pains, "flu") that were found to have no medical basis. The persistence of these complaints interfered with constructive use of interviews for problem solving. Explanations to the client that her complaints had no medical basis were ineffectual in decelerating the complaints, as were efforts to "change the subject." It was the worker's impression that these complaints were maintained by the attention which they coerced from listeners, including herself. As the first step in a modification plan, the worker recorded the baseline frequency of such complaints during two five-minute periods in each of five interviews—one period at the beginning of the interviews, the other in the middle. The rate averaged almost one complaint per minute (see Figure 4.3). The worker shared this data with the client, discussed the reasons for changing the behavior, and explained the following modification procedure, which was then put into effect. Whenever the client mentioned unsubstantiated physical symptoms, the worker would ignore the client and pointedly look away. Whenever the client verbalized positive attitudes about her physical health, the worker would give special attention and approval.

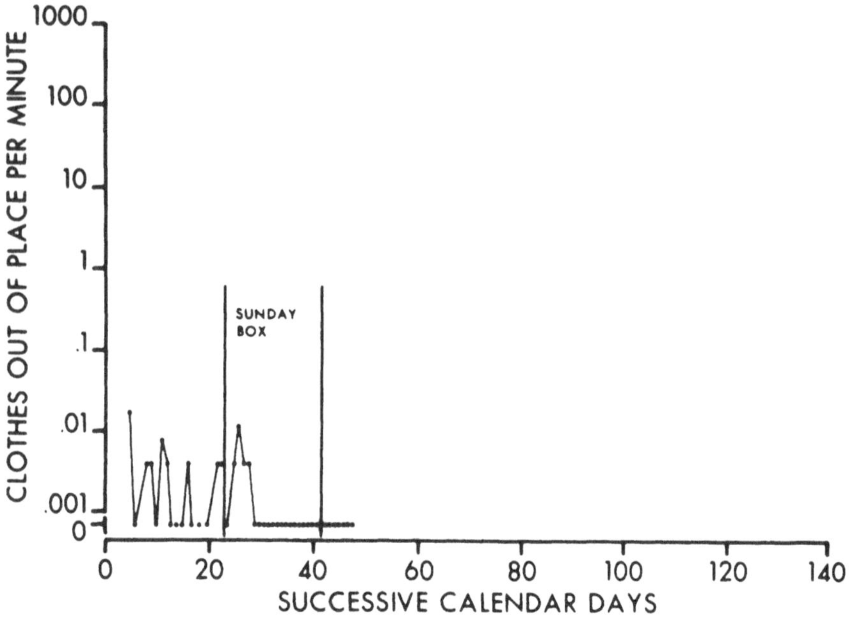

FIGURE 4.2 *Client's daughter's rate of leaving clothes out of place: before phase; phase using "Sunday Box" consequence; and after phase (same conditions as before phase).*

Following an interview in which there were no unsubstantiated physical complaints, the worker would take the client out for coffee. As shown in Figure 4.3, this plan was relatively successful in decelerating hypochondriacal complaints ($p = .002$).

CONCLUDING COMMENTS

The above summary and illustrations of student projects with clients suggest the practical utility and almost unlimited range of applicability of the precision social work model. More rigorously controlled evidence for the effectiveness and broad applicability of behavior modification technology is available in numerous published studies. See, for example, Bandura (1969); Bijou and Baer (1967); Eysenck (1960b, 1964); Franks (1969: part I); Krasner and Ullmann (1965); Krumboltz and Thoresen (1969); Ullmann and Krasner (1965).[10]

The material presented also suggests the practicality and instructional values of incorporating such an assignment in field instruction for social work students. Most students completed the assignment successfully—the majority, through projects serving agency clients. They thereby demon-

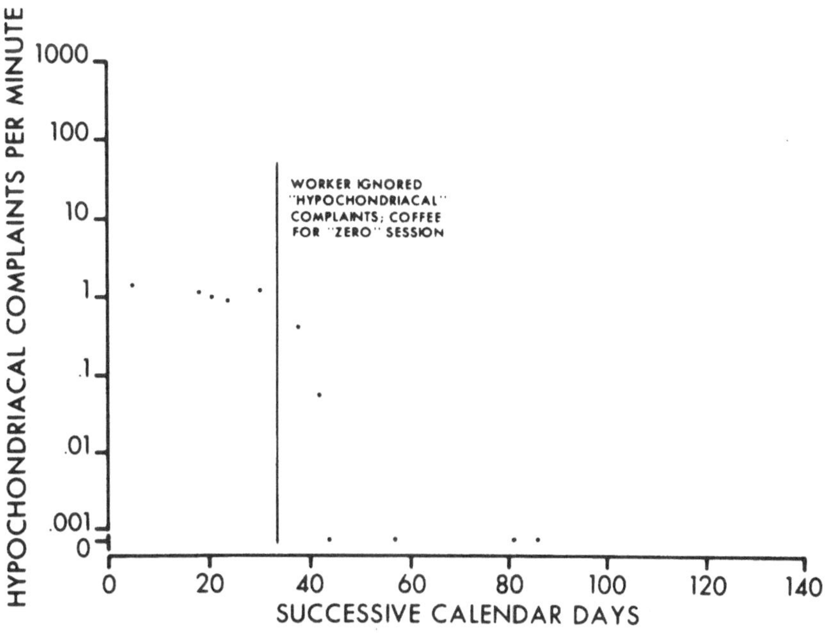

FIGURE 4.3 *Hypochondriacal complaints of pregnant client: before phase, and phase when worker ignored such complaints but offered coffee after each session with zero hypochondriacal complaints.*

strated beginning skills in specifying problematic and desired behaviors operationally, in using procedures for observing and recording and graphing such behaviors reliably, and in applying behavior modification procedures for helping clients to alter target behaviors.

Most of the students expressed to us informally their personal satisfaction with the learning values of this assignment in preparing them for social work practice. In addition, a number of them, after working in agencies following completion of the MSW degree, have volunteered to us their judgment that training in behavior modification principles and in the precision social work model was one of the most valuable aspects of their preparation for social work practice.

On the other hand, many of the student projects had limitations from the standpoint of service to the client. In some, for lack of sufficiently detailed information gathering, the choice of consequences did not seem to be adequately individualized. The arrangement of consequences often did not apply what is known regarding the effects of different schedules of reinforcement; consequences were sometimes arranged so as to occur too long after the behavior, and too infrequently relative to the amount of behavior required, to be maximally effective. Many projects were not continued long enough during modification phases to assure that stable change of the target behavior had been achieved. Few projects included an after or follow-up phase, as a check on whether control of the target behavior had shifted to natural consequences present in the everyday life situation. Finally, although most of the target behaviors were important for the client to change in order to "get along better" in their everyday environments, many clients presented additional important problems for which precision social work procedures were not offered.

This incompleteness of service probably reflected in part limitations in knowledge and skill on the part of both students and field instructors, as well as the latter's discomfort with a body of knowledge and skills that was new to them and challenged some of their traditional assumptions. The effectiveness of field instruction in this regard may require more adequate preparation and in-service training of field instructors.

Notes

1. James Daniels.
2. See below, section on "Recording," for discussion of graphing; and see note 7 for information on where copies of this graph form may be obtained.
3. The mid-median test is an approximation of Fisher's exact test of significance for 2 x 2 contingency tables. In this application the 2 x 2 table is formed by first determining the median data-point within each phase (e.g., before phase or during-modification phase, respectively), and then determining the mid-median of the two phases being compared. The mid-median is the point numerically half-way between the respective phase-medians. The 2 x 2 table is formed by counting the number of data-points in the first phase which lie above or below the mid-median, respectively, and doing likewise for the second phase. To simplify computations, Fisher's exact test is applied using a table of approximate (grossly rounded) values of factorials and rounding the resulting p-value to a single significant digit.
4. Doing projects with a friend, associate, relative, or oneself as subjects was permitted as an "out" for students who might have difficulty in completing successful projects with clients.
5. This total excludes six second-year transfer-in students to whom the assignment did not apply, but includes three community organization students for whom the requirement was administratively ambiguous.
6. See note 3.
7. See Figure 4.1. Copies of this graph form are available from Behavior Research Company, Box 3351, Kansas City, Kansas 66103, @ $20 per ream.
8. Sara Copman.
9. Jo Ann Sheeley.
10. Also see research reports published in four journals devoted exclusively to this area, *Behavior Research and Therapy*, *Behavior Therapy*, the *Journal of Applied Behavior Analysis*, and the *Journal of Behavior Therapy and Experimental Psychiatry*.

References

Bandura, Albert. *Principles of behavior modification.* New York: Holt, Rinehart and Winston, 1969.

Bijou, Sidney W., and Baer, Donald B. *Child development: Readings in experimental analysis.* New York: Appleton-Century-Crofts, 1967.

BRIAR, SCOTT. Family services. In Henry S. Maas (Ed.), *Five fields of social service: Reviews of research.* New York: National Association of Social Workers, 1966.

BROWN, GORDON E. (Ed.) *The multi-problem dilemma: A social research demonstration with multi-problem families.* Metuchen, N.J.: Scarecrow Press, 1968.

EYSENCK, HANS J. The effects of psychotherapy. In H. J. Eysenck (Ed.), *Handbook of abnormal psychology.* London: Pitman Medical Publishers, 1960. (a)

EYSENCK, HANS J. (Ed.) *Behavior therapy and the neuroses.* New York: Pergamon, 1960. (b)

EYSENCK, HANS J. *Experiments in behavior therapy.* New York: Pergamon, 1964.

EYSENCK, HANS J., and RACHMAN, STANLEY. *The causes and cures of neurosis.* San Diego: Robert R. Knapp, 1965.

FRANKS, CYRIL M. (Ed.) *Behavior therapy: Appraisal and status.* New York: McGraw-Hill, 1969.

HOLLAND, JAMES G., and SKINNER, B. F. *The analysis of human behavior.* New York: McGraw-Hill, 1961.

HONIG, WALTER K. (Ed.) *Operant behavior: Areas of application.* New York: Appleton-Century-Crofts, 1967.

KIMBLE, GREGORY A. *Hilgard and Marquis, conditioning and learning,* 2nd ed. New York: Appleton-Century-Crofts, 1961.

KIMBLE, GREGORY A. (Ed.) *Foundations of conditioning and learning.* New York: Appleton-Century-Crofts, 1967.

KRASNER, LEONARD, and ULLMANN, LEONARD. (Eds.) *Research in behavior modification.* New York: Holt, Rinehart, and Winston, 1965.

KRUMBOLTZ, JOHN D., and THORESEN, CARL E. (Eds.) *Behavioral counseling: Cases and techniques.* New York: Holt, Rinehart, and Winston, 1969.

LEVITT, EUGENE E. The results of psychotherapy with children: An evaluation. *Journal of Consulting Psychology,* 1957, *21,* 189–196.

LEVITT, EUGENE E. Psychotherapy with children: A further evaluation. *Behavior Research and Therapy,* 1963, *1,* 45–51.

LINDSLEY, OGDEN R. An experiment with parents handling behavior at home. *Johnstone Bulletin,* 1966, *9,* 27–36.

LINDSLEY, OGDEN R. Operant behavior management: Background and procedures, *and* Training parents and teachers to precisely manage children's behavior. University of Kansas Medical Center, Children's Rehabilitation Unit—Special Education Research, mimeo, 1967–68.

MEYER, HENRY J., BORGATTA, EDGAR F., and JONES, WYATT C. *Girls at vocational high: An experiment in social work intervention.* New York: Russell Sage Foundation, 1965.

STUART, RICHARD B. Analysis and illustration of the process of assertive conditioning. Paper read at National Conference on Social Welfare 94th Annual Forum, Dallas, May, 1967.

STUART, RICHARD B. *Trick or treatment: When and how psychotherapy fails.* Champaign, IL: Research Press, 1969.

TEUBER, N. L., and POWERS, E. Evaluating therapy in a delinquency prevention program. *Proceedings, Association for Research in Nervous and Mental Diseases,* 1953, *31,* 138–147.

THOMAS, EDWIN J. Selected sociobehavioral techniques and principles; An approach to interpersonal helping. *Social Work,* 1968, *13,* 12–26.

THOMAS, EDWIN J., and GOODMAN, ESTHER. (Eds.) *Socio-behavioral approach and applications to social work*. New York: Council on Social Work Education, 1967.

ULLMANN, LEONARD, and KRASNER, LEONARD. (Eds.) *Case studies in behavior modification*. New York: Holt, Rinehart, and Winston, 1965.

VERHAVE, THOM. (Ed.) *The experimental analysis of behavior*. New York; Appleton-Century-Crofts, 1966.

5

SIDNEY W. BIJOU, ROBERT F. PETERSON,
FLORENCE R. HARRIS, K. EILEEN ALLEN, AND
MARGARET S. JOHNSTON

Methodology for Experimental Studies of Young Children in Natural Settings

Child psychology began with the direct observation of children in natural settings as the writings of Darwin, Preyer, Hall, Baldwin, and Taine will attest. Over the years, variations on this procedure have produced a wealth of information describing the flow of behavior changes. These variations have not been nearly as successful in providing data for an experimental analysis of child development.

Typically, experimental observational studies of children in natural settings have been weak because they have not taken into account advances in methodology in laboratory (contrived) investigations. The procedures described in this paper attempt to do that and will be seen to differ from traditional methods in three major ways.

The first difference is in experimental strategy. Most field-experimental studies have used the group S strategy; here we advocate the single S design. In the single S design (Dinsmoor, 1966; Gelfand and Hartmann, 1968; and Sidman, 1960), data on a child are usually collected under four conditions to evaluate the functional relationships between the conditions manipulated and changes in behavior. In condition one, baseline, the situation remains unchanged except for the addition of an observer; in condition two, a change is made; in condition three, the altered condition is eliminated or negated; and in condition four, the experimental condition is reinstated. On the other hand, in the group S strategy, data are obtained to ascertain functional relationships between groups of children observed in different situations. Usually data on individual children are pooled to obtain a value for children receiving similar "treatment," and the performance of one group is compared with other groups subjected to different experimental or control

Reprinted with permission of *The Psychological Record,* 1969, Vol. 19, pp. 177–210.

conditions. Studies by Lambert (1960) and Bandura and Walters (1963) exemplify this type of design.

The second difference between the method described here and conventional methods is in the way stimulus and response events are derived. Here they are defined in observable terms. Inferences and hypothetical concepts are avoided. In the Lambert-Bandura-Walters method, for example, they are also defined in observable terms but inferences about the observed events are admissible. Thus hypothetical concepts such as "intent," "wish," and "desire" are often included as part of the "raw" data.

A third difference is in the method for measuring response strength. In this presentation, the strength of a response is its frequency of occurrence. In the Lambert-Bandura-Walters approach, the strength may be frequency of occurrence, latency, intensity, duration, or a combination thereof. The advantages of the *consistent use* of a frequency measure have been repeatedly stressed by Skinner (1966). More on this point later.

We shall consider the procedures for a field-experimental study as characterized in the preceding paragraphs, under the following headings: (*a*) Specifying the field-experimental situation; (*b*) Defining response events; (*c*) Defining stimulus events; (*d*) Evaluating observer reliabilities; (*e*) Collecting data; and (*f*) Analyzing and interpreting data.[1]

The Field-Experimental Situation

The field-experimental situation consists of the physical and social circumstances in which the study is conducted. The physical setting may be part of the child's home, hospital, institution, school, or child guidance clinic. In the home the situation might include the living room and kitchen (Hawkins, Peterson, Schweid, and Bijou, 1966); in the hospital, the child's ward and his bedroom (Wolf, Risley, and Mees, 1964); in the public school, a special classroom or elementary classroom (Becker, Madsen, Arnold, and Thomas, 1967; Birnbrauer, Wolf, Kidder, and Tague, 1965); in the nursery school, the nursery school room and the play yard (Hart, Allen, Buell, Harris, and Wolf, 1964); and in the clinic, the play therapy room with the usual furniture and equipment (Wahler, Winkel, Peterson, and Morrison, 1965).

During the course of a study the physical situation may change despite the investigator's efforts to the contrary. Some changes may be so extreme as to preclude further study until the original situation has been restored (e.g., power failure for several days); others might be routine and would not warrant disrupting the study (e.g., old chairs in the child's hospital bedroom being replaced with new ones).

Let us now consider the social circumstances of field-experimental situations. In the child's home, the social conditions might involve the behavior of the mother (Zeilberger, Sampen, and Sloane, 1968) or the mother and a younger sibling (Hawkins *et al.* 1966). Variations which would preclude continued observations might be the additional members of the family or friends, illnesses, or any other event which would disrupt the regular routines of family life. Transient interruptions may also occur: the phone may ring, a salesman may appear, a neighbor may visit—all at the wrong time from the point of view of the study. Intrusions such as these can be minimized if the parent is instructed how to handle them beforehand.

In a nursery school study, the social conditions might include the head teacher, two assistant teachers and the children in the group, as in the study of motor skills in a nursery school boy (Johnston, Kelley, Harris and Wolf, 1966). Absence of the head teacher or an assistant teacher, or presence of the child's mother would probably vary the situation enough to preclude data collection. Marked reduction in class attendance due to illness, inclement weather, or holiday preparations at home would also be considered a cardinal alteration in the field situation. Holiday preparations, parties for parents, or widespread debilitating colds would constitute setting factors that would call a halt to research until the standard situation is restored.

In summary, the physical and social conditions in a field-experimental situation should be specified at the outset of a study. Whether subsequent variations are judged major or minor will depend, in large measure, on the nature of the problem, practical considerations, and the investigator's experience with similar events in the past. In any event, all the changes that occur during the study should be reported as part of the data.

Response Events

The purpose of an investigation will dictate which response events will be selected for study (Bijou and Baer, 1966). Investigations which aim to demonstrate an empirical relationship involving an antecedent stimulus condition, a reinforcement contingency, or a setting event might use behaviors which are relatively easy to measure and record (Bijou and Baer, 1961), while investigations designed to analyze prototypes of larger sets of responses ("personality" characteristics, for example) might use responses with features intrinsically related to the problem. One might study hyperactivity to determine whether it is modifiable by the manipulation of social contingencies. Studies which aim to test theory would, of course, use response classes which center on the problem. For example, the investigator who is interested in analyzing the interaction between operants and respondents in emotional behavior would select response classes which clearly have both properties. Studies which aim to provide information on a clinical problem would probably employ the response class indigenous to the problem. Hence, certain responses would be observed because in their mild form they constitute a problem in normal children and in their more severe form they constitute the core of a problem in deviant development, such as temper tantrums.

How should the responses selected for study be defined and measured? Procedures for defining the responses are considered in detail beginning with the next topic.

As noted earlier, the strength of the response may be measured in terms of its latency, intensity, duration, frequency of occurrence, or some combination thereof. It is our opinion that a *frequency of occurrence* measure is most serviceable for a natural science approach to field-experimental studies. First, it readily shows changes over short and long intervals, and second, it gives a measure of the amount of behavior displayed (Honig, 1966). Finally, and perhaps most importantly, it has been demonstrated to be workable for many species observed in a wide range of situations. Witness, for example the orderliness and interrelatedness of data reported in the *Journal of the Experimental Analysis of Behavior.*

Skinner (1966) has argued frequently for a rate measure of behavior. The following is a particularly cogent statement:

> Rate of responding is important because it is especially relevant to the principal task of a scientific analysis. Behavior is often interesting because of what might be called its *character*. Animals court their mates, build living quarters, care for their young, forage for food, defend territories, and so on, in many fascinating ways. These are worth studying, but the inherent drama can divert attention from another task. Even when reduced to general principles, a narrative account of *how* animals behave must be supplemented by a consideration of *why*. What is required is an analysis of the conditions which govern the probability that a given response will occur at a given time. Rate of responding is by no means to be equated with probability of responding, as frequency theories of probability and comparable problems in physics have shown. Many investigators prefer to treat rate of responding as a datum in its own right. Eventually, however, the prediction and control of behavior call for an evaluation of the probability that a response will be emitted. The study of rate of responding is a step in that direction [pp. 15–16].

Deriving Response Terms from Preliminary Observation

We recommend that response terms be derived from observations in the field-experimental situation. This procedure provides the investigator with an opportunity to observe the kinds of responses that actually occur and their rates, to infer probable functional relationships, and to evaluate the situation for a field-experimental study. The following is an account of the preliminary procedures in a parent-child study in a child guidance clinic (Wahler *et al.*, 1965):

> For the first two sessions, the mother was instructed, "Just play with——— as you might at home." These instructions were modified for one of the cases when a later analysis of the data revealed little or no evidence of what the parents had earlier described as deviant behavior. In this case the mother was

given other instructions, based on her description of her typical behavior at home.

During these sessions, two observers, working in separate observation rooms, obtained written records of the child's and the mother's behavior. Analysis of these records began with a selection of the child's deviant behavior. This selection was based upon similarities between the recorded behavior and the behavior which the parents reported to create problems at home. A second classification of the child's behavior was made to establish a class of behavior which the experimenter regarded as incompatible with the deviant behavior. Later, strengthening of this class was used in eliminating the deviant behavior.

A second analysis of the written records involved a description of the mother's ways of reacting to her child's deviant behavior, and to his incompatible behavior. Essentially, this analysis provided a description of possible reinforcers provided by the mother for the two classes of the child's behavior [p. 115].

Another example of a preliminary procedure in a field situation is the following narrative of an autistic child and members of his family in the home situation (Zimmerman and Ferster, 1961).

I arrived at 4 p.m. simultaneously with Mrs. Doe. I walked into the house with them and sat down on the couch. She asked if there were any questions. I said, "No, just go about your usual routine and ignore me." She proceeded into the kitchen to prepare dinner.

John and the little girl walked around the dining room and living room for about two minutes.

Mrs. Doe said, shouting from the kitchen, "Go play with your records, John." John ignored. She repeated the same, coming into the dining room where the phonograph lay on the floor. She put a record on for him. John approached the record player, sat down on the floor next to it. He removed the needle and disrupted the record. John's mother, upon hearing the scratching from the kitchen, shouted, "John, just one record at a time! You know just one record at a time!" He got up, left the record player, played with another toy on the floor. It was a heavy metal top. He then approached the basement door which was open. He was holding the top. He paused at the top of the stairs and then proceeded to throw the top down the stairs.

The mother shouted from the kitchen, "John, what did you do now? Go get the top and bring it into the house." Upon his mother's command, John walked slowly down the stairs, got the top, came up again, and repeated the procedure of throwing it down the stairs. The mother shouted again but did not appear. "John, go get the top. Bring the top into the house. I told you to bring the top into the house." John stood at the basement door while his mother commanded. At the end of her comments, John went slowly down the stairs, got the top and brought it back into the house and placed it on the floor. He did not proceed to play with it. The mother gave no verbal reinforcement when John got the top. She is still in the kitchen most of the time, peering out periodically demanding of John, "Do this, don't do that!" John did have a small amount of time to himself because his mother was preparing dinner. He approached me several times. At first when I arrived, he picked up my pocketbook and started playing with it. I ignored him.

Mrs. Doe said, "John, put the lady's pocketbook down." He continued his behavior nevertheless. I finally took the purse away from him fearing that he would empty the contents on the floor. I put it in an inaccessible place. Twice

John approached me as I was reading a book. He tapped the book, he pulled the book. I ignored him. He went away for the remainder of my visit.

The mother left the kitchen several times. She went to John.

"Come dance with me," she said on one occasion. She put a record on the phonograph and dragged him around on the floor for 2 minutes.

Several times, when the little girl was nearby, John smilingly pinched her. John's mother, upon hearing the cries, shouted, "Leave your sister alone, leave your sister alone!" He did not let her alone until the little girl ran away or was taken away by her mother.

Some investigators follow the practice of taking a narrative and then transforming it into a three-column table, patterned after the three-term contingency (Skinner, 1953), to obtain a clearer impression of the relationships among the antecedent stimulus events (cues for action), responses, and consequent stimulus events. Consider the following running account of a child's behavior in a nursery school play yard.

Timmy was playing by himself in a sandbox in a play yard in which other children are playing. A teacher stands nearby. Timmy tires of the sandbox and walks over to climb the monkeybars. Timmy shouts at the teacher, saying, "Mrs. Simpson, watch me." Timmy climbs to the top of the apparatus and shouts again to the teacher, "Look how high I am. I'm higher than anybody." The teacher comments on Timmy's climbing ability with approval. Timmy then climbs down and runs over to a tree, again demanding that the teacher watch him. The teacher, however, ignores Timmy and walks back into the classroom. Disappointed, Timmy walks toward the sandbox instead of climbing the tree. A little girl nearby cries out in pain as she stumbles and scrapes her knee. Timmy ignores her and continues to walk to the sandbox.

If this episode were recorded in terms of antecedent stimulus events, operant responses, and consequent social events, it would take the following form:

Setting: Timmy (T.) is playing alone in a sandbox in a play yard in which there are other children playing. T. is scooping sand into a bucket with a shovel, then dumping the sand onto a pile. A teacher, Mrs. Simpson (S.), stand approximately six feet away but does not attend to T.

Time	*Antecedent Event*	*Response*	*Consequent Social Event*
9:14		1. T. throws bucket and shovel into corner of sandbox. 2. T. stands up. 3. T. walks over to monkeybars and stops. 4. T. turns toward teacher. 5. T. says, "Mrs. Simp-	

Time	*Antecedent Event*	*Response*	*Consequent Social Event*
	6. Mrs. S. turns toward Timmy.	son, watch me."	6. Mrs. S. turns toward Timmy.
		7. T. climbs to top of apparatus.	
		8. T. looks toward teacher.	
		9. T. says, "Look how high I am. I'm higher than anybody."	
9:16	10. Mrs. S. says, "That's good, Tim. You're getting quite good at that."	11. T. climbs down.	10. Mrs. S. says, "That's good, Tim. You're getting quite good at that."
		12. T. runs over to tree.	
		13. T. says, "Watch me climb the tree, Mrs. Simpson."	
	14. Mrs. S. turns and walks toward classroom.	15. T. stands, looking toward Mrs. S.	14. Mrs. S. turns and walks toward classroom.
9:18	16. Girl nearby trips and falls, bumping knee.		
	17. Girl cries	18. T. proceeds to sandbox.	
		19. T. picks up bucket and shovel.	
		20. T. resumes play with sand.	

Note that a response event (e.g., 5. T. says, "Mrs. Simpson, watch me.") may be followed by a consequent social event (e.g., 6. Mrs. S. turns toward Timmy.) which may also be the antecedent stimulus for T's next response (e.g., 7. T. climbs to top of apparatus). Note too, that antecedent stimulus events (e.g., 16. Girl nearby trips and falls, bumping knee, and 17. Girl cries) are not followed by responses on the part of the subject. These have a neutral function for him; or stated differently, they are not part of his functional environment. Note, finally, that the child's behavior is *described*. Inferences about his feelings, intentions, and other presumed internal states are excluded.

Defining and Recording Response Events

The main problem in defining a response event is establishing criteria so that two or more observers can agree on its occurrence. For example, if it is desired to record the number of times a child hits other children, the definition of hitting must be described so that an observer can discriminate among hitting, patting, and shoving responses. Or, if it is desired to record the number of times a child says, "No," the definition of "No" must be specified so that an observer can discriminate it from other words the child utters, and from nonverbal forms of negative expressions. Sometimes response definitions include criteria for magnitude and duration. For example, in a study by

Hart *et al.* (1964), crying was defined in a way to distinguish it from whining and screaming, and in addition, it had to be "(a) loud enough to be heard at least 50 feet away, and (b) of 5-seconds or more duration."

Response events which are composed of several classes of responses such as isolate behavior, fantasy-play, aggressive behavior, and temper tantrums must, of course, have definitions with objective criteria for each response included in the category. We can best elaborate on the problem of adequate response definitions by looking at the procedures for establishing behavioral codes.

There are two major approaches to coding responses. The first involves making a *specific response code* for each investigation. For example, at the Child Behavior Laboratory at the University of Illinois a code was prepared for studying attending-to-work behavior in a distractible seven-year-old boy. Attending-to-work included: (1) counting words, (2) looking at the words, and (3) writing numbers or letters. When any of these behaviors occurred during a 20-second interval, it was scored as an interval of work. In a second study involving a six-year-old boy with a similar problem, this code was modified slightly. In order for the observer to mark occurrence of attending-to-work behavior in the 20-second interval, the child had to engage in relevant behavior for a minimum of ten seconds. The reliability on both codes averaged 90 per cent for two observers over twelve sessions. (See section 3 for methods of determining observer reliability.) Another code involving spontaneous speech was developed for a four-year-old girl who rarely spoke. Incidences of speech were recorded whenever she uttered a word or words which were not preceded by a question or a prompt by a peer or teacher. Reliability averaged 80 per cent for two observers over 15 sessions. In a third instance, a code was made to study tantrum behaviors in a six-year-old boy. The responses which defined tantrum behavior included crying, whining, sobbing, and whimpering. The average reliability for this class of behavior was 80 per cent for two observers over 11 sessions.

In contrast to this highly vocal form of tantrum behavior, Brawley, Harris, Allen, Fleming, and Peterson (1969) developed a code which recorded temper outbursts centering around vigorous motor responses. In their investigation a tantrum was noted each time the child engaged in hitting himself plus any one of the following: (1) loud crying, (2) kicking, or (3) throwing himself or objects about.

The second approach to coding responses is through the construction of a *general response code,* one that can be employed to study almost any behavior in a given field situation. An example of such a code is one prepared by the nursery school staff at the University of Washington. It is presented in Table 5.1. The symbols in the left-hand column of the table are recorded on a data sheet such as is shown in Table 5.2. Each 3-box segment represents a time interval of 15 seconds and each block of 12 boxes represent 1 minute.

TABLE 5.1 *General response code for studying children in a nursery school*

Symbol	*Definition*
	Top row
V	v = subject (*S*) verbalizes. Possible variations: v̶ = *S* addresses teacher or answers teacher's question Ⓥ = *S* directs, requests of, demands of, "bosses" another child (*O*) ↓ = *S* calls *O* by name from a distance of more than three feet
	Middle row
P	1. *S* and *O* within 3 feet of each other for at least half of 10-second interval. Brief encounters—e.g., *S* walks past *O*—are not entered. 2. *S* and *O* on separate trikes within 6 feet. 3. The following pieces of equipment or activity areas are assumed to give proximity to *S* and *O*: a. swings b. tunnel c. easels d. chairs at a table
T	*S* touches *O*, or *O* touches *S* (a single physical contact during any 10-second interval).
	Bottom row
E	*S* and *O* in or on one of the following pieces of outdoor equipment at the same time. The equipment is not used as the location for a "parallel-play" or "shared-play" activity. ("Props" brought in—e.g., large blocks, dishes, blankets, rocks, sand, leaves—change the play to *A* or *C*): 1. swings 2. boat 3. trees 4. jungle gym, rope ladder, climbing frame 5. packing boxes 6. logs 7. rocking board, teeter-totter 8. little house (inside or roof area) 9. tunnel 10. tumble tub 11. trikes (*S* and *O* on separate trikes, within 15 feet) 12. fence 13. rope connected equipment
	S and *O* engaged in a "parallel-play" activity, that is, an activity in which their staying together can be attributed primarily either to the reinforcing properties of the play material or to the structure given to the situation by some outside agent. 1. An activity supervised by the teacher or resulting from teacher direction (creative materials, feeding and looking at pets). 2. An activity taking place in a predetermined location. For example: a. easel painting b. table play

TABLE 5.1—*Continued*

A

c. rug areas in creative room and large room
d. doll corner play (rug in area included)
e. sand box

3. An activity involving identical or related material, in which *S* and *O* play relatively independent of one another. For example:
   a. *S* and *O* digging with separate shovels in same general location.
   b. *S* and *O* building separate block structures in general location.
   c. *S* and *O* with separate wheelbarrows, wagons, or other pull-push toys.
4. Children's attention around focal objects—e.g., rabbit, worms, magnifying table, thermometer, pets.

C

S and *O* engaged in a "shared-play" activity, in which reinforcement is derived largely from the mutual use of materials or from the presence of the other child.

1. An activity involving a common object, with "object" defined as
   a. any movable item (single toy, rope) or items (*S* and *O* adding blocks to same structure; taking beads from same box).
   b. a particular part of a nonmovable item which is the direct object of play for both *S* and *O* (*S* and *O* digging or filling the same hole; *S* and *O* jumping on board together; *S* and *O* washing in same basin or bucket).
2. An activity involving an exchange of objects (*S* and *O* throwing pine cones or leaves at each other; *S* handing *O* a rolling pin).
3. A cooperative activity—e.g., *S* and *O* teetering; *S* pulling *O* in a wagon; *S* and *O* in tumble tub.
4. A "unified" or "organized" activity involving intimate movements or gestures or common verbalizations (*S* and *O* crawling around on ground, roaring like lions). A "game"; a parade.
5. A shared-play activity identified as such through verbal approach and response between *S* and *O*, e.g., *S*: "Let's build a house." *O*: "O.K."; or *O*: "Let's build a house"; *S* starts building.
6. A sustained physical encounter. (*S* and *O* wrestling. *O* hits *S*, who hits back.)

S and *O* moving together from one area to another.

Note: In *time sampling*, when more than one child is being observed, this notation can be used to express the fact that *S* and *O* have moved together from one location to another. Thus, if when last observed *S* and *O* were in the sand box and are now on the swings (but were not observed moving together to the swings) the information can be coded as follows:

Interval 1 Interval 2

S and *O* remaining together for more than one interval.

1. In a situation involving no activity, equipment, etc. (*S* and *O* simply standing beside each other at the fence for more than one interval).

TABLE 5.1—*Continued*

Interval 1 Interval 2

2. On a piece of equipment not being used in active play. (*S* and *O* sitting together inside packing box or in boat for more than one interval).

Interval 1 Interval 2

Count for Social Behavior Data

Isolation = V alone, or no entry in 10-second interval.

Low = P, A, E, / alone, or in combinations.

High = C, T. / / alone or in combination with anything else.

Table 5.2 shows a segment of data on a nursery school girl who changed activities with high frequency (Allen, Henke, Harris, Baer, and Reynolds, 1967). Entries were made in the top row to indicate occurrences of vocalizations (V), in the middle row to show proximity (P) or physical contact (T) with another person, and in the bottom row to indicate contact with objects (E) or with children, and whether the interaction was parallel play

TABLE 5.2 *Sample line from a data sheet of nursery school girl who changed activities with high frequency*

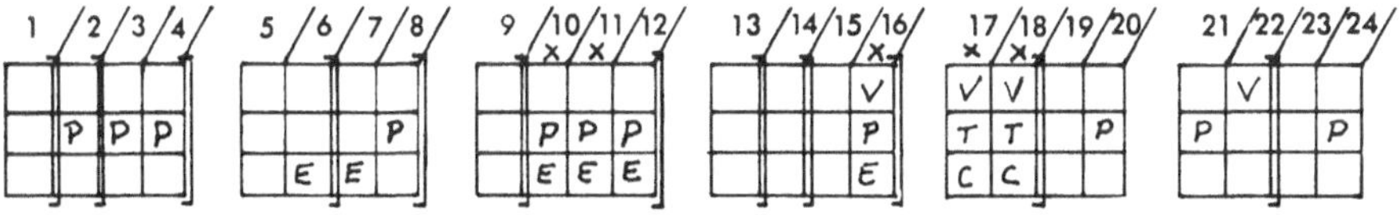

(A) or shared play (C). Other marks and symbols are added in accordance with the problem studied. For example, each bracket in Table 5.2 indicates leaving of one activity and embarking on another. During the 6-minute period in which records were taken (24 15-second intervals), the child changed her activity 12 times. During that time the teacher gave approval five times contingent upon her verbal or proximity behavior as indicated by Xs above the top line (intervals 10, 11, 16, 17, and 18). A tally of the data indicated that she spent most of the 6-minute period alone or in close proximity to another child, sometimes on the same piece of play equipment.

During three intervals (16, 17, and 18) she talked (V) and was close to or touched a child (P or T) while physically engaged in interaction with another child (C or E). Even though rate of activity change, and not peer interaction, was the subject of the study, the other data on social behavior provided interesting information: decline in rate of activity change was related to an increase in rate of appropriate peer behavior.

The Washington code can be readily modified to record more complex interactions. For example, it was used to study a nursery school boy who shouted epithets, kicked, and hit other children. Ordinarily these aggressive acts would appear in the record sheets undifferentiated from a nonaggressive interaction. To distinguish them from other behaviors, the symbol letter was circled if the behavior met the criteria of an aggressive act. Thus, in Table 5.3, intervals 13, 22, and 23 contain a V with a circle which indicates aggressive verbalizations, while intervals 19 and 20 contain a T within a circle which indicates physical attack (hitting, kicking or pinching). Other in-

TABLE 5.3 *Sample line from a data sheet of nursery school boy displaying aggressive behaviors*

1	2	3	4	5	6 X	7 X	8 X	9	10	11 X	12 X	13	14	15	16	17 X	18 X	19	20	21	22	23	24	25	26 X	27 X	28	29 X	30
V					V							(V)				V	V	V	V	V	(V)	(V)						V	
P	P				P	P	P	P								P	P	(T)	(T)	P		P	P	P	P	P	P	T	P
C	C		C	C	C	C	C	C	C	C	A	A	A	A	A	A	A	A	A	A	A	A			A	A	C	C	
					B	B	B	B	B	B	B					B	B	B	B	B	B	B	B	B	B	B	B	B	

formation was incorporated in the recording system. The letter B was entered in the fourth row to indicate that the child was playing with or aggressing against a specific child. This additional notation was made midway in the study when teachers observed that the *S* and *B* usually behaved aggressively toward each other. Data collected prior to this change served as a baseline against which to judge the effects of changing social contingencies. Subsequently, teachers gave approval contingent on nonaggressive interactions between these boys as shown by the Xs above intervals 6, 7, 8, 11, 12, 17, 18, 26, 27, and 29.

Another example of a *general observational code* which may be employed with young children in the elementary school classroom has been developed by Becker, *et al.* (1967). Like the nursery school code, it consists of symbols and definitions designed to cover the range of interactions that ordinarily occur in an elementary classroom.

The Mechanics of Recording

The procedures discussed and the examples cited thus far describe the collection of data as a process in which an observer makes entries with a pencil on a sheet marked with successive time units. These data could just as well have been recorded with electromechanical devices. In a series of studies on autistic children, Lovaas and his co-workers (Lovaas, Freitag, Gold and Kassorla, 1965a; and Lovaas, Schaeffer, and Simmons, 1965), have painstakingly developed apparatus and procedures for recording up to 12 responses. They have also devised an apparatus for training observers (Lovaas, Freitag, Gold, and Kassorla, 1965b).

> The apparatus for quantifying behaviors involved two units: an Esterline-Angus twenty-pen recorder and an operating panel with twelve buttons, each button mounted on a switch (Microswitch: "Typewriter pushbutton switch"). When depressed, these buttons, activated a corresponding pen on the Esterline recorder. The buttons were arranged on a 7 x 14-inch panel in the configuration of the fingertips of an outstretched hand. Each button could be pressed independently of any of the others and with the amount of force similar to that required for an electric typewriter key.
>
> The child and attending adult were observed in a nursery playroom setting through a one-way mirror. Various behaviors of the child and the adult were defined. Each behavior corresponded with the designated button on the panel and, consequently, with a specified pen on the recorder. When the child or teacher initiated any one of the defined behaviors, the observer pressed the button on the operating panel assigned to that behavior. The button was pressed down at the time the behavior occurred and was held down until the behavior terminated. In this way, the apparatus kept a running account of both frequency and duration of each behavior [p. 109].

In a sequence of parent-child studies in a child guidance clinic, observers activated microswitches to indicate the occurrences of critical events (Wahler *et al.*, 1965).

> . . . the observers recorded only three classes of behavior—two for the child (deviant behavior and incompatible behavior) and one for the mother (*her* reactions to her child's behavior classes). This was done by depressing selected microswitches every five seconds for any of the previously classified deviant or incompatible behavior patterns which occurred during the five-second intervals. Another microswitch was reserved for any behavior of the mother's which occurred immediately after the child's two classes of behavior [p. 115].

Electromechanical recording devices have certain advantages over paper-and-pencil methods. The former require less attention than the latter, thus allowing the observer to devote more of his effort to watching for critical events. Furthermore, instruments of this sort make it possible to assess more carefully the temporal relationships between certain stimulus-and-response events, as well as to record a large number of responses over the same time period. On the other hand, paper-and-pencil recording methods are more flexible and more mobile. They can be used in any setting since they do not require special conditions such as power supply.

Whether the data are recorded by hand or by electromechanical devices, the investigator has to decide whether to log incidences of response (and in many situations, durations), or register the frequencies of occurrences and nonoccurrences within a time interval. For the most part, the nature of the data is the deciding factor.

Recording the frequencies of occurrences and nonoccurrences requires the observer to make a mark or activate a switch in each time interval in which the response is observed. It is immediately apparent that in this procedure, the maximum frequency with which a response can occur is determined by the size of the time unit employed. If a 5-second interval were used, the maximum frequency would be 12 per minute; if a 10-second interval were employed, the maximum rate would be 6 responses per minute, and so on. Thus, in studies with a high frequency of behavioral episodes, small time intervals are employed to obtain high correspondence between the actual and recorded frequencies of occurrences.

Stimulus Events

The ease or difficulty of defining a stimulus event is related to its source. Some stimuli originate in natural and man-made physical objects, some in the biological makeup of the subject himself, and some in the behavior of people and other living organisms (Bijou and Baer, 1961).

Defining stimuli from physical objects does not pose a serious problem since such stimuli are ordinarily available for observation by any member of the community. The only requirement made by a science of behavior is that these stimuli be described in the usual dimensions of space, time, size, velocity, color, texture, and the like (Skinner, 1953).

The greatest difficulty in deriving objective definitions of stimuli which originate in the biological makeup of the subject is their obscurity, especially under field conditions. Consider what must be available to an observer for him to record the frequency and duration of a toothache, "butterflies" in the stomach, general bodily weakness, dizziness, or hunger pangs. Nevertheless, the exact description and function of specific biological stimulus variables must be studied in an experimental analysis of behavior. It seems clear that at present, the field-experimental method, especially with human Ss, is not particularly suited for exploring the relationships between biologically anchored stimulus variables and behavior variables. Research into these variables must be postponed until it is practical to monitor physiological events through sophisticated telemetric devices. We may, however, be closer to this possibility than we think (Pronko, 1968). Until the time when it is practical to externalize biological events by means of telemetry, we must look to studies conducted in laboratories for information on the functional role of biological stimulus variables in a systematic analysis of behavior.

Defining stimuli from social events poses problems identical to those inherent in defining response events, discussed above. Hence, social stimuli have been defined with the aid of *specific stimulus codes* and *general stimulus codes.*

An example of a specific stimulus code is found in a study of an autistic child by Brawley *et al.* (1969). The social stimulus, attention of an adult, was made contingent upon certain behaviors of the child. Giving attention was defined as: "(1) Touching the child; (2) being within two feet of and facing the child; (3) talking to, touching, assisting or going to the child." Using such criteria, the investigators catalogued the types of behaviors which constituted social interaction involving attention and excluded other stimuli originating in the behavior of an adult in contact with the child. Another example of the use of a specific stimulus code is in a study of the hyperactivity in a nursery school child (Allen *et al.*, 1967). Giving social reinforcement involved "talking" to S while facing him within a distance of three feet, or from a greater distance using his name; touching S; and giving him additional materials suitable to the ongoing activity. Withholding or withdrawing social reinforcement consisted of turning away from S; not looking or smiling at him; and directing attention to some other child or activity (p. 232). A third example of a specific stimulus code comes from a study of the reinforcing function of a teacher's commands to "sit down" in the classroom (Madsen, Becker, Thomas, Koser, and Plager, 1968). There were two categories. (1) "Sit-down" commands. This class consisted of instructions for children to return to their seats or to sit properly, such as: "Please sit down, Johnny." "Everyone please go back to your seats." and "The rules say that we should stay in our seats while we are working." (2) Praise for sitting. This category included remarks to children who were seated, indicating approval, e.g., "You are sitting nicely." "Mary is working very well; I like that." "I like the way Jimmy is sitting and working." It also included comments to the entire class or to the other teacher in team teaching, such as: "I like the way Johnny has been sitting at his seat working for a *long* time." "Mary and Jane are doing a good job of working today."

Becker and his colleagues have also developed a more general stimulus code which may be used to record teacher behaviors in the elementary classroom situation (Madsen, Becker, and Thomas, 1968). This code includes approving reactions to both appropriate and inappropriate behavior, disapproving reactions and instructional reactions. Each of these major classes is in turn broken down into sub-classes. For example, approving reactions may be divided into (1) praise, (2) physical contact, (3) head reactions such as nodding, and (4) granting privileges. In addition, the observer may score whether the teacher's behavior was audible to the entire class and what student behaviors preceded it.

The discussion on defining, coding, and recording stimulus events has focused on stimuli which are *consequent* to response events. However, a field-experimental study may be concerned with stimulus events which *precede* responses such as asking a question or making a request. Stimuli which precede responses are quantified and recorded the same way as stimuli which follow responses. A field-experimental study may also be concerned with stimuli which function as a *setting event,* i.e., a condition that affects the strengths of many specific stimulus-response relationships (Bijou and Baer, 1961). Suppose a young child was observed over 10 days during the music period in the nursery school with respect to his social behavior and sustained activity. Suppose, too, that on the eleventh day the nursery school teacher was informed that on doctor's orders the child was given a tranquilizing drug before coming to school and that he will receive such medication during the next two weeks. What effects will the drug have on the child's behavior? Research aimed at giving a partial answer to this question would be concerned with discerning the relationship between a setting event (dosage of the transquilizing drug) and changes in school behaviors (social behavior and sustained activity during the music period as recorded).

In concluding this section, two points should be stressed. (*a*) Since social stimuli are the behavior of individuals in relation to the S of a study, the problems of defining and recording social stimulus events are the same as defining response events. Therefore everything discussed in the previous section on response events holds for social stimulus events. The only difference is procedural. Stimulus events are the conditions ordinarily manipulated in a study of functional relationships. (*b*) The task of defining social stimuli from an adult is somewhat eased since the time and form of the adult's behavior is specified by the investigator and monitored by the observer.

Observer Reliabilities

A high level of agreement by observers on the occurrence of a stimulus or response event is usually ascertained before baseline observation is taken. The degree of agreement, or observer reliability, is dependent upon a number of factors, including: (*a*) adequacy of the observational code, (*b*) training of the observers, (*c*) method of calculating reliability coefficients and (*d*) frequency of observations over sessions (time sampling). We shall discuss each in turn.

The Observational Code

The method of defining stimulus and response events has been discussed earlier. We need add here only that reliability of the recording of an observed event is directly related to the specificity of the definitions in the code. Thus, single response classes (hitting the head on the floor) tend to be more reliable than multiple response classes (aggressive behavior composed of hitting, spitting, throwing objects, and the like) and specific criteria for a response, whether single or a member of a multiple response class, tend to be more reliable than general response classes.

Initial definitions are likely to be crude and in most cases are refined after evaluation in the actual observational situation. In final form the descriptions of responses in the code should be comprehensive, delineating clearly all responses in each category. It is also desirable to develop codes so that each response class is mutually exclusive—there is no overlapping of definitions.

Observer Training

Even if the observational code employed is adequate, two observers will not necessarily record the occurrence of the same event at the same time unless each has learned his task thoroughly and has been instructed in conducting himself while recording. Here are some suggestions on the training of observers.

The observer should be made familiar with the tools for recording, i.e., the clipboard, stopwatch, and data sheets. He should also be required to memorize which events are to be recorded, over what intervals, and with which symbols. Training in recording with a second observer should follow, with frequent intervals to discuss which behaviors are to be recorded and which are not. In some instances it is difficult to train observers because the behaviors occur at low frequencies or irregular times. In this case a short film or video tape of these or other similar responses might enhance and accelerate the training procedure. Training sessions should continue until the observational accounts reach the criterion of reliability established at the outset of the study.

After the observer has had experience with the code in practice situations he is ready to collect data for the study. He should be instructed to seat himself on the perimeter of the room or play yard and be as inconspicuous as possible. Thus he should be told not to interact with the child being observed. He should ignore all questions or other behaviors on the part of the child. He should not laugh or smile at the S or any of the children. If he finds himself in eye-contact with the child, he should break this relationship by looking away for a short time. If the S moves to a distant corner of the room or yard where it is difficult to see or hear him, the observer should move to another location without appearing to follow him. In general, the child's behavior, with special emphasis on the frequency of the child looking at the observer, should indicate whether or not he is or is not oblivious to the presence of the observer. In some instances the child may require several weeks to acclimate, especially if the field-experimental situation is for him a new school room, hospital ward, or play therapy room.

The Reliability Coefficient

Since the index of the reliability between the records of two observers is, to some degree, a function of how it is calculated, the advantages and disadvantages in the various methods of reliability determination require some discussion.

One method involves obtaining data from two observers who record the

TABLE 5.4 *General response code for studying children in a classroom*

Symbols	*Classes*	*Class Definitions*
X	Gross Motor Behaviors	Getting out of seat; standing up; running; hopping; skipping; jumping; walking around; rocking in chair; disruptive movement without noise; moves chair to neighbor; knees on chair.
N	Disruptive Noise	Tapping pencil or other objects; clapping; tapping feet; rattling or tearing paper; throwing book on desk; slamming desk. (Be conservative, only rate if could hear noise when eyes closed. Do not include accidental dropping of objects or if noise made while performing X above.)
∧	Disturbing Others Directly	Grabbing objects or work; knocking neighbor's books off desk; destroying another's property; pushing with desk.
⟶	Aggression (Contact)	Hitting, kicking; shoving; pinching; slapping; striking with object; throwing object at another person; poking with object; biting; pulling hair.
⌒→	Orienting Responses	Turning head or head and body to look at another person, showing objects to another child, orienting toward another child. (Must be of 4 seconds duration, not rated unless seated; or more than 90° using the desk as a reference.)
V	Verbalizations	Carrying on conversations with other children when it is not permitted. Answers teacher without raising hand or without being called on; making comments or calling out remarks when no question has been asked; calling teacher's name to get her attention; crying; screaming; singing; whistling; laughing loudly; coughing or blowing loudly. (May be directed to teacher or children.)
//	Other Tasks	Ignores teacher's question or command; does something different from that directed to do, includes minor motor behavior such as playing with pencil eraser when supposed to be writing; coloring while the record is on; doing spelling during arithmetic lesson; playing with objects; eating; chewing gum. *The child involves himself in a task that is not appropriate.*
———	Relevant Behavior	Time on task; e.g., answers question, looking at teacher when she is talking; raises hand; writing assignment. (Must include whole 20-second interval except for orienting responses of less than 4-seconds duration.)

frequency of events for a standard period such as an hour. Each observer obtains a sum of events for that period. Unless the sums from each observer are identical, the smaller sum is divided by the larger to obtain a percentage of agreement score. If the sums are identical, the reliability coefficient would be 100 per cent. This method is often used when the investigator is interested in frequencies *per se* and not in the time of occurrences since the index gives only the amount of agreement over the total number of behaviors observed in the standard period of observation. It does not indicate whether the two observers were recording the same event at exactly the same time. Thus it might be possible that one observer was recording few behaviors during the first half-hour and many during the second, while the second observer was doing the opposite. To ascertain whether this is the case, one could divide the hour's observational period into shorter segments and calculate the reliability for each. As the segments become shorter, one can determine with increasing confidence whether the observers are scoring the same event at the same time. In fact, one may measure the agreement on recording in a very short interval such as five or ten seconds. With such a method, reliability is calculated by scoring each interval in terms of whether the two observers agree or disagree and the number of agreements is totaled and divided by the number of agreements plus the number of disagreements. Note that one may score several agreements or disagreements in an interval if several classes of events are being recorded at the same time. In this case the interval is broken down according to the number of different events being scored with each class of events scored as an agreement or disagreement.

Let us consider the data in Table 5.4. Observer 1 and Observer 2 recorded the occurrence or nonoccurrence of events in four categories (1–4). There were 24 agreements and 10 disagreements over a 4 minute period. The circles indicate disagreements. The reliability index would be:

$$\frac{24}{24 + 10} = \frac{24}{34} = 71\%$$

The intervals without an entry were not counted as agreements in the calculation. Inclusion of empty intervals, especially with low-rate behaviors, would inflate the reliability coefficient. For example, the number of agreements in the two records shown in Table 5.5 is 4, while disagreements equal 11. The reliability index is

$$\frac{4}{11 + 4} = \frac{4}{15} = 27\%.$$

If one included the empty intervals as agreements, the reliability index equals

$$\frac{34}{34 + 11} = \frac{34}{45} = 76\%.$$

There are problems with both methods of calculating the index. In recording events of low frequency, the observers may not agree on which interval an event occurred, or on how it should be classified (A, B, or C). If this occurs, it is clear that something is wrong; yet when empty intervals

TABLE 5.5 *General stimulus code for teacher's behavior in an elementary classroom*

General Class	*Sub-Symbol*	*Sub-Class*	*Definitions and Illustrations*
I. Approving reactions to appropriate behavior (following the behavior)	P	Praise	Verbal approval or praise. Examples: That's good; You are doing well; I like the way you're working; You make me happy; Thank you; I like you; I like that.
	C	Contact	Physical contact such as embracing, kissing, patting, holding arm or hand, having sit in lap.
	H+	Approving head reactions	Smiling, winking, nodding. (Rate only if P is not rated.)
	G	Granting Privileges	Helping teacher; choice of games; doing something "first." Choice of activity. (All response contingent.)
		Promise of Privilege	If occurs, note in comments.
II. Supporting reactions to inappropriate behavior (following the behavior)	(Sub-Codes same as above but followed by /)		
III. Disapproving reactions to inappropriate behavior (following the behavior)	V−	Critical verbal comment	Yelling, scolding, raising voice, screaming. Need not be of high intensity, e.g., Don't do that; Stop talking; Did I call on you; You are wasting your time; Don't laugh; Go to the office; You know what you are supposed to do.
	H	Holding the child	Forcibly restraining child; forcibly removing child from room; grabbing, hitting, spanking, slapping, or shaking child.
	VR−	Critical use of rules	You know we don't talk during work time.
	H−	Disapproving head reactions	Frowning, grimacing, side-to-side head shaking. (Not rated if V−.)

TABLE 5.5—*Continued*

General Class	*Sub-Symbol*	*Sub-Class*	*Definitions and Illustrations*
	TW	Threat of withholding privilege or of punishment	Statements of loss of privilege or punishment at some time in future.
	W	Withholding privileges	Keeping in from recess; (action); depriving child of classroom privileges; (specify)
	Q	Termination of social interaction	Turns out lights and says nothing; turns back on class and waits for quiet; stops talking and waits for quiet; isolate from group.
		Sending out of room	To hall, office, principal, etc. Note if occurs.
IV. Instructional reactions	R	Stating rules	Any reminders of classroom rules; asking a child to repeat the rule; point to the rule on the board; etc. (Do not rate if VC— is rated.)
	I	Do this	Giving instructions as to what to do. "Do this." "Turn to page x." "Get out your books."
	T_1	Explanation	Stating why things should be done a certain way; giving "reasons"; explaining meanings of concepts, etc.
		Prompting	Help the child give the right answer with partial or total prompts.
		Academic recognition	Call on child for an answer.
		Probing	Asking questions to elicit information from child.
	T_2	O.K.+ Confirmation	That's right, O.K., marking correct, etc. (Do not rate if P is ratable.)
		Error	That's wrong, checking wrong, etc. (Do not rate if V is ratable.)
	T_3	Other	Interacting with child; can't tell if T_1 or T_2.

are recorded as agreements, it appears that the observers are in adequate agreement. The problem of disregarding agreement that an event did not occur in an interval is further complicated by the fact that by so doing, the calculations do not take into account all instances of agreement. After all, both observers looked and agreed that the event did not occur. It would appear then that two other factors enter into calculating inter-observer reliability. The first involves the frequency of the event and the second the length of the observational period. Thus, if empty intervals are scored as agreements, a low-frequency event observed over a long period of observation will produce a high reliability coefficient. This problem may be resolved by computing not one but two reliability coefficients, one for occurrence and one for nonoccurrence.

One way of increasing the number of intervals with identical entries is to score events which are recorded as occurring in adjacent intervals as agreements. If this formula is applied to the data in Table 5.4, agreement rises from 27 per cent to 73 per cent.

A technique of "noncontinuous" observing over the standard time interval may also increase the reliability index especially if disagreement is defined as the placement of an event in one of two adjacent intervals. In this procedure, the observers record for shorter portions of time. For example, instead of taking consecutive 10-second observations, the observer might record for 10 out of every 15 seconds, or for 20 out of every 30 seconds. During the period in which the observer is not attending to his Ss, he may be recording the behaviors he had just viewed. This method was used by O'Leary, O'Leary, and Becker (1967) in a study of deviant sibling behavior in the home.

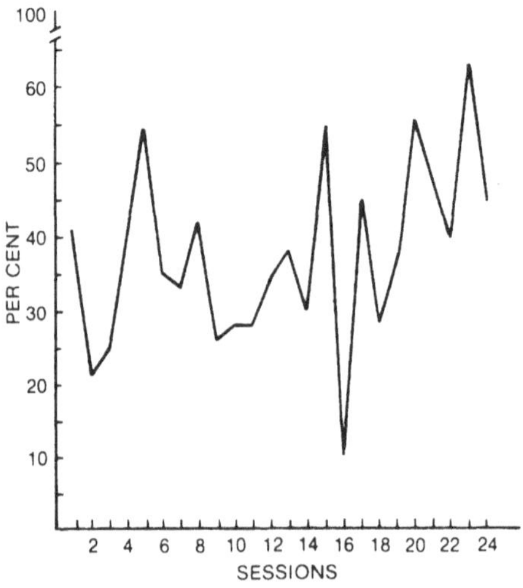

FIGURE 5.1 *Verbalization frequency during play*

The use of a second observer does not necessarily insure high reliability of the raw data since it is possible for both observers to agree on the scoring of certain events and at the same time be incorrect (Gewirtz and Gewirtz, 1964). Thus both observers might record some events which should not be noted and ignore others which should. Hence, it is advisable to use a third observer on occasion as a check on this possibility.

Frequency of Observations Over Sessions

In some instances, it may not be practical to observe each day or each session in which the events of interest occur. This may be true if the observer is available for a limited time or if the investigator would like to collect data on several children during the same activity. Under such circumstances, a time-sampling procedure with repeated but brief observational periods may be indicated.

Data from a recent study of a four-and-a-half year old boy in a laboratory nursery school (Bijou, Peterson, and Ault, 1968) provide an example of the differences if recordings were taken intermittently over sessions. Figure 5.1 shows the boy's frequency of verbalization to other children during the play period. The average frequency of his verbal output over 26 sessions was 36 per cent. Let us assume that instead of observing him each day as shown in Figure 5.1, he was observed every other day, beginning with the first day. Figure 5.2 shows the result. Although only half as many observations

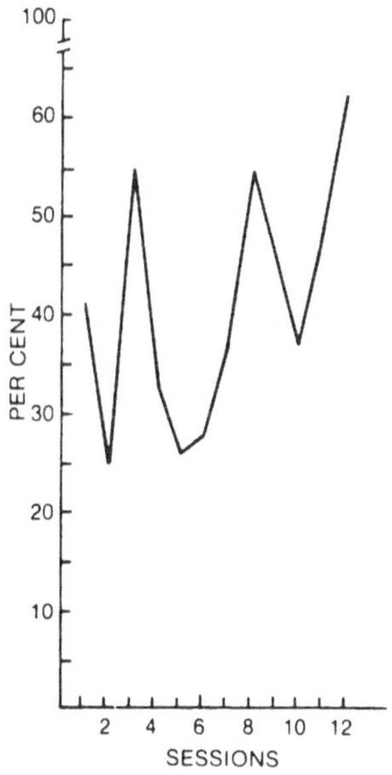

FIGURE 5.2 *Sample of verbalization frequency based on odd-numbered sessions in Fig. 5.1.*

are plotted, the average frequency changes little and is now 38 per cent. Similar results are obtained when the observer records every other day beginning with the second day. This result may be seen in Figure 5.3. In this instance there is somewhat more variability than in Figure 5.2, and the overall average is slightly reduced, to 33 per cent. It can be seen that in all three figures the general trend is the same.

As the number of days of observation is reduced, trends in the data are modified. For example, sampling every third day (beginning with the first session in Figure 5.1) yields an average of 34 per cent, only a slight deviation from the average of daily recording.

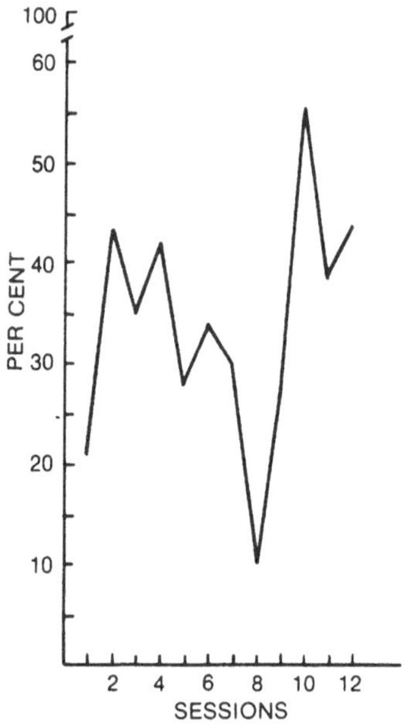

FIGURE 5.3 *Sample of verbalization frequency based on even-numbered sessions in Fig. 5.1.*

COLLECTING DATA

As pointed out in the introduction, in a typical field-experimental study, data are collected in a series of conditions designed to explore the possibilities of a functional relationship between stimuli and responses. The first is the baseline condition, i.e., the situation prior to experimental manipulation. The next is the experimental condition, or the one in which a stimulus event is changed. Following that is a return to the baseline condition and then to the experimental condition. Other baseline and experimental conditions may follow depending on the nature of the study.

First Baseline Period

Data are taken during the first baseline condition as soon as the situation has been demonstrated to be feasible, the observers have met the criterion of adequate training, and the child has adapted to the situation. Data are collected under this condition for as many sessions as are necessary to demonstrate stability. Stability is defined as a trend which is more or less horizontal or slightly in the direction opposite to that anticipated during experimental manipulation. Thus, estimates of the mean and variance of the response rate observed should fall within certain arbitrary limits. If the baseline is characterized by unsystematic variability, or a persistent accelerated or decelerated trend, data collection is stopped and a reassessment is made of the code, specifications of the field-experimental space, and the training of the observers. Further checks and reassessments may be necessary before adequate baseline data are obtained.

How many responses should be recorded in the baseline period? The number depends on the purpose of the study since data are collected to provide the investigators with findings upon which to draw conclusions about the relationships at issue. That is, an investigator may be only interested in the relationship between one response class and a simple type of experimental manipulation, e.g., a change from material to social reinforcement. In such a study, obviously only one class of response need be recorded. In another situation the investigator may be interested in seeing whether the experimental manipulation planned (e.g., using "time-out" following physical aggression) not only alters the main response variable (e.g., physical aggression) but also another class not directly involved in the manipulation (e.g., verbal aggression). He would have to take data during baseline on the two classes of responses involved (e.g., physical and verbal aggression). If it is planned to record two or more response classes during the baseline and succeeding experimental conditions, and if one or more of the response categories contain multiple sub-classes, it would be expedient to use an electromechanical recording system such as described in Section 2, or to employ several observers working in concert.

First Experimental Period

In the first experimental period a change in the field situation is made. This experimental manipulation may involve an alteration in antecedent or consequent stimuli or a setting event. For example, in the Wahler, *et al.* (1965) study mentioned previously, changes in antecedent and consequent stimuli are described as follows:

> Following the baseline sessions, *E* made systematic attempts to change the mother's reactions to her child's behavior. These attempts involved the use of instructions to the mother before and after the playroom sessions, plus signal light communications to her during the sessions. During initial sessions, *E* used

> the signal light as a cueing system, essentially to tell the mother when and how to behave in response to her child's behavior. As the mother improved in her ability to follow instructions, *E* eventually changed the function of the signal light from cueing system to reinforcement system. The mother was now required to discriminate and respond appropriately to her child's behavior without *E*'s cueing. *E* used the signal light to provide immediate feedback to the mother concerning her correct and incorrect discriminations, thus teaching her appropriate discrimination responses [p. 116].

How long should the experimental condition remain in effect? It depends on the data—on the stability shown in the curves. In some studies the change is abrupt and stability is apparent within a few sessions. A study on the social behavior of a four-year-old girl provides an example (Allen, Hart, Buell, Harris, and Wolf, 1964). During the first of five baseline sessions, the child interacted with other children 10 per cent of the day. Data from the remaining four sessions showed interaction percentages of 21 per cent, 14 per cent, 12 per cent, and 12 per cent. For this child, interaction with other children averaged 14 per cent of the time. When the experimental condition (teacher's approval contingent upon the child's social contact with peers) went into effect, there was an increase in the child's peer relationships on the *first* experimental day. The rise was from about 12 per cent to 55 per cent and the increased rate continued during the entire experimental period.

In other studies the change in behavior may be gradual, extending over several sessions. For example, in a study by Hart *et al.* (1964) a change in the frequency of operant (spoiled) crying in a preschool boy did not occur until after the *fifth* experimental session. During the baseline period the child cried from five to ten times in the morning hours at school. Five days after introduction of the experimental condition (extinction procedures for crying and positive reinforcement for desirable social behavior) his crying decreased to zero. From the fifth to the tenth day, the final day of the experimental condition, his crying episodes remained between zero and two per day.

When establishing the duration of the experimental phase, the investigator should not only take into account the lag between the application of the experimental condition and the response, but should also consider the functional properties of the variables to be manipulated. In studies involving stimuli with reinforcing properties, relatively short experimental periods are advocated, since long ones might allow enough time for the establishment of new conditioned reinforcers. If this occurs, withdrawal of the experimental condition in the next experimental phase of a study may not result in a decrease in rate of responding because of the power of the newly acquired reinforcers. For example, in a study by Ault, Peterson, and Bijou (1968) the frequency with which an elementary school child worked on academic tasks was observed. Then the child was given attention and praise contingent upon his behavior. This procedure resulted in a sharp increase in working as

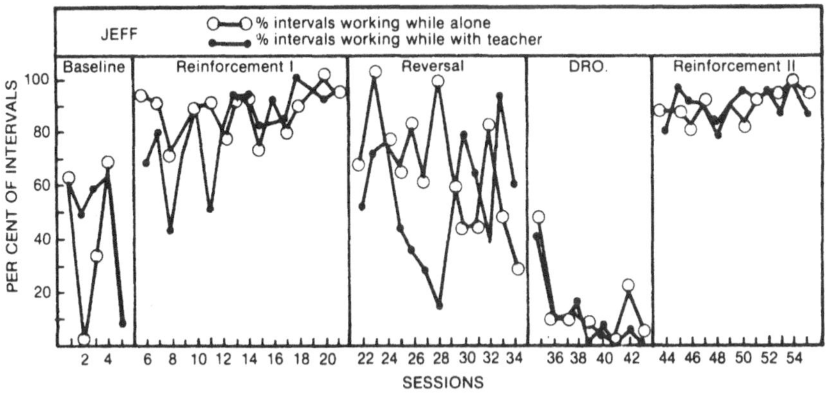

FIGURE 5.4 *Per cent of time engaged in academic work.*

can be seen in Figure 5.4. Later, reinforcement was withdrawn for some 13 sessions. Although the behavior declined in comparison to the previous reinforcement period, it was still twice as frequent when compared to the baseline period.

It is possible that failure of the rate to approximate baseline levels may have been due to the operation of other reinforcers which, once the behavior was generated, functioned to maintain it, at least partially.

Another example may be found in a study on the relationship between a mother and her preschool boy observed in their home (Hawkins *et al.*, 1966). In this case the rate of objectionable behaviors was very high during the first baseline period. During the treatment phase of the study these behaviors were reduced markedly. However, a return to baseline did not result in a sharp increase in objectionable behavior. Their frequency remained relatively low. Observation suggested that the rate was depressed in the second baseline period not only because new acquired reinforcers were in operation but also because the contingencies delivered by the mother had changed. She apparently learned in the first experimental period to be more sensitive and responsive to the behaviors she should reinforce, extinguish, or punish.

In experimental situations in which the rate of responding during baseline is very low, the child may not react to the newly introduced experimental condition for several days. Under these circumstances, auxiliary procedures may be used to speed up the onset of initial interaction. One such technique, referred to as "shaping," consists of differentially reinforcing behaviors that approximate more and more the desired behavior. For example, in a study designed to increase a nursery school boy's climbing behavior on a climbing frame (Johnson *et al.*, 1966), the teacher gave attention and praise when S came near (defined by markers on the ground) the equipment. After the behavior of moving toward and being within the prescribed area occurred with high frequency, she changed the criterion for delivering the contingencies so that only closer approaches to the equipment would receive the teacher's attention. After the program resulted in a high frequency of coming closer to the climbing frame, the teacher gave praise and supportive comments contingent only upon actual contact with the apparatus. Since the child displayed a low rate of contacts with the frame during the baseline phase, it probably would have taken many weeks to obtain the high rate of interaction with the apparatus described in this study.

Another technique for getting S in contact with the experimental condition is to force the required behavior and then strengthen it. Thus, if *E* were studying the effects of social contingencies on the development of a motor skill such as riding a tricycle, he might, instead of differentially reinforcing successive approximation to the tricycle, actually place the child on it and give social approval for his being there. Additional sessions of the same sort and then a shaping procedure could follow as soon as the child seemed comfortable when on or near the tricycle. A procedure similar to this was used to help a three-year-old girl to gain gross motor skills on the playground equipment in a laboratory nursery school (Harris, 1967). In this case, the percentage of time the child spent on outdoor equipment was practically zero. On the first experimental day the teacher lifted the child onto a piece of equipment and enthusiastically praised and encouraged her as long as she remained on it.

Each morning for nine successive mornings the teacher placed her on a different piece of climbing equipment. She did this only once for each piece. Thereafter, whenever the child touched that piece of equipment, the teacher at once came to reinforce her with verbal and tactual appreciation and any necessary help. After the ninth day, all cueing was terminated, but reinforcement continued as before. Climbing dropped slightly when cueing ceased but soon recovered its previous rate.

Second Baseline Period

The third phase of the experimental procedure usually consists of an operation designed to reduce or eliminate the experimental condition. The purpose of the second baseline period is to determine whether the relationship observed during the experimental phase was in fact related to the experimental condition. The second baseline period may consist of the *removal* of the experimental condition. The procedure is clear and straightforward: the condition instituted in the experimental period is discontinued. Or the second baseline period may consist of *reversing* the contingencies. In a study by Harris, Johnson, Kelley, and Wolf (1964)on crawling in a nursery school girl who seldom walked, crawling regularly attracted the teacher's attention and evoked sympathy, while upright postures and brief episodes of walking did not receive a great deal of attention. After baseline data were collected on "on-feet behavior," there followed an experimental period during which the teacher gave attention and praise for upright posture and upright locomotion, but not for crawling, thus reversing the contingency in operation during the first baseline period. During the second baseline period the teacher's attention and sympathy were again given for crawling and only scant notice was given to incidences of upright postures and locomotions.

Still another procedure for the second baseline period would be to distribute the experimental contingencies on a *random schedule.* For example, *E* may wish to determine the effect of negating contingent adult attention without causing emotional outbursts. To do this, he could dispense adult attending behavior in a way that *S* would continue to receive the same number of social reinforcers given in the experimental period but randomly rather than contingently. Such a procedure was employed in a study by Hart, Reynolds, Brawley, Harris, and Baer (1966), where the effects of teacher attention on cooperative play were observed. Attention was given both contingently and noncontingently. Even though the amount of attention was higher during the noncontingent portion of the study, only contingent attention resulted in a significant increase in cooperative play.

What is the minimum number of sessions required for an adequate second baseline period? No set number can be established since the purpose of the second baseline observation is not to see whether the data obtained in the first baseline period can be duplicated in the second, but to determine whether changes that occurred during the experimental phase can be attributed to the experimental manipulation. In some of the studies cited in this paper, the second baseline period is as long or longer than the first. For example, see Figure 5.4. In others, the second baseline period is somewhat shorter than the first (e.g., Johnson *et al.,* and Hawkins *et al.,* 1966); and in still others, the second baseline is quite short (e.g., Brawley *et al.,* 1969).

A short baseline period is sometimes indicated out of consideration for the child's welfare, as in the case of severe aggression or self-destructive behavior. Thus if the data showed that during the first experimental period aggressive behaviors were reduced, the baseline condition would be reinstated for a brief time, only long enough to see whether the alteration affected the behavior in the direction observed during baseline. In a study by Peterson and Peterson (1968) on self-destructive behavior in a young retarded child, the second baseline period consisted of a reversal of contingencies for only three sessions. There was a sharp increase in self-destructive behavior which was taken as evidence that the contingencies in operation during the first experimental period were functional.

Second Experimental Period

In the fourth phase of a study the procedures used in the first experimental period are usually reinstated. If the rate of responses under this condition approaches the rate observed in the first experimental period, added information is provided on the strength of the functional relationship between the stimulus and response functions observed.

Other Periods

In many instances the demonstration of a functional relation is only the first segment of a study. It may be a prelude to explore several schedules of reinforcement, or different modes of dispensing reinforcers, or various forms of stimulus control, or the effects of different setting events. For example, *E* may wish to study the effects of one versus three adults dispensing the reinforcement on a variable ratio schedule and he might approach the problem as follows: (*a*) Establish the functional properties of the selected stimulus and response events by the procedures described above: first baseline period, first experimental period, second baseline period, and second experimental period. (*b*) Institute an experimental period with one person dispensing reinforcers on a variable ratio schedule. (*c*) Return to the baseline condition. (*d*) Set up an experimental period with three persons dispensing reinforcers on the same variable ratio schedule. (*e*) Return to the baseline condition. (*f*) Repeat the experimental period with one person on the same variable ratio schedule.

Analyzing Data and Interpreting Results

Analyzing the data of a study and interpreting the results are procedures which describe the *behavior of the investigator* with respect to the symbols (usually numbers) representing the interactions observed. In analyzing the raw data, the investigator transforms his numbers in various ways in the hope of revealing in a clear fashion the relationships contained therein. In interpreting the results of his transformations he makes inferences, in the form of verbal statements, about the generality of the relationships demonstrated.

Analyses of Data

Typically the investigator translates the raw data into graphic, tabular, arithmetical, or statistical representations. Which specific forms he selects will depend upon the purpose of the study, the nature of the data, and his cherished theoretical assumptions.

Graphic representations of the data are usually in the form of curves or bar charts with *discrete* or *cumulative* values. Discrete curves or bar charts show values in the form of sums for each successive session. Cumulative curves present values based on the sums for all previous sessions. Therefore, discrete curves go up, stay at a level, or go down; cumulative curves go up or stay at a level. Examples of discrete curves are shown in upper half of

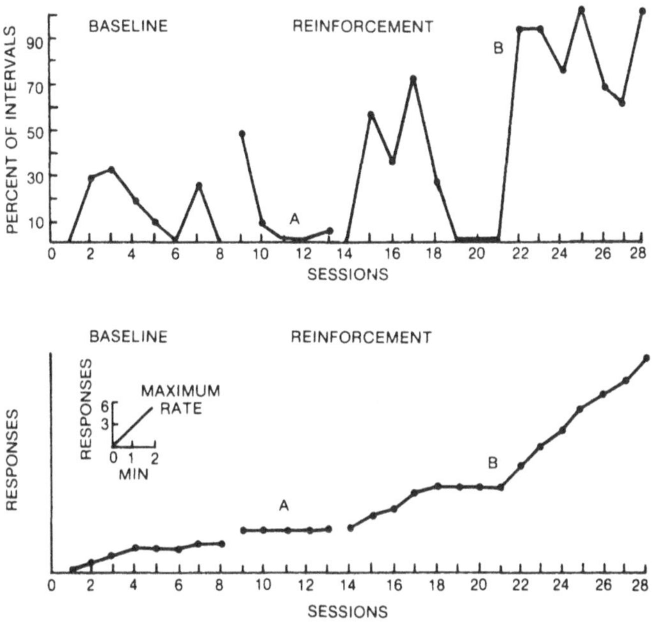

FIGURE 5.5 *Cumulative and discrete plots of appropriate eating behaviors.*

Figure 5.5 and of cumulative curves on the same data in the lower half of Figure 5.5.

What determines whether the data should be presented in discrete or cumulative form? It depends on which type of plot will show the relationships more clearly. An example of the way the same raw data look when plotted in discrete and cumulative forms is shown in Figure 5.5. Here we see rates of eating and deviant behaviors (e.g., getting out of chair, touching food with fingers, contacting his brother) of a 4-year-old boy during lunch and in the presence of his mother and younger brother. In the upper half of Figure 5.5, the values are plotted in discrete form; in the lower half in cumulative form. During the first manipulative period the mother gave her son all of the dessert at the end of the luncheon period. In the second, she placed a small bit of dessert in a separate plate each time the boy ingested a spoonful of the main course. The dessert accumulated in the plate during the meal was given to the youngster at the end. In the cumulative version it is apparent that the second procedure was more effective than the first in changing the child's behaviors at mealtime.

Data are often presented in the form of percentages to clarify differences among experimental conditions and to show trends within and between experimental periods. In most instances they are coordinated with graphs of the data.

Viewing the child in each experimental condition as a population of responses, statistical operations may be performed on the data from an individual subject. Measures of central tendencies, variances, and correlations may be calculated, and tests of significance of the differences made to assess relationships among the response rates observed in the different conditions of the study. However, when the differences are large and the relationships are clearly apparent there is little need for statistical tests. When they are small the investigator can do one of two things: (*a*) He can revise his procedures and start over, or (*b*) he can resort to statistical techniques to determine whether the differences found may be attributed to sampling errors. The investigator who is interested in demonstrating a functional relationship would probably modify his procedures and launch a new study. The investigator who is oriented toward testing a learning or personality theory would probably apply statistical tests to ascertain whether the difference found is acceptable as evidence for or against the theory.

Interpretation of Results

The investigator's interpretation of the results is the *raison d'etre* of a study. Basically his interpretations are statements about the relationships found and their generality. The nature of the statements made will be highly compatible with the investigator's theoretical position and philosophy of science. Interpretations of results in a study which aims to test a theory or an hypothesis usually consist of statements supporting or not supporting a deduction of an inference. Comparisons are made with findings from related studies and issues are raised about the soundness of the theory or hypothesis evaluated.

Interpretations of results in a study which aims to demonstrate basic, empirical, behavioral principles usually consist of descriptions of what was done and what was found, and of comparisons with other studies performed under similar conditions and procedures. Analysis of findings in this manner restricts generalizations to the data obtained. It also precludes the use of "explanatory terms" based on hypothetical mental and physiological states and variables. Interpretations of findings from studies which are designed to *apply* behavioral principles directly to practical problems usually consist of descriptions of the conditions and procedures, the findings, and a statement of the effectiveness of the application. Examples of this style of interpretation may be found in the *Journal of the Experimental Analysis of Behavior*, *Journal of Applied Behavior Analysis,* and in Honig's volume on operant research and application (1966).

Note

1. This paper summarizes the efforts of numerous individuals working in the field-experimental situations since 1962 at the University of Washington and the University of Illinois. Among them are D. M. Baer, M. M. Wolf, T. R. Risley, and Betty Hart,

University of Kansas; J. S. Birnbrauer, University of North Carolina; R. Wahler, University of Tennessee; H. N. Sloane, University of Utah; Marion Ault, University of Illinois; Susan G. O'Leary, Stony Brook, New York; Sophia Brown, Jacksonville, Illinois; and Eleanor Brawley, Richmond, Virginia. We are especially indebted to Andrew Wheeler who obtained the data presented in Figure 5.5. Support for this paper and for many of the studies cited in it was from the U. S. Public Health Service, National Institute of Mental Health (M–2208, M2232, and MH 12067) and from the Division of Research, Bureau of Education for the Handicapped, U. S. Office of Education, Grant No. OEG–0–9–2322030–0762(032).

References

Allen, K. E., Hart, B. M., Buell, J. S., Harris, F. R., and Wolf, M. M. Effects of social reinforcement on isolate behavior of a nursery school child. *Child Development*, 1964, *35*, 511–518.

Allen, K. E., Henke, L. B., Harris, F. R., Reynolds, N. J., and Baer, D. M. The control of hyperactivity by social reinforcement of attending behavior. *Journal of Educational Psychology*, 1967, *58*, 231–237.

Ault, M. E., Peterson, R. F., and Bijou, S. W. The management of contingencies of reinforcement to enhance study behavior in a small group of young children. Unpublished manuscript, 1968.

Bandura, A., and Walters, R. H. *Social learning and personality development.* New York: Holt, Rinehart, and Winston, 1963.

Becker, W. C., Madsen, C. H., Jr., Arnold, C. R., and Thomas, D. R. The contingent use of teacher attention and praise in reducing classroom behavior problems. *Journal of Special Education*, 1967, *1*, 287–307.

Bijou, S. W., and Baer, D. M. *Child development: A systematic and empirical theory*. Vol. 1, New York: Appleton-Century-Crofts, 1961.

Bijou, S. W., and Baer, D. M. Operant methods in child behavior and development. In W. K. Honig (Ed.), *Operant behavior: Areas of research and application*. New York: Appleton-Century-Crofts, 1966.

Bijou, S. W., Peterson, R. F., and Ault, M. A method to integrate descriptive and experimental field studies at the level of data and empirical concepts. *Journal of Applied Behavior Analysis*, 1968, *1*, 175–191.

Birnbrauer, J. S., Wolf, M. M. Kidder, J. D., and Tague, C. Classroom behavior of retarded pupils with token reinforcement. *Journal of Experimental Child Psychology*, 1965, *2*, 219–235.

Brawley, E. R., Harris, F. R., Allen, K. E., Fleming, R. S., and Peterson, R. F. Behavior modification of an autistic child. *Behavioral Science*, 1969, *14*, (2), 87–98.

Buell, J. S., Stoddard, P. L., Harris, F. R., and Baer, D. M. Patterns of social development collateral to social reinforcement of one form of play in an isolate nursery school child. *Journal of Applied Behavior Analysis*, 1968, *1*, 167–173.

Dinsmoor, J. A. Comments on Wetzel's treatment of a case of compulsive stealing. *Journal of Consulting Psychology*, 1966, *30*, 378–380.

Gelfand, D., and Hartman, D. P. Behavior therapy with children: A review and evaluation of research methodology. *Psychological Bulletin*, 1968, *69*, 204–215.

Gewirtz, H., and Gewirtz, J. L. Caretaking settings, background events, and behavior differences in four Israeli child-rearing environments: Some preliminary trends. In B. M. Moss (Ed.), *Determinants of infant behavior* IV. London: Methuen, 1967.

Harris, F. R., Johnston, M. K., Kelley, C. S., and Wolf, M. M. Effects of positive social reinforcement on regressed crawling of a nursery school child. *Journal of Educational Psychology,* 1964, *55,* 35–41.

HARRIS, F. R. The use of reinforcement principles with nursery, preschool, and kindergarten children. Paper delivered to the Annual Meeting of the AERA, New York City, 1967.

HART, B. M., ALLEN, K. E., BUELL, J. S., HARRIS, F. R., and WOLF, M. M. Effects of social reinforcement on operant crying. *Journal of Experimental Child Psychology,* 1964, *1,* 145–153.

HAWKINS, R. P., PETERSON, R. F., SCHWEID, E., and BIJOU, S. W. Behavior therapy in the home: Amelioration of problem parent-child relations with parent in a therapeutic role. *Journal of Experimental Child Psychology,* 1966, *4,* 99–107.

HONIG, W. K. (Ed.). *Operant behavior: Areas of research and application.* New York: Appleton-Century-Crofts, 1966.

JOHNSTON, M. S., KELLEY, C. S., HARRIS, F. R., and WOLF, M. M. An application of reinforcement principles to development of motor skills of a young child. *Child Development,* 1966, *37,* 379–387.

LOVAAS, O. I., BERBERICH, J. P., PERLOFF, B. F., and SCHAEFER, B. Acquisition of imitative speech by schizophrenic children. *Science,* 1966, *151,* 705–707.

LOVAAS, O. I., FREITAG, G., GOLD, V. J., and KASSORLA, I. C. Experimental studies in childhood schizophrenia: Analysis of self-destructive behavior. *Journal of Experimental Child Psychology,* 1965, *2,* 67–84. (a)

LOVAAS, O. I., FREITAG, G., GOLD, V. J., and KASSORLA, I. C. Recording apparatus and procedure for observation of behaviors of children in free play settings. *Journal of Experimental Child Psychology,* 1965, *2,* 108–120. (b)

LOVAAS, O. I., SCHAEFER, B., and SIMMONS, J. Q. Building social behavior in autistic children by use of electric shock. *Journal of Experimental Research in Personality,* 1965, *2,* 99–109.

MADSEN, C. H., JR., BECKER, W. C., and THOMAS, D. R. Rules, praise, and ignoring: Elements of elementary classroom control. *Journal of Applied Behavior Analysis,* 1968, *1,* 139–150.

MADSEN, C. H., JR., BECKER, W. C., THOMAS, D. R. KOSER, L., and PLAGER, E. An analysis of the reinforcing function of "sit down" commands. In R. K. Parker (Ed.), *Readings in Educational Psychology,* Boston: Allyn & Bacon, 1968.

O'LEARY, K. D., O'LEARY, S. G., and BECKER, W. C. Modification of a deviant sibling interaction pattern in the home. *Behaviour Research and Therapy,* 1967, *5,* 113–120.

PETERSON, R. F. and PETERSON, L. The use of positive reinforcement in the control of self-destructive behavior in a retarded boy. *Journal of Experimental Child Psychology,* 1968, *6,* 351–360.

PRONKO, N. H. Biotelemetry: Psychology's newest ally. *Psychological Record,* 1968, *18,* 93–100.

SIDMAN, M. *Tactics of scientific research.* New York: Basic Books, 1960.

SKINNER, B. F. *Science and human behavior.* New York: Macmillan, 1953.

SKINNER, B. F. Operant behavior. In W. K. Honig (Ed.), *Operant behavior: Areas of research and application.* New York: Appleton-Century-Crofts, 1966.

THOMAS, D. R., BECKER, W. C., and ARMSTRONG, M. Production and elimination of disruptive classroom behavior by systematically varying teacher's behavior. *Journal of Applied Behavior Analysis,* 1968, *1,* 35–45.

WAHLER, R. G., WINKEL, G. H., PETERSON, R. F., and MORRISON, D. C. Mothers as behavior therapists for their own children. *Behaviour Research and Therapy,* 1965, *3,* 113–124.

WOLF, M. M., RISLEY, T. R., and MEES, H. L. Application of operant conditioning procedures to the behavior problems of an autistic child. *Behaviour Research and Therapy*, 1964, *1*, 305–312.

ZEILBERGER, J., SAMPEN, S. E., and SLOANE, H. N., JR. Modification of a child's problem behaviors in the home with the mother as therapist. *Journal of Applied Behavior Analysis*, 1968, *1*, 47–53.

ZIMMERMAN, E. H., and FERSTER, C. B. Observations of child in treatment at the Psychiatric Institute, Indiana University Medical School. Unpublished manuscript, 1960.

6

SHELDON D. ROSE

A Behavioral Approach to the Group Treatment of Parents

Group work, like casework, has been defined as a method of treatment whose purpose is the improved social functioning of clients.[1] Although the social work literature abounds in descriptive typologies and case studies aimed at facilitating the practitioner's diagnostic skills, few articles have pointed to a specific set of procedures of intervention available to the social worker for the emelioration of the client's problems. In the absence of a theoretical foundation that would aid in specifying the worker's actions, little progress in this direction could be made. With the introduction of learning theory into social work, however, conceptual tools became available for describing in detail a large number of procedures of intervention, many of which have been systematically evaluated and effectively demonstrated in a variety of contexts.

In contrast to the recent introduction of learning theory in social work, the small group has long been used by social workers. Social-psychological studies have demonstrated the power of the group to modify its members' behavior and attitudes.[2] Many operational hypotheses concerning the group's specific attributes are available to the social worker.

In developing a behavioral approach to the group treatment of parents,[3] the author has taken advantage of the empirical findings derived both from learning theory and from small group theory.[4] Since social workers are more familiar with small group theory, this paper will emphasize the procedures and principles derived from learning theory. Examples will be given that have been drawn from the experiences of five second-year students at the University of Michigan School of Social Work who worked with groups of parents and utilized some or all of the procedures reported here. The stu-

Reprinted with permission of the National Association of Social Workers, from *Social Work,* Vol. 14, No. 3 (July 1969), pp. 21–29.

dents worked primarily with parents from the lower socioeconomic strata in a settlement house, child guidance clinic, family service agency, public welfare agency, and school service agency. The groups ranged in size from three to eight members and met once a week for as few as five to as many as 16 weeks.

Assessment

One of the major difficulties of parents who come to an agency is the inadequacy or inappropriateness of their child's management procedures—the skills necessary to cope with their child's behavior. The purpose of behavioral group treatment is to increase their repertoire of procedures and to teach them the appropriate conditions under which these techniques should be applied.

Before the parent can be taught these skills, it is necessary to determine the child's presenting behavioral problem.[5] The parent learns to state the problem in terms of observable behaviors that occur or fail to occur in specific situations. He is also shown ways of estimating (or counting) how often they take place, since it is the frequency that is most often changed. Because most parents are not accustomed to speaking in specific terms about behavior and many lack observational skills that are a prerequisite to any description or counting, in most groups considerable time is given to training them to do so.

This training involves observing social situations, counting specific behaviors, charting these behaviors, and reporting the results to the group. In order to increase the probability of success, the parents first observe and count behaviors with which they are not especially concerned, e.g., the number of times the child leaves and enters the room, the context and number of situations in which he smiles or laughs. As they gain skill in observation, they note the frequency of the behaviors with which they are concerned, e.g., complaining, temper tantrums, soiling, teasing a sibling, being a truant. At this point a baseline—an estimate of the frequency of the behavioral problem prior to any endeavor at change— is established.

The baseline makes it possible to evaluate the degree of the child's behavioral changes as treatment progresses. However, in the experiences described in this paper, several difficulties arose that frequently made it necessary to rely on indefinite estimates or to forgo a baseline completely. Some of these problems were the parents' different levels of comprehension, their inadequate training, "forgetting," and a lack of cooperation by one of the spouses.

There is considerable evidence to support the contention that the events that follow a given behavior or the immediate consequences of that behavior have a strong influence on subsequent performance of it (see Krasner and Ullmann, 1965: chaps. 5–12; Staats and Staats, 1963: 35–115). This is one of the basic precepts of learning theory and it forms the foundation for many forms of intervention. For this reason, parents are taught to observe and describe the immediate results of all their child's behaviors with which they are concerned. One set of consequences over which the parents have the most control are their own reactions—emotional, verbal, and motor. Once the parents are able to describe their responses, a major part of the treatment involves assessing them and training the parents in new or more appropriate ones.

In order to determine which behaviors should be modified, the worker also reviews the long-range consequences of each behavioral problem with the parents. In this process, many parents discover that the ultimate effects of one set of behaviors are relatively unimportant or, because of the consequences of previously unconsidered behaviors, they warrant immediate attention.

The following example is an excerpt from a group meeting in which some of the aspects of assessment are demonstrated:

> Mrs. M complained that her 11-year-old daughter had frequent temper tantrums. The members inquired about the conditions that led to them. Mrs. M, after reflecting a moment, indicated that her daughter responded this way whenever the mother said "no" or she became frustrated in any way. When asked what happened when she had these tantrums, Mrs. M said she usually gave her daughter exactly what she wanted in order to quiet her down. Mrs. W asked what might eventually happen if this habit were to persist. Throwing up her hands, Mrs. M replied that it would drive the whole family out of their minds and probably her teacher and friends, too.

The members then suggested to Mrs. M that she was maintaining the behavior she wanted to eliminate by rewarding her daughter after the temper tantrum. This implied the change procedures to be used: Mrs. M would have to find some alternative response to the temper tantrum, such as ignoring her, walking away, using calm verbal expressions, and/or isolating her until the tantrum wore off.

Goal-Setting

After assessing the problem, each set of parents is helped by other parents to establish a goal of the desired frequency or intensity of behavior they would like to see their children achieve. The goals are formulated along the same dimension as those in relation to the presenting behavior or the conditions under which a behavior is appropriate. As is true of initial behavioral problems, the criteria of specificity and the description of the impinging conditions are essential in the statement of goals. The kind of goals dealt with include increasing the frequency of studying to one hour or evening, eliminating temper tantrums, reducing the frequency of fighting with a sibling to twice a week, learning new ways of responding to external stress or limitations, discriminating between situations in which loud, raucous play is appropriate or inappropriate, and increasing the frequency of coming home on time to every evening.

The worker also evolves with each parent or set of parents the goal each parent expects to achieve for himself by the end of treatment. Many parents are initially hesitant to look at ways in which they themselves must change in order to establish the desired changes in their children and, as a result, prefer to focus solely on the changes in the child. The worker may postpone encouraging the parent to make explicit the goal of his own behavioral change in the first phase of treatment. However, the need for parental change usually becomes obvious as soon as the children's behaviors are evaluated.

Examples of goals for parental change include ignoring temper tantrums and providing attention for more desirable behaviors, establishing rules and routines and ways of maintaining them, giving rewards in a consistent rather than haphazard manner, and learning and practicing the forms of manifesting interest in the child's school and recreational activities.

The processes of assessment and goal-setting begin in an intake interview and are continued in the group. Dealing with these tasks in the group provides each parent with an opportunity to help others specify their problems and impinging conditions and to observe on repeated occasions the relation of these conditions to the problem. The group members gradually take over from the worker the responsibility of determining whether the problem and goal are sufficiently specific and the conditions adequately described. By analyzing and dealing with problems other than their own, they increase their problem-solving skills in general and are better able to cope with new problems that may arise after the group terminates (see Goldstein, *et al.*, 1966: 212–259).

Modifying Children's Behavior

After each set of parents decides which behavior they will seek to modify first, they begin to learn procedures for altering it. These procedures usually involve modifying antecedent and consequent conditions to improve the performance of desirable behaviors and decrease the performance of less desirable ones.[6]

Some examples of modifying antecedent conditions are the use of routines (when none existed previously), the introduction of models who have acceptable characteristics that are likely to be imitated, the elimination of seductive parental behaviors that previously triggered off undesirable behavior, and the use of cues to help the children remember the desired behavior. Examples of modifying consequent conditions are systematically applying limits, rewarding on a frequent and consistent basis, time-out procedures, and withholding attention or other rewards when they seem to be maintaining the undesirable behavior.

Extensive case examples of these techniques are to be found in the literature.[7] For this reason, in the remaining part of this paper the author will largely concentrate on the procedures used by the worker in teaching parents to become behavior modifiers.

Modifying Parents' Behavior

In order to teach the parents the techniques to be used, the following behavioral teaching procedures are utilized by the worker: programmed instruction, model presentation, behavioral rehearsal, and behavioral assignments. These should be included in a total group plan in such a way that each client may achieve his stated goals. Each of these procedures also involves the other group members in some way in helping work toward the goals of treatment.

Since most parents are not able to learn to do everything at once, simple techniques are taught first, which are followed gradually by more complex procedures and combinations of different procedures. Usually parents try out each step between sessions. Although these techniques are usually integrated into a sequential plan, for purposes of analysis each will first be discussed separately.

Programmed Instruction

When treatment is viewed as a learning process, one can use the same techniques to teach new behavior that have proved effective in teaching academic subjects. One such technique is programmed instruction.[8] In the project, extensive use was made of a programmed instruction book on child management in which the writers train the parents to use a number of basic concepts and principles for working with their children (see Smith and Smith, 1966). Some of the principles on which the book focuses are increased consistency in parental behavior, the use of rules to provide increased consistency, and guidelines for selecting and enforcing rules. The book is especially effective for disorganized parents or those who have difficulty in limiting their children. It seems to be less effective for excessively orderly parents and strict disciplinarians. The following example from the book is a discussion followed by an exercise:

A. SELECTING A RULE

1. What Is a Rule?

Any demand made on a child by a parent is a rule. Any task he must perform is a rule. Any decision regarding what he may have or may not have, what he may do or may not do—any such decision is a rule. Many parents dislike establishing rules. Usually they feel guilty when they require the child to do something which is unpleasant. They are not aware that consistent enforcement of a rule makes the world safer and more comfortable for the child.

Parents sometimes disguise rules to ease their guilt. They say, "Wouldn't you like to do the dishes?" or "Do you want to take a nap?" If the only acceptable answer to the question is "yes," it is a rule—regardless of the way it is stated. It would be much less confusing to the child if Mother said, "Do the dishes now," or "It's naptime."

Some rules are "long term." They must be enforced again and again over a long period of time. These rules usually govern the performance of a chore or a family routine. In each item below, choose the long-term rule.

. . . . . .

23.—a. Mark must cut the grass every Saturday afternoon.
—b. Mark can earn 50¢ by weeding the garden.
24.—a. Mother provides Joan with an alarm clock.
—b. Joan must dress herself without help before she leaves for school.
25.—a. Jeanine has to do the dishes on Monday and Friday.
—b. Jeanine's brother asks her to substitute for him on Wednesday.
26.—a. Everyone must wash his hands and face before eating dinner.
—b. It is often necessary to turn on the light in the dining room if the sun has set [Smith and Smith 1966: 19–20].

There are several ways in which the program can be used. The first is to assign a number of principles and exercises each week to be completed at home. In the group meeting, the responses are discussed and applications to the parents' specific situations are suggested. Since the Smith and Smith program requires approximately a seventh-grade level of reading, some variation was required for several of the groups with whom the project members worked. In one group, the worker would prepare simplified excerpts from the program that were then discussed in the group. He asked the parents to complete the exercises during the meeting and helped them with concepts or words they did not understand. In most groups the entire book was not used. In some groups additional exercises were designed that taught other principles. Programmed instruction was the major basis of treatment in one group. In another group the parents thought the program was for parents with younger children and preferred discussing their own examples. In the remaining groups, programmed instruction was used to supplement the many other procedures used.

Model Presentation

When situations are presented in which some of the parents think the principle is difficult or impossible to enforce, the worker may suggest appropriate parental responses and/or may encourage the other members to make suggestions. But such advice, although helpful, is seldom sufficient to add new behaviors to the parent's repertoire or to eliminate ineffective ones.[9]

To demonstrate appropriate behavior, the worker or a parent who has solved a similar problem plays the role of the parent. The other group members play the others significant in the situation. The parent whose problem is being enacted is the director. In this capacity he instructs the other members in performing their roles and defines the conditions that have led to the problem.[10]

In training the members, the worker may initially play all the roles.[11] When the parents begin role-playing, the situation is highly structured, i.e., the roles are predetermind in discussion. If notes describing each of the roles are distributed to the participants, anxiety about role-playing is usually reduced. The worker points out that dramatic ability is not essential and that as soon as the point has been made, the action will be terminated. Another way to reduce initial anxiety is to announce in advance that no situation should be played longer than five minutes. After some discussion the role-playing may be continued.

The role-play situation may be repeated several times until the parent feels comfortable enough to try it himself. The cast may be modified or various aspects of the situation may be adapted to simulate more nearly the varied conditions of real life.

In evaluating the role play, the entire group is encouraged to discuss the appropriateness of the parent's actions. The worker first discusses with the group what the probable consequences of these actions would be. Then the group discusses alternate actions and examines their probable effects. The members may also discuss the problems of applying any of these actions to their own situations.

There are several additional techniques for model presentation that do not involve role-playing and may be used instead of or, preferably, in addition to it. One is to invite parents from previous groups to tell their techniques for handling similar problems. Another is to present the case histories of such parents. Popular films or television programs in which characters have coped with similar problems may also be used.

Behavioral Rehearsal

Behavioral rehearsal refers to the client's performance of behavior in the treatment situation that he would like to perform in the real-life situation. Lazarus, in a controlled experiment, has demonstrated the greater effectiveness of behavioral rehearsal in comparison to "advice-giving" or a "reflective-interpretive approach" in the treatment of persons who are unassertive (see Lazarus, 1966: 205–212). Experience suggests that the approach can be used in the treatment of a wider range of behavioral problems than those used by Lazarus. It has been used by the parents to practice such behaviors as setting limits, establishing new reward procedures, ignoring situations that previously they could not ignore, and even using behavioral rehearsals with their children. Practice in the simulated situation seemed to facilitate performance in the real situation by reducing the anxiety associated with it.[12]

Behavioral rehearsal usually follows some form of model presentation.

Prior to a person's performance of his own role in a family situation, the worker and the group members review exactly what new behaviors the parent is to perform. After the first rehearsal, the other members evaluate the performance and make additional suggestions for alterations. The situation is repeated at least once. Then the parent is given a behavioral assignment to perform some of the behaviors rehearsed with the group in the real-life situation. It is seldom possible in one session for each person to rehearse his situation. In the course of several meetings, however, it is helpful if everyone who is willing has the opportunity to perform at least once. It is preferable to begin with situations that have implications for several, if not most, of the group members.

Behavioral Assignments

One of the major problems of group and individual treatment is a lack of concern about generalizing change to situations outside the treatment situation. Although role-playing focuses on extra-group situations, it is performed within the group context. Moreover, it demonstrates and provides practice but does not assure performance in the real-life situation. For these reasons, at each meeting behavioral assignments are given to group members so that they may try out newly learned behaviors outside the group prior to the next meeting. The following are four requisites for the successful performance of a behavioral assignment:

1. The assignment should be highly specific. The client should know exactly what he must do and the conditions under which the given responses should be performed. Furthermore, if certain unexpected conditions arise (e.g., illness), or if the appropriate conditions do not occur, alternate behaviors, such as telephoning the worker, should be developed.

2. The client should be able to handle the assignment, i.e., there should be a high probability of success. If the client succeeds early in treatment, it is more likely that he will continue to try behavioral assignments.[13] On the other hand, an assignment should not be so easy that no new learning takes place.

3. The client should commit himself, at least verbally, in front of his fellow group members to attempt the performance of his assignment. If the client states exactly what he is going to do, it will be more difficult for him to hedge or explain away his failure.

4. The client should report the details of his attempt to carry out the assignment to the group. Without such monitoring procedures, it seems that assignments are soon neglected. Monitoring by the other group members serves both as a reward for trying the task and a source of information about how it can be done more effectively the next time.

Initially, the assignment may be suggested by the worker on the basis of the previously mentioned criteria. The client, together with the other group members, works out the details. The worker then asks the client if he understands and thinks he can perform the assignment within the allotted time. If not, the assignment is adjusted accordingly. Once he has had some experience in applying the criteria, each client develops his own assignment with assistance from the others.

Each assignment must be viewed as being part of the sequence. As one assignment is completed, a slightly more difficult one should be given. The sequence should ultimately lead to the attainment of the treatment goal. The completion of each assignment is, in a sense, the achievement of a subgoal.

Two examples that point up the interrelationship and sequence of the aforementioned techniques are the following:

> Mrs. L, Mrs. A, and Mrs. B complained that their children never did chores in the house. After the Smith and Smith program on enforcing rules had been discussed, Mrs. M demonstrated in a role-playing incident (model presentation) how she set and enforced rules. She was followed by Mrs. L who rehearsed behaviors in which she enforced a daily bed-making rule (model presentation). Then Mrs. A played her own role in a situation in which her daughters refused to do the dishes (behavioral rehearsal). Mrs. M prompted Mrs. A about what she should say. Finally, the group gave Mrs. L, Mrs. A, and Mrs. B the assignment of developing and enforcing a rule with one of their children (behavioral assignment) and reporting to the group at the next weekly meeting.
>
> . . . . .
>
> Mr. and Mrs. N had difficulty limiting the acting-out behavior of their son, aged 11. The group members discussed the antecedent conditions of the child's behavior and the previous ways in which Mr. and Mrs. N responded to it, which included showering him with attention, arguing with each other, and pleading with the child to stop.
>
> The worker suggested several alternative responses, such as immediately removing the child from the scene of the acting out without discussion. Mrs. McA, who had used this procedure effectively, demonstrated how it should be done. The worker played the role of the son (model presentation).
>
> Mr. and Mrs. N were hesitant about role-playing but were willing to describe exactly what they would do (behavioral rehearsal). They agreed to try it out during the week (behavioral assignment). The worker pointed out that they could expect an increase in the undesired behavior before the situation got better, and Mrs. McA affirmed this from her experience.
>
> Other group members thought it would be helpful if, after this first attempt, Mr. and Mrs. N would call Mr. and Mrs. McA to tell them what had happened so they would not have to wait until the next meeting (monitoring the behavioral assignment).

Relationship

Since relationship is a core concept in the present-day practice of social work, a description of its place in the behavioral approach seems necessary.

Although the worker does not focus on relationship-building as a means of intervention, the low rate of discontinuance and the frequent verbal expressions of satisfaction suggest that quite rapidly he becomes a highly attractive individual.

The factors that contribute to relationship-building appear to be the following: (1) The worker provides a highly structured situation in which answers are given to the clients' specific problems. (2) The worker readily recognizes and rewards achievement. (3) Accomplishments are clearly defined in such small steps that everyone achieves something between and during every meeting, which affords the worker ample opportunity to be rewarding. The feeling of success even in small things may be in itself an important internal reward for many parents. (4) Since goals, procedures, and assumptions of treatment are made explicit, the situation is not ambiguous. This reduces anxiety and, in turn, increases the worker's attractiveness.[14]

The social worker does not set aside his natural warmth, understanding, or acceptance of the clients with whom he works. He adds to his skills in relationship the more specific techniques espoused in this paper. The parent, too, is taught that the techniques are to be applied in a warm and understanding social climate. Since the parents cannot be taught warmth, it is sometimes helpful to teach them the physical manifestations of it. In doing so, there is some support for the assumption that the appropriate feelings will eventually follow the behavioral manifestation.[15]

Value of the Group

There are many therapeutically facilitating aspects of the group, most of which are common to all group treatment approaches. In a group there is an abundance of models for the client to imitate. Although clients are treated for the absence of behaviors necessary to deal adequately with their children, almost all parents have within their repertoire adaptive behaviors they can demonstrate or teach to other parents in the group. The worker encourages and structures imitation of those behaviors appropriate to each client in terms of his individual treatment goals. The group also provides a large variety of role-players for model presentation and behavioral rehearsal.

When the cohesiveness of the group is high, approval and disapproval of the group members function as effective controls.[16] Encouraged by the worker, members tend to create a norm of accurate accounting of extragroup activities. Thus the group may be an especially efficient means of monitoring behavioral change outside it. With the worker's help, the group members also develop norms for working on their problems, being specific as opposed to global, and participating in discussion and role-playing. Thus the parent, in observing and participating in the treatment of others, develops a range of solutions for a range of problems.

Conclusion

In the groups in which the behavioral approach was used, most parents claimed at termination that they were better able to handle their problems and many felt they would be better able to cope with any new problems their children might have. The workers, too, stated that it was helpful to have prescriptions for what they could do to help the parents. They also indicated that it was easier to prepare for meetings and evaluate outcomes than in previous treatment situations.

Although the outcomes reported in this paper are the results of a demonstration project and are anecdotal in nature, they are sufficiently promising to encourage an expansion of this approach and an exploration of the use of additional behavioral precedures to facilitate still further the treatment of parents in groups.

Notes

1. For a detailed description of this specific orientation to social group work, see Vinter (1965).

2. For a review of findings pertaining to the implication of power for the behavior of group members, see especially Collins and Guetzkow (1964:152–165).

3. The author wishes to express his appreciation to Paul Glasser and Tony Tripodi for their helpful comments on this paper.

4. A behavioral approach refers to a treatment approach that focuses on behavioral change and is based, at least in part, on learning theory. The author is by no means the first to describe a behavioral approach to the treatment of parents. Within the same theoretical framework, the following authors suggest a variety of procedures for parental training, many of which are not included in this article: Walder *et al.* (n.d.); Patterson *et al.* (1967); Shah (n.d.); Russo (1964); Wahler *et al.* (1965).

5. In this paper the author has tried to avoid the technical terminology that assumes the reader has a background in learning theory.

6. The reader could rightfully raise the question of what is desirable and who determines the desirability of behavior. For purposes of this paper, the author has avoided such a discussion. The behavior modifiers more frequently allude to adaptive and maladaptive behaviors. See Ullmann and Krasner (1956:20) for a definition of maladaptive behavior from the learning theorist's point of view.

7. A large selection of such case examples is to be found in Ullmann and Krasner (1965) and recent issues of behavior modification journals.

8. See Staats and Staats (1963:415–424). In this section, the writers discuss the principle of and values underlying programmed instruction as it applies to academic subjects. For a bibliography of programs applicable to social work practice, see Thomas and Lind (1967).

9. For empirical evidence of this statement, see Lazarus (1966).

10. For an excellent summary of the principles and implications of model presentation for behavioral change, see Bandura (1965).

11. For an extensive discussion of the possibilities and limitations of role playing for treatment, see Corsini (1966).

12. The empirical evidence for this assumption has been discussed by Goldstein, Heller, and Sechrest (1966 : 97–109).

13. Success in task performance has been shown by Marquis, Guetzkow, and Heyns (1963:55–67) to be related to several indications of satisfaction. Success is probably experienced as an intrinsic reward and, therefore, according to learning theory, should function to increase the probability that the behaviors that preceded it would occur with greater frequency or intensity.

14. For a discussion of the relation between ambiguity, message threat, and the therapist's attractiveness, see Goldstein, Heller, and Sechrest (1965:171–177).

15. See Brodsky (1967). Brodsky demonstrates how verbal behavior follows non-verbal learning. If it is assumed that verbal behavior is an indication of the feelings of the individual, this supports the present author's contention that feelings can best be changed by first changing behaviors associated with them (the author's limited experience also supports this contention).

16. Compare Bass (1960:60). On the basis of extensive research experience, Bass points out that the more attractive the group, the greater the rewards that may be earned by its members.

References

BANDURA, ALBERT. Behavioral modifications through modeling procedures. In Leonard Krasner and Leonard Ullmann (Eds.), *Research in behavior modification.* New York: Holt, Rinehart and Winston, 1965.

BASS, B. M. *Leadership, psychology and organization behavior.* New York: Harper and Bros., 1960.

BRODSKY, GERRY. The relation between verbal and non-verbal change. *Behavior Research and Therapy,* 1967, *5,* 183–182.

COLLINS, BARRY E., and GUETZKOW, HAROLD. *A social psychology of group processes for decision-making.* New York: John Wiley, 1964.

CORSINI, RAYMOND (with the assistance of Samuel Cardone). *Role-playing in psychotherapy: A manual.* Chicago: Aldine, 1966.

GOLDSTEIN, ARNOLD P., HELLER, KENNETH, and SECHREST, LEE B. *Psychotherapy and the psychology of behavior change.* New York: John Wiley, 1966.

KRASNER, LEONARD, and ULLMANN, LEONARD. (Eds.) *Research in behavior modification.* New York: Holt, Rinehart and Winston, 1965.

LAZARUS, ARNOLD A. Behaviour rehearsal vs. non-directive therapy vs. advice in effecting behaviour change. *Behaviour Research and Therapy,* 1966, *4,* 209–212.

MARQUIS, D. G., GUETZKOW, HAROLD, and HEYNS, R. W. A social psychological study of the decision-making conference. In H. Guetzkow (Ed.), *Groups, leadership and men: Research in human relations.* New York: Russell Sage Foundation, 1963.

PATTERSON, G. R. *et al.* Reprogramming the social environment. *Journal of Child Psychology and Psychiatry,* 1967, *8,* 181–196.

RUSSO, SALVATORE. Adaptations in behavioural therapy with children. *Behaviour Research and Therapy,* 1964, *2,* 43–47.

SHAH, SALEM A. Training and utilizing a mother as the therapist for her child. Mimeo, n.d.

SMITH, JUDITH M., and SMITH, DONALD E. P. *Child management: A program for parents.* Ann Arbor, MI: Ann Arbor Publishers, 1966.

STAATS, ARTHUR W., and STAATS, CAROLYN R. *Complex human behavior.* New York: Holt, Rinehart and Winston, 1963.

THOMAS, EDWIN J. (Ed.) *The socio-behavioral approach and applications to social work.* New York: Council on Social Work Education, 1967.

THOMAS, EDWIN J., and LIND, ROGER. Programmed instruction as potentially useful in social work education: An annotated bibliography. *Social Work Education Reporter,* 1967, *15,* 22–27, 33.

ULLMANN, LEONARD P., and KRASNER, LEONARD. *Case studies in behavior modification.* New York: Holt, Rinehart and Winston, 1965.

VINTER, ROBERT D. Social group work. In Harry L. Lurie (Ed.) *Encyclopedia of social work.* New York: National Association of Social Workers, 1965.

WAHLER, R. G., *et al.* Mothers as behavior therapists for their own children. *Behaviour Research and Therapy,* 1965, *3,* 113–124.

WALDER, LEOPOLD O., *et al.* Teaching behavioral principles to parents of disturbed children. Manuscript, University of Maryland, n.d.

7

HARRY LAWRENCE AND
MARTIN SUNDEL

Behavior Modification in Adult Groups

Social workers, clinical psychologists, and psychiatrists have become increasingly interested in behavior modification—"the application of the results of learning theory and experimental psychology to the problems of altering maladaptive behavior" (Ullmann and Krasner, 1965:2; Thomas, 1968; Wolpe, 1969). Utilizing the principle that both maladaptive and adaptive behavior are acquired, maintained, or reduced by conditioning, therapists have analyzed and treated a variety of problems such as phobias, depression, school disruption, and interpersonal hostility and passivity.

The basic procedures of behavior modification are (1) identifying the problem and specifying the relevant behavior that must be changed, (2) discovering the reinforcers that maintain the problem behavior and those that can be manipulated to change it, (3) programming reinforcement schedules, and (4) teaching new adaptive behaviors when they are missing from the client's repertoire.

Relevance to Group Work

Although the uses of behavior modification in group work have been limited, the results have been promising. See, for example, Hastorf (1965); Liberman (1970); Rose (1969); Rose *et al.* (1970); Lawrence (1967). This article describes the application of behavior modification pinciples to time-limited group treatment of adults. The major procedures include (1) developing protreatment group norms, (2) teaching behavioral assessment and other problem-solving skills that can be used during and after

Reprinted with permission of the National Association of Social Workers, from *Social Work,* Vol. 17, No. 2 (March 1972), pp. 34–43.

group treatment, (3) maximizing the therapeutic effects of social reinforcement, and (4) developing desired client behavior within the group that members can apply in their own environment.

In this treatment model of social group work, the client becomes a member of the group to solve a problem that concerns him and significant others. The treatment objective is to change the behavior of each member in relationships outside the group where his problem is manifested.

Group functioning objectives, such as group cohesiveness, democratic leadership, self-revealing communication, or warm group experiences are relevant only to the degree that they help achieve treatment goals. Group functioning objectives vary according to the tasks required to solve a problem. They are means to an end, not ends in themselves.

Treatment goals for solving each member's problems are specified early in the group's history. Although initial goals may be revised or changed later, both the member and the worker must have a concrete understanding of what these goals are. Success of treatment is based on the degree to which a member's specified goal has been reached.

Once the group has assessed a member's problem with him and has delineated the goal he wants to achieve, the workers must find the most efficient and effective interventions for achieving the desired outcome. These interventions may involve direct, indirect, and extragroup means of influence (Vinter, 1967a). Appropriate interventions are selected in part on the basis of social science knowledge (e.g., small-group, social role, and behavior theory) about how people acquire, maintain, and change their behavior. In this respect, the group worker is like the physician who applies his knowledge of anatomy, physiology, and pharmacology to treat an abscess or the engineer who uses his knowledge of physics, metallurgy, and geology to construct a bridge.

Other group work approaches define their goals in terms of the interventions they use. As a result, their utilization of social science knowledge is limited because they emphasize how skillful the worker is in following uniform methods that have been predetermined by social work practice wisdom. For example, a meeting is often evaluated in terms of whether the worker observed a subtle communication or facilitated a member's participation in a discussion. These skills are important, but if they supersede or become detached from concern for the treatment goals, they become an art rather than a science. Such practice is like that of an architect who becomes so enthused about a building's design that he disregards its function. Science is relevant to him only if he is concerned with both structure and function.

The group therapy described in this article was conducted at a family service agency. Most of the clients had been known to the agency for one to five years. Their problems included child management, anxiety, marital discord, depression, and interpersonal difficulties with friends, family, and coworkers. Seventeen men and women were divided into three groups, with two workers serving as cotherapists for each group. The groups met for 2½ hours once a week, and a time limit of eight weeks was set for the treatment process. Success of treatment was determined by the degree to which each member's concrete goals were achieved in relation to his initial problem. The treatment sequence of study, diagnosis, treatment, and evaluation closely approximated that described by Vinter (1967b).

INTAKE

Vinter defines intake as "the process by which a potential client achieves client status (1967b:9). During this process the client presents his problem and the worker makes a preliminary diagnosis. The worker and client then decide whether treatment should be continued.

Prior to forming the groups, the workers held intake interviews with each client. In the interview the client (1) presented the problem(s) he wanted to work on in the group in behaviorally specific terms, (2) tentatively specified the goal(s) he hoped to achieve in treatment, (3) stated whether he wished to participate in group treatment, and (4) verbally agreed to abide by the rules for group participation.

To achieve these objectives, the workers used five specific procedures that were designed to be used as guidelines, rather than prescriptions. The workers also considered the idiosyncracies of each client and the immediate circumstances that unfolded during the interview.

Typical difficulties encountered during interviews included value differences between worker and client, the client's fear of treatment, refusal to admit the severity of his problem, and anxiety about talking to the worker. Although each of these situations required alterations in the intake strategy, the workers successfully completed the intake objectives with each client in one interview.

Procedure 1

The client was oriented to the initial interview. Each prospective group member completed a problem checklist before his intake interview. He checked those items that indicated the areas in which he was having role difficulties, e.g., with a parent, spouse, or employer. He then double-checked the relationships that concerned him most and described in writing how they were a problem and what he hoped to change.

By examining the client's checklist the worker knew what to focus on in the interview. In addition, the form partially structured how the client presented his problems.

Procedure 2

The client's problems were delineated in behaviorally specific terms. Clients often described their problems in the form of vague statements that were devoid of interpersonal or situational circumstances (e.g., "What's the point of going on?" "Everything's going wrong in my life"). In addition, they made assumptions about what caused their problems (e.g., "Once I discover why I fear my father, I'll be able to handle my boss") or how they could be solved (e.g., "I've come to the conclusion that the only way to solve my marital difficulties is to get a divorce").

To avoid choosing treatment interventions on the basis of such faulty definitions, the worker asked the client to describe a specific problem of his own or someone else within the context of the person(s) and circumstances involved. For example, "whenever I get ready to leave the house in the evening, my mother shouts at me and accuses me of 'sleeping around' with men." "When the boss asks me to explain my reports, I tremble and answer in monosyllables."

Frequently a client described his problem in terms of another person's undesirable behavior, rather than recognizing his own contribution to it. However, he was not confronted with this fact during intake because he would learn to recognize his role in maintaining the problem during the group assessment process.

The worker then asked the client to give two or more recent examples of each problem. If these examples were inconsistent with the client's statement of his problem, his statement was revised.

Procedure 3

Client and worker selected the problems to work on in the group and determined the order in which they would be considered. It sometimes became apparent during treatment that the client's initial problem was less serious or of less concern to him than others he had neglected to mention during intake. Therefore, to increase the chances that the appropriate problem was selected during the intake, the problem areas on the client's checklist were reviewed with him.

Criteria for establishing problem priorities included (1) the client's expressed preference for one problem over another, (2) the problem's suitability for time-limited group treatment and its relationship to the problems of other group members, (3) the negative consequences of the client or significant others of failing to solve the problem, (4) the benefits that might accrue to the client or significant others if the problem was solved, (5) the likelihood of solving the problem, given the client's existing behavioral repertoire, barriers, and available resources, and (6) the problem that required attention before others could be dealt with. The problem that met most or all of these criteria was given highest priority.

Procedure 4

A tentative treatment goal was established for each problem selected. The tentative treatment goal included what the client could reasonably expect to achieve in group treatment and the client's definition of the conditions he wanted to alter.

Although high specificity was attempted during intake, goals could not be formulated completely until the more detailed process of behavioral assessment took place during group meetings. The following example illustrates a tentative treatment goal:

> Problem: Mr. S shouts loudly when he tells his daughter to do her chores. She responds by crying, kicking the furniture, and avoiding him.
>
> Tentative goal: Mr. S's daughter will perform reasonable chores without being shouted at by her father.

Procedure 5

An initial treatment contract was established with the client. The initial contract consisted of the worker's statement of the conditions for group participation and the client's agreement to abide by these conditions and his decision to enter treatment. During the contract discussion, the worker answered the client's questions and explained the rationale for the procedures that would be used during treatment. (These procedures were reconfirmed during the first group meeting.)

If short-term group treatment is to be an effective means of achieving each member's treatment goals, the following set of group conditions must be established as rapidly as possible: (1) The group conforms to and enforces a set of protreatment norms. (2) It makes further decisions on problem priorities and clarifies treatment goals. (3) It contributes to the assessment of each member's problems. (4) It makes appropriate prescriptions for solving each member's problems and teaches each member to carry out these prescriptions successfully. (5) It socially reinforces its members.

Group Norms

The first procedure was to establish the following protreatment norms, to help the group internalize an effective set of rules and methods of enforcing them:

1. *Members must attend every meeting.* The meetings were designed according to a systematic progression of behavioral concepts, problem-solving steps, and tasks to be accomplished. If a member missed one meeting, his subsequent participation could be seriously hindered. Therefore, it was made clear to each member that one absence could lead to his removal from the group.

2. *Members must refrain from outside socializing until the series of meetings is completed.* Because the group was task oriented, i.e., it existed to solve the members' problems rather than as an end in itself, outside alliances among members might have conflicted with its purpose. For example, when a married man described his problem of social isolation, an unmarried fe-

male member of the group responded by inviting him to a party at her home. The worker's brief reminder about the contractual rule forbidding outside socializing effectively stopped what could have had negative consequences for these members and the rest of the group.

3. *Group discussions must be focused on contemporary events related to the member's problems.* Treatment was focused on problems that each client agreed to work on in the group, rather than on understanding or changing his total personality. Thus members were asked to refrain from discussing their personal histories.

4. *Members must refrain from hostile confrontation with each other.* Ventilation of hostile feelings was viewed as detrimental because it diverted the group's attention from problem-solving to exploring relationships among group members. Speculating on members' motives was also considered counterproductive to problem-solving because it could stimulate angry interactions and preoccupation with unstable hypotheses. For example, a member asked Mrs. M why she did not want to be assertive with her employer—implying that she enjoyed being abused. The worker explained that this line of inquiry might lead to time-consuming speculations about Mrs. M's childhood experiences and prior marital difficulties, which were not relevant to the conditions that influenced the problems with her employer.

5. *Members must work on assigned tasks between group meetings.* Assignments were formulated for the members at every session. Each client carried out his assignment in his own environment and reported on the results at the next meeting. By observing environmental events related to his actions, he thus increased his awareness of how his behavior maintained the objectionable actions of others.

Because the workers stated these five rules during intake interviews and group contract discussions, it was easier to enforce them during treatment. Initially, the workers assumed the responsibility for enforcing the rules. However, they also instructed the group to comment when a member broke a rule. The rules soon became group norms and the members enforced them when necessary.

The second procedure was to help the group clarify problem priorities and treatment goals. At the first group meeting the workers presented each client with a written statement of the previously agreed-on treatment goals. Each client was then given the option of rearranging his priorities. A client might change his priorities because his life circumstances had changed or because he had concealed his major concerns during the intake interview.

Behavioral Assessment

To be effective problem-solvers, clients had to know how to assess behavior correctly. Thus in the third procedure the workers taught the essentials of behavioral assessment to the group, keeping in mind the following considerations: concepts must be explained with a minimum of jargon and qualifications, concepts must be taught in the order they are applied to concrete tasks required for problem-solving, and each member must use one concept correctly before going on to the next.

Components of Behavioral Assessment

Behavioral assessment involves the following components: response, antecedents, consequences, and frequency (hereafter referred to as the RAC-F assessment).

A response is an observable verbal or motor behavior, such as laughing, smiling, stealing, fighting, arguing, or hitting. Each response is described in precise terms, e.g., "John hits his sister," rather than "John is aggressive toward his sister." Concepts such as hostility, passive-aggressiveness, or low motivation are not responses because they do not express what a person is doing in observable terms.

Problem responses indicate either a behavioral deficit or surfeit. Behavioral deficit refers to appropriate behavior that is absent or occurs with low frequency (e.g., a 10-year-old child does not speak in complete sentences, a man rarely compliments his wife's cooking). Behavioral surfeit refers to inappropriate behavior that occurs with undesirable frequency (e.g., a boy loudly curses other children in the classroom, a child regularly soils his pants, a man beats his wife).

Antecedents are events that precede a specific response. For example, Bob struck Joe with his fist because Joe said he was stupid (first antecedent). Bob's friends urged him to strike Joe (second antecedent).

Consequences are events that follow a response and cause the frequency of the response to increase or decrease. For example, Mr. S's shouting increases if Mrs. S complies with all the demands he makes while shouting. Miss A's bragging decreases when her boyfriend ridicules her for it.

Frequency refers to the number of times or the length of time a response occurs within a specific interval. For example, "Mrs. S shouted at her daughter 12 times during the past week." "Sally cried at the dinner table for ten minutes last Friday."

Teaching the Assessment Procedure

The first step in the assessment procedure was to teach the concept of response. After explaining his concept, the workers conducted a role play in which one worker depicted a client who was having dating problems. The other worker interviewed him and demonstrated how to identify the response the client was complaining about. One of the workers then assumed the role of a husband who was having marital problems. The husband complained that although he had not done anything, his wife had yelled at him.

With cuing from the second worker, the group interviewed the "client" and identified his problem response—he read the newspaper while his children damaged the furniture.

Following the role plays, the group helped each member identify a problem response in his own situation. Each member was then told to observe this response in its natural setting and to record on a RAC-F assessment form how often it occurred. When the clients reported on their behavioral assignments the following week, the workers made sure each client understood the concept of response before progressing to the discussion of antecedents and consequences.

The concepts of antecedents and consequences were explained and diagrammed on an easel, and role plays were used to illustrate them. The members were then given a behavioral assignment to observe the problem response and record its antecedents and consequences. For example, Mrs. D was concerned because her son George hit his younger sister Darlene. For the first assignment, Mrs. D reported ten instances in which George hit his sister. In the second report, she reported 12 instances. She also identified the antecedents of George's behavior: Darlene tattled on him, teased him, or disrupted his toys. The consequences of George's behavior were that his mother yelled at him and threatened him with physical punishment.

Problem-Solving

A major advantage of group treatment is the broad range of observations and experience that can be focused on a client's problem. However, group members usually lack the basic problem-skills required. These must be taught to them. Therefore, the fourth procedure was to shift the problem-solving responsibility to the group in progressive steps as the members demonstrated that they had acquired the requisite skills.

The steps in effective problem-solving are as follows: (1) the problem must be clearly defined, including the problem response, antecedents, and consequences, (2) the frequency of the problem response must be determined, (3) goals must be formulated, (4) viable alternative methods of reaching these goals must be developed, and (5) the best method must be chosen from among these alternatives.

To carry out these steps, the members were taught to interview one another in ways that minimized irrelevant remarks and references to unobservable states. For example, the group refused to accept Mrs. M's irrelevant comment: "My boss is always out to get me." Instead they asked her to descripe a representative encounter with her boss and what each of them did in the interchange. When Mr. J said that his wife was hostile to him, the group asked him to describe what his wife actually did.

Behavioral Reenactment

Clients frequently find it difficult to describe accurately their own actions in a situation. In these instances, behavioral reenactment can be used to identify a member's problem response. The client describes a situation that illustrates his problem. He then reenacts the situation, with other group members performing the roles of other persons involved. After the reenactment, the group tells him what they have observed about his behavior.

For example, Mr. J complained that his wife constantly criticized him, but he insisted that nothing he did before or after her criticism was responsible for it. In one incident, Mrs. J had accused him of giving inadequate directions to get to a picnic. In the reenactment of this incident, Mr. J played himself and two other members portrayed his wife and daughter. After the reenactment, the group pointed out the discrepancies between Mr. J's description of his behavior and his actual behavior. He talked in a monotone, never looked at his wife, made irrelevant remarks, and rarely answered her questions. Thus Mr. J observed how his behavior served as the antecedents and consequences of his wife's criticism.

Prescribing New Responses

After a client's behavioral assessment is completed, the workers and the group develop an intervention plan with him based on behavior modification principles. In many instances, a prescription for altering the antecedents and consequences of a problem behavior is sufficient for a client. Sometimes, however, he may not know how to perform the required behavior or he may be afraid to try it. Behavioral rehearsal and assertive training can help him develop the necessary skills. For example, when Mr. J found it difficult to understand what the group told him about his behavior with his wife, a group member demonstrated it for him. The group then discussed appropriate ways he could respond to her, e.g., he should look at her when she spoke to him, make explicit statements in response to her questions, and so forth. One member demonstrated the group's recommendations. In progressive steps, Mr. J imitated the performance until he responded appropriately. Finally, he was given the assignment to use these assertive behaviors whenever his wife criticized him.

An important aspect of group treatment is the social reinforcement that members provide for one another. Studies have shown that a group's reinforcement potential is increased when a member is successful and is rewarded in the group's presence (Lott and Lott, 1960; Bandura, 1969). Therefore, assigned tasks should have a high probability of being accomplished successfully. In addition, it is important to make certain that only appropriate behavior is reinforced.

To enhance the group's ability to reinforce its members socially, the workers served as models during group discussions. When members made satisfactory comments, carried out their assignments, or engaged in prescribed behaviors in group meetings or elsewhere, they received verbal approval from the workers. The members gradually learned to give one another verbal approval when the workers provided cues and reinforced this behavior. For example, if someone reported he was successful in carrying out a prescribed intervention, the workers often asked the group to make approving comments. Later the members reinforced one another without prompting.

Once the group members learned to reinforce each other, their encouragement and approval could be used to increase task-related behavior, such as problem-solving, carrying out prescribed assignments correctly, and reporting on the results of these assignments.

The important concepts of negative and positive reinforcement were also taught to the group. Negative reinforcement was the self-defeating behavior that members used most frequently in their relationships with others. For example, Mrs. B complained that her husband left the house immediately after dinner each night and stayed with his friends until past her bedtime. Assessment revealed that Mrs. B constantly criticized and nagged Mr. B when he was at home. Thus he got away from her nagging by leaving the house.

Group members rarely used positive reinforcement to increase the frequency of desired behavior. For example, Mr. C, who led an isolated life devoid of any interests or friends, complained that none of his co-workers liked him. Assessment revealed that because he always rejected his co-workers' social invitations and responded sarcastically to their friendly overtures, they left him alone. The group encouraged Mr. C to use positive reinforcement with the men at work, i.e., to respond with interest and approval when they approached him. Mr. C. soon had longer, more pleasant conversations with his co-workers and developed new friendships.

The workers also explained to the group that to change undesirable behavior in others, one often had to change his own behavior. A striking example of such change involved Mr. C's wife. Mr. C complained that his wife often rejected his sexual advances. However, when he used positive reinforcement and reduced his overly aggressive demands, Mrs. C became sexually responsive to him.

Treatment Evaluation

The advantage of a time-limited group is that the client can reasonably expect to solve his problem within the specified time if he follows the prescribed treatment procedures. Under these circumstances, he is willing to commit himself to the work and regular attendance required. Thus the workers found that most clients adequately resolved their problems in eight group meetings. However, additional assistance was provided, if necessary, during two scheduled follow-up sessions.

The basis for evaluation of treatment was the extent to which the client's agreed-on treatment goals were accomplished. These goals were tentatively formulated with the client during intake interviews. After his behavioral assessment was completed in the group, the goals were more clearly specified in terms of this assessment, i.e., the desired frequency of his appropriate response was determined within the context of identified antecedents and consequences. For example, Mrs. D's goal was to reduce the frequency with which her son hit his sister until the hitting rarely occurred. However, in stating a goal to eliminate a negative behavior, it is also important to include a second goal, which indicates a positive behavior that will replace it. Mrs. D's second goal was to increase the amount of time her son played with his sister.

After the groups were terminated, one-month and six-month interviews were held with each client.[1] One purpose of these interviews was to evaluate the extent to which the desirable behaviors achieved during group treatment had been maintained. A second purpose was to provide additional interventions, if needed, for the problem considered during group treatment.

Before each interview, the client again filled out a problem checklist. With this instrument, it was possible for the worker to determine the degree to which the client could identify the problem he had worked on in the group. In addition, it was possible for the client to evaluate the extent to which his treatment goals had been achieved.

The six-month follow-up interviews revealed that clients had either maintained the improvements made during treatment or had improved their situations substantially. Mr. C, for example, reported that his sexual relationship with his wife was highly satisfying. Also, he had developed friendships with several of his co-workers, had started a hobby of collecting tropical fish, and was studying for a job promotion. Mrs. B reported that her husband was spending a considerable amount of time at home. He engaged in social activities with her for the first time in years, shared the household duties, and helped her discipline the children.

Mrs. D needed additional help, however. Her son had stopped fighting with his sister Darlene. But after that problem was eliminated, Mrs. D realized that Darlene was overly dependent on her and made inappropriate demands on her time and attention. The workers helped Mrs. D understand how the problem-solving techniques she had learned in the group could be used to eliminate her daughter's demanding behavior.

During the follow-up interview, the workers also tried to determine whether the client needed additional treatment for problems that had not been dealt with during group meetings or difficulties that developed after treatment had been terminated. There were no instances in which further treatment was indicated. However, the authors' treatment approach does not preclude the possibility that a client would need treatment for other problems following termination.

Summary

Behavior modification principles and procedures were integrated with a small-group approach to short-term treatment of adult problems, which included child management, anxiety, marital discord, depression, and interpersonal difficulties with friends, family, and co-workers. During individual intake interviews, the workers assessed each client's problems. In treatment, the members learned to apply the principles of behavioral assessment and problem-solving to their own and other members' problems. Intervention strategies, behavioral reenactment and rehearsal, and behavioral assignments were used to teach these principles. After eight weeks, most of the problems the group members had presented in the group were solved or significantly ameliorated. Through systematic data collection and group discussions, the clients and workers were able to evaluate the extent to which treatment goals had been achieved. Follow-up interviews were held with each client one month and six months after treatment was terminated. In a few cases, the workers suggested additional interventions to help a client make further improvements. In other situations, the client was shown how to subject a new problem to the same behavioral analysis that he had learned in the group.

The results obtained with the group work model described in this article have been encouraging. Six months after treatment, fifteen of the seventeen group members reported that the problems for which they had sought help were solved or ameliorated significantly through the group experience. This outcome indicates that further refinement and testing of the model under controlled experimental conditions would be useful.

The groups were highly structured and task oriented, and the clients had a limited range of interpersonal problems. However, this did not preclude the importance of attending to the socioemotional needs of the members. The workers used their skills to establish a trusting and accepting group environment and they were responsive to spontaneous events, such as a crisis in a member's life.

The authors' intent was to illustrate how behavior modification can be used with groups and to explain the rationale for the procedures they developed. It was not to provide a rigid prescription for others to follow. These procedures would have to be altered when used with different client populations and types of problems.

Note

1. Members were seen separately so that follow-up evaluation would closely approximate the pregroup situation. In practice, however, group follow-up meetings have also been used effectively.

References

Bandura, Albert. *Principles of behavior modification.* New York: Holt, Rinehart and Winston, 1969.

Hastorf, Albert H. The "reinforcement" of individual actions in a group situation. In Leonard Krasner and Leonard P. Ullmann (Eds.), *Research in behavior modification.* New York: Holt, Rinehart and Winston, 1965.

Lawrence, Harry. The effectiveness of a group-directed vs. a worker-directed style of leadership in social group work. Ph.D. dissertation, University of California, 1967.

Liberman, Robert. A behavioral approach to group dynamics. *Behavior Therapy,* 1970, *1,* 141–175.

Lott, Bernice B., and Lott, Albert V. The formation of positive attitudes toward group members. *Journal of Abnormal and Social Psychology,* 1960, *61,* 297–300.

Rose, Sheldon D. A behavioral approach to the group treatment of parents. *Social Work,* 1969, *14,* 21–29.

Rose, Sheldon D., *et al.* The Hartwig Project: A behavioral approach to the treatment of juvenile offenders. In Roger Ulrich, Thomas Stachnik, and John Mabry (Eds.), *Control of human behavior,* Vol. 2. Glenview, Ill.: Scott, Foresman, 1970.

Thomas, Edwin J. Selected sociobehavioral techniques and principles: An approach to interpersonal helping. *Social Work,* 1968, *13,* 12–26.

Ullmann, Leonard P., and Krasner, Leonard. *Case studied in behavior modification.* New York: Holt, Rinehart and Winston, 1965.

Vinter, Robert D. (Ed.) *Readings in group work practice.* Ann Arbor, Mich.: Campus Publishers, 1967. (a)

Vinter, Robert D. Essential components of group work practice. In R. D. Vinter (Ed.), *Readings in group work practice.* Ann Arbor, Mich.: Campus Publishers, 1967. (b)

Wolpe, Joseph. *The practice of behavior therapy.* New York: Pergamon, 1969.

III

Interviewing Guidelines and Styles

The interview is important for the behavior modifier because it is often an essential source of information, and a very convenient medium to employ to effect behavior change within and outside of the interview situation. As employed by the behavior modifier, the interview is made use of in several characteristic ways. First, the nature of the information sought is of course that most germane to the behavioral approach. Such information embraces such areas as identifiable responses (e.g., response topography and frequency), and identifiable stimuli that immediately precede or follow the emission of the responses in question and which might be possible controlling conditions for the emission of the responses in question. These controlling conditions include possible reinforcers, punishers, and discriminative and eliciting stimuli. The interviewee is viewed in this context as a source of information and as a reporter on his own behavior, the relevant behavior of others, and on other aspects of his environment.

A second characteristic of the behavioral interview is an endeavor of the interviewer to obtain information so that unwanted bias may be reduced to a minimum. For example, it now appears that for purposes of obtaining information, selected techniques of research interviewing, such as the creation of a relatively objective and nondemanding situation, asking neutral questions and employing a nonpartisan and objective but friendly demeanor toward the client, would all tend to reduce possible unwanted bias. Less attention has been given to the techniques of behavioral interviewing than to the question of what the behavioral interview should be concerned with and its general purposes.

Third, the behavioral interview is a medium of influence to be employed in behalf of given behavioral objectives. Thus the interviewer may endeavor to educate clients, to guide and control the production of verbal behavior in the interview, to set the emotional events of the client favorably in view of the interviewer's objective, and, if appropriate, to persuade the client to follow a certain course of action.

A fourth feature of the behavioral approach to the interview is a healthy appreciation of its fallibility and limitations as a source of information. Although certain types of information can only be obtained by in interview (and interview data often augment other types of data) there are often other sources of information that may be used to corroborate the interview; indeed, in many cases, the behavior modifier can and should obtain more direct measures of the behavior in question by using observational techniques or electromechanical devices.

Two of the articles in this section involve interviewing guidelines. The selection by Holland entitled "An Interview Guide for Behavioral Counseling With Parents" places emphasis on traning parents in the princples of behavior modification, relying heavily upon teaching aspects of the operant approach. The 21 topics recommended for the interview format embrace information that should be gathered in order to complete an assessment, plan for modification, and implement a behavior modification program. This interview format covers many areas also specified in the procedural guidelines presented in previous sections, except here the emphasis is upon the use of the interview to obtain the information and to conduct the training.

The paper by Wahler and Cormier entitled "The Ecological Interview: A First Step in Out-Patient Child Behavior Therapy," is an interview guide to be used for purposes of systematically collecting data from clients, parents, teachers and other mediators. The ecological interview explicitly recognizes the high degree to which behavior is situationally specific to given environmental settings and prevailing conditions. Information is accordingly sought concerning the problem behaviors emitted in a variety of home and school situations. Several pre-interview checklists are presented that parents and teachers may complete and which yield information concerning the particular problem behaviors, the situations in which they occur, and the consequences. Results from these pre-interview checklists are then used to guide the interviewer with the child, his parents, and teachers. The interviewer then summarizes the relevant information concerning the particular problem behavior, social consequences, and desirable competing behavior for the setting of the home and school—all this yielding a much more comprehensive picture than that afforded by most other approaches to the interview. The information is then used to collect further data by observation and to plan the modification.

The selection entitled "Transcript of an Initial Interview in a Case of Depression," by Joseph Wolpe, illustrates one style of behavioral history taking that places emphasis upon defining the areas of disturbance and determining their stimulus antecedents. The transcript contains examples of behavioral specification, the isolation of possible controlling conditions, the content of behavior education for this patient, and, in the case of Wolpe's approach, an endeavor to persuade the client to abandon the feelings of guilt and the patient's belief about certain negative aspects of her condition. The therapist's objectives are explicated in many footnotes. As the author indicates, this is not a typical first interview because it was a transcript based upon a consultation demonstration. Ordinarily, in the early stages of assessment, there would be considerably less therapist interpretation and therapeutic recommendations would be withheld until the completion of the assessment.

The final selection, by Thomas entitled "Bias and Therapist Influence in Behavioral Assessment," is addressed expressly to the nature of unwanted bias and therapist influence in behavioral assessment, with particular emphasis upon behavioral interviewing. This article was prompted by a concern of the author that many practitioners, ostensibly working within the greater procedural rigor of behavior modification, carry out interviews containing needless bias and influence. Examples of unwanted bias and influence are presented along with suggestions for reducing unwanted influence. Aspects of behaviorally neutral interviewing are covered along with the desirability of withholding recommendations and advice about modification until assessment has been completed.

8

CORNELIUS J. HOLLAND

An Interview Guide for Behavioral Counseling with Parents

This paper outlines a procedure found helpful by the author as an interview guide when counseling parents for behavior problems of their children. A modified form of the present procedure based on "The Analysis of Human Operant Behaviour" by Reese (1966) and *Child Development I* by Bijou and Baer (1961) was found to be readily understood by parents with secondary school education who attended a clinical group led by the author to teach parents to apply behavioral principles, generally operant in nature, to a wide range of problems the parents were experiencing with their children.

The guide serves not only as a method for the interviewer to assemble the necessary data but simultaneously as a training aid for parents, especially when used in conjunction with such a book as *Living With Children* by Patterson and Gullion (1968). When the interview guide has been completed, most of the information necessary for behavioral analysis will have been gathered as well as a selection of the procedures required by the parents to bring about change.

The points for analysis should be carried out as exhaustively as possible before the actual reinforcement program is introduced by the parents. It is better to have too much information than too little, and only with patient and repeated observation of the behavior and the environmental conditions within which the behavior occurs will the necessary clarity of the determinants emerge. For example, behavior such as tantrums may be a function of either positive reinforcement or avoidance. Although the topography of the behavior is similar, it is important to locate and specify the major controlling stimuli, i.e., whether they occur antecedent or consequent to the behavior in question, and whether they have positive reinforcing or aversive properties.

Reprinted with permission of Academic Press, Inc. from *Behavior Therapy*, 1970, Vol. 1, No. 1, pages 70–79.

Not every point covered will be equally appropriate for every behavior problem. With some cases such as tantrums, simple extinction procedures may be sufficient; with others, such as attempting to shift behavior from competition to cooperation, extinction, punishment, and positive reinforcement may be indicated and subsequently used in the total program. Nevertheless, it is well to cover every point. Often a complete coverage introduces the possibility of using simultaneously two or three techniques for behavior modification, and as such, enhances the possibility of success.

Readers will recognize the outline to be focused on the single child. However, other children in the environment present no need for additional principles. If parents experience some difficulty in modifying a child's behavior because of the intrusions or interferences of a second child, they merely must see these intrusions as behaviors on the part of the second child and apply the same principles to them accordingly. An example of this would occur when one sibling teases another and the teasing behavior is maintained by the reactions of the second child. In addition to reinforcing either positively or negatively nonteasing behavior of the first child, the parents may reinforce positively the second child whenever he does not react to the teasing in his usual manner, thus indirectly instituting an extinction procedure for the unwanted behavior.

A final point should be kept in mind. Although the author believes the outline follows the principles of reinforcement theory closely, the points covered are in a sequence which the author finds helpful to himself. Counselors who wish to use the outline may find other sequences more appropriate. It is also to be understood that the guide does not suggest the use of a mechanical gathering of information devoid of the rhythm and pace found in the counseling experience. The points covered in the guide are logical in nature and are not intended to place artificial constraints on the counselor or the parents. Neither are they intended as substitutes for the more traditional skills of a sensitive ear or a judicious tongue.

1. *Have the parents establish general goals and complaints.* This step usually presents no problem for the parents or the psychologist since most of what the parents say concerning their child implicitly contains the present complaints (symptomatology) and goals (what the parents want the child to do or become). Usually much of this is revealed in the first interview. Subsequent interviews may serve to clarify, but it is the author's experience that general complaints and goals are readily isolated even though not explicitly stated by the parents.

The above does not imply that the interviewer is merely a passive recipient of information. It is surprising how often parents voice complaints about their children without being able to state clearly what they want the child to do, even in the general way discussed here. It is the job of the interviewer to make this vagueness on the part of the parents known to them so that they may become more definite about it themselves. Some problems with children probably find their inception just in this area, where demands are made by parents without any clear notion of what they want the child to do. Consider the frequent exhortation from parents for their child to be "good" without clarifying the terminal behavior which defines "goodness" for the parents. An interesting result of this clarification is that behavior often changes to some extent spontaneously in the desired direction before the parents put into operation any of the specific procedures for behavior change.

2. *Have the parents reduce the general goals and complaints to a list of discrete behaviors which require an increase or decrease in frequency.* A procedure commonly used and found by the author to be helpful is to have the parents make a list of five or ten behaviors they wish to increase and five or ten they wish to decrease, and then have the parents rank order them in terms of severity or nuisance value. It has been the experience of the author that a generalized change in the child's behavior usually takes place after three or four behaviors have been systematically altered so that going through the entire list is unnecessary.

3. *Have the parents select from the ranked list a single problem behavior on which to concentrate their efforts.* The behavior that is selected is often the one causing the most difficulty or the one most dangerous to the child's welfare. This suggestion of focusing on a single problem while ignoring the others is one of the most important ways of bringing about some kind of manageable order into the entire attempt at behavior modification. Often parents who make contact with child guidance centers feel overwhelmed and confused by the difficulties their children are having or causing. By suggesting a focus on one problem behavior, the parents can be relieved of dealing with the many other problems for the present. Also by reducing the immediate requirements of the parents to more manageable proportions, it is more likely that any efforts at behavior change will meet with success. This in turn helps develop confidence in the methods used, and more importantly gives the parents some sense of control over what they formerly considered an almost hopeless situation.

4. *Have the parents specify in behavioral terms the precise behavior that is presently occurring and which they desire to change.* This will require on the part of the parents a detailed observation of the behavior in concrete terms. By doing so the parents get closer to the actual behavior they want changed so that it becomes salient for them. Also, when they focus on the actual behavior, and not on inferences from the behavior, they are able to get a better idea of the frequency with which the behavior occurs. It is the change in frequency, consistent with operant psychology, which is the criterion of success or failure of the program.

5. *Have the parents specify in behavioral terms the precise behavior which they desire.* This rule is very similar to the requirements of Number 4, but here the parents must articulate in behavioral terms the terminal behavior, or goal, for any problem which they wish to modify. The task for

the interviewer is to help make the goals as clear and precise as possible. Not only is this rule important in terms of measuring the success of the program, but it often reveals the first step toward the goal.

6. *Have the parents discuss how they may proceed to the terminal behavior in a step-by-step manner.* It is important for the parents to realize that it is often self-defeating to insist upon the terminal behavior immediately. For various reasons the child may not be capable of it either because the final behavior necessarily requires the foundation of prior learning, or the final behavior desired is of an aversive nature to the child.

Also important is the implication that in proceeding in such a step-by-step fashion the parents are required to make clear to themselves what is the first step toward the final goal. Often the first step or steps are already present in the child's repertoire but are ignored by the parents and thus remain at an operant level.

It is well, therefore, as an exercise for the parents to have them rehearse the steps required by the child in moving from his present behavior to the terminal behavior. By doing so, the parents are less likely to insist upon too much too soon, and will also better appreciate approximations already being made by the child toward the terminal behavior.

7. *Have the parents list positive and negative reinforcers which they think will be effective in bringing about behavior changes.* Although the assumption being made throughout this interview guide is that behavior is maintained by environmental consequences of the behavior, it is not always easy for parents to isolate the reinforcers effective in controlling their children's behavior. Some of course are quite common, such as candy, but others and probably the more important ones are or may be quite specific to the child, such as being given the opportunity to make an independent choice. But it must be emphasized that discovering a reinforcer as being either positive or negative is an empirical matter for the most part which usually must be tested in a trial and error fashion. One complaint by parents heard by counselors in a guidance clinic is that what they consider rewarding for their children often has the opposite effect. As an extreme example, certain forms of praise or attention if applied following behavior may act as an aversive stimulus and thus be functionally punishing if the reinforcement history of the child were appropriate. More commonly, what are considered rewards by the parents are neutral for the children. There are, however, good guesses that can be made based on the fact that the child shares a common culture in which certain stimuli take on positive values for most of the children in it.

The task of the interviewer is to determine as completely as possible the total resources which are accessible to the parents or anyone else dispensing the reinforcers. It is helpful to explore systematically the social resources available to the parents, such as praise, attention, affection, or recognition; the physical resources available in the home such as radio, TV, games; and the activity resources available to the child, such as riding a bicycle or making a phone call. A list of these made by the parents is helpful in fitting the reinforcer to the desired behavior in as natural a manner as possible as well as helping the parents realize the many reinforcers available to them which may be used when any unexpected situation occurs which makes immediate reinforcement desirable.

8. *Have the parents discuss what deprivations are possible.* The value of a reinforcer fluctuates with the child's being either deprived or satiated with it. Withholding toys, for example, will enhance the value of a toy when it is given following a behavior which is desired. If toys are given haphazardly, they should not be expected to be effective in behavioral control. The same can be said for affection or praise or any other stimulus serving as a reinforcer.

Many parents are reluctant to deprive their children of praise or affection for obvious reasons even though an indiscriminate use of these reinforcers may actually be doing harm to the child. It has been the experience of the author, however, that children whose behavior is being modified by these procedures do not suffer a loss of positive reinforcers in the long run; in fact, there is usually a gain when the problem behavior begins to diminish and the parents are more comfortable with the child. It has also been the experience of the author that deprivation of such activities as watching TV or using the phone are often the only deprivation necessary to bring about the desired change. More importantly, the child is usually in some deprived state already. Some pieces of sports equipment that the child greatly desired but cannot have at present is a deprived state for these purposes; also such things as a pet, a watch, a toy which the child values but does not have can be considered instances of deprived states. Therefore it is helpful to discuss with the parents the usually many things the child greatly desires but does not have, or is not obtaining as often as he desires.

9. *Have the parents clearly establish what they want to do, either to increase or decrease a behavior or to do both.* This information has already been determined from the ranked list of behaviors which the parents wish to change. It is introduced again because in many instances parents do not merely wish to decrease a behavior but also to increase an incompatible behavior. It is helpful if they have clear what is required for the total modification desired. Much of the success of this method depends on the readiness on the part of the parents to act immediately, either by reinforcing or withholding a reinforcer, and a clear notion of what they desire helps them to do so.

10. *Have the parents discuss the situation in which the desired behavior should occur.* The requirements for this step are to determine the discriminative stimuli for the desired behavior. If, for example, the parents desire to change their child's behavior from a withdrawn, isolated social style to one of more social participation with peers, the presence of the child's peers

would be the discriminative stimuli at which time any increase in social participation would be reinforced. If the parents desire an increase in obedience on the part of their child, the situation or discriminative stimulus would be the verbal statement of the request or demand made by the parents. The behavior that is desired need not occur all the time but only under certain specifiable stimulus conditions, and isolating these stimulus conditions allows the parents to become aware of the precise circumstances in which reinforcement is to take place.

11. *Have the parents discuss the situation in which the undesired behavior should not occur.* The behavior that is unwanted and should be decreased occurs under specifiable stimulus conditions. These also have to be made known for they constitute discriminative conditions for some positive reinforcer which they must become aware of and withhold if possible. A not uncommon occurrence is found when children throw tantrums in stores but do not do so at home. The child has learned that tantrum behavior does not yield to positive reinforcers except under the discriminative conditions in which the mother will give in to the child in order to terminate the aversive tantrum which for the mother occasions social embarrassment.

12. *Have the parents determine a situation which increases the likelihood that some form or portion of the desired behavior occurs.* If, for example, the parents desire to increase their child's obedience, it is likely that sometimes the child is obedient. It is also likely that the obedience often goes unrewarded. It is precisely at these times that the program should focus its initial efforts, for strengthening the behavior under a structured situation will usually increase the likelihood of its occurrence under those conditions in which it is not now occurring.

Another example would be the attempt to increase cooperative behaviors between sibs who show too much hostile competition. It is unlikely that competition occurs every time the children are together. Those times in which the children are together and are either cooperative or at least noncompetitive can be used by the parents as a situation in which they introduce some structure for the desired behavior. If the parents know, for example, that a certain toy or activity usually results in some cooperative behavior on the part of the sibs at least for a while, this could be used by the parents as the structured situation to begin the reinforcing of the desired behavior. If it were decided that the first step toward the final terminal behavior of prolonged cooperation was to have one minute of cooperative or noncompetitive play, the parents would reinforce after that period.

13. *Have the parents discuss how they may increase desired behavior by immediately giving a positive reinforcer following the behavior.* This of course is a basic principle of reinforcement theory. The crucial requirement is the immediate application of the reinforcer. The efficiency of this program depends on the availability to the parents of effective primary or secondary reinforcers which can be given immediately. Parents with whom the author

has worked are usually quite able to develop star systems or other token economies, a certain number of which could be exchanged for backup reinforcers.

A most effective reinforcer of course is the verbal stimuli of the parents which constitutes praise or recognition. It has sometimes been found, however, that the parents' verbal behavior must first be paired with backup reinforcers for it to become effective as a viable acquired reinforcer in a program such as this.

It has also been found necessary at times to work out a system whereby any token reinforcer is at first able to translate almost immediately into a backup reinforcer which the child can enjoy. It is often too much to expect a child to accumulate 15 or 20 tokens in order to obtain a backup reinforcer when one of the problems the child is having is an intolerance for delay of gratification.

In any event, the parents should be instructed to give some form of praise whenever they give another reinforcer. Social reinforcers are ultimately more relevant because they are less arbitrary and less artificial reinforcers in the child's broader social world.

14. *Have the parents discuss how they may increase desired behavior by immediately terminating a negative reinforcer following the behavior.* Both positive and negative reinforcement strengthen preceding behavior, and both can be employed effectively in the program, although usually the positive reinforcement method is the chief instrument for change. However, if parents insist on certain activities on the part of their children, such as doing the dishes, and the child finds this to be aversive, a relief from this chore can be an important source of negative reinforcement and could be effectively used.

15. *Have the parents discuss how they may decrease undesired behavior by withholding the reinforcers which follow it.* The requirements here on the part of the parents are to discover what stimuli are at present maintaining the undesired behavior, and to institute an extinction procedure. This often runs into several difficulties. The parents themselves may be providing the maintaining reinforcer. For example, a child of nine who was a chronic complainer apparently was being reinforced by his mother's concern and her getting upset. Since she had developed a habit of responding to him in this way, it was especially difficult to have her withhold this reinforcer. Again, children are often systematically taught by their parents that positive reinforcers will occur only under forms of tantrum behavior which are so shrill and upsetting to the parents that they cannot tolerate it for any length of time. It is important for the interviewer to show the parents that "giving in" after prolonged or especially shrill tantrums is a learning experience for the child leading to a prolonging or intensification of the undesired behavior.

Another difficulty is that extinction procedures often increase the undesired behavior initially. In the example cited above with the nine-year-old boy, when the mother began to ignore him, his first reaction was to increase the complaining both in frequency and intensity.

A third difficulty is that extinction is a vastly different procedure from intermittent reinforcement. Unless the parents are made to see the differential effects of each, withholding of the maintaining reinforcer may not be complete and may lead to a resistance to extinction. It is for the above reasons that the author has found extinction to be most effective when there exists the possibility of combining it with positive or negative reinforcement of incompatible behavior.

The fourth difficulty, and perhaps the most serious, is the fact that often the parents do not have control over the maintaining reinforcer. Another way of saying that parents have lost control over their child's behavior is to say that the undesired behavior is being effectively controlled by other people, agencies, or circumstances. Although this situation introduces real difficulties, some of which may never be overcome, a solution can often be achieved by the reinforcement of incompatible behavior if the reinforcer used for the incompatible behavior is of greater value to the child than the reinforcer presently controlling the undesired behavior.

16. *Have the parents discuss how they may decrease undesired behavior by removing a positive reinforcer.* This is a punishment-by-loss technique which may prove effective in suppressing behavior long enough for the desired behavior to occur. Although many children who come to guidance clinics have been punished often enough already, the author believes such a procedure may at times be the only technique effective in suppressing a behavior whose necessity to change is obvious. Behaviors such as running out into the street between parked cars, fire setting, and physically abusive behavior toward another child readily come to mind as behaviors in which the parents cannot wait for the reinforcement of incompatible behavior to occur, or for extinction to take place.

The threat of punishment-by-loss can also be used, the threat being seen as a conditioned aversive stimulus.It must be discovered, however, whether or not threats from the parents have actually acquired aversive properties, as often threats have not been followed up by the parents in the past and are therefore looked on by the child not as a discriminative stimulus for punishment but as neutral stimuli.

17. *Have the parents discuss how they may decrease undesired behavior by time-out.* Time-out is any procedure in which the child is removed from the source of positive reinforcers. Putting the child in his room for a certain period of time or in the familiar corner is a common time-out procedure. It must be carried out in such a way, however, that the child does experience a loss of reinforcers; putting a child in his room where many of his toys are available to him could not be considered a time-out procedure.

Often when a child has been given a time-out period, at least if this has not been a common punishing procedure in the family, the child will react very strongly in a negative manner. It is well to establish at the beginning the time-out procedure as a punishment by making the relief from the room or corner contingent upon a set period of time in which none of the negative behavior has occurred. If it does occur, relief from the time-out period should be made contingent upon the absence, for a specified period of time, of the undesired negative behavior.

18. *Discuss with the parents how they may pattern the reinforcers they give to the child.* The parents should give reinforcers every time the desired behavior occurs until it becomes strongly established, then they should give them randomly. This is the familiar shift from a continuous reinforcement schedule to a variable interval or variable ratio. There are no ready rules with which the author is familiar to move from a continuous to an intermittent schedule. It seems desirable, however, to tell the child that he shouldn't expect a reward every time the desired behavior occurs, even when the child is still being reinforced continuously. It also seems desirable to move from a continuous through a fixed schedule before establishing a random one.

19. *Have the parents discuss how they may vary the reinforcers they give to the child.* The parents will have available to them a list of reinforcers which they are reasonably sure are positive for the child. The parents have options of giving different amounts of the same reinforcers or different reinforcers. Varying the reinforcers enhances the probability that desired behavior, when it occurs, will be maintained for long periods of time.

20. *Have the parents discuss how they may apply two or more procedures simultaneously.* Success is enhanced by the parents having at their disposal as many procedures as can be applied to the behavior in question. The most obvious situation is an extinction procedure coupled with positive reinforcement of incompatible behavior, but other combinations are also possible and should be explored depending on the nature of the behavior the parents wish to change.

21. *Have the parents rehearse verbally the entire program.* This will require that they are able to specify clearly each step covered by the program. Such rehearsal enhances the success of the program by making salient to them such crucial issues as the terminal behavior stated in behavioral terms, any incipient behavior present, the initial steps toward the goal, the discriminative stimuli involved, and the reinforcers which must be withheld or supplied.

References

BIJOU, S. and BAER, D. *Child development I: A systematic and empirical theory.* New York: Appleton-Century-Crofts, 1961.

PATTERSON, G. R. and GULLION, M. E. *Living with children: New methods for parents and teachers.* Champaign, Illinois: Research Press, 1968.

REESE, E. The analysis of human operant behaviour. In J. Vernon (Ed.), *Introduction to psychology: A self-selection text.* Dubuque, Iowa: William C. Brown, 1966.

9

ROBERT G. WAHLER AND
WILLIAM H. CORMIER

The Ecological Interview: A First Step in Out-Patient Child Behavior Therapy

Deviant children display their problem behaviors in a variety of environmental settings. A child referred for treatment because of unusual behavior may produce this kind of behavior in his home, his school classroom, his playground, and perhaps on the streets of his city. In addition, deviant child behavior may occur in several subsettings within a particular setting. For example, the negativistic child may be negativistic at bedtime and at mealtime, but he may be quite cooperative at other times (of his day) at home. Also, the same child at school may be considered difficult to manage during the arithmetic lesson but no problem during the social studies lesson.

The above information is important to the clinician whose actions are guided by reinforcement theory (Bijou and Baer, 1961). According to this viewpoint, child behavior is to an important extent a function of its immediate environmental contingencies. Thus a child's problem behavior in his school classroom might be a reinforcement function of teacher and peer social attention; his problem behavior at home might be a similar function of parent and sibling social attention. The essence of the theory is that behavior is situation specific; it is controlled by stimuli dispensed by agents of the environmental setting in which the child behaves. This being the argument, one could contend that the child's actions in one particular setting are independent of his actions in another setting (Wahler, 1969a). If this assumption is valid, the adequately prepared clinician must be a skilled ecologist, as well as a psychologist. In other words, the clinician's skill as an intervention

Reprinted with permission of Pergamon Press, from *Journal of Behavior Therapy and Experimental Psychiatry*, Vol. 1, 1970, pp. 279–289.

agent might well be dependent on his skill in mapping the child in his social environment.

If social contingencies are to be therapeutically rearranged for the deviant child, one must know who provides these contingencies, in what behavioral form they are provided, for what child behaviors they are provided, and in what specific settings or subsettings they are provided. Given this information, the clinician is in position to intervene—to train the significant "contingency dispensers" (e.g., parents and teachers) to modify their interactions with the child. The specific nature of the modifications is based not only on the above ecological information, but also on certain principles of reinforcement theory (see Bandura, 1969).

The Interview

Workers in child behavior therapy have typically emphasized direct observation as an indispensable part of the ecological assessment (see Bijou, Peterson, and Ault, 1968). Observers, ranging from indigenous community members (Wahler and Erickson, 1969) to the child himself (Lovitt and Curtiss, 1969), have been utilized to obtain such data. However, before any observational system can be implemented, the observers must be told what to observe and where to observe it. In clinical situations, this kind of information is obtained by talking to members of the deviant child's social community (e.g., parents and teachers) and perhaps to the child himself. While an interview was undoubtedly involved in every reported child behavior therapy study over the past 10 years, it has never been reported in systematic fashion.[1] In view of the procedural rigor that usually defines behavior therapy, this state of affairs is truly amazing.

The ecological interview serves two important and often interdependent functions: (1) to develop a language system that will allow the client to communicate with the interviewer, and (2) mapping the child's behavior. The first function is illustrated by Goldiamond (1969). According to Goldiamond, the client's conception of human behavior may be radically different from that of the interviewer making it difficult if not impossible for useful information to be produced. Thus, either the interviewer must be capable of translating the client's language or the client must learn the interviewer's language. While clinicians operating from other theoretical bases vary in their choice of tactics at this point, behavior therapists invariably select the latter. Since the client (e.g., parents and teachers)is required to serve as therapist and perhaps observer, it follows that he must be somewhat conversant with reinforcement theory and the analysis of behavior from this point of view. The task of teaching this new language to the client is often facilitated through pre-interview "homework" provided by some recently available texts (e.g., Patterson and Gullion, 1968).

The second function of the ecological interview involves mapping the child's behavior as it is reported to occur in various environmental settings. The mapping, of course, is intended to specify what is to be observed and where it is to be observed. The authors have found the pre-interview checklists (Tables 9.1, 9.2, and 9.3) to be useful sources of information in reaching these goals.

The following portions of this paper are designed to describe the ecological interview in detail, particularly its mapping function. One should keep in mind that the mapping can and should also be an educational experience for the client; he should learn something about the clinician's language and his method of behavioral analysis.

THE CLIENT

The client in child behavior therapy is that person who, in the clinician's judgment, is capable of changing natural social contingencies for the child's behavior. Tharp and Wetzel (1969) use the term "mediator" to describe this function. Most often the child's parents and his teachers fit this definition, although recent work has suggested that members of the child's peer group (Wahler, 1970) and the child himself (Lovitt and Curtiss, 1969), may also meet the criterion.

A second criterion for client selection derives from the presenting complaint. If the child is reported to produce problems only at home, then his parents are the clients of choice; but, if his problems extend to the school classroom, his teachers must be included as well. Since evidence for generalization across natural environmental settings is sparse, one should presently assume that the child's behavior is situation specific.

THE CHILD'S BEHAVIOR

A child's behavior, deviant or otherwise, is meaningless unless its environmental setting is considered as the context for therapeutic intervention. Clients frequently have difficulty in describing the child's observable behavior and in specifying the particular subsetting in which the behavior was produced. For example, parents and teachers are inclined to be mentalistic in their descriptions of child behavior. Like most people, their units of description are abstractions of what the child did: hitting little brother is reported as "jealousy"; out of seat behavior in the classroom is reported as "inattention." Further, the typical clinical interviewer is apt to foster this style of reporting by accepting the abstraction or by translating it into another abstraction. Examine this sample taken from a clinical psychologist's interview report: "This child experiences frequent periods of depression, often to the point that he entertains thoughts of self-destruction. He is constantly angry because of his mother's attempts to keep him dependent on her. Yet, because of his anxiety concerning the expression of affect, he cannot

TABLE 9.1 *Child home behavior checklist*

The following checklist allows you to describe your child's problems in various home situations. The situations are listed in the column at left and common problem behaviors are listed in the row at the top. Examine *each* situation in the column and decide if one or more of the problem behaviors in the row fits your child. Check those that fit the best—if any.

	Always has to be told	*Doesn't pay attention*	*Forgets*	*Dawdles*	*Refuses*	*Argues*	*Complains*	*Demands*	*Fights*	*Selfish*	*Destroys toys or property*	*Steals*	*Lies*	*Cries*	*Whines*	*Hangs on or stays close to adult*	*Acts silly*	*Mopes around*	*Stays alone*	*Has to keep things in order*	*Sexual play*
Morning:																					
Awakening																					
Dressing																					
Breakfast																					
Bathroom																					
Leave for School																					
Play in house																					
Chores																					
Television																					
Afternoon:																					
Lunch																					
Bathroom																					
Play in house																					
Chores and homework																					
Television																					
When company comes																					
Evening:																					
Father comes home																					
Dinner																					
Bathroom																					
Play in house																					
Chores and homework																					
Television																					
Undressing																					
When company comes																					
Bedtime																					

TABLE 9.2 *Child community behavior checklist*

The following checklist allows you to describe your child's problems in various situations outside the house. The situations are listed in the column at left and common problem behaviors are listed in the row at the top. Examine *each* situation in the column and decide if one or more of the problem behaviors in the row fits your child. Check those that fit the best—if any.

	Always has to be told	*Doesn't pay attention*	*Forgets*	*Dawdles*	*Refuses*	*Argues*	*Complains*	*Demands*	*Fights*	*Selfish*	*Destroys toys or property*	*Steals*	*Lies*	*Cries*	*Whines*	*Hangs on or stays close to adult*	*Acts silly*	*Mopes around*	*Stays alone*	*Has to keep things in order*	*Sexual play*
In own yard																					
In neighbor's yard or home																					
In stores																					
Public park																					
Downtown in general																					
Church or Sunday School																					
Community swimming pool																					
In family car																					

direct his hostility outward. Consequently, he internalizes his aggression; he berates his abilities in many areas; he sees himself as inadequate and his self-esteem is extremely low."

An "abstraction count" of this sample yields a total of nine broadly judgmental terms that may be of value to many clinicians—but not to the behavior therapist. No doubt each term refers to a number of specific verbal and non-verbal child behaviors, spread over several environmental settings. Unless these behaviors are specified in terms of concrete actions, operations by the behavior therapist are impossible.

One must always keep in mind that the client will be expected to serve as the child's therapist. These nonprofessionals vary tremendously in translating psychological jargon into observable behaviors. Thus, to insure that all concerned are observing and treating the same child behaviors, these behaviors must be enumerated through labels that allow little variance in translation. If abstractions such as aggression and dependency are used, they must clearly appear as summary terms, designating lists of observable verbal and nonverbal child behaviors. Thus, the interviewer's account of the child's behavior must provide a wide sampling of what the child is reported to do and say—not inferences concerning these events.

TABLE 9.3 *Child school behavior checklist*

The following checklist allows you to describe your student's problems in various situations. The situations are listed in the column at left and common problem behaviors are listed in the row at the top. Examine *each* situation in the column and decide if one or more of the problem behaviors in the row fits your student. Check those that fit the best —if any.

	Out of seat	*Talks to others*	*Always has to be told*	*Doesn't pay attention*	*Forgets*	*Dawdles*	*Refuses*	*Argues*	*Complains*	*Demands*	*Fights*	*Selfish*	*Destroys toys or property*	*Steals*	*Lies*	*Cries*	*Hangs on or stays close to adult*	*Stays alone*	*Whines*	*Acts silly*	*Mopes around*	*Has to keep things in order*	*Sexual play*
Morning: Teacher explains lesson																							
Teacher discusses with group																							
Silent work time																							
Cooperative work with other students																							
Oral reading or class presentation																							
Line up for lunch or recess																							
Hall																							
Playground																							
Lunch																							

TABLE 9.3—*Continued*

Afternoon: Teacher explains lesson	
Teacher discusses with group	
Silent work time	
Cooperative work with other students	
Oral reading or class presentation	
Line up for recess or dismissal	
Hall	
Playground	

Naturally, the interviewer will tend to focus his behavioral enumeration on the child's problem behaviors—as defined by the client or the interviewer, or both. However, there is also good reason to notice other parts of the child's behavioral repertoire. Any child, regardless of his degree of behavioral deviance, displays some behaviors that would be considered "normal," "positive," or otherwise desirable. Some of these behaviors may be incompatible with the child's problem behaviors and their more frequent occurrence could change client and clinician judgment about the child's degree of behavioral deviance. These behaviors warrant further attention by the interviewer.

For most deviant behaviors a child produces, one could easily imagine another more desirable behavior that would physically compete with it—compete in the sense that the two could not occur simultaneously. For example, an oppositional child cannot be oppositional and cooperative at the same time; a withdrawn child cannot avoid and approach others simultaneously. Since these kinds of competing behaviors are immediately defined when their deviant counterparts are defined, they need not be a subject of further inquiry. However, there are situations in which desirable competing behaviors are not so obviously present, and thus interviewer inquiry will be necessary. That is, some desirable behaviors may be functionally, but not physically, incompatible with the child's deviant behavior. Consider the "school phobic child" in a classroom setting. We have ofter received information from teachers similar to this teacher's report: "I can tell when he's going to start crying. If he starts to stare out the window I know he's thinking of home and then he's going to get frightened." This statement implies the presence of behaviors that may be functionally incompatible with crying. The logical question to this teacher would be directed at detecting those child behaviors that are rarely correlated with crying. Perhaps reading or cooperative work with other children would fit this definition. If so, these desirable behaviors should be listed as target behaviors for more systematic observation.

In summary, the interviewer's enumeration of child behaviors should include both deviant and desirable behaviors. Whatever behaviors the interviewer selects as later observational targets, they must be countable—countable by parents, teachers, and possibly the child himself.

Environmental Settings and Subsettings

It has been traditional to think of the deviant child's problem behavior as emanating from a single grossly defined environmental setting—namely, his "home life." It is commonly argued that parental interactions with the child "broadly defined" are responsible for developing and maintaining the child's deviance. Such an assumption is erroneous for two reasons. First, there is good evidence that other people (teachers and peers), while they may not be the primary developmental factors in the child's deviance, do *maintain* or support the child's problem behavior in settings outside the home (Cormier, 1969; Thomas, Becker, and Armstrong, 1968; Buehler, Patterson, and Furniss, 1966). In fact, their support in school settings may be quite independent of parental support in home settings (Wahler, 1969a). Secondly, "home life" is too broad an environmental setting to be of much use in behavior therapy. True, inappropriate parental reactions to the child's behavior are usually a source of support for the child's deviance at home. But, few parents provide such reactions on a continual basis. It is common for parents to report that their deviant child is "fine" at certain times of the day and "terrible" at other times. The clinician needs to know those subsettings that set the occasion for deviant behavior, if for no other reason than practical use of observer time.

As stated earlier, detection of environmental settings is usefully accomplished at the same time as one constructs a list of the child's behaviors. To these goals, the enclosed pre-interview checklists for parents and teachers (Tables 9.1, 9.2, and 9.3) are very helpful. Essentially, the interviewer needs to specify environmental settings and subsettings for each of the child's deviant and desirable behaviors. To ignore the stimulus settings for these behaviors is to place unfounded trust in the phenomenon of generalization. Until evidence is accumulated to show that changes in child behavior transfer across settings, one should assume that each setting must be dealt with separately.

The multiple settings of deviant child behavior are of some advantage in the training of clients as observers and therapists. Although training of parents and teachers must be directed to specific subsettings, it might be unwise to instruct a mother to count child behaviors when she is in the process of fixing dinner, even though her child's deviant behaviors occur mainly at that time; it might also be a poor move to instruct a teacher to count deviant child behaviors during the arithmetic lesson. Client training ought to be geared to the success of the client's learning efforts. Therefore, why not start training in those settings that will insure such success?

Part of the interviewer's inquiry concerning environmental subsettings should be aimed at evaluating the client's opportunity to learn observational skills. In other words, to what degree does a client have free time to observe the child and his interactions with the client? Such an evaluation should permit the interviewer to select a subsetting in which to begin the training; that is, parental observations might begin during the child's bedtime and the teacher might develop her counting skills during the silent reading period. As the clients become skillful in these settings, they should be capable of similar operations in other subsettings where less client time is available for these purposes.

Social Consequences of the Child's Behavior

Ideal interview information would include a picture of how parents, teachers and peers support the child's deviant behavior and how they fail to develop his desirable, competing behaviors. Theoretically, one would expect the clients to be more attentive to the child's problem behavior than they are to his desirable behavior; or if not, the attention following desirable behavior should be aversive to the child. Limited research support for this assumption exists (Buehler, Patterson, and Furniss, 1966; Patterson, Ray, and Shaw, 1969).

However, the interviewer should not be optimistic in expecting this kind of information from a client. Partly, this may be due to the fact that the client is usually the primary attention dispenser in question, and self-observation is not an easy skill to acquire. In addition, other dispensers in the setting (e.g., peers and siblings) may complicate the support issue. Thus in all likelihood, direct observation may be required to understand how the child's deviant behavior obtains social reinforcement.

Despite these problems, useful information concerning social consequences can be obtained from the client. While this information might not jibe with later observational data, it can be of use in the later planning of therapeutic contingencies for the child.

Following the principles of reinforcement theory, the clinician has two options in programming therapeutic consequences for the child's deviant behavior. He may choose to instruct all social agents to ignore the behavior (extinction) or he may decide to utilize an aversive contingency (usually time-out from social attention; see Wahler, 1969b). A rule of thumb in picking tactics has to do with the social environment's ability to tolerate the child's deviant behavior. For ethical reasons, ignoring should probably always be the tactic of choice. However, this assumes that the child's deviant behavior does not produce harmful consequences to the environment, and it also assumes that the client is capable of ignoring the child. For example, suppose that a mother reports that her child's demanding behavior angers her to the point that she throws things at him. Although later observations by her or by others may reveal that she does other things as well, this information should be considered in selecting therapeutic tactics. To tell his mother to ignore her child's demanding behavior would probably be disastrous—she probably could not do it. Thus, either time-out or utilizing other social agents within the home setting would be required.

Examples like the above can easily be generated. The point is that the interviewer's assessment of a client's reaction (consequences) to the child's deviant behavior should allow him to make a judgment concerning the probable success or failure of various tactics in the later training of therapists for the child.

A Case Illustration

The following case study is presented to illustrate the previously discussed procedures of the ecological interview. This case is ideal in the sense that it clearly presents the ecological complexities of an apparently simple problem.

Willie V (age 10) was referred for psychological treatment because of his refusal to attend school. According to the school principal's referral statements, Willie often cried in class and his parents had to "drag" him to school to ensure his attendance. All concerned were mystified by the sudden onset of this problem, since Willie had been a model student up to this point (grade 4). Willie's complaints to his teacher were extremely vague. He referred to excessive noise in the classroom, inability to think, and fears that unspecified other children would hurt him.

The clients for the interview were Willie, his teacher, and his parents. Prior to their interviews, the parents and the teacher completed appropriate pre-interview checklists (Tables 9.1, 9.2, and 9.3).

Willie's parents reported their concern about a variety of his behaviors, including his refusal to attend school in the morning. Table 9.4 describes the interview outcome, based on the parents' responses to the pre-interview checklist. According to the parents, Willie's problem behavior reliably occurs in ten different home settings; the problem behaviors appear to be best described as noncompliance with parental instructions, demands that mother obey him, various complaints, and "checking on mother." Notice that all of these behaviors are "countable" in the sense that Willie's parents could now be instructed to record their occurrence in any of the listed settings.

Parental social consequences for these behaviors, while they would be difficult to count, appear to provide a logical source of reinforcement for some of Willie's problem behaviors. Since one immediate goal of treatment would be to eliminate *all* parental attention following Willie's undesirable behaviors, the interviewer could simply instruct the parents to record instances of social attention provided as consequences for Willie's behaviors. (Many behavior therapists have been able to conduct effective behavior therapy programs at home and in the classroom through modifying one general, and quite countable, class of parent or teacher behavior. This class, referred to commonly as *social attention,* is a summary term for any verbal or physical action following those child behaviors one wishes to change.)

The interviewer's discussion with the parents also revealed that Willie's mother provided most social contingencies for his home behavior. Thus, she would be required to carry the major direct role of therapeutic action. Further discussion revealed that the "inside play" and "outside play" settings would be good beginning points for the mother's observational training. According to her, she would either be too busy, too angry, or too nervous to

TABLE 9.4. *Summary of home settings for Willie's behavior including social consequences**

Home setting	*Problem behavior*	*Social consequences*	*Desirable competing behavior*
Awakening (school days only)	Complains about stomach or head pains	Mother gives medication and tells him he's OK	Defined by problem behavior
Dressing	Very slow	Mother prompts and sometimes helps	Defined by problem behavior
Breakfast (school days only)	Refuses to eat	Mother prompts	Defined by problem behavior
Leave for school	Refuses to go	Mother and father argue with him and sometimes spank him	Defined by problem behavior
Chores	Refuses to work or does jobs "halfway"	Mother argues or reasons with him	Defined by problem behavior
Outside play	Frequently returns to house to "asks if mother is there"	None obvious	Defined by problem behavior
Inside play	Asks or demands mother's help	Mother helps	Cooperative play with siblings
When mother attends to siblings	Asks or demands mother's help	Mother argues with him or helps	Cooperative play with siblings
When mother plans shopping trip or visit to friends	Asks or demands to go with her	Mother complies	Defined by problem behavior
Bedtime	Complains of fears of dark and "crooks" breaking into house	Mother reasons with him and leaves room light on	Talk with siblings

* Data based on mother's report.

begin the systematic observation of Willie in the other settings listed in Table 9.4.

At the conclusion of this interview, Willie's parents were clearly informed of the interviewer's suspicions concerning the maintenance of Willie's problem behaviors and the infrequent occurrence of his probable competing behaviors. Reinforcement theory had been discussed with them (following their reading of Patterson and Gullion, 1968) and the following observational duties had been given to Willie's mother—to be completed before the next meeting: record in longhand any requests or demands to mother during inside play and any returns to mother during outside play. Finally, record mother and father reactions to these behaviors.

During the interview, Willie's parents were told that his teacher was to be interviewed that day and a school program would soon be initiated similar to the home program. The parents were told to be certain he arrived at school the next day.

Willie was interviewed following the discussion with his parents. He was told of his parents' report concerning his behavior at school and at home, particularly his fears of school, bedtime, and what appeared to be his mother's safety. While he readily admitted his fears, he did not agree that he was demanding or oppositional at home. In addition, he pointed out that his peers seemed to dislike him and "picked on him" frequently. The latter problem and worries about his mother's health[2] were his explanations for his recent dislike of school.

Table 9.5 summarizes interview information from Willie. Willie pointed to five settings as the source of his difficulties. Worries concerning his mother and his peers plus his avoidance and complaints in peer presence appear to constitute his major problems. Except for Willie's observation that other children "picked on him" his version of social consequences for these problems was not helpful.

After obtaining the above information, Willie was given a brief explanation of reinforcement theory, with particular emphasis on the concepts of reinforcement and extinction. He was then told that a first step in changing any behavior involves learning how to record it. A further discussion of settings and Willie's behavior led to his agreeing to record his behavior and its social contingencies in four of the five settings (he explained that his recording would be too obvious to the other children during the free play period at school.) Complaining, avoidance of other children, and worries about mother, crooks and other children were to be checked in his school notebook or in a small notebook kept in his pocket or at his bedside. In addition, Willie was asked to record social attention from his peers, teacher, and parents whenever it occurred following this behavior.

Finally, Willie was told to begin his observational duties the next day and his teacher and parents would be keeping records as well.

In an interview with Willie's teacher she immediately reported her im-

TABLE 9.5 *Summary of home and school settings for Willie's behavior, including social consequences**

Home and school settings	*Problem behavior*	*Social consequences*	*Desirable competing behavior*
Outside play at home	Worries about mother	None obvious to him	Talk with siblings or peers
Silent work time at school	Worries about mother and likelihood that peers will "pick on him" later. Cries.	None obvious to him	Writing or drawing
Lunch at school	Avoids peers. Complains to teacher about peer behavior	Peers "pick on him"	Talk to peers
On playground at school	Avoids peers. Complains to teacher about peer behavior	Peers "pick on him"	Talk or play with peers
Bedtime	Worries about crooks breaking into house	None obvious to him	Talk to siblings

*Data based on Willie's report.

TABLE 9.6 *Summary of school settings for Willie's problem behavior, including social consequences**

School setting	*Problem behavior*	*Social consequences*	*Desirable competing behavior*
Arrival	Complains about many things	Teacher and mother argue with him	Defined by problem behavior
Morning silent work time	Cries and complains	Teacher reasons with him	Writing
Lunch	Complains about other children "picking on him"	Peers laugh at him and teacher reasons with him	Talks to peers
Playground	Complains about other children "picking on him"	Peers laugh at him and teacher reasons with him	Talks or plays with peers

*Data based on teacher's report.

pression that Willie was "very insecure" and that his problems undoubtedly were caused by his "overprotective" mother. After some persuasion, his teacher eventually directed her attention to Willie's school behavior, and particularly that noted by her on the pre-interview checklist. An explanation of reinforcement theory appeared to be somewhat helpful in redirecting the discussion.

Table 9.6 summarizes the results of the discussion with Willie's teacher. She said that she could obtain observational records during the morning silent work period and during the lunch period. She agreed to check the occurrence of complaints and crying and their possible competing behaviors as well. Although she argued that school events had little to do with Willie's problems, she agreed to record her reactions and those of the peers whenever they occurred following this behavior. Because Willie's crying in the classroom was rather disruptive for all concerned, the interviewer agreed to begin the school behavior program after the teacher had obtained two days of "countable" data.

On the basis of the above interview data, it proved possible to obtain some very useful observational data. All of the data were supplied by the clients' daily tallies. For validation purposes, another observer (college undergraduate) made one home and school observation. However, since this observer's frequency data were similar to those obtained by Willie's mother and teacher, his information contributed little to the behavior therapy program.

The training of Willie's parents, his teacher and Willie himself, is too complex to describe here. Essentially, the teacher and mother were trained to reinforce differentially, behaviors competing with Willie's problem behavior and Willie was encouraged to produce some of these competing behaviors when he observed himself "worrying." All clients continued to record the designated behaviors on a daily basis, and eventually were capable of covering the behaviors in all home and school settings. [Frequency counts of the behaviors and subjective reports from all concerned indicated marked improvement in Willie.]

Selection of Observers

Interview information alone is usually insufficient to construct a successful treatment program. Its primary purpose is to instruct observers what to observe and where to observe it. For the sceptical, the danger of operating on the basis of interview information alone are vividly illustrated by Patterson, Ray, and Shaw (1969). The reader should examine Patterson and Gullion, 1968; and Bijou, Peterson, and Ault, 1968; for information on the training of observers.

Most of the reported child behavior therapy studies have utilized observers not indigenous to the child's natural environment. This tactic was employed to insure observer objectivity as required for research purposes. However, for clinical purposes it is desirable to utilize the client, and when possible the child himself. This is not to say that outside observers should not be used for objectivity; in fact, every clinician concerned with this approach to child therapy should obtain this experience.

The advantages of using parents, teachers, peers, and the child himself as observers should be clear. They will be required to implement "contingency contracts": a shift in the reinforcement ground rules for the child's deviant and desirable behaviors. If a child is asked to change his behavior, he must first be aware of how he is currently behaving.

The pre-interview checklists (Tables 9.1, 9.2, and 9.3) may function as a setting operation to facilitate communication between the therapist, the client and the child. In addition, checklists can assist in mapping the kind of social attention (positive, negative, neutral or none at all) the child is receiving in a particular subsetting as a consequence of deviant as well as desirable behavior.

Notes

1. Such is not the case for behavior therapy based on principles of respondent learning (e.g., Wolpe, Salter, and Reyna, 1964) where investigators have been quite concerned with a systematic approach to the interview.
2. Willie's mother had no serious health problems.

References

Bandura, A (1969) *Principles of Behavior Modification.* Holt, Rinehart and Winston, New York.

Bijou, S. W., and Baer, D. M. (1961) *Child Development. Vol. I, A systematic and empirical theory.* Appleton-Century-Crofts, New York.

Bijou, S. W., Peterson, R. F., and Ault, M. H. (1968). A method to integrate descriptive and experimental field studies at the level of data and empirical concepts. *J. Appl. Behav. Anal. 1,* 175–191.

Buehler, R. E., Patterson, G. R., and Furniss, J. M. (1966) The reinforcement of behavior in institutional settings. *Behav. Res. & Therapy 4,* 157–167.

Cormier, W. H. (1969) Effects of teacher random and contingent social reinforcement on the classroom behavior of adolescents. Unpublished doctoral dissertation, The University of Tennessee.

Goldiamond, I. (1969) Justified and unjustified alarm over behavioral control. (pp. 235–240) In *Behavior Disorders: Perspectives and Trends.* (Edited by O. H. Milton and R. G. Wahler.) J. B. Lippincott, New York.

Lovitt, T. C. and Curtis, K. A. (1969) Academic response rate as a function of teacher and self-imposed contingencies. *J. Appl. Behav. Anal. 2,* 49–53.

Patterson, G. R., and Gullion, M. E. (1968) *Living with Children.* Champaign, Illinois.

Patterson, G. R., Ray, R. F. and Shaw, B. A. (1969) Direct intervention in Families of Deviant Children. *ORI Research Bulletin 8.*

Tharp, R. G. and Wetzel, R. J. (1969) *Behavior Modification in the Natural Environment.* Academic Press, New York.

THOMAS, D. R., BECKER, W. C. and ARMSTRONG, M. (1968) Production and elimination of disruptive classroom behavior by systematically varying the teacher's behavior. *J. Appl. Behav. Anal. 1*, 35–45.

WAHLER, R. G. (1969a) Setting generality: some specific and general effects of child behavior therapy. *J. Appl. Behav. Anal. 2*, 239–246.

WAHLER, R. G. (1969b) Oppositional children: A quest for parental reinforcement control. *J. Appl. Behav. Anal. 2*, 159–170.

WAHLER, R. G. and ERICKSON, M. (1969) Child behavior therapy: A community program in Appalachia. *Behav. Res. & Therapy 7*, 71–78.

WAHLER, R. G. (1970) *Peers as classroom behavior modifiers.* Paper read at the American Association on Mental Deficiency, Washington, D.C., May.

WOLPE, J., SALTER, A., and REYNA, L. J. (1964) (Eds.) *The Conditioning Therapies.* Holt, Rinehart and Winston, New York.

10

JOSEPH WOLPE

Transcript of Initial Interview in a Case of Depression

The interview recorded in the following transcript took place as a consultation-demonstration that was viewed on closed circuit television by a group of psychiatric residents. In the one hour available, it was necessary both to reach an evaluation and make therapeutic recommendations. It was therefore not a typical first interview. Nevertheless, it followed the basic lines of behavioristic anamneses, being primarily directed at determining the stimulus conditions, external and internal, that elicit neurotic responses.

Several features of the behavior therapy approach will be apparent to the reader. He will see that, contrary to a fairly prevalent conception, the strategy does not consist of attacking target symptoms in isolation, and that all measures are planned within a broad conspectus of the patient's major functions and life situation. He will also note that pains are taken to insure that the patient clearly understands the interrelations between stimulus conditions and responses, so that she can become an informed partner to the therapist in whatever therapeutic endeavors he may later undertake.

An important reason for selecting this case was the fact that its diagnosis was "depression." There are many who believe that such a diagnosis places behavior therapy out of its depth, for they suppose its applications to be confined to "simple" cases like phobias. What emerges here is that this woman's depression, like all other reactive depressions, is clearly relatable to specific stimulus situations. Hers is one of the common class of depressions that are secondary to the evocation of anxiety or other emotional disturbance. In this case, the relevant anxiety was unadaptive—being evoked in the context of exposure to social groups or the context of sexual guilt. At

Reprinted with permission of Pergamon Press, from *Journal of Behavior Therapy and Experimental Psychiatry,* Vol. 1, 1970, pp. 71–78.

other times the depression was related to a "normal" physiological response to sexual frustration.

Programs for procuring an adaptive *modus vivendi* for the patient were suggested for each of two alternative future life courses that she brought forward.

Dr: How long have you been here, Mrs. B?
Pt: About nine days.
Dr: How old are you?
Pt: 41.
Dr: Why are you here?
Pt: I wasn't feeling too well, but I do feel much better now.
Dr: Good. What was your complaint?
Pt: Depression. I was very nauseous to my stomach, headaches, and my mouth was tightly closed. I cried constantly for about ten days. I hadn't eaten for four days when I came in. But I do feel much better now.
Dr: Good. How long were you feeling this way?
Pt: It was sort of a downward thing, Doctor. I got the nausea about a a month ago and it would keep getting worse. Well, about six weeks ago it started.
Dr: What do you think started it?
Pt: I am not sure. It could be one of several things. One thing that is bothering me, although I don't know if I am not making this one big thing and just looking at this. My husband and I have been separated for two years, and I have been dating a gentleman for six months. We have not had intercourse. I have had no affair with him. But one time (this is very hard for me to talk about) six or seven weeks ago, I had my head on his lap one night and I don't know how it happened—his penis was out and I put my mouth down on it. I am shaken just talking about it.
Dr: Now, what's wrong with that? [During the next dozen interchanges (until "There is no union"), the therapist endeavors to reduce the patient's guilt about this sexual activity of hers—first, by putting its "wrongness" in question, and then by pinpointing the sources of her negative reaction. Eventually he is in a position to challenge the moral reasoning that is the wellspring of the guilt.]
Pt: It is horrible.
Dr: Why? I mean, was it unpleasant?
Pt: Yes.
Dr: Let me get one thing straight. Was it physically unpleasant? Is that the point? Does it taste bad, for example?
Pt: Yes. It had like a urine taste to it.
Dr: Is that what upset you?
Pt: Yes. And we didn't do the act. I put my mouth down and drew it away. It was a split second like that, so it was not oral.

Dr: It was just the taste? If it hadn't had any taste, would everything have been okay?

Pt: Well, it was sort of soft and mushy.

Dr. It was the physical unpleasantness of it? If it hadn't been physically unpleasant, you wouldn't have minded it?

Pt: Morally I would, because my conscience is just eating me away right now.

Dr: Your conscience? Will you explain that to me.

Pt: To me this is such a dirty thing.

Dr: What is?

Pt: I wouldn't have intercourse with this man, yet I went ahead and did this. If I had intercourse it would have been just as bad.

Dr: Why won't you have intercourse with this man? Do you like him?

Pt: Yes.

Dr: Would you like to have intercourse with him? If so, why won't you?

Pt: Because I am still a married woman, and I don't believe people should have intercourse unless they are married.

Dr: What do you mean by marriage? What is a marriage?

Pt: The union of two people.

Dr. Is there a union between you and your husband? [Her relationship with her husband is explored.] You are separated, there is no union. Tell me about that? Why are you separated?

Pt: I think—it was an accumulation of many things over the years. I had been ill for five years (off and on) with this depression—to one psychiatrist after another. I was in a hospital—I don't remember the name of the place. I think that he just got fed up with me being ill. I was a pest, a pain, a drag, I was always sick, and I think any man would have got fed up with it.

Dr: This is since five years ago when you were 36 years old?

Pt: Yes.

Dr: Can you say what made you depressed?

Pt: My husband owns a restaurant and he had an affair with one of the girls and wanted to marry her. [This, of course, immediately makes it important to elucidate what the patient's husband found unsatisfactory about her.] It ended up to be the biggest scandal. We live in a small town. The girl ended up in the hospital with a nervous breakdown, and it was a year or so after. I just couldn't accept it.

Dr: Wait a minute. He had an affair, but before that you were quite happy and healthy.

Pt: I always kept myself so busy that I never realized the symptoms. I think I have always been depressed—all my life, but I got by. It wasn't that bad.

Dr: By depression, what do you mean? ["Depression" is too easily taken for granted. It has different meanings for different people. Here, asking for its meaning leads to evidence of social anxiety which is then investigated.]

Pt: I never enjoy anything, Doctor. I can go out to a party and anticipate it and get all dressed, but the minute I get in there I want to go home.

Dr: Is there anything about parties that upsets you?

Pt: I don't only mean parties. It is just like when I went swimming with a group yesterday. I wanted to go, but as soon as I got there I wanted to go home.

Dr: Is there anything about groups that upsets you?

Pt: No. I just feel bored with it and I want to go home.

Dr: If there wasn't a group and there had been only one or two people, would the same thing have happened?

Pt: No.

Dr: Does this feeling have something to do with the number of people that you go to meet?

Pt: Yes. I guess so. If it is going to be a group. Now, today they told me there would be doctors in here with you and I was really frightened, but now that it is only you and I, that doesn't bother me.

Dr: So being watched by people bothers you? [It is evident that she has a neurotic habit of responding with anxiety to being watched by several people. In such cases the anxiety is often found to increase as a function of the number of watchers.] And that has interfered with your enjoying group situations?

Pt: I don't know if it is that or if I am just bored. Just nothing interests me.

Dr: But if there are only one or two people, have you then been able to enjoy situations?

Pt: Yes, if I can converse with someone. What I want to tell you before I forget. This illness of mine is something I want. It is my security.

Dr: Is it?

Pt. Yes.

Dr. Did you come to that conclusion or did somebody tell you that?

Pt: No. I did. [Nevertheless, as she had previously had a considerable amount of psychoanalytically oriented psychotherapy, it is likely that the idea was originally planted by a therapist. The conversation that follows appears to uphold this inference.] It is my security, and when I am in the hospital I don't think I am sick or don't feel as though I am sick because I feel secure that I am here.

Dr: What do you mean when you say it is your security?

Pt: Like at home, it is something to hang on to. When I am sick I feel secure. It is a big point there. I know I want to be ill. Something inside of me wants to be ill. I am punishing myself, and the more angry I get at myself, I dislike myself intensely.

Dr: Wouldn't it be nice not to be ill?

Pt: That will never happen to me.

Dr: I wouldn't say that; but in some sense then it must be true that you prefer not to be ill?

Pt: Yes. There is a part of me that doesn't want to be ill. The confident side of me. When I have good days, I could lick the world. But when I have those down days I am ready to die.

Dr: Well, doesn't that mean you would really prefer to have good days all the time?

Pt: Yes.

Dr: And isn't that why you are here in the hospital, because you hope this may be brought about. Although I realize you are not very optimistic about this, this is why you are here. Let me see if we can piece this together clearly. You have always been aware that there are certain situations which you should have enjoyed but couldn't, and one of the things that got in the way was the presence of a number of people. (There may be other things too.) Are you saying that the fact that this happened may have been a kind of damper on your husband? It might have made him dissatisfied with you. [The reasons for her husband's dissatisfaction are brought out.] That might have been a reason for his having this affair.

Pt: That he was dissatisfied with me? Oh, yes. Our sexual life was very bad, too.

Dr: Why, what was bad about it?

Pt: I never had a climax in 20 years. Never in my life have I had a climax.

Dr: Do you think you could have?

Pt: Yes.

Dr: What prevented you from doing so?

Pt: I don't think my husband knew enough.

Dr: Can you describe to me what used to happen?

Pt: Well, we would get in bed and he would kiss me and feel my breasts and things like that, but it would last about five or ten minutes and then he was ready to go and it was done. I think that maybe he was too small for me, because sometimes I could barely even feel it.

Dr: And you would sort of be left high and dry?

Pt: And then he is done and he turned over and went to sleep.

Dr. Would you feel frustrated?

Pt: Yes. For days. [A major complaint against the husband is brought to light. Both parties thus have strong negative reactions in major recurrent situations. The elements are presented for a vicious cycle of mutual repulsion that can generate growing negative emotions.]

Dr. Didn't he recognize that there was a problem. Did you tell him that this was not satisfactory to you?

Pt: Yes, but I don't think he— —Since I have met this other man, from just the petting that we have done (I told you that we didn't have intercourse), I realize that my husband didn't know anything about making love. I don't know how I even got pregnant to tell you the truth. I mean other than the fact of the actual act, it could have been anybody getting me pregnant. I don't know why. I think that I didn't feel as a woman as I should because I never had a climax. I think that in doing what I did with this other man, I in a way wanted to prove that I was a woman, too.

Dr: Well, why shouldn't you? [Another attack is made on the "rationale" of her guilt from the therapist's authoritative pedestal.]

Pt: My conscience is just eating me alive.

Dr: We will come back to that in a minute. Do you think (I am just asking you—I am not trying to suggest this to you), is it possible that because you found your sex life so unsatisfactory, you were not a very willing partner as far as your husband was concerned?

Pt: Yes. That's true.

Dr: So, we now have two reasons for him being dissatisfied with you, even though he himself was to blame for the one. You were a bit of a spoilsport in company, and you weren't very willing in bed, so he may have become dissatisfied and that may have led to him going to another woman. Now, did he tell you this? Or did he, out of the blue, tell you, "I am tired of you and I want to marry this waitress"? Is that what happened or what?

Pt: Yes, he did. I don't know how it came about. He said that he wanted to marry her. I took the car and I don't know where I drove that night. The next morning he changed his mind and asked for my forgiveness, and he went and told the girl that it was all over with. She ended up before the day was over in the hospital with a breakdown.

Dr: You took him back?

Pt: Yes, and a couple of months later I got pregnant and had my son. For a couple of years it was good after that.

Dr: You really forgave him and you didn't think about it? [The therapist is not content with "it was good."]

Pt: Oh no, I didn't forget it. I was (there is a word I could use for myself) I let him live in hell because of it. I brought it up to him every time I could.

Dr: From your point of view, in terms of the way you feel, you are not married to him anymore. There is no relationship?

Pt: But I never really let him go.

Dr: That is just on paper. In fact, you have let him go. I mean, he is supporting you economically, but there is no relationship. There is no personal situation which you could call a marriage. It is just a piece of paper with money stuck onto it. Let me ask you this. Here is this other man; does he love you? [In the following passages the potentialities of the other relationship are investigated.]

Pt: Yes.

Dr: Is he in a position to marry you?

Pt: Yes.

Dr: Could he support you?

Pt: Yes.

Dr: Is there any good reason then why you shouldn't divorce your husband and marry him? Do you like him?

Pt: Yes. I am very physically attracted to him, but he drinks—sometimes a little and sometimes a lot.

Dr: If you were to marry him, would he give it up?

Pt: I don't know. He has been a bachelor for 20 years.

Dr: He wants to marry you?

Pt: Yes.

Dr: How old is he?

Pt: He is 53, and I am 41.

Dr: Well, that's not a bad difference.

Pt: He doesn't look it. He looks very young and he is very vivacious. He is entirely different than I.

Dr: Let me ask you this. Suppose he could put himself into a position where he could have treatment for his alcoholism? If you could have a reasonable assurance that he loved you enough to want to do something to give up the drinking and if this could be controlled, would you marry him?

Pt: I don't know because I still love my husband.

Dr: You still love your husband? But you also hate your husband?

Pt: Do I? I don't know if I do.

Dr. Well, the way you kept on attacking him until you separated.

Pt: He left, but he would keep telling me to snap out of it and he was just disgusted.

Dr: There is another possible solution to this problem. If you feel basically that you love your husband, and if it is conceivable that you could contemplate the fact that he had an affair without being distressed, then you could take him back. [In what follows the possibility of restitution of the marriage is explored.]

Pt: I would take him back right now if he walked in.

Dr: You would? And would you attack him every day?

Pt: No.

Dr: But would you feel okay about it?

Pt. I think so. I can understand it better now.

Dr: Even if you may be deceiving yourself in saying that you would comfortably take him back, it is possible for you to get treatment that would enable you to tolerate it and forgive it [The rationality of what has happened would be driven home; and desensitization would subsequently be performed if nonrational emotional disturbance remained evocable by any aspects of these past developments.] I believe that your husband had good reason to be dissatisfied with you. Now, it is very possible for him to be retrained sexually so that you would not need to go on being frustrated [Means are proposed for overcoming the husband's impotence]. The question is: Is there any practical possibility of your making an approach to your husband to try to get things set right, or is he now tied up with someone else?

Pt: I don't know. He was. He was dating another waitress—he always has the waitresses. But I don't think so. We live in a small town and it took a lot of nerve for him to walk out and leave me, because there are people in town who still won't talk to him after two and a half years. It would take an awfully big man to come back and say—you know.

Dr: Either he is mixed up with somebody else now or he is not. If he is not, then there is probably quite a good chance, but it depends on the way you approach it. I think you would need to make an approach and say that you now understand the situation and understand why he did what he did; that you can accept it; that you would like to come together with him and see whether a new future could be worked out between the two of you. [It is generally a good rule to pursue objectives in the order of the patient's preferences.] That accords with the way you feel, doesn't it?

Pt: Yes. I would be very glad to do anything.

Dr: Then, at the very least you should give yourself that chance. It may not work, he may refuse, but at least you should feel that you have done everything that is possible. Then, if he doesn't under any circumstances want to come back, you must cut your losses and resign yourself to not having him and see if you can find somebody else with whom you can make a life. Do you agree or not?

Pt: Yes. I am not getting anywhere, just standing still.

Dr: Well, that seems to be the logical sequence. You must make the approach to him, and tell him that you will accept it. The two of you should not only come together, but try to come together in such a way that, by getting psychiatric help [The main targets, of course, are the patient's social anxieties and her husband's sexual inadequacy] you can remove the factors which led to the breakup of the marriage.

Pt: He doesn't believe in psychiatrists.

Dr: People often have good reason for this, because they have unsuccessful experiences; but I think what would happen here would be a constructive experience for both of you. It would really be quite different from the ordinary psychiatry that you have been thinking of. [This distinction often needs to be emphatically made, and must sometimes be spelled out in detail.]

Pt: It is just that I have been to about three or four of them, and I just don't get over my problem. He has no faith in them, because they are not doing me any good. Yet, I realize that it could be that it is not the psychiatrist's fault, but it is just me. I just don't understand or I am not getting the point of what they are trying to tell me, or I just don't want to.

Dr: I don't think it is really that. It may have something to do with the approach of the psychiatrist. I am giving you a practical program. [The targets of therapy are reiterated.] Speak to your husband and say that you accept what he did and that you want to do everything for yourself—to change yourself so that you can make the marriage work. Say that you have discovered that the two of you can get counsel to obtain the satisfactory sex life which you didn't have before. You would like to give it a go, that you feel much more mature, and so on. See what happens.

Pt: Well, I will do that. Right now he is very angry with me for coming to the hospital.

Dr: He is angry with you?

Pt: My whole family is angry. I have had hardly any visitors. They are all angry. I packed up and I left and came here myself and signed myself in.

Dr: You mean because it puts a blot on the family name?

Pt: Probably. I was in ——— Hospital, and I came out of there worse than I went in, and he just felt it wasn't going to do me any good and that I should stay home and fight it. That is what he would tell me.

Dr: At this stage, it may be a good idea for you to tell him that one of the results of your being in the hospital this time has been to reveal to you that you would like to give it another go with him and that there are ways to make it a success.

Pt: But I feel dirty now.

Dr: Look, in the same way that what he did with that waitress is understandable because of the unsatisfactory situation in which he found himself, what you have done is also understandable. [The justifiability of her sexual behavior is reiterated.] You would have been absolutely justified in having intercourse with this other man. There is no question about it. From the human point of view—you need companionship and love and so on, and if you are not getting it from your husband it is natural to do something else—the same way as when he wasn't getting affection from you, he got it from somebody else. From a rational point of view it is remarkable to me that you didn't have intercourse with this man. I think you should have.

Pt: The problem is that I am really frustrated.

Dr: Yes.

Pt: It makes me nervous because we pet and then we stop. After all I am 41 years old, and it is not easy. You know, I have not had intercourse in two and a half years.

Dr: Well that's ridiculous, and you should have, but now look—you have come to this point. [The sequential possibilities are brought together.] You have told me that you would rather have your husband. So you will try and get him to come back with you. You will try and overcome these things that have made you sort of a damping influence socially. This can be done very easily. This is a new kind of psychiatry which you can get right here. There may be other things I don't know about. We haven't been into them. These faults in you which have impaired the marriage can be overcome. Your husband's difficulty can be overcome. The other things which have interfered with marriage can be overcome. If he is prepared to go along with this, the marriage can be rebuilt. If he is not, then you have to cut your losses and get yourself another man. In any event, the fear that you have of being looked at needs to be overcome.

Pt: Doctor, do you think it is fair for me to marry any man with this depression over me?

Dr: We know what the depression came from. At least we know some of the things that can cause it. [Knowing the sources of her depression has the immediate effect of making individual attacks of depression easier for the patient to tolerate. The next stage in the therapist's strategy will be to decondition the unadaptive emotional habits that are the sources of depression. Systematic desensitization should be applied to the patient's interpersonal anxiety reactions. It would embrace her reactions to social disapproval, and her guilt in relation to having "transgressed" in various contexts of extramarital sex. A counterconditioning schedule entailing the use of sexual responses will probably be needed to overcome her husband's sexual problem (Wolpe, 1969)]. We haven't had much time together, so I haven't gone into many details. You have been depressed because you haven't enjoyed social situations due to tension in the presence of people; and that can be cured. If it is cured, that source of depression will be gone. You have also been depressed because you have been sexually frustrated. If the sexual situation can be remedied, that source of depression will be gone. If there are other things that I don't know about which can cause depression, they can be modified as well. The depression is not just a thing inside you which has got to be accepted. It is pretty clear that it comes from specified things that can be changed. Let me build a picture of a possible future. You have rejoined your husband. You no longer get disturbed by going into groups and crowds—you enjoy them. He has learned how to handle you sexually so that you have climaxes. Will there be any need for you to be depressed? But we have also noted another thing. You have a kind of anxiety at not having the approval of certain people. [This is a reference to her excessive concern about the opinions others have of her, which probably has a great deal to do with her sexual guilt reaction.] Now this can be overcome, too, very simply.

Pt: Suppose things don't work out with my husband. What would happen if I really went through and did the whole sex thing with the other man? I don't know where I would go the next day.

Dr: Well, I don't think it is all that easy. You have an emotional attitude about it, and that would have to be overcome, so that you could accept sexual relations with this man without being disturbed. But now that you have told me that you want to go back to your husband, the immediate program is different. You may want to go ahead with this man later. Now you are going to make an approach to your husband. Therefore, why should we concern ourselves about this other thing now? I really don't want to pursue this any further. I wish you luck.

Pt: You have been very kind, Doctor. Thank you.

Reference

Wolpe, J. *The practice of behavior therapy*. Oxford: Pergamon, 1969.

11

EDWIN J. THOMAS

Bias and Therapist Influence in Behavioral Assessment

Despite its rapid growth, the field of behavior therapy has developed unevenly. In general, more work has been done on the principles and techniques of modification than in the operational details of assessment and clinical procedure. Interviewing in behavior modification is an area particularly deserving of explication and codification. The interview is important because it is frequently a principal source of information for the behavior therapist and what the therapist says and does during assessment as well as modification may be very active in altering the behavior of patients. The purposes and areas of content to be covered in behavioral interviewing have been discussed by several writers (e.g., Kanfer and Phillips, 1970; Wolpe, 1969) and Wolpe has published instructive transcripts on such subjects as the identification of antecedents (Wolpe, 1970a; 1970b, 1971a), the handling of resistance (Wolpe, 1971b), and the correction of misconceptions (Wolpe, 1971c). However, little attention has been given to interviewing technique and style, especially as they relate to interviewing bias and therapist influence.

The behavior of the interviewer is of course a continuing and complex influence upon those whom he interviews. Through his eyes, face, body position, vocal expression, and words the interviewer elicits emotional states, cues behavior, and provides feedback that may reinforce or punish portions of the patient's verbal and nonverbal repertoire. Unwanted biases and *ad hoc* and premature verbal interventions can be introduced all too easily during assessment. Because the interviewer provides a continuing stream of potentially active stimuli for the interviewee, the question is not how to make assessment completely neutral behaviorally. The question, rather, is how to reduce unwanted bias and intervention and still guide the interview toward

Reprinted with permission of Pergamon Press, from *Journal of Behavior Therapy and Experimental Psychiatry,* Vol. 4, 1973, pp. 107–111.

objectives of assessment and modification. This article identifies instances, types, and adverse effects of unwanted bias and influence during assessment, suggests some ways to reduce such biases and influence, and discusses areas of desirable behavioral activity of the therapist during assessment.[1]

Examples, Types, and Adverse Effects

The author has been impressed with what would appear to be a fairly common practice during assessment of giving *ad hoc* advice, interviewing in a needlessly biased fashion, and engaging in *ad hoc* and premature intervention. Evidence of this is to be found in published transcripts of behavioral interviews, selected articles that describe aspects of assessment procedure, case studies, audio and visual tapes, and the practices of students and practicing behavior therapists as evidenced in consultation, reports, and supervision. The examples given below are not intended to be comprehensive, but they do illustrate several different types of unwanted bias and influence.

Example 1.

Patient: "I enjoy the swinging life."
Therapist: "Is that right?"
Commentary: Even if the therapist had not expressed amazement or surprise in the vocal or nonverbal aspects of his behavior, his words were literally a question and could of course be construed as expressing reservation or objection.

Example 2.

Pt: "Oral-genital sex makes me very anxious."
T: "What's wrong with oral-genital sex?"
Commentary: This question directly challenges the patient and very nearly is the equivalent of saying that there is nothing wrong with oral-genital sex. The expression of this value judgment may be totally unnecessary and, in fact, may serve to inhibit the patient from describing openly what it is about oral-genital sex that makes him anxious. If one objective of assessment is to learn about what makes the patient anxious, then more information should be sought about the eliciting stimuli for the anxiety and nothing should be done to inhibit the reporting of this information.

Example 3.

Pt: "I had a nervous breakdown two months ago and I was in the hospital for . . ." (therapist interrupts).
Commentary: If this area of information is relevant to the interviewer's objectives, his interruption may suppress subsequent responding on this subject.

Example 4.

T: "Let me ask you something about your frigidity. What do you think it does for you?"

Commentary: The therapist's question of course presumes that the frigidity actually has consequences of a given sort, which need not be the case. It is a "loaded" question.

Example 5.

Pt: "I don't enjoy the company of my children."

T: "You mean to say that you don't get anything at all out of your children?"

Commentary: The therapist's question expresses some disbelief in what the patient said and is an inappropriate way to obtain additional information on the subject of the possible aversive and nonaversive features of children for the patient.

Example 6.

T: "In other words, by drinking excessively you get back at your wife. Is that what you're saying?"

Commentary: Assuming that this was not precisely what was in fact said by the patient and that the therapist was making a presumption, it is a very biased question that could lead to a distortion of patient responses. The information presumed could be obtained by less biasing methods.

Example 7.

T: "When you hurt yourself, do you have a sexual orgasm?"

Commentary: The question should be asked in a more open-ended way to find out the possible range of reactions concerning what happens when the patient hurts himself. A direct question such as this might be appropriate, if at all, under very particular conditions such as when the patient had already indicated that sexual feelings of at least a fairly intense sort were aroused by hurting himself.

Example 8.

T: "Why do you discipline your children so harshly?"

Commentary: This is a variation of the proverbial, "Do you still beat your wife?"

Example 9.

T: "Behavior therapy has had a dramatic record of success with problems of alcoholism and I am confident we can cure you of your drinking problem."

Commentary: This optimism is much more than is justified by the research on the effectiveness of behavior therapy with problems of alcoholism and could lead to false optimism and to later disappointment or resentment.

Example 10.

T: "When was the last time you had to discipline your son? How often do you discipline him? What did he do?"

Commentary: Because the answers to each of these questions would probably be different, it would have been preferable simply to ask one question and then to ask others subsequently.

Example 11.

T: (In the first interview with the client just after he described problems of child management) "You should try rewarding your children for the good things they do and ignoring the bad . . ."

Commentary: If this were a noncontracted area, the advice would be *ad hoc* and if the assessment had not been completed, the advice would be premature intervention.

Example 12.

T: (In the first interview with marital partners) "Now I would like each of you to indicate four ways in which you would like to have your partner change and then we will proceed from there to work out a contract by which you would agree to do some of the things your partner wanted in exchange for having him do things you want done."

Commentary: Formation of a contingency contract or an exchange arrangement prior to the completion of assessment presumes information concerning the nature of problems, the controlling conditions, and the behavioral and environmental resources that may be entirely unjustified and unwarranted.

From examples such as these it is evident that there are several important types of bias and influence, and each can have adverse consequences. Information may be distorted through influences brought to bear upon the display of the patient's responses. Thus, the negative or problematic aspects of behaviors can be emphasized at the expense of obtaining information about the prosocial features; the flow of information may be interrupted; the patient may be hurried by the interviewer's pace or questions; there may be excessive dwelling on a given topic; there may be questioning of the validity and the accuracy of the patient's information; and there may be selective attention to some and not other aspects of what the patient says.

Labeling of client behavior, whether done subtly or blatantly, may create problems where there were none before, exacerbate existing problems, or contribute to the fulfillment of labeling prophecies. A false attribution of cause, in addition simply to being incorrect, may alter greatly the way the patient behaves toward himself. Any false representation of behavior therapy may lead to an incorrect commitment of the client to pursue therapy when a more accurate representation might not have encouraged him to continue. False hopes may clearly produce later disappointment and resentment. The providing of *ad hoc* or premature advice and modification is unwarranted if an assessment has not been completed. In cases not involving crises, assessment ordinarily yields several important classes of information needed in order to formulate rationally a modification plan and to select the appropriate technique of modification.

Toward Less Bias and Unwanted Influence

The objectives of assessment include obtaining the requisite information so that planning and modification can be undertaken, establishing the contract regarding the problem area upon which to work, and conveying information about behavior therapy and the regimen the patient is likely to experience. Behaviorally neutral interviewing is one way to increase the likelihood of meeting these objectives satisfactorily. While such interviewing does not guarantee the reduction of unwarranted influence, the verbal features of what the interviewer says can be expunged of most if not all distortion. When asked in a neutral way without biasing vocal inflection, questions can greatly increase the likelihood of producing undistorted information. The interviewer should not interrupt, hurry, or pace the interview too rapidly, and should let the interviewee finish what he is saying before going on to the next question. Questions of course should be asked in an unbiased way, and queries should not be used editorially to express opinions, judgments, and values.

It is also desirable to explain to patients that information will be collected and appraised during assessment and that the therapist will delay making recommendations and giving advice until the assessment has been completed. As part of this socialization of the patient, it should further be indicated that at this time, accuracy, specificity, and frankness are what is required. *Ad hoc* and premature advice should in fact be avoided until modification is undertaken. Behaviorally neutral interviewing oriented toward the above-mentioned objectives can be done without losing a lively give-and-take or a pleasant and friendly relationship.

Acceptable Behavioral Activity

There are areas in which the interviewer should be active behaviorally in that he intentionally engages in influence to facilitate therapeutic objectives. Thus, it is generally necessary to cue and guide topics in the interview and have an agenda of topics to be covered that relate to an explicit or implicit procedure of assessment and modification.[2] In the interviewer's demeanor to patients, he should endeavor to be friendly, civil, and courteous. The contract to work in the given problem area should be maintained as should cooperation with the regimen associated with the modification procedure being employed. Other activities that call for departures from strict neutrality involve socialization of the patient and the reinforcement of appropriate patient behavior, such as that involved in the production of good data. There are of course occasional crises that require the therapist to depart from a planned schedule on a given contracted problem and to work in a different area, at least temporarily. When such crises occur, the therapist may find it necessary to give advice and to engage in modification without having completed a customary assessment.

Notes

1. The research upon which this report is based was supported in part by grant SRS 10–P 5602315–02, Social and Rehabilitation Service, Department of Health, Education, and Welfare. I wish to acknowledge the helpful assistance of Claude L. Walter and Robert D. Carter who worked on the project from which parts of this paper were derived. I also wish to acknowledge the competent assistance of Ms. Joyce Morgan in preparing the manuscript.

2. For example, in the work that my colleagues and I have done on procedural guidelines for behavioral practice in open settings, we have followed steps that very much determine the particular topics to be considered in each session. These 15 steps are as follows: (1) problem inventory; (2) problem selection and contract; (3) commitment to cooperate; (4) specification of focal behaviors; (5) baseline of focal behaviors; (6) identification of probable controlling conditions; (7) assessment of environmental and behavioral resources; (8) specification of behavioral objectives; (9) formulation of a modification plan; (10) execution of a modification plan; (11) monitoring the outcomes of intervention; (12) formulation of a maintenance plan; (13) execution of a maintenance plan; (14) monitoring the outcomes of maintenance; and (15) follow-up. (Thomas *et al.*, 1970; Gambrill *et al.*, 1971; Thomas and Walter, 1973.)

References

Gambrill, E. D., Thomas, E. J., and Carter, R. D. Procedure for sociobehavioral practice in open settings. *Social Work*, 1971, *16*, 51–62.

Kanfer, F. H. and Phillips, J. S. *Learning Foundations of Behavior Therapy*. New York: Wiley, 1970.

Thomas, E. J., Carter, R. D., and Gambrill, E. D., eds. *Utilization and appraisal of socio-behavioral techniques in social welfare—pilot phase*. Final report on research supported by the Department of Health, Education and Welfare, Social Rehabilitation Service, Grant SRS-CRD 425-C1-9, Ann Arbor, Michigan, University of Michigan School of Social Work, 1970.

Thomas, E. J. and Walter, C. L. Guidelines for behavioral practice in the open community agency: Procedure and evaluation. *Beh. Res. & Therapy*, 1973, *11*, 193–207.

Wolpe, J. *The Practice of Behavior Therapy*. New York: Pergamon, 1969.

Wolpe, J. Transcript of initial interview in a case of depression. *J. Behav. Ther. & Exp. Psychiat.*, 1970, *1*, 71–79. (a)

Wolpe, J. Identifying the antecedents of an agoraphobic reaction: A transcript. *J. Behav. Ther. & Exp. Psychiat.*, 1970, *1*, 299–305. (b)

WOLPE, J. Identifying the anxiety antecedents of a psychosomatic reaction: A transcript. *J. Behav. Ther. & Exp. Psychiat.*, 1971, *2*, 45–51. (a)

WOLPE, J. Dealing with resistance to thought-stopping: A transcript. *J. Behav. Ther. & Exp. Psychiat.*, 1971, *2*, 121–127. (b)

WOLPE, J. Correcting misconceptions in a case of frigidity: A transcript. *J. Behav. Ther. & Exp. Psychiat.*, 1971, *2*, 251–259. (c)

IV

Observation, Recording, and Monitoring

Observational skills are an essential and widely employed tool in behavior therapy and research. Systematic observation using code categories tailored to the events of particular interest is a valuable and versatile technique that may be employed in the natural life settings of the home, school and institution, as well as in clinics and community agencies. The practitioner should be able to code antecedent and consequent stimulus events, obtain satisfactory observer reliabilities, collect the data as part of single-case experimental design, and analyze and interpret the results. These are some of the topics treated in the selection included earlier in Part II by Bijou, Peterson, Harris, Allen, and Johnston entitled "Methodology for Experimental Studies of Young Children in Natural Settings." The reader interested in observation is encouraged to turn back and examine this selection carefully for its discussion of observational techniques.

The coding procedure described by Bijou and his associates calls first for the development of case-specific code categories for the target behavior in question, followed by establishment of coder reliability, and then the coding itself. These writers generally use 10-second intervals as the periods within which given events are recorded as having occurred or not occurred. The article included in this Part by Kubany and Sloggett entitled "Coding Procedure for Teachers" describes an observational technique for estimating the percentage of time a student engages in appropriate or inappropriate classroom behavior. The teacher observes and records on a variable interval schedule, making use of a timer which is set according to preestablished times. This article describes the use of this technique, the validity of the sampling, alternative coding procedures, and the use of this system of recording as a basis for reinforcement. Although expressly developed for the classroom so that the teacher can utilize it without deviating from the regular routine, the procedure may be applied equally well with parents as observers in the home, or with regular personnel to observe in hospitals and other closed institutions.

Recording is generally the first step involved in bringing behavior under control. Response specification, baselining, monitoring, and follow-up are important aspects of behavior modification procedure for which some form of recording is necessary. The behavioral events to be recorded generally consist of response frequency, duration, magnitude, or latency. In the early stages of assessment, when specification is undertaken, these data serve to define the nature of the responses that may be addressed in modification. Baseline records indicate to the practitioner the extent to which the behavior is, in fact, problematic prior to modification. When compared with the monitoring records of the same responses during and after modification, baselines serve as comparison points to evaluate the efficacy of the modification. Likewise, follow-up records make it possible to appraise efficacy after intervention has been undertaken.

To record properly, one must be able to denote the target responses in question and to represent them appropriately as tallies or counts in the case of frequencies, as length of time in duration measurement, or as scalar amounts where magnitude of response is calibrated. Work with individuals can often yield large amounts of data, and practice with couples, families, or larger groups can frequently produce staggering amounts of information. In consequence, the practitioner faces many of the data management problems associated with information systems. Large amounts of data, gathered for purposes of continuous monitoring of the events in question and with an eye toward adjusting practitioner maneuvers, require that the data be recorded early and accurately, stored for further analysis or display, processed as necessary from the raw form (e.g., converted to rates), displayed rapidly and intelligibly and, finally, that early and suitable action is taken by the practitioner following review of the output. This entire information-processing sequence, beginning with input and moving through storage, processing, display, and commensurate therapist action, should ideally involve no unnecessary delays or complications. Many technical and managerial challenges confront behavior modifiers who wish to negotiate properly the steps of this sequence. The selections in this section are addressed to some of the technical innovations that have been developed to facilitate the successful accomplishment of one or more steps in processing recorded information.

The selection by Johnston entitled "A Universal Graph Paper" presents a standardized and flexible format useful for recording, graphing and displaying a large variety of responses that may interest the behavior modifier.

Such graph paper may be useful in teaching behavior modification as well as in practice and research. In the description of the many ways in which the paper may be used, the author presents in capsule form some of the graphing decisions that behavior modifiers will encounter when preparing to graph. Graphing using log axes is not covered here. For certain purposes, especially for comparison of highly diverse types of data, log or semi-log axes are desirable. See the selection by Green and Morrow for examples using Lindsley's graphing format in which rates are recorded on semi-log chart paper.

Frequencies are generally converted to rates so that the events can be expressed as events per unit of time. To facilitate the conversion of frequencies to rates, Branch and Sulzbacher have prepared a method of fast calculation which is given in their selection entitled "Rapid Computation of Rates with a Simple Nomogram."

The paper by Colman and Boren entitled "An Information System for Measuring Patient Behavior and its Use by Staff" represents an endeavor to come to grips directly with how to process the mass of information that often needs to be processed when using a point or token system. The authors describe a system that yields continuous monitoring of information relating to individual point earnings and spendings, an economic profile for the group, plus several other group indices, such as ward participation, and indicators of the effectiveness of individual staff members. This selection is important in illustrating the types of data that should be collected when monitoring earnings and expenditures for a group and ways in which such data can be employed effectively to control staff behavior. The particular method of bookkeeping is perhaps of less significance today because it is becoming increasingly clear that electromechanical devices and computers can be effectively enlisted to assist in the rapid and accurate processing of information.

The selection by Logan entitled "A 'Paper Money' Token System as a Recording Aid in Institutional Settings" illustrates some of the ways in which paper money may be better than other media of exchange in point and token systems. The selection by Lehrer, Schiff, and Kris entitled "The Use of a Credit Card in a Token Economy" illustrates a system that may be useful in the later stages of a token economy, after participants have had some experience with a "cash" token system. Each individual has a credit card that is used to produce point slips, and the records of weekly transactions are produced using some of the bookkeeping methods of business accounting. The last selection by Aitchison entitled "A Low Cost, Rapid Delivery Point System with 'Automatic' Recording" provides an evaluation of several different recording methods for exchange systems. The author then describes a point book that contains pages to be punched for points earned and spent, thus providing a continuing record of earnings and expenses. Like paper money and credit cards, this approach has advantages and shortcomings, depending upon one's objectives, clientele, and other aspects of the entire information-processing system.

12

EDWARD S. KUBANY AND
BARBARA B. SLOGGETT

Coding Procedure for Teachers

Ongoing observation and objective evaluation have been hallmarks of behavior modification research and application. However, in most classroom experiments dealing with frequently occurring deviant behavior, the record keeper has been an outside observer, typically a psychologist or research assistant (Kubany, Weiss, and Sloggett, 1971; Wasik, Senn, Welch, and Cooper, 1969). Such extravagant and often inconvenient use of outside personnel is certainly justifiable for research purposes but is probably uneconomical for widely accepted practical application.

In most cases, the teacher has not been solicited as an observer on the assumption that she has too much else to do; she cannot conduct her class efficiently and record behavior reliably at the same time. When teachers have been recruited for observing purposes, they have usually been asked to obtain only a simple frequency count of a target behavior, and the reliability of these observations is often in doubt. Even wrist counters are easily forgotten under the pressures of teaching, and observational reports from teachers are often vague. ("I think he had two or three tantrums last week.") When the referrals have concerned questions such as what per cent of the time a student spends on-task or disrupting the class, outside observers have been employed almost exclusively.

The present report[1] describes an easily learned observing and recording procedure that can be utilized by the regular classroom teacher without requiring her to deviate more than momentarily from regular classroom routine. The procedure can yield an objective statement as to approximately

Reprinted with permission from the *Journal of Applied Behavior Analysis,* Vol. 6, 1973, pp. 339–344.

how much time a given student spends doing his work, wasting time, and bothering others.

The Code Sheet and Timer

The code sheet shown in Figure 12.1 was designed to accommodate different kinds of classroom situations. Depending upon which one of the three coding columns is utilized, the teacher observes and records a student's behavior on either a 4-, 8-, or 16-min variable-interval schedule. If the teacher has the problem student for only one class period daily, it would be advisable to use the 4-min recording schedule. On the other hand, if the teacher has the student in her class all day long, she might choose to use the 8- or 16-min schedule. The numbers beside each space on the code sheet designate the number of minutes for which a kitchen timer is to be set. One of the three time schedules should be selected, and then only that column should be utilized. At the beginning of the class period, the time should be set for a time interval that corresponds to one of the numbers in the selected column. When the times "goes off," it should be reset without delay at the next number (immediately below) in the same column.

The timer should be placed in such a position that the clock face is not visible to the class. With the clock face out of sight and the intervals variable, the student has no way of telling when the timer will "go off."

Observing and Recording

When the timer bell rings, the teacher glances at the student and identifies what he is doing *at that instant.* Is he: (1) "On-task" (A)—that is, doing what the teacher wants him to do; (2) "Passive" (P)—not doing what he should be doing, but not disrupting others; or is he (3) "Disruptive" (D)—*e.g.*, out of seat, talking without permission, or making other noise. The teacher enters the appropriate code symbol—either "A," "P," or "D" in the space next to the number representing the time interval just passed. The timer should then be reset without delay.

To minimize the time spent recording, it is recommended that the teacher carry a pencil and a clipboard with the code sheet attached. To minimize any inconvenience, the teacher might allow a conscientious student to set and reset the timer. It would sit on his desk, and he also would have a code sheet so that he would know how to schedule the appropriate time intervals.

Initial Instructions to Class

"May I have your attention please? Every once in a while this timer will ring. Do not pay any attention to it. I am doing this to keep track of certain things I want to do. Simply disregard the bell and continue with your work." After the first several times the timer rings, certain class members may attend to the bell and even make comments about it. The teacher should ignore all references to the timer. In a short period of time, the class should adapt to the bell, and it will not disrupt the students when they are working.

Interpretation and Validity of the Recording

For any given day, and for longer periods of time, it is possible to calculate the approximate percentage of time that the student spends "on-task," "passive," and "disruptive." Simply divide the total number of spaces marked "A," "P," or "D" by the total number of observations. For example, if seven out of ten observations are coded as "on-task," the student may be estimated to have been on-task approximately 70 per cent of the time.

Although the teacher will record relatively few observations at infrequent intervals, there is evidence that the percentages yielded are likely to reflect the total population of behaviors occurring during the entire period. In a classroom study by Kubany *et al.* (1971), observations were made and recorded over a 50-day period. During the daily 20-min observation sessions, an outside observer would glance at the first-grade subject every 15 seconds, classifying his behavior at that moment, and then record on the code sheet. During the 20-min session the boy's behavior was observed and coded 80 times, and the daily per cent of "disruptive" behavior was estimated and plotted graphically. Using the variable-interval 4-min (VI 4-min) schedule on the teacher's observation code sheet, a sampling of these daily recordings was used for recalculating the daily percentages of "disruptive" behavior. For example, the percentage of "disruptive" behavior for day one of baseline was computed on the basis of observations recorded only at the 2-, 7-, 14-,

TABLE 12.1 *A comparison of results obtained using two different observation schedules.*

	Daily Mean Per Cent of Observations Coded as Disruptive	
	4-min Variable-Interval Schedule (four or five observations per 20-min session)	*15-sec Fixed-Interval Schedule (80 observations per 20-min session)*
Baseline (11 days)	88	90
Reinforcement (31 days)	17	15
Reversal (two days)	99	95
Reinforcement (six days)	13	16

15-, and 18-min junctures (five times during 20 minutes). Figure 12.2 shows graphically how the percentages compare under the two different recording schedules. One can see that making only four or five observations per 20-min session yielded a record remarkably similar to the one in which 80 observations were recorded.[2] These comparisons are summarized in Table 12.1. During baseline, the average per cent of "disruptive" behavior was calculated at 88 per cent based on the fixed-interval 15-sec (FI 15-sec) schedule. Based on theVI 4-min schedule, the percentage was 90—only two percentage points difference. During the first intervention period, the percentages were 17 and 19, under the FI and VI schedules respectively. A similar correspondence of results was obtained during the reversal and second reinforcement periods.

Date ____________________
Student ____________________
Teacher ____________________
Starting Time ________________
Activity ____________________

COMMENTS		FOUR		EIGHT		SIXTEEN
	2		12		12	
	5		2		8	
	7		10		28	
	1		4		2	
	3		6		24	
	6		14		6	
	4		8		24	
	6		2		6	
	4		10		30	
	1		14		12	
	2		8		16	
	5		10		4	
	3		6		8	
	7		4		30	
	2		12		28	
	1		4		6	
	7		12		24	
	3		14		16	
	4		2		12	
	5		6		2	

FIGURE 12.1 *Teacher's observation code sheet. 4-, 8-, and 16-min variable schedules.*

Under certain circumstances, the teacher's code may yield even more representative information than that garnered from an outside observer who spends 20 or 30 minutes in the classroom daily. Intervention programs frequently run all day, and there certainly is no basis for assuming that the 20- or 30-min observation period is a random sample of the total population of behaviors of concern. On the other hand, the teacher is in a position to collect data all day on a systematic interval basis that can be representative of the entire population of relevant behaviors. And different patterns of behavior at different times of the day might provide insights about reinforcing stimuli or sources that maintain inappropriate behavior.

Finally, when the teacher is the observer, neither the teacher nor the students have to adapt to visitors in the classroom, and there need be no concern about possible experimental effects due to the presence of an outside observer (Surratt, Ulrich, and Hawkins, 1969).

Alternate Procedures

When a misbehavior of interest occurs only sporadically (*e.g.*, swearing, fighting, occasional outbursts, or tantrums), it might be preferable to record simply whether or not the behavior of interest occurs or does not occur during an entire interval period (that is, from one bell ring to the next). Say, for example, that the problem behavior is "Swearing," and the first timer setting is 10 min. If swearing occurs at any time during this 10-min interval, the teacher immediately records the symbol "Y" (Yes) in the recording space for that interval. It is no longer necessary to record any further swearing behavior for that 10-min interval. The symbol "Y" simply means that at least one swearing behavior occurred during the entire time interval. If no swearing behavior had occurred during the entire interval, the teacher should record the symbol "N" (No) when the timer bell rings.

It would also be possible to use both of the two general coding procedures simultaneously. For example, the teacher would record "on-task" behavior when the bell sounds—at the end of an interval—and record "fighting" behavior if and when it occurred during that interval.

Recording as the Basis for Reinforcement

Once a baseline of target behavior has been obtained, the teacher may utilize the observing procedure as an explicit basis for dispensing reinforcement for appropriate behavior. For example, if the target student is behaving appropriately when the bell rings, he might earn a point, which could be "backed-up" by or redeemed for an infinite variety of privileges or tangible reinforcers. The reinforcers might be dispensed in the classroom, or a note indicating the daily number of points earned might be sent home for redemption there. The teacher would then have additional motivation to con-

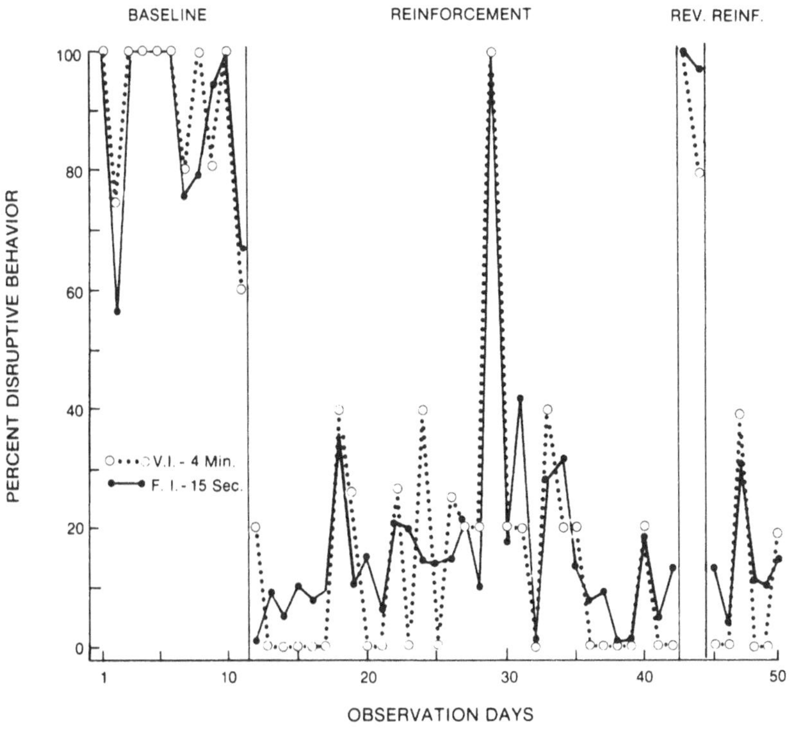

FIGURE 12.2 *Graphic comparison of results obtained under two different observational schedules. Daily percentages of observations per 20-min session during which student's behavior was coded as disruptive, obtained with FI 15-sec and VI 4-min observational schedules.*

tinue recording, because setting the timer is an integral part of remediation. As long as the teacher goes along with the intervention procedures, she would at the same time be collecting evaluation data.

Timers set on variable-interval schedules have been used successfully in numerous studies as the basis for dispensing token reinforcement (Broden, Hall, Dunlap, and Clark, 1970; Schmidt and Ulrich, 1969; Wolf, Giles, and Hall, 1968; Wolf, Hanley, King, Lackowicz, and Giles, 1970; Wolf and Risley, *unpublished*). In none of these studies, however, was the bell ring related to the evaluation/recording procedures. In each case, an outside observer coded the target behaviors.

ILLUSTRATIVE EXAMPLE

During the last month of the school year, a seventh-grade social studies teacher was experiencing difficulty with a particular student "who never does her work" (Sloggett and Kubany, *unpublished*). The teacher's coding procedure was described to the teacher and on the first day of observation, an outside observer (a new-teacher supervisor) established interrater reliability with the teacher. Utilizing the VI 4-min schedule, the teacher and the teacher trainer agreed on eight of nine observations (89 per cent) during the 50-min

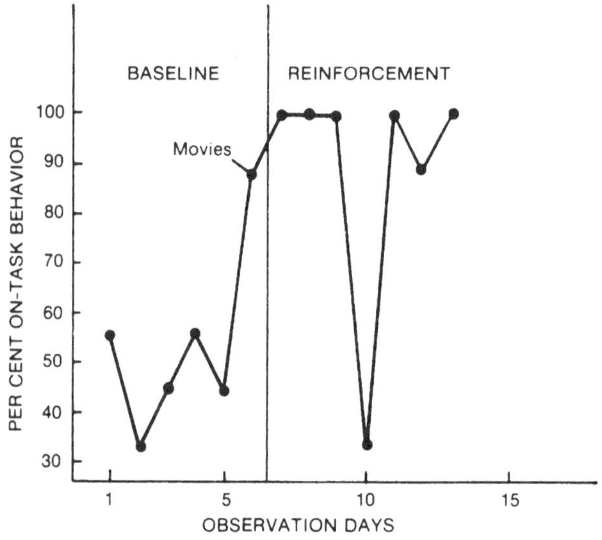

FIGURE 12.3 *Daily percentage of observations that student's behavior was coded as on-task. Her behavior was coded eight or nine times per 50-min class period on a VI 4-min schedule.*

class period. Figure 3 shows that during a six-day baseline, the remiss student was "on-task" when the timer sounded 53 per cent of the time. During the remainder of the observations, the coded behaviors were relatively equally distributed as "out of seat," "passive," and "disruptive." As an intervention procedure, it was decided to award the entire class one minute of free time for card playing at the end of the class period each time the referred girl was "on-task" when the timer sounded. Figure 12.3 shows that during the intervention period, on-task behavior increased to an estimated 89 per cent. It might be added that the teacher reported that, for her, recording the data and resetting the timer were not inconvenient and did not require her to deviate from her regular routine. She also reported that after the first few bell rings, the class paid no attention to the ringing bell.

DISCUSSION

One of the distinctive features of this coding procedure is that it relieves the teacher of the responsibility of keeping track of when to record. The timer bell provides an explicit discriminative stimulus for observing/recording behavior.

Of course, it should be stressed that development of this procedure was motivated primarily to minimize the amount of professional time necessary to implement behavioral intervention programs in the classroom and still maintain a rigorous means for monitoring and evaluation.

NOTES

1. The authors wish gratefully to acknowledge the assistance of Mrs. Annette Murayama and the editorial advice of Ronald Gallimore.

2. One implication of this finding is that many researchers may have spent more time observing than was necessary in order to make reliable inferences about the frequency of occurrence of certain behaviors. Elementary probability theory tells us that even with relatively few randomly selected observations, there is good reason to expect that the observed relative frequency will be quite close to the true state of affairs (Hays, 1963).

REFERENCES

BRODEN, M., HALL, R. V., DUNLAP, A., and CLARK, R. Effects of teacher attention and a token reinforcement system in a junior high school special education class. *Exceptional Children,* 1970, *36,* 341–349.

HAYS, W. L. *Statistics for psychologists.* New York: Holt, Rinehart and Winston, 1963.

KUBANY, E. S., BLOCH, L. E., and SLOGGETT, B. B. The good behavior clock: A reinforcement/timeout procedure for reducing disruptive classroom behavior. *Journal of Behavior Therapy and Experimental Psychiatry,* 1971, *2,* 173–179.

SCHMIDT, G. W. and ULRICH, R. E. Effects of group contingent events upon classroom noise. *Journal of Applied Behavior Analysis,* 1969, *2,* 171–179.

SLOGGETT, B. B. and KUBANY, E. S. *Training the school counselor as a behavioral consultant: A participative-modeling approach.* Unpublished paper presented at Hawaii Psychological Association, Honolulu, May, 1970.

WASIK, B. H., SENN, K., WELCH, R. H., and COOPER, B. R. Behavior modification with culturally deprived school children: two case studies. *Journal of Applied Behavior Analysis,* 1969, *2,* 181–194.

WOLF, M., GILES, D., and HALL, R. V. Experiments with token reinforcement in a remedial classroom. *Behaviour Research and Therapy,* 1968, *6,* 51–64.

WOLF, M., HANLEY, E., KING, L., LACKOWICZ, J., and GILES, D. The timer-game: A variable interval contingency for the management of out-of-seat behavior. *Exceptional Children,* 1970, *36,* 113–117.

WOLF, M. and RISLEY, T. *Analysis and modification of deviant child behavior.* Unpublished paper presented at American Psychological Association. Washington, D.C., 1967.

13

JAMES M. JOHNSTON

A Universal Behavior Graph Paper

In any setting where behavior is recorded, a great deal of time is expended in the manual tasks of creating linear graphs with the appropriate features. The resulting graphs differ widely in appearance and may lower accuracy of recording and complicate interpretation. The semi-log chart paper of Lindsley (1968) represents an attempt to deal with this situation.[1]

A solution to these problems would be the development of a standardized universal behavior graph with the following features: (1) it must allow for a variety of labels on the ordinate, (2) it must have the capacity for a wide range of numbers on the ordinate, (3) it must include a wide variety of units of time on the abscissa, (4) it must include space for basic information about the circumstances of the behavior recorded, and (5) it must be simple and quick to use. A universal behavior graph meeting these qualifications is shown in Fig. 13.1.

This is a linear graph with 100 units (16 to the in.) on both axes. Medium-weight lines mark the units in multiples of five and heavy-weight lines denote ten units, thus facilitating quick and accurate reading.

The top horizontal line is labelled calendar weeks, and Sundays are numbered through 14 weeks.

The abscissa is labelled in such a manner that most units of time can be easily chosen. These include consecutive, daily, or intermittent minutes, hours, days, or sessions. The appropriate label is designated by filling in or blackening between the dotted lines, as on a machine-scored test answer sheet. The four blank spaces divided by a decimal point are for designating the unit of a single lightweight line on the graph and must be filled in appro-

Reprinted with permission from the *Journal of Applied Behavior Analysis,* Vol. 3, 1970, pp. 271–272. Copyright 1970 by the Society for the Experimental Analysis of Behavior, Inc.

priately. For instance, if an experimenter were recording a subject's rate of responding during a daily 2-hr experimental session, the abscissa would be notated as daily 2.0-hr sessions. If a teacher were recording a child's rate of behavior during different periods of the day, the abscissa would read intermittent 1.0-hr sessions (each light-weight line referring to a single session, the sessions being recorded with a variable frequency on any one day). If the graph were being used cumulatively, the abscissa might read consecutive 10.00 min. This would mean that each line adds 10 minutes to the previous one, so line 20 would indicate 200 minutes. A therapist recording his patient's behavior on variable days of the week could look at the data across the seven days of the week (daily) or independently of the weekdays (intermittently), in which case the data points would be plotted on successive lines. It can be seen that this form of labelling for the abscissa allows for a wide variety of specific choices while retaining a simplicity in notation and interpretation.

The ordinate utilizes the same basic format of notation as the abscissa. By blackening between the lines (connecting the words), one can label the axis rate, percentage, or number; or cumulative rate, percentage, or number.

When plotting data cumulatively, the data line may reset as an automatic cumulative recorder does. The line may be reset after the top line is reached, each reset designating the maximum number of responses possible with the multiplicative and/or additive factor(s) used. This number is always a multiple of 10, thus facilitating reading of the data. The data line may also be reset upon reaching other fixed cumulative totals, or it may be reset on a time basis, such as weekly.

The range of numbers assigned to the ordinate may be widely varied by using a multiplicative and/or additive factor. By placing a decimal point in the appropriate position in the multiplicative factor, the range on the ordinate may include numbers from 0.001 to 0.01 or from 1000 to 10,000. Thus, use of this multiplier simply means that each number (or position) on the ordinate is multiplied by the appropriate factor of 10. The additive factor operates in the same manner. For instance, if data points were being recorded that typically varied between 1700 and 1800, the correct notation would be × 00100.0 + 001000.

However, if the data usually varied between 90 and 110 responses, using the left-hand ordinate the multiplier would have to be 00100.0, which would place the data points low on the graph and within a very narrow range. The solution to this and similar problems is to use the right-hand ordinate, where the data would be centered on the graph over a larger range. The labels and the multiplicative and the additive factors apply to whichever ordinate is being used, and this choice is indicated by blackening the appropriate dotted arrow at the bottom of that axis. An even greater degree of flexibility might be obtained by designing the graph without numerical values on the right-hand ordinate (and even the abscissa); however, this would also detract from the standardized appearance of the graph paper.

Information identifying the graph may be recorded on the right-hand side. This way of displaying identifying information is particularly easy to read. Figure 13.1 uses terminology appropriate to an experimental situation (sub-human or human). Of course, a variety of labels may be used for these blanks depending on the setting. In a school system, they might be Behavior, Student, Code, Teacher, Class, and School. In a hospital or clinic it could read Response, Patient, Code (or Number), Therapist, Ward, and Institution. The blank space beneath the last label may be used for notes, contingency arrangements, schedules of reinforcement, *etc.*

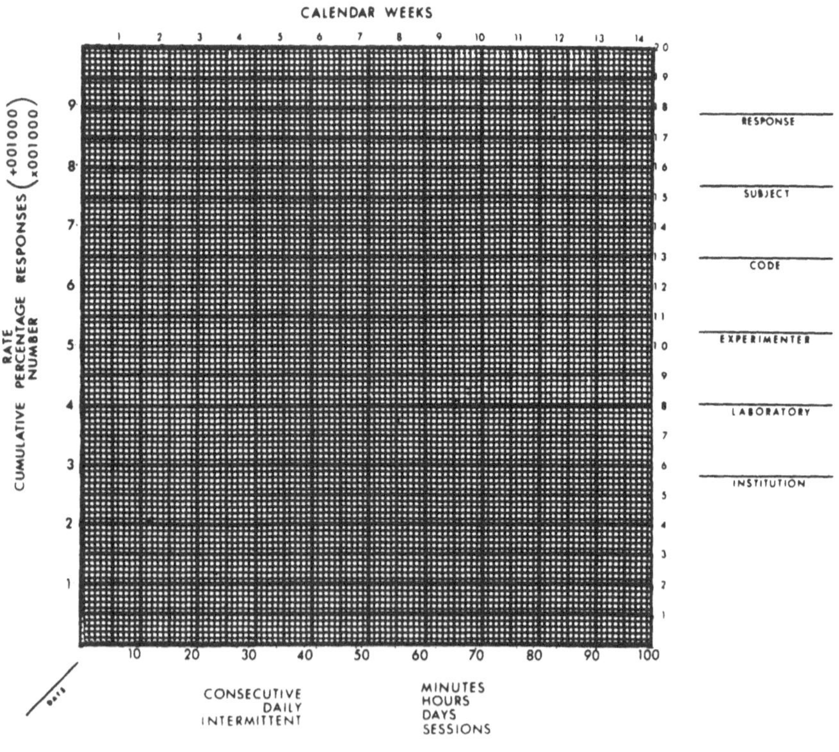

FIGURE 13.1. *Universal behavior graph paper.*

Copies of this Universal Graph Paper may be obtained by having a double-sized art copy drawn on heavy white posterboard. The camera-ready art copy can then be photographed, reduced, and copies may be offset printed at a very reasonable cost per 500 sheets.

NOTE

1. The author would like to express appreciation to Dr. H. S. Pennypacker for his cooperation and contributions in the development of this graph paper.

REFERENCE

LINDSLEY, O. R. Advertisement. *Journal of Applied Behavior Analysis,* 1968, *1,* inside back cover.

14

ROBERT C. BRANCH AND
STEPHEN I. SULZBACHER

Rapid Computation of Rates with a Simple Nomogram

Nomograms have been devised to aid in rapid calculation of body surface, basal metabolism rate, *etc.* (Geigy, 1962). Lindsley (1968) has also suggested their use in education. Figures 14.1 and 14.2 show two nomograms for obtaining rapid approximation of response rate. The right vertical axis is graduated along a time dimension, while the left axis is in a frequency dimension. When a straight edge is aligned across given values of time and frequency, the value on the diagonal at the point of intersection with the straight edge is the corresponding rate (frequency per unit time).

The nomograms shown are for two rate ranges commonly found in the classroom performance of children. However, a nomogram can be constructed for any values of time or frequency.

Keeping accurate records of the performance of ten to 40 children in a public school classroom is at best a time-consuming task. It is important, however, that such data be kept on a daily basis so that they may provide a basis for decisions about the curriculum for the following day. The teacher must be provided with rapid methods of obtaining meaningful information from her data. Unless such methods are devised, the teacher can hardly be expected to keep data which will be of only historical interest by the time it is processed.

References

Geigy Pharmaceuticals Division. *Documenta Geigy Scientific Tables.* 6th ed. Ardsley, N.Y.: Author, 1962.

Lindsley, O. R. Personal communication, 1968.

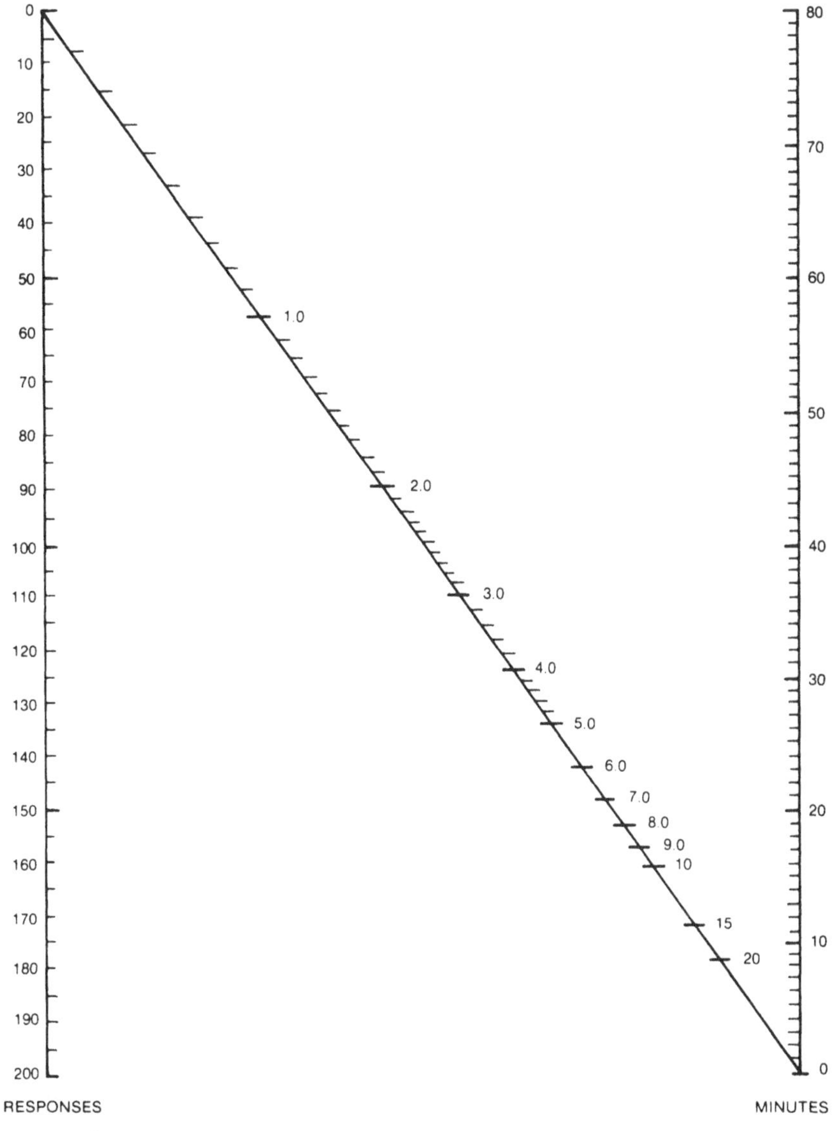

FIGURE 14.1 *Nomogram for determination of response rate.*

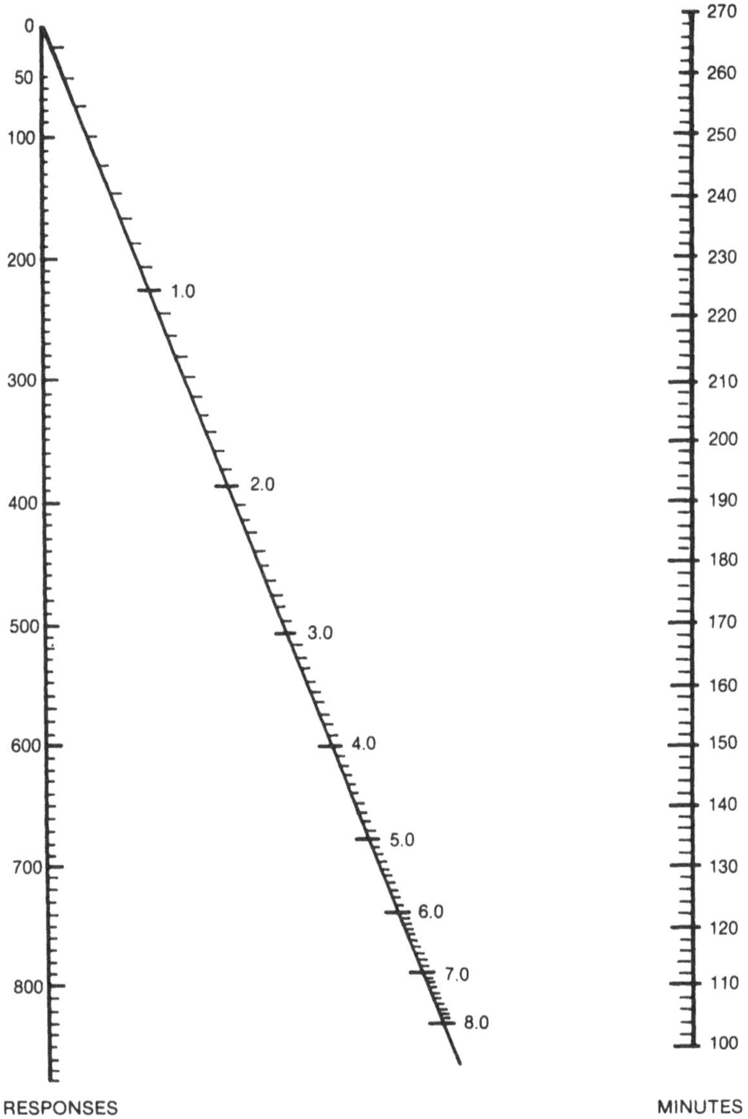

FIGURE 14.2 *Nomogram for determination of response rate.*

15

ARTHUR D. COLMAN AND
JOHN J. BOREN

An Information System for Measuring Patient Behavior and its Use by Staff

We have recently designed a 24-hr point economy ward to prepare delinquent soldiers for successful completion of their regular tour of duty in the Army. A distinctive feature of this ward is its use of an information system for measuring patient behavior in which individual and group earnings and spendings are used as the primary data measurement. This paper describes the development and operation of the measurement system and emphasizes its use by the staff in the treatment process.[1]

Background

The treatment program is detailed elsewhere (Colman and Baker, 1969; Ellsworth and Colman, 1969). Briefly, a research ward, begun in January 1967 at Walter Reed, treated patients diagnosed as having character and behavior disorders for approximately 16 weeks and discharged them to active duty. The ward housed 16 men at a time and was staffed by the normal complement of phychiatric staff, including one of us (A.C.), who had administrative control of the program.

Typically (according to their records), the patients were 21, single, and had enlisted in the Army after difficulty with a court, school, or family. They had a long history of school dropouts, job failure, and trouble with the police. Many had difficulty handling the routine of the Army field posts, were unpopular with peers in their unit, often went AWOL, had recurrent fights, and made "manipulative" suicide gestures.

Reprinted with permission of the *Journal of Applied Behavior Analysis,* 1969, Vol. 2, No. 3, pp. 207–214.

In designing the treatment program, we assumed that these men failed in the military (and previously in civilian life) because of behavioral repertoires that provided inadequate reinforcements when operating legally in social situations. Our curriculum emphasized training in educational, occupational, and "group skills," such as written reports, drafting and roles in ward administration. (See point-recording matrix in Fig. 15.1.) A point system was used to "pay off" desirable behavior. Points were paid to the men for behaviors that we believed would be reinforced in the future outside the ward. They could exchange these points for reinforcers in the system, such as cards, TV, passes, and extra education. The complete list is shown in Fig. 15.1. Although fines were levied infrequently, a board consisting of staff and patients met weekly to consider substracting points for inappropriate behavior.

After ten weeks on the ward, some of the patients were given a new status, Phase II membership, which offered access to most of the ward's reinforcements without the use of points. In order to maintain Phase II membership, patients were required to perform general leadership duties such as teaching courses, running the unit at night, and supervising the ward work program. Members could be removed from Phase II if performance fell below the standards set by staff and the other Phase II individuals. This program offered a transition from control by the relatively immediate, consistent, positive reinforcement of the point system to more delayed, variable, aversive, and more naturalistic control systems of most environments. It also functioned as a test system for evaluating how much of the behavior learned under the control of the point system would transfer into a less-explicit control condition.

Behavioral Measurement System

The primary data used for measurement was patient behavior that resulted in point earning or spending. These points were recorded directly on a data matrix designed as a daily economic balance sheet. Further data processing developed individual behavioral indices and group behavioral indices which summarized more complicated and long-term behavioral patterns of patients. The description of these measures includes techniques for data review designed to focus staff attention on objective measures of patient behavior. Our aim was to put the staff under the control of the data system so that they could (1) evaluate their effect on the patients objectively and (2) devise more effective procedures for modifying the patient behaviors designated by the information system.

Data Matrix

Figure 15.1 shows the final version of a point-recording matrix used as the primary data collection and first-order display device. Earnings and spendings for each patient were immediately entered into the appropriate boxes.

THURSDAY
20 JUNE '68
CENSUS: 14

FIXED INCOME / ADDITIONAL INCOME

SOLDIERS ON PHASE "1"	FORMATION	INSPECTION	DETAILS	UNIT MEETING	P.T.	WRITTEN REPORT	TASK GROUP	COURSE	VERBAL REPORT	MISSION ASSIGN.	Q.O. POINTS	ADJ. PTS. OWED	SPEC. CLEAN/UP	TOTAL WAGES	BONUS/W/REPORT	TEACHING CLASS	SOFTBALL PTS.	EVE. CLASS	TOTAL ADD/INC.	BAL. FROM WED.	TOTAL EARNINGS
EVANS	10	10	5	20	12		10		35	87				194	5		40		45	335	574
MARTIN	10	9	5	20	12		10	10	35					146					0	156	302
COLLINS	10	10	5	20	12					87				194			40		40	327	511
PRINCE	10	10	5	20	12		10	10	35	86				198		25			25	327	650
SOBOL	10	9	5	20	12		10	10	5	87				168		49			49	460	677
DUGAN	10	10	5	20	12		10	10	35	87				199			40	10	50	504	753
PICK											200	8		208			40	7	47	160	415
COLTER	10	9	5	20	12	15	10	10	5	86			25	207			40	5	45	742	994
CARLTON	10	10	5	20	12	15	10	10	35	87				212		25	40	10	75	448	736
POST	10	10	5	20	12					86				143				9	9	380	532
QUICK	10	10	5	20	12	15	10	10	35	86				213				9	9	370	592
SOLDIERS ON PHASE "II"																					
LONER	10	9		20	12		10	10	5	96				172					0	682	854
KASE	10	10		20	12		10	10	35	93				200		40			40	1121	1161
RODMAN	10	10		20	12		10	10	35	100				207			40	8	48	1036	1036

SPENDINGS

SOLDIERS ON PHASE "1"	PASSES	"JIF" PASS	MOVIE PASS	CARDS	PLAYING POOL	TV EARLY	TV LATE	FEES/AREA	FEES/EARLY LUNCH	FEES/CONTRACTS	COFFEE FUND	BUYING FOOD	ADJ. PTS. NC	TYPEWRITER (OLD)	IRON 8 BOARD	INTERVIEW/DR	BUYING FOOD	TOTAL SPENDINGS	BAL. TO FRI.
EVANS					30	8		[illegible]				20					32	90	484
MARTIN					24	8	16										37	85	217
COLLINS	20					8		25				12						65	446
PRINCE			45															45	605
SOBOL							16	25			10							51	626
DUGAN								25				71						96	657
PICK						8	16				10	99					70	203	412
COLTER					30	8					10							48	946
CARLTON								25				22						47	689
POST												12					22	34	498
QUICK								25										25	567
SOLDIERS ON PHASE "II"																			
LONER						24					10							34	854
KASE	165																	165	1161
RODMAN							8	25										33	1036

FIGURE 15.1 *Point-recording matrix for a day's activities. The earnings are organized into two categories: (1) "Fixed income" from standard activities, such as the inspection and the educational course; and (2) "Additional income" from extra activities, such as teaching a class or playing on the softball team. The spendings on the right side of the matrix illustrate the reinforcers that the patients purchased with their points. The patients' names are fictitious.*

Cumulative totals such as total wages, total spending, and daily balance were calculated daily. Point balances at the end of the week were put in a "bank" to use for special passes or additional discharge leave. Patients shifted to Phase II had their earnings and spendings recorded as a continuing measure of their behavior. The matrix was kept on a desk top, readily visible to staff and patients at all times.

In setting up the ward, we assumed that the record of earnings and spendings would be important in controlling the patients' behavior. They would have to refer to it to plan their activities; point totals would soon become powerful conditioned reinforcers and stimuli for appropriate behavior. We only gradually realized the importance for staff of the point matrix. One of the first clues was staff's spontaneous substitution of the matrix for conventional nursing notes (which had been abandoned because of their usual focus on pathological behavior). In the absence of these notes, we noticed that when staff personnel changed shifts, they referred to the matrix in describing how individuals had behaved on the ward that day. It was being used as a visual record of performance in ward activities, educational and leadership roles, spendings, and fines. In fact, these records were discriminative stimuli for the staff; they carried an implicit set of instructions about how to behave toward each patient as a function of the level of behavior measured by the point earnings and spendings.

We noticed that certain parts of the original data system seemed to cue inappropriate staff behavior. For example, the early form of the matrix recorded negative balances, which were circled in red. But the red circles called staff's attention to the poorly functioning patients at the expense of those patients whose accounts were balanced. The economy and matrix were redesigned to exclude negative balances; patients were fined once a week and point balances reduced to zero, with the remaining debt made up as a work detail. These changes in the data system were consistent with ward policy of reinforcing appropriate behavior while ignoring disruptive behavior. Simply recording fines once a week further minimized staff's attention to negative behavior. Techniques were devised to direct the staff's attention to positive, objective performance. For example, staff calculated moment-to-moment sub-totals so that patients could keep track of their point balances. This had the effect of keeping staff aware of the patients' positive behavior (how different from the patient asking the staff: "How much did I get fined today?"). As another technique, the staff was asked to select a "Soldier of the Week." Since a major criterion of merit was total earnings, the staff had to examine the weekly point totals of each individual. In monitoring the "long-term" contingency, the staff was asked to attend to six weeks of patient behavior. Here, a patient earned an extra day off on a long weekend or holiday pass if he fulfilled specified requirements such as a minimum six-week earning total, five verbal reports, and no fine actions. All of these devices insured that staff members were in continued contact with the daily, weekly, and monthly patterns of patient behavior.

Individual Behavioral Indices

We soon found that the data matrix could not provide a practical measurement for patient behavior for more than a few days. Since one aim of treatment was to teach the man to behave consistently over many weeks under the control of longer-term contingencies, we needed a data display to help the staff evaluate long-term behavioral patterns.

To meet this need we developed an instrument for studying an individual's economic profile for the duration of his ward stay. An example for one patient is shown in Fig. 15.2. The graph is divided into sub-units illustrating the individual's cumulative earnings and spendings for a week. The first 12 weeks show many flat earnings and spending curves, indicating little control by the ward program. During five of these weeks he was either AWOL or received fine actions. However, during the week of 26 June he showed an appropriate behavior pattern, which although gradually decreasing over the next three weeks, suggested that the problem was not a behavior deficit but rather that we had not found an appropriate reinforcer to maintain longer-term behavior. These data influenced the staff to search for alternative reinforcing procedures. We discovered that he liked a particular staff member whose job included buying food snacks for the ward store. We allowed him to help with the job contingent upon perfect attendance at work periods. This and other treatment strategies resulted in the strengthening of positive behavior apparent by early September. On Phase II, his spendings soared (a common response to the sudden availability of noncontingent reinforcements), but despite an initial reduction in total earnings, his positive behavior was maintained at the same level as on Phase I.

Group Behavioral Indices

As part of the research program on the ward, we had planned a number of experiments in which the dependent variable was the patient's participation in a given ward activity. We reviewed the results in a weekly meeting with research personnel. To our surprise, ward staff, traditionally hostile to research, wanted to be included in our meeting. They wanted to see how the experiments came out. They were even more interested in developing objective data on all aspects of the ward operation, particularly their "own" activities. They felt it would help them to know what was going on.

We saw in their interest an opportunity to add to the data review techniques for staff by plotting the daily and weekly per cent participation of the men in each activity. Staff could then evaluate new procedures more objectively. For example, we developed the weekly ward index shown in Fig. 15.3. This was a weekly sum of the per cent participation of the entire patient group in eight representative daily activities. It provided a measure of the overall participation of the men in the ward program, much as the Dow Jones Index alerts the investor to stock market trends. A daily ward

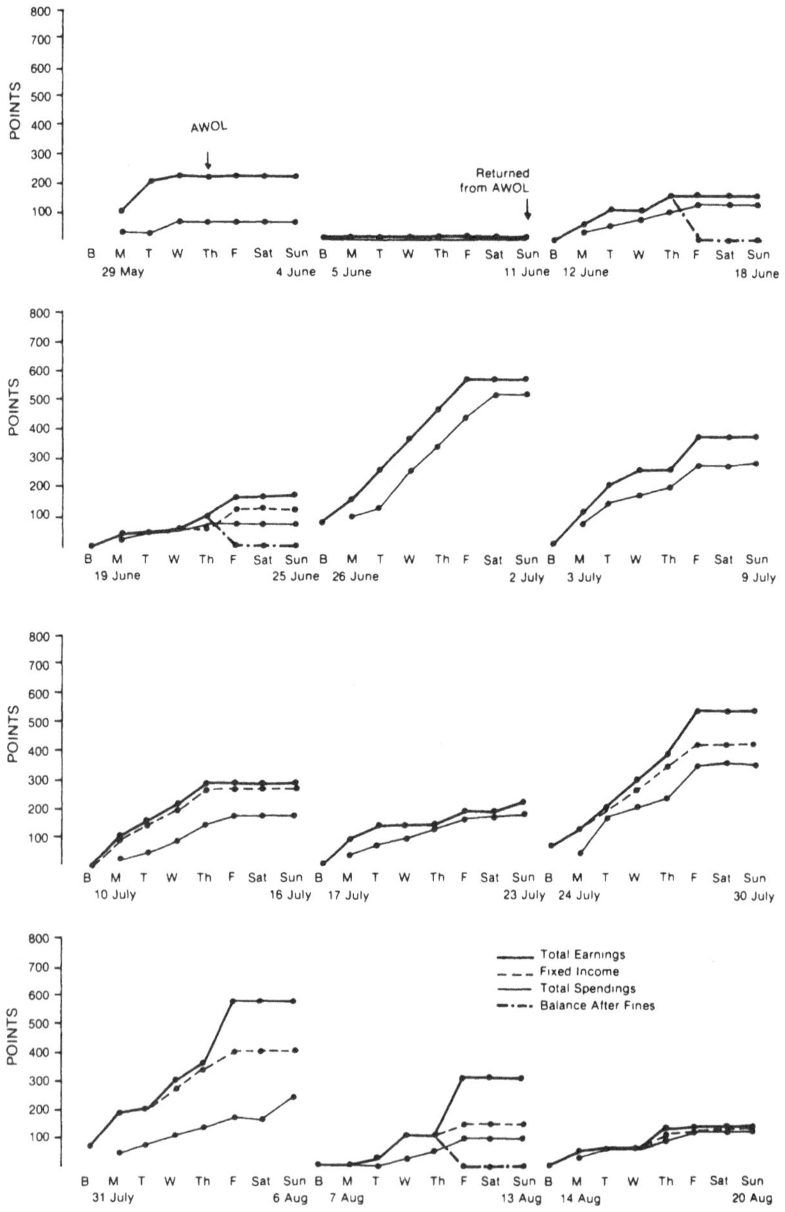

FIGURE 15.2A *Weekly graphs of point earnings and spendings for one patient. "Balance after fines" was calculated by subtracting the amount of the fine from the total earnings. These graphs illustrate a technique for examining the pattern of behavior and the reinforcements of the individual patient.*

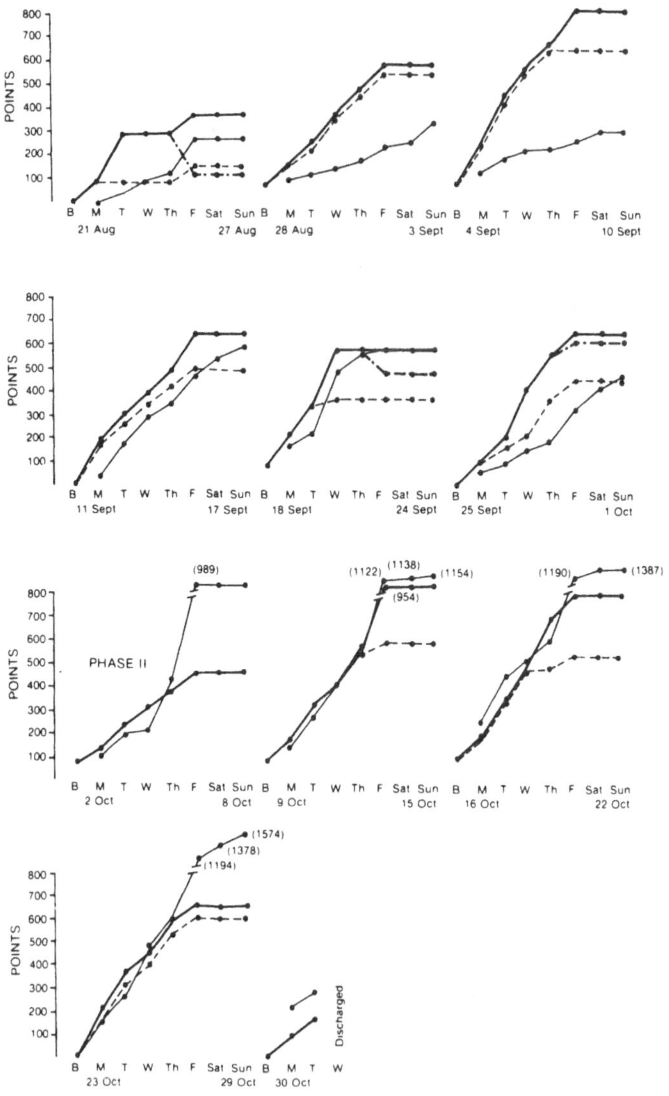

FIGURE 15.2B *Continued weekly graphs for the patient in Fig. 15.2A. The patient depicted above had a history of fighting, disorderly drinking, and trouble with the police both before and after entering the Army. He was ad-admitted to Walter Reed Psychiatric Service after four months' active duty for threatening suicide and homicide with a recently purchased mail-order gun that he kept hidden in his bunk. He has since returned to active duty and for the last nine months has functioned successfully as a data processor on a nearby Army post, an outcome predicted by the ward staff from his response to Phase II.*

index provided a more fine-grain analysis. These indices allowed staff to measure the consequences of their behavior on the ward. For example, we found a consistent drop in the ward index during the three to four weeks surrounding the departure of the psychiatric resident or sergeant. This information led to an important advance in ward procedures; we added long-term contingencies during crisis periods. As a result of adding long term contingencies, we seemed to be able to maintain behavior at a baseline level through such difficult times.

In addition to overall ward index, the per cent participation of the men in each activity was graphed and reviewed. Each activity graph allowed the staff member in charge of that activity to become an experimenter, devising methods for increased participation or performance in his activity. Figure 15.4 shows the weekly per cent participation in the ward sergeant's daily inspection over a six-month period during which a new sergeant came to the ward. For many weeks before Sgt. Sturges' arrival on July 24, the inspection participation had varied between 35 and 50 per cent, except for a drop to 18 per cent on July 17 which preceded the loss of the retiring sergeant. With Sgt. Sturges' arrival there was a transient increase to 50 per cent but for the next three weeks a strong downward trend developed. To counteract this trend he first changed the inspection time to a more favorable hour and on September 25 introduced the "lagniappe"[2] reinforcement system. These changes and the parallel increase in inspection participation are *not* construed by us as experimental demonstrations of behavioral control. Rather, they demonstrated the effective use of objective feedback from

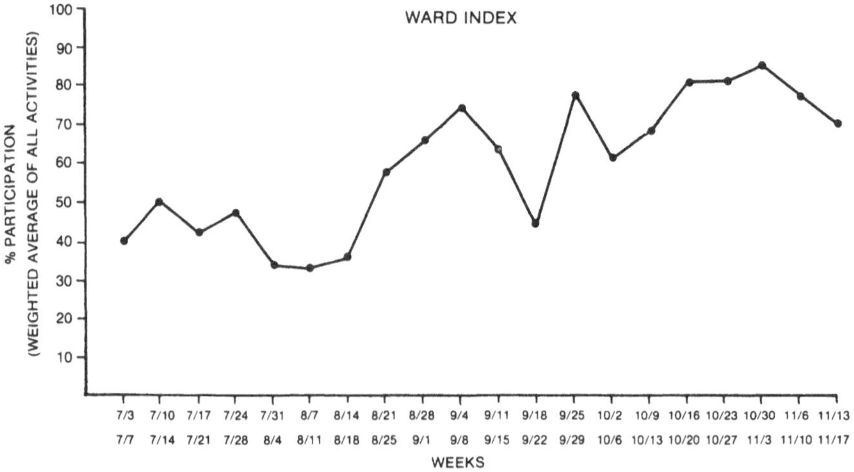

FIGURE 15.3 *The weekly ward index over a period of more than four months. This graph illustrates a technique for recording the overall participation of all men in all ward activities.*

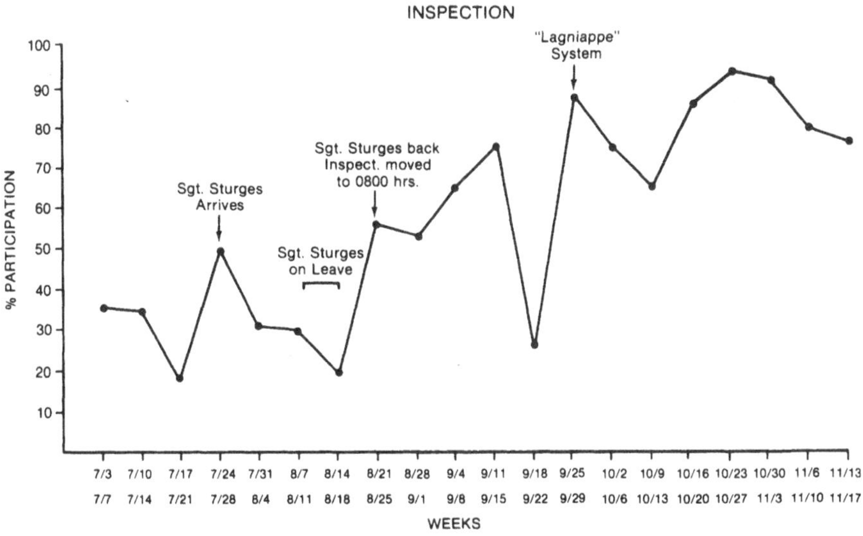

FIGURE 15.4 *Participation in the inspection activity over four months. This graph illustrates a technique for measuring the participation in a ward activity, permitting the staff member in charge of that activity to evaluate the effectiveness of his procedures.*

a data review technique to improve one aspect of Sgt. Sturges' work performance. He was able to identify a problem and experiment with changes with the assurance of having some measure of their effect. This kind of continually available learning opportunity seemed to have a major impact on staff's competence in modifying patient behavior.

An additional use of the activity graphs was to guide the ward administrator in exercising quality control over the activities and modifying the point economy. For example, a systematic drop in one course compared to other activities suggested analysis and observation of the course, with the aim of changing the teaching technique or the subject matter. As another example, while comparing graphs on several activities, it was noted that the work program was less well attended than the unit meeting. Then it was found that the work program, which required hard work for several hours, offered fewer points than the half-hour unit meeting. As a result, points were shifted into the work program and participation increased.

Maintenance of the Information System

The reliability of the behavioral recording was not formally studied. However, the accuracy of the data was constantly monitored by both patients and staff. The patients audited their own accounts to insure that they received credit for all points earned. They also complained if points were improperly awarded to other patients. For example, since the "Soldier of the Week" was selected largely on the basis of a high point total, one man was likely to point out mistakes in another's earnings. As another example, if the ward sergeant awarded points to one man during inspection for neatness of dress, another man not receiving points would want to know why. Repeated questioning of this nature appeared to force the sergeant to award points on a fair and objective basis. Although a ward technician was assigned to record attendance at every activity, we arranged alternate checks. Course instructors were asked to turn in a separate attendance record. Furthermore, the ward sergeant monitored each activity because she was held responsible for the accuracy of the data matrix by the ward administrator (A.C.), who spot-checked the accuracy of the recording.

Some aspects of the information system were automatically maintained by inherent reinforcement contingencies: since the point awards were public knowledge, the patients could audit their own accounts. However, the appropriate use of the information system required the intervention of the senior staff. The ward administration had to reinforce the staff behavior of using the behavior indices in Fig. 15.1 to 15.4. This was accomplished largely through two weekly meetings where the ward data was reviewed. Here, the ward administrator and his staff carefully scrutinized the week-to-week changes in the graphs and commented favorably on effective new procedures.

Discussion

In the experimental analysis of animal behavior, the investigator's ability to control behavior is largely dependent on his ability to measure it; he has a large number of sophisticated measuring instruments at his disposal. Just as the cumulative recorder of the pigeon's responses can control the investigator's next responses in his experiment, so the point records can influence the staff's responses in the treatment program.

The information system had the following main features:

(1) The record of points earned and the behavioral measurement system were identical. Other measures, such as rating scales and nurses' notes, were not essential.

(2) The staff's attention and work were directed toward increasing objective, positive behaviors of the patients.

(3) Data review techniques allowed the staff to evaluate the effectiveness of their procedures on patient behavior.

Point economy "managers" are increasingly finding that the control of staff behavior is as important and often more difficult than control of patient behavior. The option of controlling staff's monetary reinforcement or job security is rarely available to the manager. On our ward, one of the few aspects of the staff environment totally under our control was the behavioral measurement system. We suggest that the techniques described in this paper can aid staff in their professional roles as behavior modifiers.

NOTES

1. The authors wish to thank Allan Berry, Sally F. Oesterling, Donald L. Sturges, Agnes T. Small, and the staff of Ward 108 for invaluable technical assistance and conscientious work. We also are indebted to the Walter Reed General Hospital psychiatric residents, Drs. James Rumbaugh, Marvin Firestone, Theodore Robertson, and David Armitage, who were assigned to the ward and made major contributions to the clinical program. Finally, we appreciate the advice and support of Drs. David McK. Rioch, Joseph V. Brady, Jarl Dyrud, Israel Goldiamond, and Ewen Clague.

2. The lagniappe is a Southern Louisiana expression meaning gratuity or tip given with a purchase to a customer as a compliment or extra bonus. For example, a New Orleans fruit dealer might give a banana along with the purchase of ten apples, calling it a lagniappe. Point payment for inspection had been on a zero to ten continuum depending on appearance, bearing, etc. Sgt. Sturges introduced into this reinforcement continuum a ten-sharp and ten-sharp-sharp at the upper end of the scale, nonexchangeable verbal gifts greatly valued by the men as reflected in the increased behavior. (This concept was first called to our attention by Dr. Thomas Lewis.)

REFERENCES

COLMAN, A. D. and BAKER, S. L., JR. Utilization of an operant conditioning model for the treatment of character and behavior disorders in a military setting. *American Journal of Psychiatry,* 1969, *125,* 1395–1403.

ELLSWORTH, P. D. and COLMAN, A. D. Occupational therapy in a military milieu unit: the application of operant conditioning principles to work group experience in the treatment of character and behavior disorders. *American Journal of Occupational Therapy,* 1969, *23* (6), 495–500.

16

DANIEL L. LOGAN

A "Paper Money" Token System as a Recording Aid in Institutional Settings

The combined tasks of contingent reinforcement of desired behaviors and accurate recording of behavioral change consume much time and effort of hospital staff whose goal is the implementation of a token economy program. The most commonly used tokens include poker chips, whose various colors can represent different monetary denominations, machine-stamped metal coins, and Mexican or other inexpensive coins. The inherent flaw in the use of such tokens is that they are easily lost, stolen, or traded.

As a means of remedying some of these problems in the token economy system at Terrell State Hospital, the print shop was asked to print a large amount of rectangular-shaped "paper money." (See Fig. 16.1). The money was color-coded according to broad classes of behavior. Money bearing the labels "Self-Care," "Ward Work," and "Social Contact" was printed in different colors to facilitate easy recognition and quick sorting. The money was also stamped according to denomination (1 cent, 5 cents, and 10 cents). The amount paid for a specific behavior, however, was based entirely on the desirability of having a given patient emit that behavior. On the face of the "paper money" is a place for the patient's name, the attendant's name, the date, and the specific response that was reinforced. Specific responses have included such items as "mopping the dorm," "emptying the trash," "playing checkers," *etc.* Tokens bearing a name other than that of the holder are not honored.

Perhaps the greatest advantage of "paper money" tokens is that they completely replace standard bookkeeping systems. When the patients exchange their tokens for perishables, personal items and clothing, the tokens become

Reprinted with permission from the *Journal of Applied Behavior Analysis,* Vol. 3, No. 3, 1970, pp. 183–184.

the permanent records. Compartmentalized bins are easily constructed to facilitate counting and storage of tokens. Although a brief amount of time is involved in filling out the information on the face of the money, staff seem to prefer this type of record keeping to previous methods that involved tedious tabulation of data at the time of token exchange. Unfortunately, the present program is not structured such that the success of the "paper money" system can be accurately compared to other recording methods.

Sorting the money according to the color provides rapid feedback regarding the frequency with which broad classes of behavior are being reinforced. Determination of specific behaviors being reinforced can be made by examining the responses specified in writing on the faces of the bills. Sorting according to attendants' names yields information regarding the number of patients and the number and kind of behaviors being reinforced by each attendant.

FIGURE 16.1 *Example of the type of "paper money" used in the token economy system.*

As a safeguard against loss and mutilation of the "paper money" tokens, patients who have earned a specified number of tokens can purchase billfolds in which to carry their money.

17

PAUL LEHRER, LAWRENCE SCHIFF,
AND ANTON KRIS

The Use of a Credit Card in a Token Economy

At the Adolescent Service of Boston State Hospital (Kris and Schiff, 1968), a credit card system has been used as the means of transaction in a token economy for the past three years.[1] The medium has been "points," where one point is worth approximately one penny. The credit card system has proven to be economical and adaptable for use in the clinical management of a diverse patient population. In addition, it insures that data are collected automatically at each points transaction. This makes the system particularly useful where treatment takes place in diverse settings, rather than on a single centralized ward, and where many staff members may not understand the importance of keeping accurate records. At Boston State Hospital this system has been used by over 100 staff members throughout the hospital with a minimum of training and supervision.

The system works as follows: each patient is given a small plastic credit card with his name and other identifying data embossed on it. The card is similar to ordinary gasoline company credit cards. Each time a patient earns or spends points his name is stamped on a "points slip" using an imprinter. (If an imprinter is not available the slip can be filled out by hand.) The cards, imprinters, and points slips are all available commercially.[2] Points slips can be produced with several carbon copies and/or a final copy suitable for use as a computer card. The Adolescent Service uses one carbon copy. The original copy is given to the patient as a receipt, and the carbon copy is given to a secretary in the central office of the Adolescent Service. In addition to the patient's name and the amount of the transaction, the following in-

Reprinted with permission from the *Journal of Applied Behavior Analysis*, 1970, Vol. 3, No. 4, pp. 289–291. Copyright 1970 by the Society for the Experimental Analysis of Behavior, Inc.

formation is entered on the slip: date, identification number of the imprinter with which the slip was stamped, initials of the staff member who filled it out, and the code of the transaction that specifies whether it is a payment or a charge and identifies the type of payment or charge (see Fig. 17.1). Extra space is available to explain the nature of the charge or payment in cases where the code may not be sufficiently specific. The current list of codes used is shown in Tables 17.1 and 17.2.

Once a week a secretary collates the carbon copies of the points slips and prints out a statement for each patient that lists all the patient's earnings

TABLE 17.1 *Codes for points transactions: Payoffs (codes 00–49)*

00. More than one payoff; specify in payoff slip

School (01–09)

01. Attendance—incomplete day
02. Attendance—complete day
03. Attendance—night school
04. School bonus, classroom productivity
06. School bonus, special program
08. Homework, describe
09. Library, describe

Activities (10–19)

10. Sports
11. Occupational therapy
13. Community meeting
14. Activity bonus (describe)
15. Evening groups
16. Other daytime groups (describe)
17. Weekend groups
18. Vacation attendance
19. Ward recreational activities

Other (20–49)

20. Occasional job
21. Regular job
22. Bonus for earning criterion number of points
23. Group bonus
24. Individual bonus (describe)
27. Points statement conference
28. Special program
29. Ward job
31. Curiosity bonus

41. Attendance—incomplete day (Vocational Training Program)
42. Attendance—complete day (Vocational Training Program)
43. Work simulated productivity (Vocational Training Program)
44. Written productivity (Vocational Training Program)
48. Other (describe)
49. Bookkeeping correction

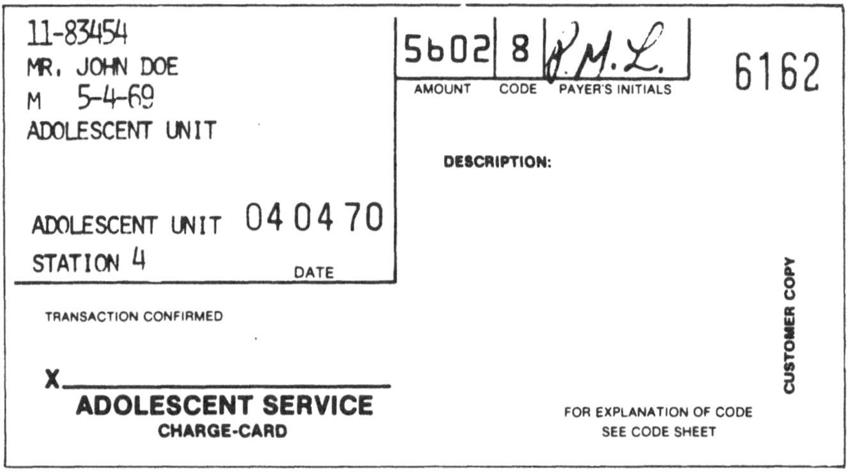
11-83454
MR. JOHN DOE
M 5-4-69
ADOLESCENT UNIT

ADOLESCENT UNIT 04 04 70
STATION 4
DATE

5602 | 8 | P.M.L.
AMOUNT | CODE | PAYER'S INITIALS

6162

DESCRIPTION:

TRANSACTION CONFIRMED

X

ADOLESCENT SERVICE
CHARGE-CARD

FOR EXPLANATION OF CODE
SEE CODE SHEET

CUSTOMER COPY

FIGURE 17.1 *Sample points slip.*

and spendings for the preceding week by code and amount. It also shows the patient's points balance for the coming week.[3] A sample points statement is shown in Fig. 17.2. The secretarial time involved is approximately eight hours per week for approximately 50 patients. The points statement provides a convenient and reliable source of data both for research and for program planning. The information about a patient's performance necessary for carrying out special reinforcement programs is available at a glance from the points statement. The points statement can thus be used as a focus for weekly sessions with staff members in which patients' programs are reviewed. For the purpose of research, carbon copies of the points slips and/or weekly statements can be filed concurrently according to several classifications (*e.g.*, by patient, by date, *etc.*) to facilitate making a statistical summary of points activity.

Although primary reinforcement is necessarily delayed until the end of each week, patients do receive immediate secondary reinforcement in the form of a receipt and the social reinforcement that accompanies the payment transaction. The delay in tallying patients' points activity is useful in teaching these relatively impulsive patients to plan ahead financially. The more regressed and/or retarded patients who cannot tolerate a week's delay in primary reinforcement are put on an "immediate payment" plan in which they use their payment receipts as cash. This is also done routinely with new patients until they become "involved" in the activities of the Adolescent Service.

A word should be added on how to handle patients who chronically spend more than they earn. Most patients are good credit risks. For those who are not, a weekly list of debtors is maintained in the canteen where most of the

TABLE 17.2 *Codes for points transactions: Charges (codes 50–99)*

50. More than one charge; specify on charge slip

Lounge (51–59)

51. Morning snack period
52. Other morning times
55. Afternoon (2:00–5:00 P.M.)
58. Evening (5:00–9:00 P.M.)
59. Special lounge charge

Specials (60–79)

60. Special purchases, personal (describe)
61. Special purchases, materials for activities
62. Rentals
63. Locker room purchases
65. Other meals (off campus)
66. Special events (on campus)
68. Personal money withdrawal
70. Off campus trip
71. Bus
72. Staff (describe)
73. Psychotherapy
74. Tutorial
75. Special course tuition (school only)
76. Special program
77. Library book deposits
78. Sheltered workshop fee
79. Other specials (describe)

Penalties (80–99)

80. Leaving lounge without paying (50 points)
81. Service charge missing card (25 points)
82. Lost card replacement (50 points)
83. Loan interest
85. Fine, group
86. Fine, individual (no summons)
87. Summons fine (describe)
99. Bookkeeping correction

points are spent. A patient's name cannot be released from the debtor's list until the following week's points statement appears, assuming that the patient has earned his way out of debt by then. Although a harassed staff member has occasionally failed to check the debtor's list and thus has occasionally allowed a debtor to spend, this has never continued very long. Illegal spending by debtors is made a major issue at community meetings and bad credit risks soon become well known to the canteen staff, who check on them more carefully. In such cases, patients soon learn that illegal spending only deepens and prolongs their indebtedness.

11-83454
MR. JOHN DOE
M 5-4-69
ADOLESCENT UNIT

ADOLESCENT UNIT POINTS SYSTEM
WEEKLY STATEMENT

OLD BALANCE 3223 NEW BALANCE 3561

TOTAL EARNINGS 1487 TOTAL CHARGES 1149

4 6 70

DATE	DAILY EARNINGS: SCHOOL CODE	AMT	ACTIVITY CODE	AMT	OTHER CODE	AMT	DAILY CHARGES: LOUNGE CODE	AMT	SPEC & SERV CODE	AMT	CHARGES CODE	AMT	DAILY BALANCE
6 APR 70	1												
6 APR 70	4	.75											
6 APR 70	5	.45											
6 APR 70	6	.55	13	.15			58	.60					33.53 •
7 APR 70	2	.55	15	.30									
7 APR 70	5	1.29	11	.40									
			11	.40			58	1.45			80	.50	34.52 •
8 APR 70	2	.80											
8 APR 70	4	.75											
8 APR 70	5	.97	11	.10									
8 APR 70	6	.25	10	.40			58	.95					36.84 •
9 APR 70	2	.80											
9 APR 70	4	.75											
9 APR 70	5	.72											
9 APR 70	5	.50	16	.50	27	.25	58	2.29	68	5.00			33.07 •
10 APR 70	2	.45											
10 APR 70	4	1.00											
10 APR 70	5	.29					55	.70					34.11 •
10 APR 70					22	1.50							35.61 •
TOTAL 10 APR 70		10.87		2.25		1.75		5.99		5.00		.50	35.61 •

COMMENTS

FIGURE 17.2 *Sample points statement.*

NOTES

1. This investigation was supported in part by PHS Grant MH 14861–04 from the National Institute of Mental Health.

2. The Adolescent Service purchased the credit cards and imprinters from the Farrington Manufacturing Company. The price of the imprinters varies between $50 and $85, and the price of credit cards is $30 per thousand. Patients' names are embossed on the credit cards using a hand embosser. The embosser used is available from Pitney-Bowes for approximately $600. If an embosser is unavailable, embossing can be done commercially at nominal cost. Also, temporary cards can be made inexpensively using an ordinary label maker that embosses the patient's name on a strip of plastic adhesive tape. The tape can then be applied to the credit card. The points slips used at the Adolescent Service were purchased from Moore Business Forms, Inc. for approximately $6 per thousand.

3. In preparing statements, the secretary uses a NCR Model 160 Billing Machine, which costs $1465. The statements can also be prepared by hand. Forms for the statements can be mimeographed or can be purchased commercially in printed form with several carbon copies. The Adolescent Service has purchased these forms from Moore Business Forms, Inc. for approximately $65 per thousand.

REFERENCE

KRIS, A. O. and SCHIFF, L. F. An adolescent consultation service in a state mental hospital: maintaining treatment motivation. *Seminars in Psychiatry*, 1969, *1*, 15–23.

18

R. A. AITCHISON

A Low-Cost, Rapid Delivery Point System with "Automatic" Recording

Token economies in environments ranging from "home" type settings (Phillips, 1968) to large wards (Ayllon and Azrin, 1968) have used a variety of procedures for dispensing tokens and points. Many such systems have relied on points and credits rather than physical tokens, perhaps because the dispensing of such tokens can become difficult and time consuming when room inspection or general ward cleanup occurs on a large hospital ward. In addition, the token's advantage of being usable in token-operated automatic dispensing machines (*e.g.*, soft drink and cigarette dispensers) is of no consequence in low-budget systems such as state hospitals that cannot afford to introduce these devices.

The use of a single, central record of behavior emitted by individuals on a ward (Colman and Boren, 1969) is only feasible when the size of the ward is small. A highly desirable feature of the Colman and Boren recording system, having a record of important patient behaviors and their rate of occurrence, is also in the system being suggested, except here, each patient's point book must be examined to determine behaviors emitted for that week. Similarly, the use of a points system that is maintained and recorded by patients (Phillips, 1968) is feasible where the patient-caretaker ratio is small enough to ensure that cheating does not occur.

The paper money system (Logan, 1970), if it is to be useful as a recording system, requires several colors of paper money, each in several denominations. Having each aide carry enough of this paper money to reinforce the behavior of many patients seems quite demanding; to require the aide to write in the patient's name, aide's name, date, and task at each token ad-

Reprinted with permission from the *Journal of Applied Behavior Analysis,* 1972, Vol. 5, No. 4, pp. 527–528.

ministration seems prohibitive in terms of the aide's time. The results of this procedure might be to endanger the aide's cooperation with the token system. Further, due to the amount of time required to administer each token, the overall reinforcement frequency probably would be reduced, and many criterion behaviors go unreinforced.

The present system was designed to allow a staff of five psychiatric aides to maintain a variety of behaviors in a ward of 50 to 60 juveniles. Specifically, this system requires each patient to carry an eight-page point book with him at all times. A page for a single day is reproduced in Figure 18.1 (actual size is 3 by 5 in.). The five psychiatric aides each carry two paper punches; one is a standard round hole punch (Gem; McGill Metal Products Co., Marengo, Ill.) and the other is a diamond-design punch (heart, spade, and club patterns are also available from the same manufacturer).[1] The shaped holes resulting from the "design" punch are slightly smaller than the standard punch, and these smaller punches are used to give points. Within this system, all behaviors earn points that are punched at the appropriate column (determined by number of points earned) at the appropriate time in the patient's daily schedule. The exchange of these points for back-up reinforcers involves using the standard hole punch to "remove" the figured hole already punched. The example page reproduced in Figure 18.1 shows

10	20	30	Name
		♦	Room
			Ward
			8:30
●			9:30
			10:30
			11:30
			12:30
			1:30
			2:30
			3:30
			4:30
			medication
			medication
			extra jobs
			extra jobs

FIGURE 18.1 *A page from the point book carried by each patient.*

30 points earned for room maintenance and 10 points earned for being on time to a 9:30 class; the 10 points have been spent so all that remains is the large round hole used to "remove" those points.

Several disadvantages of the described system may limit its application: (1) there is no easy way to determine the rate of reinforcement used by each aide or staff member, except to give different shaped punches to different staff; (2) some patients have attempted to hold out two pages of the point book at once, thus getting twice as many punches; (3) there is less flexibility in the payoff rates: this could be changed by giving each patient a card where many different values could be punched out, but this would sacrifice the records of what behaviors the patients engaged in on each day.

Although it is possible that the patients could obtain punches from retail sources, it was initially difficult for the author to find retail sources for shaped punches in the area. After six months of successful operation, one patient used an Xacto knife and attempted to forge the diamond-shaped punch. Although the boy was a skilled model builder, his forged punches were easily detected. It appears that the club, heart and spade shapes would be far more difficult to forge. Within two weeks of the initial forging attempt, a punch was stolen from an aide; in anticipation of that event, a second set of punches had been obtained and was quickly substituted when the theft was reported. The thief continued to use his punch after all others were replaced and thus his and his friend's point books showed punches of the discontinued shape and they were quickly apprehended. There have been no subsequent forgings or thefts, but an additional set of punches has been obtained and the diamond-shaped punch has been permanently retired due to its potential forgeability.

A number of important advantages appear to derive from the described system for point delivery: (1) delivery is very rapid and points may be delivered to many individuals in a few minutes, (2) on a ward with high rates of stealing, these points cannot be stolen, exchanged, or forged. All of these are serious problems whenever a large number of juvenile delinquents are in the care of a very few individuals. (3) Each patient carries his point book at all times so off-ward behavior (*e.g.*, school performance, therapy, promptness to appointments, etc.) can be reinforced without relying on memory or additional communications to record points at a central location. Also, the spending of points can be recorded in the same book, and again at off-ward locations (*e.g.*, canteen, hospital dances, movies, *etc.*). (4) The books are exchanged each week for new ones, and thus provide a record of individual patients' rates of emitting room-cleanup behaviors, ward-cleanup behaviors, and on-time behaviors for classes, therapy, appointments, and medication. (5) The entire system was implemented for a cost of $7.00. Finally, (6) all procedures were carried out by psychiatric aides who had for the most part finished high school but who had no professional training beyond that level. Professional time involved in maintaining the system was approximately 20 hours per week and that was mainly for data summation, which could have been handled by persons with less training had they been available. The amount of professional time required and the ease and simplicity with which untrained persons can use an experimental procedure are important design criteria if a procedure is to be useful beyond a single experimental setting.

These specific advantages of the described token-dispensing procedures combine with the presented data on selected behaviors within the ongoing token system to suggest that token reinforcement can be used to modify the behavior of large wards of institutionalized adolescents.

Note

1. Available from Hoover Educational Equipment, 1511 Baltimore, Kansas City, Missouri for $7 per dozen.

References

AYLLON, T., and AZRIN, N. *The token economy.* New York: Appleton-Century-Crofts, 1968.

COLMAN, A. D., and BOREN, J. J. An information system for measuring patient behavior and its use by staff. *Journal of Applied Behavior Analysis,* 1969, *2,* 207–214.

LOGAN, D. L. A "paper money" token system as a recording aid in institutional settings. *Journal of Applied Behavior Analysis,* 1970, *3,* 183–184.

PHILLIPS, E. L. Achievement Place: token reinforcement procedures in a home-style rehabilitation setting for "pre-delinquent" boys. *Journal of Applied Behavior Analysis,* 1968, *1,* 213–223.

V

Schedules and Checklists

Schedules and checklists are category systems for reporting aspects of behavior that are filled out by the patient or others. The data reported are generally self-reports or observations of others. Although commonly in the form of ratings, the behavioral events thus reported may be based upon response frequencies, durations, or magnitudes. Among the advantages of using schedules and checklists is that data may generally be recorded and scored rapidly.

In the early years of behaviorism, self-reports and reports of others were held in poor repute among behaviorists, especially reports used as indicators of behaviors that could be measured more directly or of hypothetical mental states not amenable to measurement. It is still true, and justifiably so, that most behaviorists and behavior modifiers would prefer direct measurement of a response to reports by the patient or someone else about the behavior. In recent years, however, behavioral researchers and therapists have found that checklists and schedules may be employed selectively to produce useful and, in some cases, indispensable data for research and therapy. Many behavior modifiers who engage in the applied analysis of behavior rely heavily upon reports in which observation schedules are employed and some behavior therapists use selected checklists and schedules as part of patient assessment and evaluation.

Critics of the self-report often overlook two important factors. The first is that self-reports are behaviors and, in some cases, they are themselves the primary responses of interest. This is especially the case when dealing with verbal reports which are "patient labels" that may be applied to the patient's own behavior—such as his level of anxiety, depression, heterosexuality, or homosexuality. When self-reports are verbal behaviors that are themselves the main focus of interest, the question of their validity as indicators of other phenomena is not central. A second factor often overlooked is that self-reports, or for that matter any reports when employed as indicators of other events, have not been shown to be any more unreliable or invalid than other types of measurement, with the possible exception of well-calibrated electro-mechanical devices. Self-reports have been shown to be valid indicators of verifiable information concerning the person (Walsh, 1967, 1968).

Self-reports may also be used as indicants or summaries of more than one event. Hilgard's (1969) research is illustrative here. Using pain-state reports of subjects which were compared with different physiological indicators and pain-inducing stimuli, Hilgard found that pain reported verbally on a simple numerical scale yielded orderly and valid results. The reported pain bore a systematic relationship to the pain stimuli, and the lawfulness of the relationship was supported by the fit of the power function which has been found to hold for other perceptual modalities (Stevens, 1957). In regard to the reports in relationship to the physiological indicators, Hilgard said: "I wish to assert flatly that there is no physiological measure of pain which is either as discriminating of fine differences in stimulus conditions, as reliable upon repetition, or as lawfully related to change conditions, as the subject's verbal report (p. 107)."

Many behavior modification techniques rely upon the dispensation of reinforcers to change behavior. Knowledge of the individual's particular profile of reinforcers may provide essential information that may assist in the selection of potentially reinforcing conditions for use in modification. The individual's reinforcer profile may also specify aspects of the person's difficulty, and it may involve reinforcers, in problems of depression, for example. An instrument that may be used to assess an individual's reinforcer profile is the Reinforcement Survey Schedule (RSS) developed by Cautela and Kastenbaum, which is described in the first selection entitled "A Reinforcement Survey Schedule for Use in Therapy, Training and Research." This article presents a description of and rationale for the four separate sections of the RSS, as well as for the uses of the schedule along with illustrative data. As the authors indicate, the RSS is a self-report checklist which may be employed in practice with individuals and families, in work in institutions, and in research.

Irrational fears and anxieties are among the most commonly encountered problems in clinical practice. The practitioner faces the task of specifying the amount and the areas of fear in those cases in which fear and anxiety are the presenting problems, as well as in other cases in which the practitioner wishes to obtain information concerning the possible relevance of fear. The Fear Survey Schedule (FSS), developed by Wolpe and Lang, is perhaps the most widely used self-report schedule in behavior therapy. In their article entitled "A Fear Survey Schedule for Use in Behavior Therapy" these authors present the FSS based upon 76 self-report items. This FSS is number III and is based upon revisions and extensions of the authors' prior efforts to develop a clinical instrument. The FSS calls for self-ratings of fear or other unpleasant feelings that relate to a variety of anxiety-evoking stimuli, such as those involving animals, tissue damage, illness, death and associated stimuli, classical phobias, social stimuli, and noises, among others.

The next selection, by Landy and Gaupp, is entitled "A Factor Analysis of the Fear Survey Schedule–III." This article is a report on a replicated factor analysis of the FSS. The fear factors that emerged were fear of animate nonhuman organisms, interpersonal events, the unknown, noise, and medical-surgical procedures. As the authors indicate, the results of this study may be used as criteria for selecting subjects, as bases for assessing behavior change in clinical work, and to investigate possible generalization effects in clinical and experimental work. There is another clinical use that might also be mentioned. This involves comparing the individual's profile of fear responses with the factors found here to determine whether similar or different patterns are present for that individual.

In the selection entitled "Some Correlates of Self-Reported Fear" Spiegler and Liebert present findings on fearfulness for males and females in different age groups. The subjects in this study completed the FSS of Wolpe and Lang containing items dealing mainly with unrealistic fears, as well as the authors' Supplementary Fear Questionnaire containing 67 items devoted to realistic fears.[1] The authors found that scores for the realistic fears were as high if not higher than those for the unrealistic fears. The women were found to report more fear than men. Whereas there appeared to be no developmental trend associated with the irrational fears, the rational fears were found to be higher in adolescence and old age as compared with young and middle adulthood. A strong positive relationship between reported fear and social acceptability is also reported.

The selection by Thomas, Walter and O'Flaherty entitled "A Verbal Problem Checklist for Use in Assessing Family Verbal Behavior" presents a checklist that may be used to specify and assess problematic and nonproblematic aspects of marital and parent-child communication. The report presents the categories of the 49-item checklist and describes a three-step procedure by which verbal behavior is presented for response display and rated. Results reported are based upon a sample of clinical couples. Among the findings presented are the ratings for response categories, problem specifications for marital partners, inter-rater and problem category reliability as well as validity. The Verbal Problem Checklist was found to be a rapid, simple, and relatively reliable and accurate instrument to assist in the specification of problems of family verbal behavior.

The final selection, by Rathus, is a paper entitled "A Thirty-Item Schedule for Assessing Assertive Behavior." Problems of assertiveness are frequently encountered in behavior therapy and assertion training is sometimes employed to alter assertive behavior. The schedule reported by Rathus is a self-rating instrument designed to yield information about the individual's assertiveness. The paper also reports inquiries into the reliability, validity, and item analysis for the schedule.

Among other checklists and schedules not included here that may be useful in practice are those of Bentler (1968a; 1968b) for the assessment of heterosexual behavior experience for males and for females.

NOTE

1. The items for the Supplementary Fear Questionnaire are the following: older people, furry animals, going blind, blushing, communism, competition, cold, being crippled, drowning, examinations, being embarrassed, bright light, rats, being lost, germs, going outside, policemen, death of a loved one, psychologists, telephones, reptiles, disease, earthquakes, fog, cancer, dreams, foreigners, mild electric shock, forests, fainting, end of the world, heat, dying, nightmares, being away from home, being poisoned, physical pain, being poor, responsibility, school, storms, sexual behavior, war, unknown, men, ghosts, hospitals, marriage, robbery, spiders, suicide, radiation, going deaf, homosexuality, lawyers, teachers, suffocation, venereal disease, being taken advantage of, loss of temper, women, social gathering, going and staying, violence, shortness of breath, sin, studying. From Document NAPS-00889, ASIS National Auxiliary Publications Service, c/o CCM Corporation, 909 Third Avenue, 21st Floor, New York, New York 10022.

REFERENCES

BENTLER, P. M. Heterosexual behavior assessment—I. Males. *Behaviour Research and Therapy*, 1968, *6*, 21–26 (a).

BENTLER, P. M. Heterosexual behavior assessment—II. Females. *Behaviour Research and Therapy*, 1968, *6*, 27–30 (b).

HILGARD, E. R. Pain as a puzzle for psychology and physiology. *American Psychologist*, 1961, *24*, 103–114.

WALSH, W. B. Validity of self-report. *Journal of Counseling Psychology*, 1967, *14*, 18–23.

WALSH, W. B. Validity of self-report: Another look. *Journal of Counseling Psychology*, 1968, *15*, 180–186.

19

JOSEPH R. CAUTELA
AND ROBERT KASTENBAUM

A Reinforcement Survey Schedule for Use in Therapy, Training, and Research

The assumptions and procedures of behavior therapy differ in many crucial aspects from traditional therapeutic approaches (Eysenck, 1960; Wolpe, 1958). However, in one aspect, psychotherapy based on reciprocal inhibition agrees with a number of therapeutic models. Both the more conventional models and the reciprocal inhibition approach place great emphasis on the concept of anxiety as an explanatory construct. Wolpe (1958, p. 33) defines neurosis as: ". . . any persistent habit of unadaptive behavior acquired by learning in a physiologically normal organism. Anxiety is usually the central constituent of this behavior, being invariably present in the causal situations." Anxiety is reduced by the application of the reciprocal inhibition procedures. These procedures are based upon the assumption that, "if a response antagonistic to anxiety can be made to occur in the presence of anxiety-provoking stimuli so that it is accompanied by a complete or partial suppression of the anxiety responses, then the bond between these stimuli and the anxiety responses will be weakened" (Wolpe, 1958, p. 71).

As can be seen from the above description of neurotic behavior it is important for the therapist employing reciprocal inhibition procedures to identify the stimuli that precede anxiety responses. What is needed is a full picture of the stimulus antecedents of the neurotic reactions. This picture should not only include the identification of the stimuli but also the extent of the anxiety reaction. Many times it is arduous and time consuming to obtain a total view of the anxiety components by use of interview procedures.

Reprinted with permission of author and publisher: Cautela, J. R., & Kastenbaum, R. A. Reinforcement Survey Schedule for use in therapy, training, and research. *Psychological Reports*, 1967, 20, 1115–1130.

Consequently fear survey schedules (Geer, 1965; Wolpe and Lang, 1964) have been developed for use by reciprocal inhibition therapists.

In practice, one often finds that it is also necessary to develop *new* behavior (approach responses) as well as to eliminate unadaptive fear responses. This leads to the necessity for using both reciprocal inhibition and operant conditioning techniques in dealing with many individual cases. As indicated above, reciprocal inhibition procedures require the identification of stimuli which precede anxiety responses. In the employment of operant conditioning techniques it is also important to identify possible reinforcing stimuli. Unless reinforcing stimuli are identified, it is exceedingly difficult to shape new responses. This is equally true concerning the treatment of neurotics in a private clinical setting and the rehabilitation of institutionalized patients.

In operant therapy the crucial procedure is the manipulation of reinforcing stimuli to extinguish unadaptive behavior or shape new responses. Often one finds there are classes of stimuli which seem reinforcing to many individuals, such as smiling and paying attention. There are also idiosyncratic reinforcers, i.e., stimuli that are especially reinforcing to one particular individual. For one person, jazz music may have some reinforcing value; for another person classical music may be reinforcing and jazz music aversive. It would be quite helpful for use in combined reciprocal inhibition and operant conditioning therapeutic approaches to employ a Reinforcement Survey Schedule to identify possible reinforcing stimuli together with their relative reinforcing values. Most of the behavior therapy done with psychotics has employed operant procedures (Ayllon and Michael, 1959) with some success. Operant procedures should also be promising for use with other institutionalized groups such as geriatric patients and juvenile offenders. At present the authors are exploring the use of behavior therapy with geriatric patients and one of the authors (Cautela) is using behavior therapy techniques with delinquents in both group and individual settings.

While the Reinforcement Survey Schedule (RSS) offered here was developed primarily within a behavior therapy model, one need not exclude other theoretical frameworks and empirical applications. It is often assumed, for example, that behavior therapy and developmental theory make a number of mutually incompatible assumptions and have very little subject matter in common. But the RSS can be employed to advantage in either conceptual framework. The RSS is also intended to be useful to investigators who favor an eclectic viewpoint. Although terminology may differ from theory to theory, most psychologists recognize the importance of identifying those stimuli which are associated with the probability of response occurrence. In this paper we are chiefly concerned with those stimuli which can be used to evoke adaptive responses in contrast to stimuli which tend to evoke maladaptive responses (anxiety stimuli).

Description of the Reinforcement Survey Schedule

The RSS is divided into four major sections (see Table 19.1). In the first three sections the respondent is asked to rate items on a five-point scale representing the degree to which the stimuli give joy or other pleasurable feelings. The extreme points of the scale are "not at all" and "very much."

Section I consists of items that actually can be presented to an *S* or client in many conventional settings. Thus, for example, item one, "Eating," includes six specific kinds of food which a therapist might present to his client in the course of a session. There are ten items in Section I, some of which are furthter subdivided. The total number of rating decisions in Section I is 33. An attempt has been made to provide a comprehensive sampling of areas of possible pleasure within the scope of a relatively few items. The items in Section I can be presented in three ways: (1) actually presenting the objects themselves; (2) presenting a facsimile of the object, for example, a picture of a beautiful woman or handsome man; (3) presenting the objects in imagination.

Section II consists of items which, for most practical purposes, can be presented only through facsimile or imagination. Usually these items will be presented in imagination. There are 44 items in Section II, eight of which have sub-categories. The total number of rating decisions is 106. It is obvious that the range of possible stimuli is greatly increased when we include imagination as a means of manipulating stimuli. It is important to note that both reciprocal inhibition procedures and new operant approaches employ the manipulation of covert stimuli (Homme, 1965) as a useful way to influence behavior; also, developmental-field theory gives particular emphasis to the structure of inner-experience as a way of evaluating the level and style of functioning (Kastenbaum, 1965, 1966a).

Although it would be possible to develop a scale with fewer sub-items, it was considered useful to provide information that is reasonably specific so there will be less of a gap between RSS rating and its clinical implementation. For example, it may be only moderately helpful to know a person enjoys reading very much, but quite helpful to know the particular kind of reading that is especially enjoyable, e.g., *True Confessions* or science fiction. Section II items include both active and spectator pursuits, solitary and interpersonal activities. These items encompass objects, people, and psychological states (such as "being perfect"). Some items portray the respondent in an initiating role with respect to other people, while other items portray the person in a recipient role.

Section III differs from the preceding section in that it presents *situations* rather than discrete objects and activities. While experimental procedures often focus upon a single reinforcing stimulus, it is often the case in an individual's daily life that he is confronted with a combination of stimuli and responses from a variety of sources. Most behavior in daily life occurs in "situations." It is, therefore, considered useful to sample a variety of situations or psychosocial fields for their possible reinforcing value, as will be seen below. The analysis of response contingency in relationship to field situations is a particularly important meeting place for behavior theory and developmental-field theory. Section III presents six brief "Situations I would like

TABLE 19.1 *Reinforcement survey schedule*

The items in this questionnaire refer to things and experiences that may give joy or other pleasurable feelings. Check each item in the column that describes how much pleasure it gives you nowadays.

	Not at all	*A little*	*A fair amount*	*Much*	*Very much*
Section I					
1. *Eating*					
a. Ice Cream	____	____	____	____	____
b. Candy	____	____	____	____	____
c. Fruit	____	____	____	____	____
d. Pastry	____	____	____	____	____
e. Nuts	____	____	____	____	____
f. Cookies	____	____	____	____	____
2. *Beverages*					
a. Water	____	____	____	____	____
b. Milk	____	____	____	____	____
c. Soft drink	____	____	____	____	____
d. Tea	____	____	____	____	____
e. Coffee	____	____	____	____	____
3. *Alcoholic Beverages*					
a. Beer	____	____	____	____	____
b. Wine	____	____	____	____	____
c. Hard liquor	____	____	____	____	____
4. *Beautiful Women*	____	____	____	____	____
5. *Handsome Men*	____	____	____	____	____
6. *Solving Problems*					
a. Crossword puzzles	____	____	____	____	____
b. Mathematical problems	____	____	____	____	____
c. Figuring out how something works	____	____	____	____	____
7. *Listening to Music*					
a. Classical	____	____	____	____	____
b. Western/Country	____	____	____	____	____
c. Jazz	____	____	____	____	____
d. Show Tunes	____	____	____	____	____
e. Rhythm & Blues	____	____	____	____	____
f. Rock & Roll	____	____	____	____	____
g. Folk	____	____	____	____	____
h. Popular	____	____	____	____	____
8. *Nude Men*	____	____	____	____	____

(continued next page)

TABLE 19.1 (Cont'd) *Reinforcement survey schedule*

	Not at all	A little	A fair amount	Much	Very much
9. *Nude Women*	____	____	____	____	____
10. *Animals*					
a. Dogs	____	____	____	____	____
b. Cats	____	____	____	____	____
c. Horses	____	____	____	____	____
d. Birds	____	____	____	____	____
Section II					
11. *Watching Sports*					
a. Football	____	____	____	____	____
b. Baseball	____	____	____	____	____
c. Basketball	____	____	____	____	____
d. Track	____	____	____	____	____
e. Golf	____	____	____	____	____
f. Swimming	____	____	____	____	____
g. Running	____	____	____	____	____
h. Tennis	____	____	____	____	____
i. Pool	____	____	____	____	____
j. Other	____	____	____	____	____
12. *Reading*					
a. Adventure	____	____	____	____	____
b. Mystery	____	____	____	____	____
c. Famous People	____	____	____	____	____
d. Poetry	____	____	____	____	____
e. Travel	____	____	____	____	____
f. True Confessions	____	____	____	____	____
g. Politics & History	____	____	____	____	____
h. How to-do-it	____	____	____	____	____
i. Humor	____	____	____	____	____
j. Comic Books	____	____	____	____	____
k. Love Stories	____	____	____	____	____
l. Spiritual	____	____	____	____	____
m. Sexy	____	____	____	____	____
n. Sports	____	____	____	____	____
o. Medicine	____	____	____	____	____
p. Science	____	____	____	____	____
q. Newspapers	____	____	____	____	____
13. *Looking at Interesting Buildings*	____	____	____	____	____
14. *Looking at Beautiful Scenery*	____	____	____	____	____
15. *T.V., Movies or Radio*	____	____	____	____	____
16. *Like to Sing*	____	____	____	____	____
a. Alone	____	____	____	____	____
b. With Others	____	____	____	____	____
17. *Like to Dance*					
a. Ballroom	____	____	____	____	____
b. Discotheque	____	____	____	____	____

(continued next page)

TABLE 19.1 (Cont'd) *Reinforcement survey schedule*

	Not at all	*A little*	*A fair amount*	*Much*	*Very much*
c. Ballet or Interpretive	____	____	____	____	____
d. Square dancing	____	____	____	____	____
e. Folk Dancing	____	____	____	____	____
18. *Performing on a Musical Instrument*	____	____	____	____	____
19. *Playing Sports*					
a. Football	____	____	____	____	____
b. Baseball	____	____	____	____	____
c. Basketball	____	____	____	____	____
d. Track & Field	____	____	____	____	____
e. Golf	____	____	____	____	____
f. Swimming	____	____	____	____	____
g. Running	____	____	____	____	____
h. Tennis	____	____	____	____	____
i. Pool	____	____	____	____	____
j. Boxing	____	____	____	____	____
k. Judo or Karate	____	____	____	____	____
l. Fishing	____	____	____	____	____
m. Skin-diving	____	____	____	____	____
n. Auto or cycle racing	____	____	____	____	____
o. Hunting	____	____	____	____	____
p. Skiing	____	____	____	____	____
20. *Shopping*					
a. Clothes	____	____	____	____	____
b. Furniture	____	____	____	____	____
c. Auto parts & supply	____	____	____	____	____
d. Appliances	____	____	____	____	____
e. Food	____	____	____	____	____
f. New car	____	____	____	____	____
g. New place to live	____	____	____	____	____
h. Sports equipment	____	____	____	____	____
21. *Gardening*	____	____	____	____	____
22. *Playing Cards*	____	____	____	____	____
23. *Hiking or Walking*	____	____	____	____	____
24. *Completing a Difficult Job*	____	____	____	____	____
25. *Camping*	____	____	____	____	____
26. *Sleeping*	____	____	____	____	____
27. *Taking a Bath*	____	____	____	____	____
28. *Taking a Shower*	____	____	____	____	____
29. *Being Right*					
a. Guessing what somebody is going to do	____	____	____	____	____
b. In an argument	____	____	____	____	____
c. About your work	____	____	____	____	____
d. On a bet	____	____	____	____	____
30. *Being Praised*					
a. About your appearance	____	____	____	____	____

(continued next page)

TABLE 19.1 (Cont'd) *Reinforcement survey schedule*

	Not at all	*A little*	*A fair amount*	*Much*	*Very much*
b. About your work	____	____	____	____	____
c. About your hobbies	____	____	____	____	____
d. About your physical strength	____	____	____	____	____
e. About your athletic ability	____	____	____	____	____
f. About your mind	____	____	____	____	____
g. About your personality	____	____	____	____	____
h. About your moral strength	____	____	____	____	____
i. About your understanding of others	____	____	____	____	____
31. *Having People Seek You Out for Company*	____	____	____	____	____
32. *Flirting*	____	____	____	____	____
33. *Having Somebody Flirt with You*	____	____	____	____	____
34. *Talking with People Who Like You*	____	____	____	____	____
35. *Making Somebody Happy*	____	____	____	____	____
36. *Babies*	____	____	____	____	____
37. *Children*	____	____	____	____	____
38. *Old Men*	____	____	____	____	____
39. *Old Women*	____	____	____	____	____
40. *Having People Ask Your Advice*	____	____	____	____	____
41. *Watching Other People*	____	____	____	____	____
42. *Somebody Smiling at You*	____	____	____	____	____
43. *Making Love*	____	____	____	____	____
44. *Happy People*	____	____	____	____	____
45. *Being Close to an Attractive Man*	____	____	____	____	____
46. *Being Close to an Attractive Woman*	____	____	____	____	____
47. *Talking About the Opposite Sex*	____	____	____	____	____
48. *Talking to Friends*	____	____	____	____	____
49. *Being Perfect*	____	____	____	____	____
50. *Winning a Bet*	____	____	____	____	____
51. *Being in Church or Temple*	____	____	____	____	____
52. *Saying Prayers*	____	____	____	____	____
53. *Having Somebody Pray for You*	____	____	____	____	____
54. *Peace and Quiet*	____	____	____	____	____

Section III–Situations I Would Like To Be In

How much would you enjoy being in each of the following situations?

1. You have just completed a difficult job. Your superior comes by and praises you highly for "a job well done." He also makes it clear that such good work is going to be rewarded very soon.

not at all ( ) a little ( ) a fair amount ( ) much ( ) very much ( )

2. You are at a lively party. Somebody walks across the room to you, smiles in a friendly way, and says, "I'm glad to meet you. I've heard so many good things about you. Do you have a moment to talk?"

not at all ( ) a little ( ) a fair amount ( ) much ( ) very much ( )

3. You have just led your team to victory. An old friend comes over and says, "You

(continued next page)

TABLE 19.1 (Cont'd) *Reinforcement survey schedule*

played a terrific game. Let me treat you to dinner and drinks."
not at all ( ) a little ( ) a fair amount ( ) much ( ) very much ( )
4. You are walking along a mountain pathway with your dog by your side. You notice attractive lakes, streams, flowers, and trees. You think to yourself, "It's great to be alive on a day like this, and to have the opportunity to wander alone out in the countryside."
not at all ( ) a little ( ) a fair amount ( ) much ( ) very much ( )
5. You are sitting by the fireplace with your loved one. Music is playing softly on the phonograph. Your loved one gives you a tender glance and you respond with a kiss. You think to yourself how wonderful it is to care for someone and have somebody care for you.
not at all ( ) a little ( ) a fair amount ( ) much ( ) very much ( )
6. As you are leaving your place of worship, a woman turns to you and says, "I want you to know how much we appreciate all that you did for us in our time of trouble and misery. Everything is wonderful now. I'll always remember you in my prayers."
not at all ( ) a little ( ) a fair amount ( ) much ( ) very much ( )

A. Now place a check next to the number of the situation that appeals to you most.

Section IV

List things you do or think about more than:

5	10	15	20 times a day?
______	______	______	______
______	______	______	______
______	______	______	______
______	______	______	______
______	______	______	______
______	______	______	______
______	______	______	______

to be in." Each situation is constructed from at least three specific reinforcing stimuli. For example, Item 1 combines the satisfaction of having completed a difficult job, praise and appreciation from a superior, and a promise of future reward. Table 19.2 details the particular reinforcing stimuli for each situation in Section III. As will be seen in Table 19.2, each situation was constructed to convey a distinct theme.

After responding to each situation separately, *S* is asked to indicate which situation appeals to him the most. From the nature of the items in Section III, it appears obvious that these items will usually be presented in imagination.

In Section IV, *S* is asked to list the things he does or thinks about more than certain designated frequencies from 5 to 20. In practice, we have found that this section may require some elaboration with particular populations. For example, with a number of juvenile offenders the authors found it necessary to give illustrations and examples. This section was included so that

Premack's *Differential Probability Hypothesis* (1959) may be used to manipulate behavior. The *Premack Differential Probability Hypothesis* states that if two responses occur with different probabilities, the response with the highest probability can be used to reinforce the response with the lower probability. For example, if someone smokes 40 cigarettes a day, "high probability," smoking may be made contingent upon reading a page in a book, "low probability." These responses may include thoughts, activities such as walking, aggressive behavior, or derogatory remarks made to oneself. If these responses are available to the therapist or researcher they can be used to increase the probability of behavior that has a low frequency. In the geriatric population, putting one's feet on the floor can be a low probability response which has to occur before the person takes a drink of water. This

TABLE 19.2 *Percentage of extreme responses for situational themes and respective components for Section III*

Situation No.	*Theme*	M *of specific reinforcers*		*Specific reinforcers*	
1.	Occupational Success 80.6	74.6	(24)*	Completion of difficult job	69.1
			(30/b)	Praise: About your work	80.0
2.	Favorable Social Attention 70.3	65.1	(42)	Somebody smiling at you	80.6
			(31)	Somebody seeking you out for company	56.4
			(30)	Heard so many good things about you	58.4
3.	Successful Competitive Performance 64.8	44.4	(19)	Playing a sport	30.2
			(30/e)	Praise: About your athletic ability	43.6
			(31)	Sought out for company	86.6
			(3)	Promise of food (1) and drink	35.8
4.	Pleasure from Nature 69.1	56.1	(23)	Hiking or walking	38.2
			(14)	Looking at beautiful scenery	70.3
			(10a)	Accompanied by your dog	54.5
			(54)	Peace and quiet	61.2
5.	Loving Intimacy 91.5	66.5	(46)	Close to your loved one	74.5
			(7)	Listening to music	40.7
			(43)	Making love	84.2
6.	Faith and Good Works 51.5	51.3	(51)	Coming from place of worship	23.6
			(35)	Making somebody happy, and helping them	92.1
			(53)	Having somebody pray for you	38.2

*Numbers in parentheses refer to specific reinforcers that are also presented as items in Sections I or II of the RSS.

section can be particularly valuable in teaching the patient self-control responses and also in establishing therapeutic activity which can occur in the absence of the researcher or therapist.

Administration of Scale

The RSS is given either individually or in group settings. When *S*s present problems in comprehension or communication, it is suggested that the size of the group be reduced. The authors' experiences suggest that administration time for college students is approximately 20 minutes and for juvenile offenders approximately 30 minutes. The extra time needed for juvenile offenders is for definition of items. This is especially true with youthful offenders from 12 to 17 of average intelligence. For certain populations who are illiterate or unable to read the questionnaire for one reason or another, the test has to be administered orally. In our experience a minimum of seventh-grade education is needed to have a fairly good comprehension of the questionnaire. It is recommended that the scale (RSS) be administered to children of high school age or younger only with the knowledge and consent of parents or guardians.

Illustrative Data

The RSS was administered to 111 male undergraduates and 54 female undergraduates. A chi-square analysis for the frequency of choice for each response category showed no significant difference ($p > .05$, $N = 165$), i.e., there was no tendency to pick any one category, such as "a fair amount," over any other category.

Comparisons of Sections I, II, and III of the RSS reveal some interesting data with respect to percentage of choice for each response category.

Section I, which consists of palpable or concrete items, has a lesser percentage of "very much" responses as compared with Section II, which contains mostly items that would involve symbolic manipulation. Preliminary data from a population of juvenile offenders indicate a greater percentage of "very much" choices for Section I over Section II. It appears from these data that Section I-type items are more effective reinforcers for delinquents than are Section II-type items. Just the reverse seems to be the case for college undergraduates. These results are consistent with investigations that report primary reinforcers to be more effective for delinquent as compared with nondelinquent populations (Johns and Quay, 1962; Bandura, 1961). Time perspective research also has revealed a similar tendency for delinquent youths to be relatively less oriented toward goals and gratifications in the future and relatively more oriented toward immediate gratifications and tension release (Barndt and Johnson, 1955). One might expect that preference for Section I over Section II items would be characteristic of culturally deprived and less mature individuals as might be predicted from data on time perspectives (LeShan, 1952; Kastenbaum, 1966b).

It can also be seen from Table 19.3 that the percentage of choice for the "very much" items for Section III is greater than Sections I and II combined. This finding is probably associated with three factors: (1) In each of the Section III situations there are a number of possible reinforcing items. It appears that the items in these situations have a cumulative effect, although perhaps not simply additive. (2) The situations require more imaginative manipulation than do the items in either Section I or Section II. (3) Presentation of a number of discrete reinforcing items in the form of a unified story may constitute a "reinforcing field." This "reinforcing field" might be regarded as somewhat analogous to a Gestalt grouping. The reinforcing value of each item is determined by its position within a (symbolic) configuration as well as its reinforcing value as established without consideration of context. From a developmental standpoint, one would expect relatively mature individuals to respond to a larger variety of reinforcing fields than would relatively immature individuals. The implication of the relatively greater choice of the "very much" response category for Section III is that a reinforcing field probably would be more effective in shaping behavior than discrete presentations of reinforcing stimuli. The present findings tend to support the value of emotive imagery in counterconditioning. As previously noted, the use of emotive imagery involves the presentation of reinforcing stimuli symbolically within a vignette.

TABLE 19.3 *Per cent of choice for each response category for males and females*

Section *N*	*No response*	*Not at all*	*Little*	*Fair amount*	*Much*	*Very much*	*Much and very much* 2
I $N = 165$	1.4	16.4	22.7	26.2	19.7	13.6	16.6
M = 111	1.1	15.1	23.3	28.1	20.3	12.1	16.2
F = 54	2.0	19.7	21.0	23.0	17.6	16.7	17.1
II $N = 165$	1.5	17.6	17.4	23.2	20.0	20.2	20.1
M = 111	1.1	16.0	18.6	24.2	22.1	18.1	20.1
F = 54	2.0	22.3	15.0	20.7	15.8	24.2	20.0
III $N = 165$	0.0	2.3	11.0	15.4	26.7	44.6	35.7
M = 111	0.0	2.9	11.3	17.4	28.0	40.4	34.2
F = 54	0.0	11.2	10.2	11.1	24.1	53.4	38.8
M_M	.73	11.33	17.03	23.23	23.47	23.50	23.49
M_F	1.33	14.40	23.15	18.27	19.17	31.43	25.30
$M_{Tot.}$	1.03	12.87	20.09	20.75	21.32	27.47	24.39

A comparison of male and female responses for each category, as presented in Table 19.3, indicates that the females tend to choose a greater percentage of "very much" responses for each of the three sections. The greatest difference occurs for Section III. Although there is no obvious explanation for the differences in male and female responses on the "very much" category, some speculation can be offered in this regard. Perhaps there is no "real" difference in choice, but the females might be less inhibited in expressing extreme response choices, in keeping with more liberal cultural sanctions for expressing affect by women than for men. Perhaps, however, the sex differences in response are related to a relatively greater dependency on vicarious satisfactions through wishing and fantasy behavior on the part of women who, in Western culture, have not been allowed as many sources of satisfaction as the male.

Clues to the differential reinforcing value of different kinds of people may also be found in the RSS data. The present findings, for example, suggest that Old Men (Sec. II, Item 38)and Old Women (Sec. II, Item 39) have rather little value as positive reinforcers for the behavior of young adults. "A little" and "a fair amount" were the most frequently cited response categories for both of these items. By contrast, "very much" and "much" were the two most popular responses for Items 36 and 37: Babies and Children. Furthermore, Old Men and Old Women were less preferred than Dogs (Sec. I, Item 10-A), although slightly more than Birds (10-D) and Cats (10-C).

These findings tend to support a recent study which found that the "psychological distance" between the efforts one would make to save a young man and an old man was significantly greater than the distance between an old man and a pet dog or cat (Kastenbaum, 1964). The situation that is suggested by these illustrative data require more extended discussion than what can be offered here. It might simply be noted that the RSS could serve as a measure of attitude change toward the aged before and after particular individuals are exposed to desensitization concerning the aged. Additionally, the young adults who presently find old men and old women to be without much reinforcement value will one day themselves fall into these categories —a circumstance that holds rich theoretical and empirical possibilities.

References

Ayllon, T. and Michael, J. The psychiatric nurse as a behavioral engineer. *J. Exp. Anal. Behav.*, 1959, *2*, 323–334.

Bandura, A. Psychotherapy as a learning process. *Psychol. Bull.*, 1961, *58*, 143–159.

Barndt, R. J. and Johnson, D. M. Time orientation in delinquents. *J. Abnorm. Soc. Psychol.*, 1955, *51*, 589–592.

Eysenck, H. J. *Behaviour therapy and the neuroses*. Oxford: Pergamon, 1960.

Geer, J. H. The development of a scale to measure fear. *Behav. Res. Ther.*, 1965, *3*, 45–54.

Goldstein, K. The mental changes due to frontal lobe damage. *J. Psychol.*, 1944, 187–208.

HOMME, L. E. Perspectives in psychology: XXIV. Control of coverants, the operants of the mind. *Psychol. Rec.*, 1965, *15*, 501–511.

JOHNS, P. and QUAY, R. The effect of social reward on verbal conditioning in psychopathic and neurotic military offenders. *J. Consult. Psychol.*, 1962, *26*, 217–220.

KASTENBAUM, R. The interpersonal context of death in a geriatric hospital. Paper read at the 17th Annual Meeting, Gerontological Society, 1964, New York.

KASTENBAUM, R. Engrossment and perspective in later life: a developmental-field approach. In R. Kastenbaum (Ed.), *Contributions to the psychobiology of aging*. New York: Springer, 1965.

KASTENBAUM, R. Developmental-field theory and the aged person's inner experience. *Geron.*, 1966, *6*, 10–13. (a)

KASTENBAUM, R. The meaning of time in later life. *J. Genet. Psychol.*, 1966, *109*, 9–25. (b)

KOGAN, N. and SHELTON, F. C. Beliefs about "older people:" a comparative study of older and younger samples. *J. Genet. Psychol.*, 1962, *100*, 93–111.

LAZARUS, A. and ABRAMOWITZ, A. The use of "emotive imagery" in the treatment of children's phobias. *J. Ment. Sci.*, 1962, *108*, 191–195.

LESHAN, L. L. Time orientation and social class. *J. Abnorm. Soc. Psychol.*, 1952, *47*, 589–592.

PREMACK, D. Toward empirical behavior laws: I. Positive reinforcement. *Psychol. Rev.*, 1959, *66*, 219–233.

WOLPE, J. *Psychotherapy by reciprocal inhibition.* Stanford: Stanford Univer. Press, 1958.

WOLPE, J. and LANG, P. A fear survey schedule for use in behavior therapy. *Behav. Res. Ther.*, 1964, *2*, 27–30.

20

JOSEPH WOLPE AND
PETER J. LANG

A Fear Survey Schedule for Use in Behavior Therapy

Behavior therapy (or conditioning therapy) is the use of techniques based on experimentally tested principles of learning to overcome persistent unadaptive habits. It has been mainly applied to the treatment of neuroses (Wolpe, 1958; Eysenck, 1960; Rachman, 1963), which, there is now good reason to believe, are persistent, unadaptive habits—most often autonomic habits of an anxiety response pattern. In all cases, it is a necessary preliminary to have a full picture of the stimulus antecedents of the neurotic reactions. While many such antecedents are easily discernible, and indeed may be brought forward by the patient among his presenting complaints, others may be quite obscure, recognized only after a great deal of questioning and observing the patient—and sometimes not even then.

The idea of determining anxiety stimuli through an inventory was, it seems, first put forward several years ago by Dixon, De Monchaux, and Sandler (1957). The present instrument was directly suggested and partly derived from a Fear Survey Schedule (FSS-I).[1] This FSS was developed to assess change in phobic behavior and generalized anxiety in experimental studies of desensitization psychotherapy (Lang and Lazovik, 1963). A second experimental form (FSS-II) has since been constructed from the responses of a college population, and a factor analysis, as well as a study of the schedule's relationship to several personality scales, has been completed (Geer, 1963).

The revised and extended schedule presented here has been designed for clinical use. It includes the most frequent neurotic anxiety stimuli that have been encountered in patients in the course of 15 years of practice of be-

Reprinted with permission of Pergamon Press, from *Behaviour Research and Therapy*, 1964, Vol. 2, pp. 27–30.

havior therapy. It provides a clinical means of surveying a wide range of reasonably common sources of disturbed reactions in a very short time. It will be noted that, without exception, the stimulus situations forming the content of the inventory are situations to which it is unadaptive for a person to have anything more than a mild anxiety (except perhaps under very special circumstances): and a persistent habit of responding with considerable anxiety in any such situation is by definition neurosis (Wolpe, 1954, 1958).

After each item in the schedule shown here there is a letter in parentheses which refers to a subclassification of the item—A for animal; T for tissue damage illness, death or associated stimuli; C for other classical phobias; S for social stimuli; N for noises; and M for miscellaneous. (These letters are not included in the forms given to patients.) Table 20.1 shows how the items are distributed into these subclasses. A few items really fit into more than one subclass and arbitrary decisions about their placement have been made. However, the classification is given mainly to facilitate clinical use and is in no sense definitive. A formal, statistical analysis of the scale is planned.

TABLE 20.1 *Distribution of classes of anxiety-evoking stimuli in the inventory*

Animal	9
Social or interpersonal	17
Tissue damage, illness and death, and their associations	18
Noises	4
Other classical phobias	16
Miscellaneous	8
Strange places, falling, failure, imaginary creatures, strange shapes, feeling angry, dull weather, making mistakes.	

Though the schedule is of general use in behavior therapy, irrespective of which of the many available techniques are employed, it is likely to be found most often relevant to systematic desensitization (the piecemeal deconditioning of thematically related neurotic habits, using imagined stimuli against a background of deep muscle relaxation [Wolpe, 1958, 1961]). It must again be stated (cf. Wolpe, 1963)that it is unsatisfactory for any therapy to be administered by persons untutored in its principles and untrained in its methods. Nevertheless, in the present lack of training facilities some therapists may feel justified in trying out the methods in some of their cases on the principle that half a loaf is better than no bread. But inventories and other aids are no substitute for the skill of the therapist.

TABLE 20.2 *Fear survey schedule (FSS-III)*

The items in this questionnaire refer to things and experiences that may cause fear or other unpleasant feelings. Write the number of each item in the column that describes how much you are disturbed by it nowadays.

	Not at all	*A little*	*A fair amount*	*Much*	*Very much*
1. Noise of vacuum cleaners (N)					
2. Open wounds (T)					
3. Being alone (C)					
4. Being in a strange place (M)					
5. Loud voices (N)					
6. Dead people (T)					
7. Speaking in public (S)					
8. Crossing streets (C)					
9. People who seem insane (T)					
10. Falling (M)					
11. Automobiles (C)					
12. Being teased (S)					
13. Dentists (T)					
14. Thunder (C)					
15. Sirens (N)					
16. Failure (M)					
17. Entering a room where other people are already seated (S)					
18. High places on land (C)					
19. People with deformities (T)					
20. Worms (A)					
21. Imaginary creatures (M)					
22. Receiving injections (T)					
23. Strangers (S)					
24. Bats (A)					
25. Journeys (C)					
a—Train					
b—Bus					
c—Car					
26. Feeling angry (M)					
27. People in authority (S)					
28. Flying insects (A)					
29. Seeing other people injected (T)					
30. Sudden noises (N)					
31. Dull weather (M)					
32. Crowds (S)					
33. Large open spaces (C)					
34. Cats (A)					
35. One person bullying another (T)					
36. Tough looking people (S)					
37. Birds (A)					
38. Sight of deep water (C)					
39. Being watched working (S)					
40. Dead animals (T)					

TABLE 20.2 (Cont'd) *Fear survey schedule (FSS-III)*

	Not at all	*A little*	*A fair amount*	*Much*	*Very much*
41. Weapons (M)					
42. Dirt (C)					
43. Crawling insects (A)					
44. Sight of fighting (T)					
45. Ugly people (S)					
46. Fire (C)					
47. Sick people (T)					
48. Dogs (A)					
49. Being criticized (S)					
50. Strange shapes (M)					
51. Being in an elevator (C)					
52. Witnessing surgical operations (T)					
53. Angry people (S)					
54. Mice (A)					
55. Blood (T)					
a—Human					
b—Animal					
56. Parting from friends (S)					
57. Enclosed places (C)					
58. Prospect of a surgical operation (T)					
59. Feeling rejected by others (S)					
60. Airplanes (C)					
61. Medical odors (T)					
62. Feeling disapproved of (S)					
63. Harmless snakes (A)					
64. Cemeteries (T)					
65. Being ignored (S)					
66. Darkness (C)					
67. Premature heart beats (missing a beat) (T)					
68. (*a*) Nude men (S)					
(*b*) Nude women					
69. Lightning (C)					
70. Doctors (T)					
71. Making mistakes (M)					
72. Looking foolish (S)					

NOTE

1. Although scored differently, the original FSS instructions and items are part of an inventory constructed by Akutagawa (1956).

REFERENCES

AKUTAGAWA, D. *A Study in Construct Validity of the Psychoanalytic Concept of Latent Anxiety and a Test of a Projection Distance Hypothesis.* Ph.D. thesis, University of Pittsburgh, 1956.

DIXON, J. J., DE MONCHAUX, C., and SANDLER, J. Patterns of anxiety: the phobias. *Brit. J. Med. Psychol.* 1957, *30,* 34–40.

EYSENCK, H. J. (Ed.) *Behaviour Therapy and the Neuroses.* New York: Pergamon Press, 1960.

GEER, J. H. Personal communication, 1963.

LANG, P. J. and LAZOVIK, A. D. Experimental desensitization of a phobia. *J. Abnorm. (soc.) Psychol.*, 1963, *66*, 519–525.

RACHMAN, S. An introduction to behaviour therapy. *Behav. Res. Ther.*, 1963, *1*, 3–15.

WOLPE, J. Reciprocal inhibition as the main basis of psychotherapeutic effects. *Arch. Neurol. Psychiat.*, 1954, *72*, 205–226.

WOLPE, J. *Psychotherapy by Reciprocal Inhibition.* Stanford: Stanford University Press, 1958.

WOLPE, J. The systematic desensitization treatment of neurosis. *J. Nerv. Ment. Dis.*, 1961, *132*, 189–203.

WOLPE, J. Behavior therapy in complex neurotic states. *Brit. J. Psychiat.*, 1964, *110*, 28–34.

21

FRANK J. LANDY AND
LARRY A. GAUPP

A Factor Analysis of the Fear Survey Schedule-III

The assessment of change in avoidance behavior and its generalized effects in experimental analogue research of behavior therapy has led to the development of the Fear Survey Schedule (FSS-I, Lang and Lazovik, 1963; FSS-II, Geer, 1963; and, FSS-III, Wolpe and Lang, 1964). While the FSS-I and FSS-II were designed for experimental use and have been statistically analyzed (Rubin *et al.*, 1968) the FSS-III was ostensibly designed for clinical application. However, the FSS-III has since been employed in experimental analogue research despite the lack of a formal statistical analysis of the schedule.

The FSS-III is a revised and extended version of the FSS-II and includes frequently encountered anxiety stimuli. The 76 items were subclassed into six categories as determined on the basis of face validity [i.e., animal (A), tissue damage illness, death or associated stimuli (T), classical phobias (C), social stimuli (S), noises (N), and miscellaneous (M)]. Experimentally, subscores based on the above categorization have been used as criteria for subject selection, to assess behavior change and to examine generalization effects of treating a target symptom.

Based on present usage of the FSS-III, as well as its potential value, it was felt that a description of the factor structure of the schedule would be useful.[1]

Method

The *S*s were 494 male and female students enrolled in the introductory psychology course at The Pennsylvania State University. Course credit was offered for the completion of the FSS-III. The response rate was approxi-

Reprinted with permission from Pergamon Press, from *Behaviour Research and Therapy,* 1971, Vol. 9, No. 2, pp. 89–93.

mately 80 per cent. Responses were made using a five-point Likert type format ranging from "Not At All" to "Very Much" fearful.

RESULTS

Due to the size of the schedule (77 items, item 70 was made into two items), neither the intercorrelation matrix nor the complete rotated factor loading matrix will be presented. Since it is the feeling of the authors that the interpretation of factors might be influenced by chance relationships in an unreplicated factor analysis, the questionnaire was administered to two independent samples of subjects and a separate factor analysis was done for each. This check on factor structure enables one to discuss underlying dimensions with a greater degree of assurance.

The factor solution consisted of a principal components factor analysis with unities appearing in the diagonal. A Varimax rotation was applied to the solution (Kaiser, 1958). The termination of factoring was determined by a Scree test (Cattell, 1966).

In the primary sample (Sample 1), a variable was considered to load on a factor if it had loading greater than 0.40 on that factor and no loading greater than 0.40 on any other factor. The loading for each of these variables was then examined in sample 2. Those loadings greater than 0.40 are reported in the column to the right of the primary sample loadings. The items, their loadings and the subclass as determined by Wolpe and Lang (1964) for the two samples appear in Tables 21.1–21.5.

TABLE 21.1 *Items and rotated factor loadings for Factor 1*

Item		*Sample 1**	*Sample 2†*
6.	Dead people	0.45	
20.	Worms (A)	0.67	0.52
24.	Bats (A)	0.63	0.74
30.	Flying insects (A)	0.45	0.53
36.	Cats	0.50	
39.	Birds	0.43	
42.	Dead animals	0.57	0.59
43.	Weapons (M)	0.51	0.49
45.	Crawling insects (A)	0.57	0.64
48.	Fire	0.44	
56.	Mice (A)	0.73	0.68
65.	Harmless snakes (A)	0.55	0.61
66.	Cemeteries (T)	0.57	0.55
70.	Nude men	0.45	
72.	Lightning	0.41	
	% Total variance	21%	

* $n = 319$.
† $n = 175$.

TABLE 21.2 *Items and rotated factor loadings for Factor 2*

Item		*Sample 1*	*Sample 2*
12.	Being teased (S)	0.47	0.57
16.	Failure (M)	0.64	0.61
41.	Being watched working (S)	0.42	0.54
47.	Ugly people	0.52	
49.	Sick people (T)	0.42	0.46
51.	Being criticized (S)	0.72	0.59
55.	Angry people (S)	0.42	0.49
59.	Parting from friends (S)	0.44	0.48
61.	Feeling rejected by others (S)	0.73	0.70
64.	Feeling disapproved of (S)	0.74	0.75
67.	Being ignored (S)	0.68	0.69
74.	People with deformities	0.53	
75.	Making mistakes (M)	0.72	0.61
76.	Looking foolish (S)	0.78	0.66
	% Total variance	6%	

TABLE 21.3 *Items and rotated factor loadings for Factor 3*

Item		*Sample 1*	*Sample 2*
3.	Being alone (C)	0.41	0.40
4.	Being in a strange place (M)	0.58	0.43
8.	Crossing streets (C)	0.41	0.49
11.	Automobiles (C)	0.45	0.45
14.	Thunder (C)	0.43	0.61
17.	Entering a room where other people are already seated	0.43	
21.	Imaginary creatures (M)	0.41	0.48
23.	Strangers	0.56	
35.	Large open spaces	0.45	
40.	Sight of deep water (C)	0.41	0.46
63.	Airplanes (C)	0.42	0.43
68.	Darkness (C)	0.49	0.54
	% Total variance	4%	

The factor analysis could have been carried out to twelve factors using a different set of criteria for the termination of factor extraction, but the additional seven factors would have collectively accounted for less than 9 per cent of the total variance.

DISCUSSION

In discussing the factors which appear, factor structure will be considered as a function of those significant loadings which are replicated over the two samples.

TABLE 21.4 *Items and rotated factor loadings for Factor 4*

Item		*Sample 1*	*Sample 2*
1.	Noise of vacuum cleaners (N)	0.50	0.56
5.	Loud voices (N)	0.65	0.41
25.	Journeys by train (C)	0.42	0.72
26.	Journeys by bus (C)	0.66	0.57
28.	Feeling angry	0.51	
34.	Crowds	0.40	
37.	One person bullying another	0.51	
44.	Dirt	0.43	
46.	Sight of fighting	0.42	
	% Total variance	4%	

TABLE 21.5 *Items and rotated factor loadings for Factor 5*

Item		*Sample 1*	*Sample 2*
2.	Open wounds (T)	0.55	0.63
18.	High places on land	0.49	
19.	Looking down from high places	0.49	
22.	Receiving injections (T)	0.57	0.54
31.	Seeing other people injected (T)	0.60	0.60
54.	Witnessing surgical operations (T)	0.61	0.68
57.	Human blood/animal blood (T)	0.56	0.70
60.	Prospect of a surgical operation (T)	0.44	0.56
62.	Medical odors (T)	0.40	0.43
73.	Doctors (T)	0.56	0.43
	% Total variance	4%	

Factor 1. This factor seems fairly well defined. It deals primarily with fear of animate, nonhuman organisms which might best be described as culturally instilled and culturally accepted fears. Factor 1 seems to account for the lion's share of the variance, as one might suspect based on the prevalence of experimental research dealing with phobic reactions related to these objects.

Factor 2. Again, this factor seems fairly clear-cut. It describes a form of interpersonal anxiety, the strongest variables being those of failure, criticism, and rejection. The percentage of variance accounted for is considerably smaller than that of the first factor, indicating that it is a lot less general, i.e., holds less sway over "anxiety responses" as mainfested in the FSS-III. The same is true for the next three factors.

Factor 3. This factor, though more difficult to interpret, seems to describe a fear of the unknown which may involve magical thinking, i.e., the fear that the unknown may bring about some misfortune or catastrophe.

Factor 4. Again, it is difficult to interpret the factor. It may be that the analysis of the primary sample capitalized on chance relationships and there is really nothing to interpret. On the surface, it appears that the common variables (items 1, 5, 25, and 26) are tied together by the dimension of noise. In cases like this, the strategy of replication of factor structure shows its worth.

Factor 5. This factor is clearly a fear of medical-surgical procedures. On the basis of variance accounted for (4 per cent) this appears to be a rather specific fear.

While it is interesting and potentially useful to know the factor structure of the FSS-III, it should ultimately be shown that the described factors have some utility in the classification of individuals. With this in mind, the scales were incorporated into ongoing research being conducted with a roach-phobic sample. The FSS-III was administered to 26 subjects who characterized themselves as roach-phobics and 26 subjects randomly selected from a "normal" population. Factor scores were computed for both groups on Factor 1 (fear of animate, nonhuman organisms). The hypothesis tested was that the phobic subjects would manifest significantly greater mean factor scores than normals. The factor score for each individual consisted of the unweighted sum of the nine replicated items in Table 21.1. The hypothesis was supported. The phobic group had significantly greater factor scores than the normals ($t = 1.85, p < 0.05$).

The data dealing with the roach-phobic subjects is similar to getting your first kiss from an ugly girl—it's comforting, but nothing to brag about. It points out the strategies which must be used to anchor the factors and capitalize on their predictive potential. Work is currently being carried on to determine the utility of the factors for the assessment of treatment effects.

One thing is clear about the FSS-III—there are a very large number of specific factors embedded within its 77 items and one is both clinically and statistically ill-advised to depend on a logical grouping of items in selecting subjects, assessing behavior change, and investigating generalization effects.

Note

1. This research was supported, in part, by a grant from the Pennsylvania State University, College of Liberal Arts Central Fund for Research.

References

Cattell, R. B. The meaning and strategic use of factor analysis. In R. B. Cattell (Ed.), *Handbook of Multivariated Experimental Psychology*. Chicago: Rand-McNally, 1966.

Geer, J. H. The development of a scale to measure fear, *Behav. Res. & Therapy*, 1965, *3*, 45–53.

Kaiser, H. F. The varimax criterion for analytic rotation in factor analysis, *Psychometrika*, 1958, *23*, 187–200.

LANG, P. J. and LAZOVIK, A. D. Experimental desensitization of a phobia, *J. abnorm. soc. Psychol.*, 1963, *66*, 519–525.

RUBIN, B. M., KATKIN, E. S., WEISS, B. W., and EFRAN, J. S. Factor analysis of a fear survey schedule, *Behav. Res. & Therapy*, 1968, *6*, 65–75.

WOLPE, J. and LANG, P. J. A fear survey schedule for use in behavior therapy, *Behav. Res. & Therapy*, 1964, *2*, 27–30.

22

MICHAEL D. SPIEGLER AND
ROBERT M. LIEBERT

Some Correlates of Self-Reported Fear

Recent investigations of college students' self-reported fear have shown that such self-descriptions are relatively reliable (Geer, 1965), have some predictive power with respect to behavioral measures (Geer, 1965; Lanyon and Manosevitz, 1966), correlate moderately with instruments which purport to measure conceptually related dispositions (Geer, 1965; Grossberg and Wilson, 1965), and show that men regularly report themselves to be less fearful than women (Geer, 1965; Grossberg and Wilson, 1965; Manosevitz and Lanyon, 1965). The self-reported fear of persons other than college students and assessment of fears relating to the realistic stresses of modern life are among the important problems to which little research has been directed. The present study was specifically designed to initiate exploration of these two issues.[1]

METHOD

Self-Report Fear Inventory

Recent research on self-reported fear has been dominated by a series of so-called Fear Survey Schedules, substantially overlapping in item content. The latest and most extensive of these has been developed by Wolpe and Lang and referred to as the Fear Survey Schedule-III (FSS-III; Wolpe and Lang, 1964). The FSS-III, like its predecessors, is said to name "situations to which it is unadaptive for a person to have anything more than mild anxiety"

Reprinted with permission of author and publisher: Spiegler, M. D. & Liebert, R. M. Some correlates of self-reported fear. *Psychological Reports,* 1970, 26, 691–695.

(Wolpe and Lang, 1964, p. 27). It is presumably for this reason that the FSS-III does not include a large number of situations which may realistically produce fear. For example, cancer, war, physical pain, and death are among the potentially fear-provoking situations not represented on the FSS-III. Thus, the 145-item self-report fear inventory used in the present study was composed of both the FSS-III (78 items; Wolpe and Lazarus, 1966) and a 67-item Supplementary Fear Questionnaire. While the FSS-III focuses primarily on unrealistic fears, the Supplementary Fear Questionnaire focuses predominantly on realistic ones. *S*s, in groups of varying size, respond anonymously to the inventory by indicating their degree of fear for each item by selecting one of five alternates: "Not at all," "A little," "A fair amount," "Much," and "Very much." These responses were assigned the scores 0, 1, 2, 3, and 4, respectively.

Sample

In an effort to explore as large an age range as seemed feasible with a self-report inventory, volunteers were drawn from high school, college, and various civic and social organizations. The total sample was comprised of 349 *S*s, 160 males and 189 females, ranging in age from 13 to 85 years. The sample was divided into four age groups, each representing a recognized period of life in our culture. Group I, to be called *Adolescents,* consisted of persons who ranged in age from 13 to 18 years; Group II to be called *Young Adults,* included persons between the ages of 19 and 30 years; Group III, called *Adults,* contained individuals between 31 and 47 years; and Group IV, called *Senior Citizens,* was composed of *S*s whose ages ranged from 60 to 85 years.

RESULTS

Reliability

Coefficient alpha was computed for the two subscales as a measure of their internal consistency. For the FSS-III, Pearsonian $r = .946$ (which is virtually the same as that reported by Geer [1965]) and for the Supplementary Fear Questionnaire, $r = .953$, indicating that both subscales possess high internal consistency reliability.

Self-reported Fear as a Function of Age and Sex

Total fear scores were obtained by summing the scores for the items on each subscale and were examined by 2×4 analyses of variance. The mean fear scores for all groups on the FSS-III and the Supplementary Fear Questionnaire are presented in Fig. 22.1.

For the FSS-III (Fig. 22.1a), a significant main effect for sex was obtained ($F = 26.81$, $df = 1/341$, $p < .0001$), with males reporting less fear than females. However, for these predominantly unrealistic fears, no significant effect for age was found ($F < 1.00$), and the Age × Sex interaction was not significant ($F = 1.21$, $df = 3/341$). In contrast, for the predominantly realistic fears (Supplementary Fear Questionnaire, Fig. 22.1b), a clear developmental pattern is apparent. Significant effects for age ($F = 6.42$, $df = 3/341$, $p < .0005$) and sex ($F = 4.84$, $df = 1/341$, $p < .03$) were obtained, as well as a significant interaction ($F = 2.62$, $df = 3/341$, $p < .05$). For both

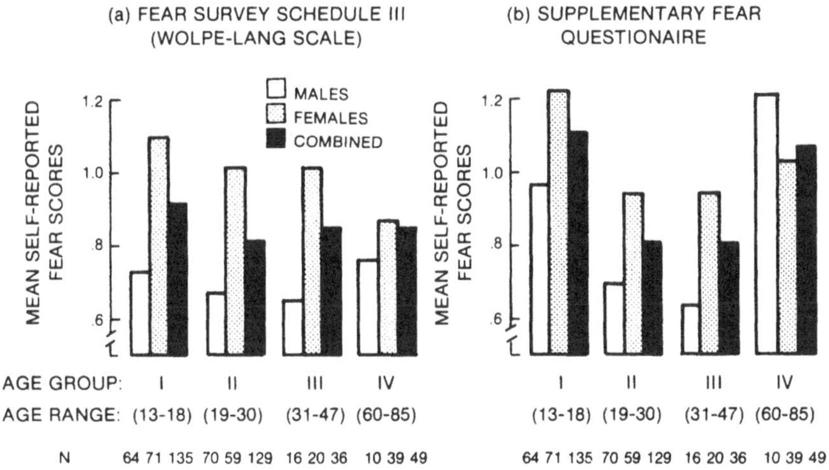

FIGURE 22.1 *Mean fear scores for all groups on the FSS-III and supplementary fear questionnaire.*

sexes, Adolescents reported themselves to be significantly more fearful than Young Adults ($t = 3.36$, $df = 132$, $p < .002$; $t = 3.14$, $df = 128$, $p < .01$; for males and females, respectively),[2] whereas Young Adults and Adults did not differ in their reported fear for either sex. Senior Citizen males reported themselves to be more fearful than Adult males ($t = 2.50$, $df = 24$, $p < .02$). The difference between female Senior Citizens and Adults was in the same direction but was not significant. Males in Groups I, II, and III were found to report significantly less fear than their female counterparts ($t = 2.75$, $df = 133$, $p < .01$; $t = 2.96$, $df = 127$, $p < .01$; $t = 1.99$, $df = 34$, $.10 > p > .05$; for Groups I, II, and III, respectively). However, in contrast to the pattern at earlier ages, Senior Citizen men tended to report themselves as *more* fearful than women of their age, although this apparent reversal was not significant. Thus, in general, there was a U-shaped pattern across the four age groups.

Self-reported Fear and Social Desirability

In order to assess the relationship between self-reported fear and social desirability, ten judges (five male and five female advanced psychology graduate students or research assistants) were asked to rate the 145 items for members of their own sex, in terms of the social desirability or acceptability to fear or feel anxious about each. The ratings were made on a seven-point Likert-style scale similar to that used by Edwards (1957). High agreement between sets of five judges was obtained (Pearsonian *r*s between each judge's ratings and the mean ratings ranged from .60 to .86; for all values $p < .001$, two-tailed). Combining across same-sexed judges, the mean social desirability ratings of the items were correlated with the corresponding mean self-reported fear scores for the two sub-scales. The four correlations obtained were positive and significant (FSS-III—Males: .85, Females: .73; Supplementary Fear Questionnaire—Males: .83, Females: .78; all values $p < .001$). Thus, the more socially acceptable it is to fear something, the higher is the self-reported fear. Additionally, on the FSS-III, the correlation was significantly higher for males than for females ($z = 2.77$, $p < .01$, two-tailed).

Highest Self-reported Fears

Considering the individual items[3] on the self-report inventory, the ten most feared stimuli, for the sample as a whole, were, in descending order: "Death of a loved one," "Cancer," "War," "Going blind," "Failure," "Communism," "Being crippled," "Drowning," "Feeling rejected by others," and "Speaking in public." Of these ten highest fears, three ("Failure," "Feeling rejected by others," and "Speaking in public") came from the FSS-III and the remaining seven from the Supplementary Fear Questionnaire. Of the ten top fears for the entire sample, four were also ranked in the top ten for all age groups and both sexes; these were "Death of a loved one," "Cancer," and "War," the three most feared items overall, and "Communism" which ranked 6.5 overall. None of these four items appeared on the FSS-III.

Discussion

The highly reliable finding that women report more overall fearfulness than men for the greater part of their lives is consistent with cultural stereotypes, with clinical observations (e.g., Noyes and Kolb, 1963), and with empirical studies of self-report fear inventories (e.g., Wilson, 1967). Nevertheless, the origin of the sex difference is far from clear. The magnitude of self-reported fear is highly related to social desirability for all groups, but for the FSS-III this relationship is significantly greater for men than women. It would be of interest to determine whether men are actually less fearful than women or merely report themselves as less fearful. Research which relates behavioral indices of fear with self-report measures is planned to help clarify these issues.

The data concerning realistic fears suggest that individuals experience increased stress at the ages which immediately precede and follow the period of life accompanied by the greatest responsibility and productivity. Adolescents and Senior Citizens in our society are typically somewhat insecure, conflicted with regard to independence-dependence, and somewhat helpless. All of these conditions may serve to elicit new fears and intensify already existing ones. Of particular interest is the tendency for the increase in self-reported fear between Adulthood and Senior Citizenry to be greater for men than for women. This difference may be due to the fact that women in general experience less of a change in their roles as housewives and mothers than do men, who relinquish their primary roles as family providers.

The differences between unrealistic and realistic fears brought out in the present study are intriguing ones. The U-shaped developmental pattern from Adolescent to Senior Citizenry holds only for realistic fears, and, moreover, those stimuli which were reported as most fear-provoking are primarily realistic in nature. Increased attention to some of the more reasonable human fears, which have been long overlooked, appears to be an important direction for future theoretical and applied research.

Finally, it should be noted that a major problem with any cross-sectional study of age differences involves the potential confounding of age with socioeconomic, educational, and intellectual factors. The Adult and Senior Citizen samples used in this study consisted of predominantly white, middle-class natives of an urban area and appeared to be relatively comparable on the dimensions named above. Since the Adolescents were drawn from a private high school and most of the Young Adults were from a comparable college population, it is likely that these latter groups were highly similar to each other but differed in intellectual level from the former ones. However, the overall pattern of results does not appear to be an artifact of these differences.

Notes

1. This study was supported, in part, by NIMH Predoctoral Fellowship MH–40781 and by NIMH Grant FR–05537 to Fels Research Institute. Grateful acknowledgement is made to the following organizations (in Nashville unless otherwise stated) for their generous cooperation: Belmont Pioneers; Belmont Methodist Church; Donelson and Franklin Road Jaycees; Maplewood Hill and Peabody Demonstration schools; Bethlehem, Donelson, Madison, and Williamson County Senior Citizen groups; Golden Age Club, Jewish Community Center; and Wertham Bag Company. Thanks are also due to Linda Chapman, Erika Lichter, Larry W. Morris, and Philip Rolnick for their assistance.

2. All probability levels for individual comparisons are reported two-tailed.

3. A copy of the questionnaire items, listing the means, standard deviations, and ranks of each, may be obtained without charge from either of the authors or by remitting $1 for microfiche or $3 for photocopy for Document NAPS–00889 from the ASIS National Auxiliary Publications Service, c/o CCM Information Corporation, 909 Third Ave., 21st Floor, New York, N. Y. 10022. [Editor's note: The items for the SFQ have been listed in a footnote to the introduction to Part V, Schedules and Check-lists.]

References

EDWARDS, A. L. *The social desirability variable in personality assessment and research*. New York: Dryden, 1957.

GEER, J. H. The development of a scale to measure fear. *Behaviour Research and Therapy*, 1965, *3*, 45–53.

GROSSBERG, J. M. and WILSON, H. K. A correlational comparison of the Wolpe-Lang Fear Survey Schedule and Taylor Manifest Anxiety Scale. *Behaviour Research and Therapy*, 1965,*3*, 125–128.

LANYON, R. I. and MANOSEVITZ, M. Validity of self-reported fear. *Behaviour Research and Therapy*, 1966, *4*, 259–263.

MANOSEVITZ, M. and LANYON, R. I. Fear Survey Schedule: a normative study. *Psychological Reports*, 1965, *17*, 699–703.

NOYES, A. P. and KOLB, L. C. *Modern clinical psychiatry*. Philadelphia: Saunders, 1963.

WILSON, G. D. Social desirability and sex differences in expressed fear. *Behaviour Research and Therapy*, 1967, *5*, 136–137.

WOLPE, J. and LANG, P. J. A Fear Survey Schedule for use in behavior therapy. *Behaviour Research and Therapy*, 1964, *2*, 27–30.

WOLPE, J. and LAZARUS, A. A. *Behavior therapy techniques: a guide to the treatment of neuroses*. New York: Pergamon, 1966.

23

EDWIN J. THOMAS, CLAUDE L. WALTER, AND KEVIN O'FLAHERTY

A Verbal Problem Checklist for Use in Assessing Family Verbal Behavior

The verbal repertoire is perhaps the largest, most complex and most elaborately developed set of human operant responses. Many of the problems of marital partners and parents and children involve the verbal repertoires of the family members. When family members seek help with such problems, the therapist must address the portions of verbal repertoires of two or more individuals that may be intricately patterned and interdependent in the interpersonal relationship. The task of assessment is unusually complex. Furthermore, the family members involved are often unable to describe precisely the problems of verbal behavior for which they seek assistance. Thus clients and patients frequently refer to their family verbal problems simply as "communication difficulties," "family arguments," or as "talking past each other." For his part, the therapist has very few procedures to assist him in specifying behaviorally the verbal responses that may be the focus of modification.

This paper describes one procedure by which the very large number of potential problems of verbal behavior may be rapidly narrowed down and specified behaviorally for purposes of assessment of family verbal behavior. A central part of the procedure is to have the therapist rate a number of categories of possible problematic verbal behavior for each member of the marital couple or family, using a Verbal Problem Checklist (VPC). In addition to the assessment procedure and Checklist, this paper reports illustrative data and initial findings on reliability and validity based upon a study of clinical couples who sought assistance with difficulties of marital communication.[1]

Reprinted with permission of Academic Press, Inc. from *Behavior Therapy,* in press.

Overview of Assessment Procedure

The assessment of verbal behavior requires at least three procedural steps. The first is response display, which makes it possible to obtain samples of the verbal responses of interacting family members for such purposes as specification, measurement and evaluation. The response display consists of having the family members discuss particular topics, such as problems in the marriage (or family), communication problems in the marriage (or family), or the strengths in the marriage (or family). Topics can generally be chosen to enhance the likelihood of obtaining a relevant sample of verbal behavior. Two to four such topics, each discussed for 15 to 20 minutes, are generally enough. The discussions are tape-recorded for subsequent analysis and during the discussions, the therapist withdraws from the room or sits inconspicuously to one side.

Response specification is the second procedural step. Unless this is accomplished with an electromechanical signal system such as SAM (Signal System for the Assessment and Modification of Behavior) (Thomas, Carter, Gambrill and Butterfield, 1970; Thomas, Carter and Gambrill, 1971), or through post-session coding of verbal responses from taped records or transcripts of tapes, the therapist must generally turn to a rating system. The VPC, described below, is a checklist intended for clinical use in the rapid and accurate rating of a number of potentially problematic categories of verbal responding.

The VPC should be completed immediately after the discussion period. During the discussion the therapist can prepare for his subsequent ratings by taking notes and actually counting many of the responses for which ratings are required. He can also record possible patterns between and among the partners and note other problems besides those of communication that may be referred to.

The third step in this procedure is to select the area of behavior for modification. Before working on a given problem of verbal behavior, however, the therapist must rule out the presence of problems not involving verbal behavior alone, such as difficulties of child management, sex, irrational fears and decision making, that could have higher priority than a problem of verbal behavior. Thus the assessment should also include some inquiry into nonverbal problems. If nonverbal problems have lower priority than those of verbal behavior, the task then is to select from among those rated highest the area or areas of verbal responding most deserving modification. At this point there are ordinarily several areas of verbal behavior that might be selected for modification and, often, any one of them could be selected as the first to modify. Illustrative criteria for the selection of one area include the pervasiveness and severity of the surfeit or deficit. These criteria, however, are still being developed.

THE VERBAL PROBLEM CHECKLIST

The categories given below apply to the verbal behavior of the speaker and involve verbal responding of a surfeit or deficit nature that may be potentially problematic. Although the responses embraced by the categories are not functional units, strictly speaking, they are intended to refer to objectively definable referents, to be concretely measurable and to require a minimum of inference on the part of the rater. The categories have been inductively derived in connection with three years of research on family verbal behavior in which target problems were selected for modification on the basis of individualized assessment. Indeed, many of the behaviors to which the categories refer have now been quantified in connection with baselining and modification in single-couple experiments. Even so, the set of categories is not intended to be fixed or final or to preclude individualized specification of the particular verbal problems of the family members.

Rating Procedure

Each family member is rated on each of the 49 categories of verbal response for amount and whether that amount of response is judged to constitute a problem. Ratings of amount range from 1 (not at all), 2 (a slight amount), 3 (a moderate amount), to 4 (a large amount). The problem ratings are 1 (no problem), 2 (for uncertainty of rater), and 3 (for the presence of a problem). After the 49 categories have been rated, the therapist then indicates any particular types of patterning. Finally, recommended areas for modification are recorded, if these are then evident.

The Categories

The 49 categories of response given below are a modification and extension of 27 categories reported in a provisional list by Carter and Thomas (1973). The categories may be grouped into several different types of response. For example, the first ten deal with vocal characteristics of speech (e.g., overtalk, undertalk, fast talk, slow talk). Dysfluent talk (43) and affective and unaffective talk (11 and 12) also deal at least in part with vocal features. Others deal essentially with referent representation and include overgeneralization (20), undergeneralization (21), and several others (23–25 and 32). Still others deal essentially with how much information is given (44–46). Six categories pertain to the speaker's behavior in relationship to the content and embrace such factors as content avoidance (26 and 27), content shifting (28 and 29), content persistence (30 and 31), detached utterance (34), and over-and underresponsiveness (15 and 16). Three of the categories pertain to the control and direction of conversation. These are obtrusions (13), excessive question asking (17) and excessive cueing (22). Finally, the largest number of categories pertains to aspects of the content proper. These involve quibbling (14), pedantry (18), dogmatic statement (19), negative talk (47 and 48), positive talk (35 and 36), acknowledgment (37 and 38), opinion (39 and 40), agreement (41 and 42), illogical talk (49), and temporal remoteness (33).

The category definitions are given below:[2]

1. *Overtalk.* An interactant speaks considerably more than his partner (or others with whom he is interacting), considering the interaction session as a whole.

2. *Undertalk.* An interactant speaks considerably less than his partner (or others with whom he is interacting), considering the interaction as a whole.

3. *Fast talk.* An interactant speaks too rapidly as indicated, for example, by the number of words per second while he is speaking.

4. *Slow talk.* An interactant speaks too slowly, as indicated, for example, by a low number of words per second while he is speaking.

5. *Loud talk.* An interactant speaks too loudly.

6. *Quiet talk.* An interactant speaks too softly so that it is difficult to hear what he says.

7. *Singsong speech.* An interactant speaks with a songlike quality, almost as if he were singing or chanting (e.g., speaking with rhythmic variations of pitch or volume or both).

8. *Monotone speech.* An interactant speaks with little variation of pitch, volume, and inflection for each word or phrase.

9. *Rapid latency.* An interactant speaks very quickly following the speech of another.

10. *Slow latency.* An interactant responds very slowly after another interactant stops speaking.

11. *Affective talk.* An interactant's speech indicates one or a variety of so-called emotional behaviors such as those indicated by crying, whining, screaming, or speaking with a shaky voice. The affective character of the speech is generally judged to be inappropriate to the content.

12. *Unaffective talk.* An interactant speaks without the vocal characteristics ordinarily associated with the content of what is being said.

13. *Obtrusions.* An interactant too frequently makes utterances while another is speaking. Such intrusions become interruptions if they produce an immediate and apparently premature termination of the speech by the other.

14. *Quibbling.* An interactant endeavors to explicate, clarify, or dispute a minor, tangential, and irrelevant detail.

15. *Overresponsiveness.* An interactant speaks too long and what he says goes beyond what is called for in responding to the partner's talk. (Overresponsiveness applies to the speeches of the interactant in response to what is requested or suggested by others whereas overtalk applies to speaking

more than one's partner, or others, in the interaction, considering the entire interaction session.)

16. *Underresponsiveness.* An interactant says too little in relation to what a previous question or comment appears to call for. (This too applies to speeches of the speaker and is to be distinguished from undertalk.)

17. *Excessive question asking.* An interactant asks too many questions.

18. *Pedantry.* An interactant uses too many big words where simpler, better-known words would be adequate (e.g., saying trepidation for fear or vicissitude for change).

19. *Dogmatic statement.* An interactant makes a statement in a categorical, unqualified, all-or-none, black-or-white manner.

20. *Overgeneralization.* An interactant misrepresents real world referents (behaviors or other events) by exaggerating such characteristics as their amounts, importance, or quality. For example, overgeneralization of amount may involve the use of the word "always" when an event occurs sometimes.

21. *Undergeneralization.* An interactant misrepresents real world referents (behaviors or other events) by understating such characteristics as their amount, importance, or quality. For example, events that sometimes occur may be said "never" to occur.

22. *Excessive cueing.* An interactant employs more verbal cues than are necessary, as indicated by asking too many questions or making too many requests, directives, commands, or suggestions.

23. *Incorrect autoclitic.*[3] An interactant misrepresents real events by making incorrect remarks regarding what he is about to say. For example, a speaker might say that what he is about to say is true and proceed to lie, or he may announce that he is about to tell a very funny joke and then tell a story that is not funny at all.

24. *Presumptive attribution.* An interactant misrepresents the meanings, motivations, feelings, and thoughts of others by incorrectly attributing non-obvious characteristics to them ("mind reading," "second-guessing").

25. *Misrepresentation of fact or evaluation.* An interactant incorrectly represents facts such as real world events or evaluations of others such as their preferences and interests.

26. *Topic content avoidance.* An interactant clearly and openly averts the opportunity to talk about an assigned or agreed upon topic.

27. *Other content avoidance.* An interactant clearly and openly averts the opportunity to talk about subjects then being discussed if these topics were not assigned or agreed-upon subjects.

28. *Topic content shifting.* An interactant introduces new or different content from an assigned or agreed-upon topic.

29. *Other content shifting.* An interactant prematurely introduces new or different content from that which is currently being discussed if the subject being discussed were not assigned or agreed upon.

30. *Topic content persistence.* An interactant speaks excessively on an assigned or agreed-upon topic.

31. *Other content persistence.* An interactant speaks excessively on a given subject that previously was being discussed by others and is not an assigned or agreed-upon topic.

32. *Poor referent specification.* An interactant fails to speak concretely and specifically in regard to the referent and, instead, his speech tends to be general and abstract.

33. *Temporal remoteness.* An interactant dwells excessively on referents pertaining to the past or the hypothetical future.

34. *Detached utterance.* An interactant talks on a subject that does not show a clear semantic connection to the immediate focus of the discussion (e.g., irrelevant examples, ideas, or hypothetical situations).

35. *Positive talk deficit.* An interactant fails to compliment or say nice things about the other as a person or about what the other says or does.

36. *Positive talk surfeit.* An interactant excessively compliments or says nice things about the other person or about what the other says or does.

37. *Acknowledgment deficit.* An interactant fails to admit or give credit when the other is correct in a statement or fails to express recognition of the other's point of view or assertion.

38. *Acknowledgment surfeit.* An interactant excessively admits or gives credit when the other may be correct in a statement or expresses excessive recognition of the other's point of view or assertion.

39. *Opinion deficit.* An interactant fails to express a preference or an opinion regarding referents when the discussion seems to call for some evaluation by him.

40. *Opinion surfeit.* An interactant expresses preferences or opinions excessively regarding the referents when the interaction does not seem to call for this much expression of opinion by him.

41. *Excessive agreement.* An interactant agrees excessively with the statements of others.

42. *Excessive disagreement.* An interactant disagrees excessively with the statements of others.

43. *Dysfluent talk.* An interactant displays an excess of nonfluencies, such as stuttering or hesitating.

44. *Too little information given.* An interactant provides too little information considering that which should or might be provided at that point in the discussion.

45. *Redundant information given.* An interactant excessively repeats information already given or known.

46. *Too much information given.* An interactant provides an excessive amount of information concerning a subject compared with that which is necessary.

47. *Negative talk surfeit.* An interactant expresses too frequent or too

lengthy negative evaluations of others, events, or other aspects of his surroundings. When these negative evaluations are applied to the behavior of others with whom he is interacting, the interactant is faulting.

48. *Negative talk deficit.* An interactant fails to express negative evaluations, especially in situations in which they would be warranted.

49. *Illogical talk.* An interactant makes an illogical statement considering what he or others have said.

FINDINGS

The early findings reported here are based upon ratings of two raters who completed the VPC following periods during which marital partners discussed assigned topics for approximately twenty minutes each. Nine couples, referred by collaborating family agencies for focused, time-limited assessment and modification for difficulties involving marital communication, discussed four topics each. These topics were expectations of one another as husband and wife (period 1), a decision-making topic of their own choosing in which they were to try to reach a decision if they could (period 2), a second discussion of expectations as husband and wife (period 3), and problems they had in their marriage (period 4).

Two raters, located outside the experimental booth where the couples discussed the topics, listened to each discussion by headphones and made ratings independently after each session was over (two topics were discussed in each session). Each of the three raters who participated in the project was familiar with the categories and the rating system. The findings reported here are based upon analyses of amount ratings. (Analogous information for the rating of problems is not presented because essentially the same results were found.)[4]

Ratings for Response Categories

The average amount ratings for response categories for husbands and wives were very similar for all discussion periods and, hence, only those for period 1 are reported here. The ranges and medians were very similar for husbands and wives (1.00 to 2.78 with a median of 1.44, for husbands, and 1.00–2.87 with a median of 1.35, for wives).[5] In the main, the ratings were low for most categories and far from the maximum for the categories having the highest ratings. Ratings of categories for husbands tended to be very similar to those for wives. For example, most of the categories that received high ratings were so rated for both husband and wife. Thus, the following categories were rated in the upper third of the distribution for husbands and wives: negative talk surfeit, excessive disagreement, positive talk deficit, overgeneralization, poor referent specification, topic content shifting, other content persistence, acknowledgement deficit, obtrusions and other content shifting. Overtalk was rated in the upper third of the distribution for wives but not for husbands whereas quiet talk and unaffective talk were so rated for husbands but not for wives.

Problem Specification for All Couples

A central question is the extent to which the VPC facilitates a narrowing down of the response areas that may be the focus for modification. To obtain information on this question, the average number of response categories rated as High and Low was determined for husbands and wives for all discussion periods. A rating for a response category was designated as High if the two raters made ratings of 3 or 4 each or one 4 and a 3. Low consisted of the two raters having given ratings of 1 each or a 1 and a 2. Analysis indicated that an average of 35 to 36 response areas for both husband and wife were rated as Low. In other words, approximately three-quarters of the potential problem areas for these couples yielded Low ratings. The analysis also indicated that an average of three to four areas were rated as High for each spouse, with a mean of about seven High ratings per couple. The VPC did indeed narrow down response areas that would be the chief candidates for possible modification.

Inter-rater Reliability

A total of 36 periods were rated, four for each of the nine couples. Inter-rater reliability was determined by calculating the association between ratings of the two raters for each response category. This was done for each of the 36 periods and for husbands and wives, yielding a total of 72 measures of association. The measure of association was the Kruskal-Goodman gamma, a measure of the strength of association of two cross-classifications of ordered items (Goodman and Kruskal, 1954) which has been recommended as a suitable measure of association for ordinal scales (Costover, 1965). Gamma expresses the conditional probability of a like order minus the conditional probability of an unlike order divided by one minus the probability of at least one tie. Values of gamma range from −1.00 through 0 to +1.00.

The gammas for the inter-rater reliabilities range from −.19 through +1.00 and most of them were moderate to very high. The median for husbands was .69 and, for wives, .66. If a gamma of .5 is taken as moderately high, we find that for the amount ratings 78 per cent exceeded this value for the husbands and 83 per cent for the wives.

Average inter-rater reliabilities for husbands and wives were also calculated for each discussion period. All of the averages were in the sixties and seventies and there were relatively small differences between periods and between husbands and wives.

Reliability of Problem Categories

To determine rater agreement for each of the 49 categories, the absolute difference between rater 1 and rater 2 was determined and averaged by couple across all discussion periods for each problem category. A score of 0 indicates no difference and 3, maximal difference. The average difference scores were low for the response categories. Thus scores ranged from 0 to slightly over 1.00, with a median for husbands of .56 and .50 for wives. It was evident, however, that some of the low difference scores could have been due to the absence of the responses being judged rather than high agreement of raters when the responses occurred.

Thus, in order to learn more about factors entering into rater reliability of items, an analysis was conducted in which the items were cross-classified by the average difference and the average rating scores. The results of this analysis are presented in Table 23.1 where it may be seen that the main factor associated with high difference scores is a high average rating score for the response category. That is, the raters disagreed most on responses judged to occur most frequently and disagreed least on responses judged to occur least frequently.

Careful inspection of the table indicates the VPC categories rated most and least reliably. For example, categories that would appear to be judged with least reliability are those for which the average difference scores are high and the average rating scores are medium (categories 9, 14, and 22).

Validity

Two response categories that had readily quantifiable referents were selected for a validity analysis. These categories were overtalk and undertalk, ratings for which were compared with the actual amount of talking. The first validation criterion was talk relative to partner and it consisted of the proportion of one partner's talk over both partners' talk. The second criterion was total talk relative to the period and this consisted of the total time spent talking in the period by the couple over the total amount of time of the discussion period.

The initial step in the analysis was to prepare rating scores. A rating difference score for overtalk and undertalk was calculated by subtracting the wife's rating from the husband's and transforming the difference scores into a seven-point scale. Using the gamma statistic as a measure of association, these rating difference scores were then cross-tabulated against talk relative to partner. The latter was calculated by subtracting the percentage of wife talk to total talk from the percentage of husband talk to total talk and transforming the difference scores into a nine-point scale. The association of the rating with this criterion indicates the extent to which talk relative to partner is associated with overtalk and undertalk.

The other analysis addressed the question of the extent to which the ratings of overtalk and undertalk related to how much the couple talked in the discussion period. This analysis required that a couple rating be worked out for overtalk and undertalk which consisted of the sum of the ratings for one measure divided by two. The results were then converted to a seven-point scale. The validation criterion of total talk relative to the period in-

TABLE 23.1 *Classification of checklist categories of verbal problem checklist for amount ratings across all discussion periods by average difference score and average rating score*

Average Difference Score	*Average Rating Score*		
	High (2.86–1.64)	*Medium (1.63–1.30)*	*Low (1.29–1.00)*
High (1.15–.72)	35[a], 42, 20, 37, 31, 32, 11, 44, 28, 13, 30, 25, 24	9, 14, 22	
Medium (.71–.36)	47, 10	16, 40, 5, 19, 39, 17, 29, 33, 12, 1, 6, 26, 15	27
Low (.35–.00)	2		3, 4, 45, 41, 46, 38, 21, 8, 18, 48, 7, 43, 49, 23, 34, 36

[a] Category numbers in each cell of this table are listed in order (from left to right) of the average rating score. Both the average difference and the average rating score are for couples (i.e., for the mean of husband and wife scores) averaged across the four discussion periods.

volved a scale of proportions that ranged from 0 to 100 which was transformed into a nine-point scale.

In the analysis, the gamma was computed on the basis of rating and talk data for 36 sessions. Four gammas were calculated for one rater and the same four for another, yielding a total of eight. There were high positive gammas for overtalk relative to partner (.79 for Rater A and .83 for Rater B) and relatively high negative gammas for the ratings of undertalk relative to partner (−.62 and −.59 for Raters A and B, respectively). Although the associations for overtalk were higher than for undertalk, the gammas indicate a high concordance between the actual amount of talking of interactants and the rated amount of talking of interactants relative to partners.

A more complicated picture is revealed by the associations between couple rating and couple talk relative to the period. For overtalk, the correlations were low and negative (−.32 and −.38 for the raters). For undertalk, very high negative associations were found (−.92 and −.75), indicating that the more the couple was rated as undertalking, the less talking they did relative to the total period of time. Both partners can undertalk, considering their talk relative to the total time available, whereas both cannot easily overtalk. This to some extent accounts for the low negative associations of −.32 and −.38. Also, the range of responses here was greatly truncated by a large number of 1's for the couple overtalk ratings.

Altogether, these findings suggest that the ratings of overtalk much more clearly specify the amount of talk relative to partner, whereas the ratings of undertalk are more indicative of the sheer amount of talk relative to the amount of time available for talking in the period.

Discussion

As an aid to response specification, the VPC was found to be even more parsimonious than originally anticipated. Although ratings were made of the amount of response as well as of whether the amount evidenced was a problem for 49 categories of potentially problematic verbal response, it turned out that the amount and problem ratings were highly correlated and that the analyses for amount produced essentially the same findings as those for the problem ratings. Because the ratings of amount are more behaviorally specific and less judgmental, they alone would probably be enough to obtain for most clinical or research purposes.

The VPC narrowed the number of possible problem areas from a maximum of 49 to an average of four for husbands and three for wives. The use of the VPC to rate areas of verbal responding after family members have discussed assigned topics was found to be a relatively rapid and simple technique of response specification. The entire procedure of which the VPC was a part was found to be a viable method to follow in the assessment of potential problems of verbal responding.

The inter-rater and response category reliabilities were gratifyingly high. Furthermore, reliability of raters was essentially unaffected by whether ratings were made of the verbal behavior of husbands or wives or by the topics discussed. These results suggest that the VPC may be employed with an adequate level of rater reliability in clinical practice and research. However, the raters disagreed most on behaviors judged to occur most frequently. The findings on reliability indicate the desirability of providing careful training in response discrimination and in rating prior to the use of the VPC.

The results on the validity of the overtalk and undertalk categories support the validity of the ratings and also explicate the basis for the ratings. Other categories of the VPC should be examined against objective validation criteria.

Notes

1. The research upon which this report is based was supported in part by SRS Grant No. 10-P 56023/5-02, Social and Rehabilitation Service, Department of Health, Education and Welfare. We wish to acknowledge the helpful assistance of Robert Hodnefield in rating marital partners and of the workers and executive personnel who referred couples from the following agencies: Child and Family Service of Washtenaw County, Catholic Social Services of Washtenaw County, Family Service Agency of Genesee County, Family Service of Metropolitan Detroit and the Monroe County Community Mental Health Center. We also wish to acknowledge the competent assistance of Ms. Virginia McIntosh and Ms. Joyce Morgan in preparing the manuscript.

2. Twenty-four of the categories in this list have earlier counterparts in the paper of Carter and Thomas (1973) mentioned before. These categories are as follows: 1, 2, 3, 4, 5, 6, 43, 11, 13, 37, 35, 26, 28, 30, 32, 33, 15, 16, 17, 19, 20, 24, 34, and 39. Two of the categories in the original list were dropped (countercomplaining and excessive compliance) and one (abusive talk) was replaced by another (negative talk surfeit).

3. The term autoclitic refers to verbal responses of the speaker that pertain to the speaker's verbal behavior and that have an effect on the listener (Skinner, 1957).

4. Furthermore, the correlation of average amount ratings with average problem ratings across the 49 response categories was high. Spearman's *rho* was .95 for the husbands and .96 for the wives.

5. Average category ratings for husbands and wives for all response categories are available from the first author upon request.

References

CARTER, R. D. and THOMAS, E. J. Modification of problematic marital communication using corrective feedback and instruction. *Behavior Therapy*, 1973, *4*, 100–109.

COSTOVER, H. L. Criteria for measures of association. *American Sociological Review*, 1965, *30*, 3, 341–353.

GOODMAN, L. A. and KRUSKAL, W. H. Measures of association for cross-classifications. *American Statistical Association Journal*, 1953, *49*, 732–764.

SKINNER, B. F. *Verbal Behavior*. New York: Appleton-Century-Crofts, 1957.

THOMAS, E. J., CARTER, R. D., and GAMBRILL, E. D. Some possibilities of behavioral modification with marital problems using 'SAM' (Signal system for the assessment and modification of behavior). *Advances in Behavior Therapy*. New York: Academic Press, 1971.

THOMAS, E. J., CARTER, R. D., GAMBRILL, E. D. and BUTTERFIELD, W. H. A signal system for the assessment and modification of behavior (SAM). *Behavior Therapy*, 1970, *1*, 252–259.

24

SPENCER A. RATHUS

A Thirty-Item Schedule for Assessing Assertive Behavior

Assertion training has received much attention as a behavior therapy technique for directly shaping assertive behavior (Rathus and Ruppert, 1972; Salter, 1949; Wolpe, 1958, 1969, 1970; Wolpe and Lazarus, 1966). Thus the need for an instrument for measuring behavioral change in assertion training has arisen. Wolpe (1969) and Wolpe and Lazarus (1966) report that they assess patients' pretreatment assertiveness by asking them several questions, but they report no method for quantifying and thus determining the reliability and validity of these data. The old "A-S Reaction Study" (Allport, 1928) comprised a quantified method for evaluating assertiveness, but many of the items on this scale appear to be in need of updating. For example, Item Three on the 1939 Revision of the Form for Women reads

> At church, a lecture, or an entertainment, if you arrive after the program has commenced and find that there are people standing but also that there are front seats available which might be secured without "piggishness" but with considerable conspicuousness, do you take the seats?

The *Guilford-Zimmerman Temperament Survey* (Guilford and Zimmerman, 1956) contains a scale of social ascendance, but this instrument also contains 270 items which assess traits other than assertiveness.

The schedule in the present study consists of the 30 items shown in Table 24.1. Some of these are based on Wolpe's (1969:63) and Wolpe and Lazarus's (1966:43) situations, and on items from the Allport (1928) and Guilford and Zimmerman (1956) scales. Others were suggested by diaries the author requested be kept by two classes of college juniors and seniors. In

Reprinted with permission of Academic Press, Inc. from *Behavior Therapy*, 1973, Vol. 4, pp. 298–406.

TABLE 24.1 *Rathus assertiveness schedule*

Directions: Indicate how characteristic or descriptive each of the following statements is of you by using the code given below.

+ 3 very characteristic of me, extremely descriptive[a]
+ 2 rather characteristic of me, quite descriptive
+ 1 somewhat characteristic of me, slightly descriptive
− 1 somewhat uncharacteristic of me, slightly nondescriptive
− 2 rather uncharacteristic of me, quite nondescriptive
− 3 very uncharacteristic of me, extremely nondescriptive

____ 1. Most people seem to be more aggressive and assertive than I am.*
____ 2. I have hesitated to make or accept dates because of "shyness."*
____ 3. When the food served at a restaurant is not done to my satisfaction, I complain about it to the waiter or waitress.
____ 4. I am careful to avoid hurting other people's feelings, even when I feel that I have been injured.*
____ 5. If a salesman has gone to considerable trouble to show me merchandise which is not quite suitable, I have a difficult time in saying "No."*
____ 6. When I am asked to do something, I insist upon knowing why.
____ 7. There are times when I look for a good, vigorous argument.
____ 8. I strive to get ahead as well as most people in my position.
____ 9. To be honest, people often take advantage of me.*
____10. I enjoy starting conversations with new acquaintances and strangers.
____11. I often don't know what to say to attractive persons of the opposite sex.*
____12. I will hesitate to make phone calls to business establishments and institutions.*
____13. I would rather apply for a job or for admission to a college by writing letters than by going through with personal interviews.*
____14. I find it embarrassing to return merchandise.*
____15. If a close and respected relative were annoying me, I would smother my feelings rather than express my annoyance.*
____16. I have avoided asking questions for fear of sounding stupid.*
____17. During an argument I am sometimes afraid that I will get so upset that I will shake all over.*
____18. If a famed and respected lecturer makes a statement which I think is incorrect, I will have the audience hear my point of view as well.
____19. I avoid arguing over prices with clerks and salesmen.*
____20. When I have done something important or worthwhile, I manage to let others know about it.
____21. I am open and frank about my feelings.
____22. If someone has been spreading false and bad stories about me, I see him (her) as soon as possible to "have a talk" about it.
____23. I often have a hard time saying "No."*
____24. I tend to bottle up my emotions rather than make a scene.*
____25. I complain about poor service in a restaurant and elsewhere.
____26. When I am given a compliment, I sometimes just don't know what to say.*
____27. If a couple near me in a theatre or at a lecture were conversing rather loudly, I would ask them to be quiet or to take their conversation elsewhere.
____28. Anyone attempting to push ahead of me in a line is in for a good battle.
____29. I am quick to express an opinion.
____30. There are times when I just can't say anything.*

[a] Total score obtained by adding numerical responses to each item, after changing the signs of reversed items.

* Reversed item.

them were recorded behaviors the student would have liked to exhibit but refrained from exhibiting because of fear of aversive social consequences.

The reliability and validity and an item analysis of the resultant instrument, the Rathus Assertiveness Schedule (RAS), are discussed below.

Reliability

Test-retest Reliability.

Test-retest reliability of the RAS was established by administering the instrument to 68 undergraduate college men and women ranging in age from 17 to 27, and then retesting them after eight weeks had passed. The mean pretest score was .29, the standard deviation 29.1.[1] Mean posttest score was 1.62, and the standard deviation 27.63. A Pearson product-moment correlation coefficient was run between respondents' pre- and posttest scores, yielding an r of .78 ($p < .01$), indicating moderate to high stability of test scores over a 2-month period.

Split-half Reliability.

Internal consistency of the RAS was determined by having 18 college juniors and seniors administer the test to 67 people off campus. They were instructed to choose three or four persons whom they knew quite well. *S*s thus chosen were male and female, ranging in age from 15 to 70. Their RAS scores varied from the +60s to the −70s.

A Pearson product-moment correlation coefficient was run between total odd and total even item scores, yielding an r of .77 ($p < .01$), suggesting that the qualities measured by the RAS possess moderate to high homogeneity.

Validity

The validity of the RAS was established by comparing self-reported RAS scores to two external measures of assertiveness.

Study 1.

In the first validating study, the 18 college students who administered the RAS to the 67 subjects they knew well then rated these subjects on a 17-item schedule (Table 24.2) constructed according to semantic differential technique (Osgood, Suci, and Tannenbaum, 1957). The modifiers "very" were attached to the extreme positions of each scale, "slightly" to the central positions, and "rather" or "quite" to the moderate positions. The extreme positive pole of each scale was assigned to the number +3, and positions were numbered consecutively, omitting zero because of the absence of a center point, to −3, the negative pole of each scale.

The factor structure of the 17-item rating schedule was determined by factor analyzing raters' responses using a principal component procedure, followed by a varimax rotation of the raw factors. Four factors, accounting for 71.2 per cent of the total variance were thus obtained: assertiveness, contentment, intelligence and prosperity, and health.[2] Pearson product-moment correlation coefficients were then run between the 67 RAS scores and the student raters' impressions of their personality traits on each of the 17 scales. RAS scores correlated significantly ($p < .01$) with each of the five scales

TABLE 24.2 *17-Item rating schedule*

1. bold	___:___:___:___:___:___	timid
2. poor	___:___:___:___:___:___	prosperous
3. quiet	___:___:___:___:___:___	outspoken
4. intelligent	___:___:___:___:___:___	stupid
5. assertive	___:___:___:___:___:___	nonassertive
6. awful	___:___:___:___:___:___	nice
7. unhealthy	___:___:___:___:___:___	healthy
8. aggressive	___:___:___:___:___:___	withdrawing
9. happy	___:___:___:___:___:___	unhappy
10. satisfied	___:___:___:___:___:___	dissatisfied
11. unfair	___:___:___:___:___:___	fair
12. ill	___:___:___:___:___:___	well
13. confident	___:___:___:___:___:___	uncertain
14. smart	___:___:___:___:___:___	dumb
15. strong-willed	___:___:___:___:___:___	weak-willed
16. active	___:___:___:___:___:___	inactive
17. discontent	___:___:___:___:___:___	content

comprising the assertiveness factor of the rating schedule: boldness ($r =$ .61), outspokenness (.62), assertiveness (.34), aggressiveness (.54), and confidence (.33). RAS scores also covaried significantly but negatively ($r = -.36$; $p < .01$) with scale No. 6, indicating niceness, but did not covary at above chance expectation with any of the 11 remaining scales. RAS scores thus serve as valid indicators of respondents' assertiveness in terms of the impressions they make on other people. Failure of RAS scores to covary with scales indicative of intelligence, happiness, fairness, and so on is suggestive that RAS scores are not confounded by a desire on the part of respondents to answer items in the manner they feel is socially desirable.

Study 2.

Another index of the RAS's validity was determined by comparing 47 coeds' RAS scores to ratings of their responses to five questions asking them what they would do in situations in which assertive, outgoing behavior could be used with profit. The questions were as follows:

1. You have worked very hard on a term paper and you receive a very poor grade, say a D or an F. What would you do? (If the subject says that

she would discuss it with her professor, she is further asked "What if the professor is uncooperative or nasty?")

2. You are seated at a restaurant counter, waiting for service. The waitress begins to serve someone who came in after you, a couple of seats away. What would you do?

3. A casual acquaintance remarks "That's a pretty sweater you're wearing." What would you do?

4. You have tried on five pairs of shoes and none of them is quite what you are looking for. The salesman seems to be a bit disgusted. He says "Lady, this is what everybody's wearing these days. If you don't find what you want here, you're not going to find it anywhere." What would you do?

5. You are trying to take a nap. Your roommate is talking to a friend on the other side of the room. They are trying to speak softly, but you are being kept awake. What would you do?

The subjects were questioned by neutral interviewers, and question and answer sessions were audiotaped. Tapes were then played for raters who knew neither the subjects nor how they had scored on the RAS. Responses to the questions were rated from "very poor" to "very good" according to the following standards: very poor—"Don't know" or would you do or say nothing; poor—attempted assertion that is inadequate; fair—some assertion shown, but not carefully thought out or "natural"; good—appropriate assertiveness shown, but with rough edges; very good—appropriate assertion shown with good expressiveness. Attention was paid to *S*s' tones of voice and credibility as well as to the content of their remarks. Answers were given from 1 point for a very poor response to 5 points for a very good response. Total ratings could thus vary from 5 to 25 points per *S*. Interrater reliability for ratings of audiotaped responses was very high: $r = .94$ ($p < .01$).

Each subject's score for these question and answer sessions was determined by taking the mean of the two raters' totals. Scores from the audiotaped sessions thus ranged from 5.5 to 23. Their RAS scores ranged between -52 and $+49$. A Pearson product-moment correlation coefficient was then run between RAS scores and scores from the audiotaped sessions, yielding an r of .70 ($p < .01$). Thus, RAS scores are also valid in terms of impartial raters' impressions of the behaviors that subjects report they would exhibit in specific social encounters.

Item Analysis

To determine each item's contribution to the RAS and its validity in terms of external criteria, Pearson moment correlation coefficients were run between item scores, total RAS scores, and semantic differential ratings of six personality traits for the 67 subjects discussed in the first of the above validity studies. Table 24.3 shows the resultant correlation matrix, indicating the correlations between each of the 30 RAS items, total RAS scores, the five semantic differential scales that comprise the assertiveness factor of the 17-item rating schedule, and the semantic differential scale indicating niceness.

Results.

Of the 30 items, 27 correlate significantly with the total RAS score. None of the remaining three detracts from the total score, however, and it is suggested that these items be maintained. Items 1 and 21 indicate, respectively, whether respondents consider themselves to be as aggressive and assertive as their peers and whether they consider themselves to be open and frank about their emotions. Although a client's own conception of his current status is not valid in terms of the impressions he makes on others, his self-concept is likely to be related to his willingness to undergo certain types of treatments. For example, the meek individual who looks upon himself as assertive is likely to resist assertion training, though he be in dire need of it. The therapist can make use of such information. It is suggested that item 18 be maintained since it is significant in its relationship to the total score at the .10 level of confidence, and it is desirable to know whether a client feels that he would contradict a respected person in a public situation.

Perusal of the correlations between test items and the independent indications of respondents' boldness, outspokenness, assertiveness, aggressiveness, and confidence indicate that 19 of the 30 items correlate significantly with at least one of these external criteria. The other 11 items may nevertheless be maintained in the scale for several reasons: none of them correlates significantly negatively with external criteria; the RAS possesses moderate to high internal consistency; and they offer useful information concerning respondents.

Of the 30 RAS items, 28 were found to correlate negatively with semantic ratings of respondents' niceness, and six of these do so significantly. The social desirability of assertiveness is thus brought into question. While this finding is further suggestive that assertiveness as measured by the RAS is not likely to be confounded with social desirability, it implies that therapists who are attempting to instigate assertive behavior in clients must take care to point out the distinction between demanding that one be treated with fairness and justice and the gratuitous expression of nastiness.

Therapists should consider that a global stimulating of clients to behave more assertively (e.g., as suggested by Salter, 1949) may result in strong aversive social feedback which the client receiving assertion training is likely to be particularly ill-equipped to handle. As has been pointed out elsewhere (Rathus and Ruppert, 1972), it is often the case that others have a stake in the client's remaining nonassertiveness, and that they will resist his efforts to reconstruct his relationships such that favors and decencies are reciprocated rather than one-sided. In so doing, they are likely to suggest that he is failing to behave "nicely." Such remarks will be highly punitive to the client who

TABLE 24.3 *Correlations between assertiveness schedule items, total assertiveness schedule scores, assertiveness factor items and the niceness item from the 17 item semantic differential rating scale*[a]

		Items from 17 Item Semantic Differential Rating Scale					
R.A.S. Item	*Total Score*	*Boldness*	*Outspoken-ness*	*Assertive-ness*	*Aggressive-ness*	*Confidence*	*Niceness*
1	.1110	−.0223	.0907	−.0033	.1177	.0926	−.0138
2	.7006**	.5680**	.5073**	.2397*	.5313**	.3065*	−.2408*
3	.4176**	.2718*	.1853	.1695	.1620	.1274	−.0896
4	.5030**	.1630	.3200**	.1860	.2749*	.1315	−.1508
5	.2362*	.1295	.0247	.0304	.0560	.0383	−.0078
6	.4149**	.3098*	.2787*	.3127*	.3505**	.3615**	−.1178
7	.3369**	.1450	.1562	.1000	.0522	.0077	−.1275
8	.4813**	.2014	.1514	−.1098	.0972	.0182	−.1206
9	.2385*	.0985	.1236	−.0928	.2388*	.1445	.1301
10	.4218**	.1734	.1773	.0072	.1696	.2246	−.0902
11	.5003**	.3359*	.4169**	.2443*	.2251	.2325	−.1193
12	.5783**	.3459**	.3069*	.1308	.2897*	.2398*	−.2165
13	.4211**	.3340**	.3621**	.1065	.2650*	.0397	−.0994
14	.4514**	.3999**	.3007*	.3550**	.4272**	.2247	−.0619
15	.4077**	.0832	.2025	.1717	.1520	.1862	−.2181
16	.3619**	.3152**	.2711*	.2369*	.2133	.0363	−.2906*
17	.6465**	.4878**	.4731**	.2627*	.4130**	.2850*	−.3160**
18	.2318	.0887	.0223	.0337	.0554	.1800	−.1633
19	.5227**	.4698**	.3796**	.2304	.3606**	.3382**	−.2040
20	.2826*	.1112	.1615	.1013	.1650	.0606	−.1048
21	.2107	−.0202	−.0125	−.0424	.0268	−.0590	−.0297
22	.4442**	.3544**	.3347**	.0997	.2205	.0225	−.2530*
23	.5236**	.3378**	.3954**	.2642*	.2845*	.2889*	−.3395**
24	.5428**	.2586*	.3925**	.2161	.2824*	.2253	−.0732
25	.4982**	.3831**	.3683**	.2566*	.3930**	.1382	−.1566
26	.3060*	.0784	.0809	.0616	.1531	.0705	.0115
27	.4198**	.0939	.1818	−.0117	.1086	−.0805	−.1245
28	.4459**	.2925*	.2947*	.1739	.1151	.0581	−.2236
29	.5507**	.4267**	.4378**	.2077	.4105**	.2151	−.2017
30	.6078**	.3100*	.3052*	.1280	.2083	.1008	−.2865**

[a] $N = 67$.
* $p < .05$.
** $p < .01$.

possesses little confidence and experiences the therapist's encouragement and approbation for but 50 minutes once or twice a week. Thus, in the early stages of assertion training assertiveness may be most effectively fostered through practice in specific situations in which the client is likely to arouse either positive social feedback or limited amounts of negative feedback. In this manner, he may gradually develop confidence and increased tolerance for negative feedback.

Discussion

The data show that the self-reporting RAS permits reliable and valid assessment of assertiveness or social boldness. Such an instrument can be used both in research that investigates the efficacies of various procedures for shaping assertive behavior and for obtaining pre- and post-measures of patients' assertiveness in clinical practice. An item analysis suggests that a shortened 19-item version of the RAS may be used with accurate results, but that retaining all items will not detract from the instrument's validity. It is recommended that all 30 items be retained since they will provide the therapist with useful information concerning his patients' impressions of their own assertiveness and frankness, and of the behaviors which are most typical of them in a variety of situations.

Notes

1. Data presented in this article were processed by the UNIVAC 1108 Computer at the State University of New York at Albany Computing Center. The author is grateful to Larry J. Siegel, currently of the College of Criminal Justice at Northeastern University, for his aid in programming.
2. Data concerning the loadings of the semantic differential scales presented in Table 24.2 with each of these factors are available from the author.

References

ALLPORT, G. *A-S Reaction Study*. Boston: Houghton-Mifflin, 1928.

GUILFORD, J. P., and ZIMMERMAN, W. S. *The Guilford-Zimmerman temperament survey*. Beverly Hills, Calif.: Sheridan Psychological Services, 1956.

OSGOOD, C. E., SUCI, G. J., and TANNENBAUM, P. H. *The measurement of meaning*. Urbana, Ill.: University of Illinois Press, 1957.

RATHUS, S. A., and RUPPERT, C. Assertion training in the secondary school and the college. *Adolescence,* 1972, *7*.

SALTER, A. *Conditioned reflex therapy*. New York: Capricorn, 1949.

WOLPE, J. *Psychotherapy by reciprocal inhibition*. Stanford, Calif.: Stanford University Press, 1958.

WOLPE, J. *The practice of behavior therapy*. New York: Pergamon, 1969.

WOLPE, J. The instigation of assertive behavior: Transcripts from two cases. *Journal of Behavior Therapy and Experimental Psychiatry,* 1970, *1*, 145–151.

WOLPE, J., and LAZARUS, A. A. *Behavior therapy techniques*. Oxford: Pergamon, 1966.

VI

Electromechanical Devices

Electrical and mechanical devices assist the behavior therapist and researcher in obtaining objective data for recording and monitoring. Such devices may also be used for purposes of stimulus transformation, alteration of neurophysiological states, consequence scheduling, and prompting and teaching (Schwitzgebel, 1968). When properly developed and in good working condition, electromechanical devices can generally be made to perform their functions more sensitively, reliably, accurately, durably, and cheaply than can their human counterparts, and may often do so with fewer reactive effects upon patients and subjects.

In his extensive survey entitled "Instrumentation in Behavior Therapy," Butterfield examines the functional characteristics, selection criteria, illustrative uses, and costs for the following types of electromechanical devices: timers, counters, shockers, and other aversive stimulation devices, telemetric devices, transducers, cameras and projectors, audio magnetic tape recorders, and chart recorders. The devices have been grouped in this way because any particular device or type of device may be employed to perform one or more function. Broadly speaking, the functions for which electromechanical devices may be used involve monitoring and recording, data display, and modification.

Among other sources are the survey of electromechanical devices by Schwitzgebel (1968), the special issue of the *American Psychologist* of March, 1969, devoted to instrumentation in psychology, and the book by Schwitzgebel and Schwitzgebel (1973).

References

Schwitzgebel, R. L. Survey of electro-mechanical devices for behavior modification. *Psychological Bulletin,* 1968, *70,* 444–460.

Schwitzgebel, R. L. and Schwitzgebel, R. K. *Psychotechnology: Electronic Control of Mind and Behavior.* New York: Holt, Rinehart and Winston, 1973.

25

WILLIAM H. BUTTERFIELD

Instrumentation in Behavior Therapy

This chapter provides basic information about devices that have been used in monitoring, assessing, or treating various behavioral problems. It focuses on the devices which are commonly used by behavior therapists, i.e., counters, timers, chart recorders, shocking devices, and transducers. Devices used less frequently are discussed but not in detail.

Each section within the chapter discusses a series of devices in terms of their operation, their important mechanical or electrical parameters, and concludes with representative examples of how the devices have been employed in behavior therapy.

Timers

Behavior therapists, finding time an important variable, may need to determine if the duration of a behavior decreases or increases as a result of treatment; for example, whether the duration of a child's temper tantrums decreases after the implementation of a timeout procedure, or whether the daily duration of a student's study time increases after the student is put on a reinforcement schedule.

Therapists may also want to know the duration following the onset or offset of stimulus, event, or response before another event, stimulus, or behavior occurs or ceases. The therapist, for example, might like to know how soon a reinforcer follows a response, or how long after shock is applied a subject continues to respond.

Therapists may also seek to program events or stimuli for specific durations. They might wish to deliver a free reinforcer every 15 seconds, or to terminate each experimental trial after 15 minutes, or to ring a stimulus bell

Prepared especially for this volume.

every five minutes, or to put a time "pip" on a polygraph chart once each second.

Types of Timers

To aid in such tasks there are two basic types of timers: indicating timers and output timers. Many, however, serve both timing functions.

Indicating timers. Simple indicating timers are basically modified clocks or watches which show either elapsed time (time since the start of an event) or the time remaining until the timer "times out" (indicating zero time). The first type of indicating timer is sometimes called an elapsed-time timer. The second type is often called a countdown timer.

Indicating timers are categorized by how they display time. There are two main categories: (a) clocklike indicators, and (b) digital indicators.

Clocklike indicators generally have dials and hands like those of clocks, though some have a dial face which moves past a fixed pointer.

Digital and numerical indicators display elapsed time or time to zero time in numbers which may show time either in minutes and decimals (e.g., 3.54 minutes) or in hours, minutes, and seconds (e.g., 3 hours, 6 minutes, and 10 seconds).

Output timers. Output timers often do not provide any means for visually determining elapsed time or the time until zero time. These timers' prime function is to signal when a preset interval has passed, commonly providing either an auditory output (a bell ringing)or an electrical output (used to turn other equipment on or off).

Some output timers produce an output after the passage of a specific fixed time interval while others produce an output after variable time intervals. The first type is commonly called an interval timer and the second a probability timer or a probability generator.

Output timers may also be nonrecycling ("one-shot") or recycling. That is, they may produce an output and stop timing until reset, or they may repeatedly produce an output at the end of a programmed interval.

Another way of classifying timers (other than by their timing function) is by the components used in their construction. Looked at this way, we find (a) mechanical timers; (b) electromechanical timers; and (c) electronic timers. An example of a simple mechanical timer is the handwound stopwatch. Electromechanical timers are similar to mechanical timers except that they are powered by an electrical source. Some also provide an electrical output to other devices. Electronic timers have no moving parts in their timing mechanisms; instead they utilize electronic methods to produce a time signal.

Kitchen timers, pocket alarms, and alarm watches. The common characteristic of these timers is that they produce an audible signal at the end of a preset interval of time. Most often this signal serves to denote the end of a behavioral trial and if the trial has been completed successfully, the availability of reinforcement (the parent who tells the children, "if you are quiet until the timer bell rings, you can have a cookie," and the teacher who says, "if you are quiet and study until the timer goes off, you can play," are examples). These timers may also be used for time sampling; that is, instead of measuring the duration of a behavior or counting all instances of a behavior, the behavior may be counted only during a specified time interval. The interval selected by the therapist for his time sample is set into the timer, which then produces a signal at the end of the interval, indicating that the time sampling period is over.

Stopwatches, stop clocks, elapsed-time meters, running time meters, and session or trial timers. These are devices used to monitor the duration of a behavior or event; for example, measuring the length of a temper tantrum, the amount of time a student attends to a teacher, the amount of time a teacher attends to his students, the amount of time it takes to complete a task, or the length of an experimental session or procedure. These timers may also be used for time sampling.

Tape timers. Tape timers utilize 16-mm movie film. Holes are punched in the film and whenever a hole passes a photoelectric cell, or whenever a switch arm drops into the hole, an electrical signal is generated which can be used to operate a variety of programming devices. The primary use of these timers is to generate variable interval schedules of reinforcement. They are not easily portable and thus are limited to use in the behavior therapist's office.

Pulse generators, precision clocks, and precision time bases. All of these devices are output timers which have as a function the provision of a reference signal for time calibration purposes. The outputs from these timers are commonly used to put time pips on a chart recorder or audio beeps on a tape recording so that the therapist can tell where in time an event has occurred. They are also used in conjunction with counters to provide outputs to other programming devices at very precise time intervals.

Special-purpose timers. Any output timer can be used as a special-purpose timer. The following paragraphs mention a few of the special purposes for which timers have been used.

Azrin and Powell (1969) used a pill dispenser with an attached timer connected to an auditory output device to train a patient to take his pills at the proper time intervals. Azrin and Powell (1968) also used a cigarette case that locked itself for a given time to help a subject reduce the frequency of his cigarette smoking.

Sanders and Hopkins (1969) used a timer to periodically operate a movie camera to photograph the ongoing behavior of subjects. Similarly timers could be used to operate tape recorders or video tape recorders for time sampling purposes.

Metronomes, which are specialized timers, have been used to treat patients with stuttering problems (Brady, 1969, 1971).

Selection Considerations

The main criteria that should be used in selection timers are (a) timing range; (b) noise level; (c) portability; (d) cost; (e) mode of control; (f) operating voltage; and (g) inherent accuracy and reproducibility of accuracy. Each of these factors is discussed below.

Timing range. Both indicating and output timers are available in many different timing ranges. Commonly available ranges are .001 to .999 sec., .010 to 9.99 sec., .050 to 500 sec., .100 to 99.9 sec., 1.00 to 999 sec., 1.00 to 1800 sec., 0 to 10 min., 0 to 15 min., 0 to 30 min., 0 to 1 hr., 0 to 2 hr., 0 to 12 hr., 0 to 15 hr., 0 to 24 hr., and 0 to 60 hr.

Noise level. Mechanical timers and electromechanical timers are generally noisy, though some manufacturers produce soundproofed timers.

Electromechanical and electronic timers can introduce noise into audio systems, producing clicks or pops in an audio system when the timers switch on other equipment. This noise can sometimes provide unintentional cues to the patient and so may have to be eliminated. It usually can be eliminated by electrical shielding, by electronically isolating the audio circuits from the programming circuits, or by purchasing timers with built-in noise suppression circuits.

Portability. In general, mechanical timers are more compact than electromechanical and electronic timers. In addition, they do not require any outside source of power. Small battery-operated electromechanical and electronic timing devices are available but their cost is often quite high. If high timing accuracy is not required, simple resistance-capacitator electronic timers can be purchased or manufactured by a local electronic technician for under $50.

Cost. In general, mechanical timers are least expensive and electronic timers most expensive. Satisfactory mechanical timers (such as kitchen timers) can be obtained for less than $10. Depending on the functions they perform, electromechanical timers cost from about $20 to about $500. Electronic timers range in price from about $150 to about $1,000.

Inherent accuracy and reproducibility of accuracy. Each timer has an inherent timing error. Mechanical timers typically have the largest error and electronic timers the smallest. There is, however, a great deal of variability. Some manufacturers specify the expected error, others do not. In any case, timers can be checked by comparing them with an accurate electric wall clock, or with a time standard such as that broadcast by the National Bureau of Standards on radio station WWV, or by calling the National Bureau of Standards time service (current telephone number: 303/499–7111). In addition to the inherent accuracy, one must take into account the reproducibility of timer settings, or the comparability of intervals in the case of recycling timers. Some timer settings can be closely replicated upon resetting while others may have errors of from several seconds to minutes. Some recycling timers also produce more consistent intervals than others. For most therapeutic purposes, tolerable timing errors can be fairly large, and thus the accuracy factor is not overly important. Even so, a therapist should know what error is involved so that he can determine if that error is acceptable.

Durability. Mechanical and electromechanical timers are prone to shock damage and, though to a lesser extent, so are solid-state electronic timers. Reasonable care should be taken to protect timers from rough handling.

Mode of control. Most manual timers must be directly controlled by the therapist, while electromechanical and electronic timers can be remotely controlled. The usual mode of remote control is through a relay contained in the timer which, when actuated, starts the timer. The voltages that can be used for actuating the relay are discussed in the following section.

Operation and control voltages. Electromechanical and electronic timers require a source of electrical energy. The most common voltage used is 117 V AC, though some timers will operate on other specified voltages. Timers which produce an electrical output or which can be remotely controlled often require an additional source of voltage. This voltage can vary but usually is low-voltage DC. Common control voltages are 3, 6, 12, and 28 V DC. Some timers, however, have built-in low-voltage power supplies, making an external low-voltage supply unnecessary. However, most of these timers still require a 117 V AC input for the operation of the timing mechanism.

COUNTERS

When there are more than a few occurrences of an event, some recording method that is more reliable than a therapist's mentally "keeping track" of events must be used. Tally marks are commonly used to record multiple occurrences of an event. Keeping a simple tally of events is sufficient for many purposes, but as the number or the rate of occurrences increases, using a tally sheet becomes cumbersome and inaccurate. Furthermore, tally sheets do not present the data in summary form. Tallies must still be counted and converted to a cumulative numerical total. Again, there are times when the use of tally sheets is inconvenient (such as a teacher recording the occurrence of a behavior as she walks around a classroom) or counterproductive (such as giving a child unintended attention and thus, perhaps, unintended reinforcement for an inappropriate behavior). Finally, tally sheets do not materially help the therapist perform other functions or operations which may be required to implement the treatment plan.

More sophisticated counting devices, developed to aid the therapist in counting behaviors, are simply called counters.

Types of Counters

There are three common classes of counters: (a) mechanical; (b) electromechanical; and (c) electronic.

Simple mechanical counters. The simplest counters, such as golf counters and mechanical tally counters usually record the occurrence of events in numerical form. Simple mechanical counters are normally cumulative, each input causing the total showing on the counter to increase by one.

Electromechanical and electronic counters. As counters become more complex, they are more likely to be electromechanical or electronic. Electromechanical counters are simply electrically operated mechanical counters. Electronic counters are also electrically operated, but they do not normally include any mechanical mechanism.

Multifunction Counters

Add-subtract counters. These counters are bidirectional; that is, single digits can be subtracted from the total on the counter as well as added.

Printout counters. These have a provision for printing or recording on paper or magnetic tape the count showing on the counter at any given moment. They usually reset to zero when they print. Some, however, allow the therapist to choose between two modes of operation: a reset or a non-reset after printing.

Preset counters. These counters produce an electrical output pulse when the event being counted reaches some predetermined number, and this output can operate other programming devices. The face of the counter always shows the number of "counts" left until the next electrical pulse is due to occur.

Steppers. Sometimes called sequencers or accumulators, steppers are similar to preset counters in that they also produce an electrical output pulse after a predetermined number of counts have occurred, but these devices do not show the number of counts remaining before the next output pulse is due.

Selection Considerations

The main criteria that should be used in selecting timers are (a) resettability; (b) counting rate and durability; (c) portability; (d) mode of control; (e) operating voltage; (f) cost; and (g) noise level.

Resettability. Many counters have limited utility for behavior therapy in that the counters cannot be reset to zero except by completing a forward cycle one digit at a time.

There are, however, many counters which can be reset to zero at any point in their counting cycle. These counters are better suited to the needs of the behavior therapist since he can easily reset the counter when he wishes to count a new behavior or to count the same behavior for a new time period.

Counting rate and durability. As with any mechanical device, the reliability of mechanical counters decreases with use. Some manufacturers specify for their counters the mean number of counts between failures, and this information can be used to select a counter that will meet the demands of a specific situation. The reliability of electromechanical counters also decreases as the rate at which they are actuated increases. All such counters have a specified maximum rate of actuation. For most, the maximum rate ranges from about four counts a second to about 25 counts a second. If the maximum rate is exceeded, the counter will not count properly. Other things considered, then, it is better to select counters which are designed to count at high rates rather than low rates.

Electronic counters can count at extremely high rates. They also are less failure-prone than mechanical and electromechanical counters. Most electronic counters, however, do lose their count if the power to the counter is momentarily disrupted. If the count must be maintained and power failure is a possibility, then most electronic counters are not suitable.

Portability. Mechanical counters are the most portable since they do not require an external power source. They are also smaller physically. Current electronic counters are still more bulky than electromechanical counters, but their size has been rapidly decreasing. If the present trend continues, electronic counters will soon be equally as portable as electromechanical counters.

Mode of control. Mechanical counters must be manually operated, whereas electromechanical and electronic counters can be remotely controlled. Remote control is often desirable and is sometimes necessary when the visibility of the therapist's monitoring is to be reduced and it is essential when the counters are actuated by other electronic devices or by automatic programming equipment.

Operating voltage. All electronic and electromechanical counters require a source of power. Some may require more than one voltage input for their operation. Counters operate on a variety of voltages, though the most common are 117 V AC, 1.5, 6, 12, and 28 V AC or DC.

Cost. Mechanical counters are generally least expensive and electronic counters are most expensive. The number of functions included in any one counter also increases the cost. Simple resettable mechanical tally counters can be obtained for under $10. Nonresettable electromechanical counters can be obtained at about the same cost. Resettable electromechanical counters range in cost from about $15 to about $500. Electronic counters cost from about $100 to $4,000.

Noise level. Mechanical and electromechanical counters are inherently noisy, even though some have been built to operate quietly. Since noise may be undesirable, the therapist should consider the acceptability of a noisy counter. Electronic counters are silent and thus do not pose a noise problem.

If an audio sound system is being used in conjunction with the counter, switch closures which operate the counters may be picked up in the audio system. These "clicks" can be eliminated by standard electronic shielding techniques.

Application of Counters in Therapeutic Situations

Counters are used in three basic ways in behavior therapy: (a) to monitor and record the occurrences of events; (b) to display data of interest to the patient; and (c) to program consequences of behavior.

Any counter may perform more than one function at a given time. The following examples serve as illustrations:

Monitoring and recording. Daly and Frick (1970) used electromechanical counters to record the number of times a subject pushed a button signifying he expected to stutter. Thomas, Carter, Gambrill and Butterfield (1970) used electromechanical counters to record the number of times spouses pushed a button to indicate that they liked or disliked what their mates were saying. Mattos (1968) reported that he used a 5-channel manual counter to simultaneously record multiple behaviors of one subject. Lindsley (1968) used a golf counter which was strapped to his wrist to record the number of times his subjects moved within given periods. Grimoldi and Lichtenstein (1969) used an automatic counter to monitor the number of times a cigarette was mashed out in an ashtray; pressure on the ashtray operated a hidden switch closure, activating the counter.

Displaying data to the patient. When counters are used to display data to the patient, they commonly show the number of reinforcers earned (Coleman, 1970), the value of the reinforcers earned (Bensen, 1971), the number of responses made (for example, the number of ahs in a patient's speech [Bick, 1971]), and the number of responses required to obtain the next reinforcer (pilot study by author).

Programming consequences of behavior. Examples of this last category of use are not often explicitly discussed in the literature, but predetermining counters or steppers are commonly used to program fixed-ratio schedules and in combination with other devices to program variable-rate schedules.

Shockers and Other Aversive Stimulation Devices

Shocking devices, sometimes called stimulators, are used as the source of aversive stimulation where punishment, avoidance, or escape contingencies are used to modify and control behavior.

Where punishment contingencies are used, a specified patient response causes the patient to be shocked. The shock may be of short duration, or it may continue to be applied for a specified period after the response has occurred. In either case, the shock is automatically terminated by the shocking apparatus rather than by the patient.

Where an escape contingency is used, the patient must make a specified response to terminate the shock. Under both punishment and escape contingencies, the patient actually experiences aversive stimulation.

In the avoidance situation, the patient prevents the occurrence of aversive stimulation by making some response (active avoidance) or by not making a response (passive avoidance). Some avoidance schedules provide the patient with a warning signal which signifies that aversive stimulation is about to occur.

There are three basic types of shockers: (a) constant current; (b) constant voltage; and (c) unregulated voltage and current.

As their names imply, constant current and constant voltage shockers have built-in regulating systems which automatically adjust the current or voltage to maintain constant voltage or current between the electrodes. This is necessary because otherwise the voltage or current would fluctuate with the internal resistance of the patient changes, as in the case with an unregulated shocker. If the voltage and current are both allowed to fluctuate, there is no way the therapist can control the shock level that is being delivered to the patient.

In addition to automatically controlling the voltage and current levels, some shockers also control other parameters of the shock administration. These parameters are (a) pulse frequency; (b) pulse duration; (c) number of pulses in pulse train; (d) time between pulse trains; and (e) the wave form. (See Figure 25.1)

Some shockers allow the therapist to mix two shock pulses. As an example, the first pulse may be a medium amplitude, long duration pulse while the second may be a high amplitude, short duration pulse delivered during the same period as the longer duration pulse.

To date, most of the therapists using shock in behavior modification have not systematically varied any parameter other than current or voltage amplitude; therefore, the parameters illustrated in Figure 25.1 are not discussed in this chapter.

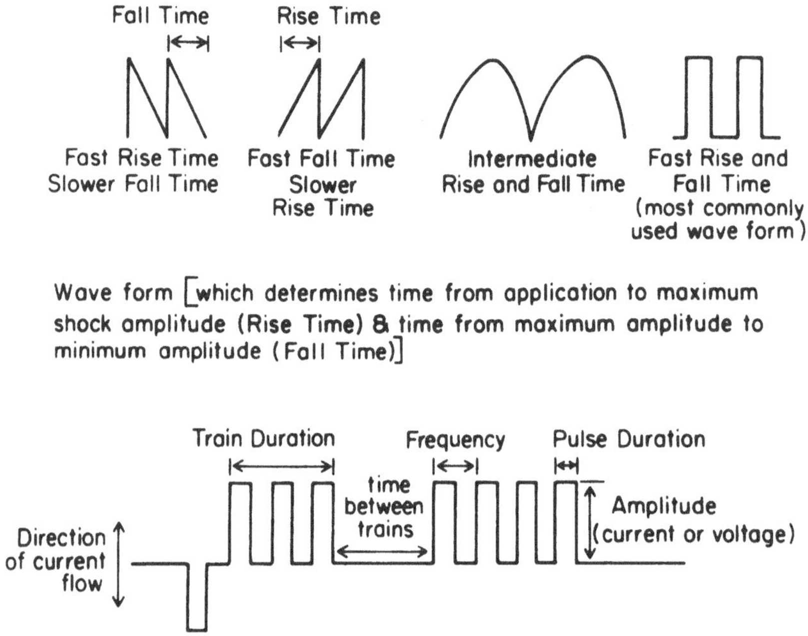

FIGURE 25.1 *Shock characteristics which can be varied.*

Specific Types of Shockers

Hand-held shockers. These are small hand-held battery-operated shockers. Some have electrodes built into the shock box so that when the electrodes are pressed against the skin, a shock is delivered. Others use finger electrodes attached to the shock box by a cable.

Cattle prods. These are standard cattle shockers. The most commonly used cattle prods are those manufactured by the Hot Shot Company and by Sears, Roebuck, and Company.

Radio-controlled shockers. These shockers consist of a transmitting unit and a wrist or belt-worn battery-powered receiver. The electrodes are connected to the receiver through a cable and are usually designed to be applied to the finger, the wrist, or the lower leg.

Visually keyed shocker. This shocker is designed so that when certain slides are projected on a screen, the subject is shocked.

Acoustic-keyed shock. This shocker shocks the subject when a certain recorded passage is presented to him.

Laboratory stimulators. These devices allow the therapist to manipulate all the parameters of shock discussed in the section on types of shockers.

Selection Considerations

Type of shocker to use. There does not seem to be any clear-cut preference in the behavioral literature for constant current, constant voltage, or for unregulated shockers. The author's strong personal preference is for a constant shocker since it is possible to ensure that the current passing through the patient's body does not exceed safe limits. In addition, the level of shock felt by the patient seems to him to be more consistent.

Safe limits of current and voltage. The safe limits for current and voltage are to be determined in part by the location of the electrodes. As a general rule, electrodes should only be used on a leg, an arm, or a finger. Furthermore, they should be close together on the same extremity. In addition, safe levels of current must be observed.

The following information is supplied by Tektronix, Inc., (Strong, 1970) and is quoted from *Popular Electronics*:

> Most of us think that a shock of 10 kV would be more deadly than one of 100 volts. This is not so. People have been electrocuted by ordinary 117 volt appliances and by voltages as low as 42 volts DC! The real measure of the degree of shock is not the voltages applied, but the amount of current forced through the body and that need not be very much [*Popular Electronics*, 1972:31].

> One has only to look at the effects various current levels have on the human body. At one milliampere through the intact, unbroken skin, the patient will probably feel a very slight tingle. At ten millamperes, he will in all likelihood think someone is trying to electrocute him [French, 1972:33].

The Lafayette Instrument Company, in its equipment literature on shockers, states that 5mA is generally considered the maximum safe level that should be allowed to pass through a human body from an external contact.

Continuing with the information from Tektronix:

> While any amount of current over 10mA is capable of producing a painful to severe shock as shown in Figure 25.2, current between 100 and 200 mA can be lethal. Currents above 200 mA, while producing severe burns and uncon-

> sciousness do not usually cause death if the victim is given immediate resuscitation (artificial respiration).
>
> Voltage is not a consideration; it is important only because its level and the body resistance between the points of contact determine how much current flows. Since resistance varies greatly, it is impossible to predict a dangerous voltage. The resistance may vary from 1000 ohms for wet skin to over 500,000 ohms for dry skin—remembering that the resistance from point to point under the skin may be only a few hundred ohms. Also remember that the contact resistance decreases with time and the fatal current may be reached rapidly.
>
> As shown on the chart, a current as low as 20 mA is very dangerous and painful, and the victim can't let go of the circuit. As the current approaches 100 mA, ventricular fibrillation of the heart usually occurs. Above 200 mA, the muscular contractions are so severe that the heart is often forcibly clamped during the shock. This clamping sometimes protects the heart from going into ventricular fibrillation and the victim's chances of survival are good.
>
> Now what lessons can be learned from all of this? First, regard all voltage sources (even some batteries) as potential killers [*Popular Electronics*, 1972].

The levels of current cited above apply where the current is flowing through intact skin. Much lower levels are considered unsafe if the skin is pierced and the current does not pass through the skin. Underwriters Laboratory, in a letter to the author, considers any current in excess of 1/10 of a milliampere unsafe under such conditions.

In summary, the currents and voltages used in aversive conditioning shockers *are potentially lethal*, thus a therapist must use utmost care and in all cases connect the *electrodes to locations close together on the same extremity*.

Given the above information, let us look at the actual shock levels used by therapists.

Daly and Cooper (1967) reported that they used between .75 mA and 2.5 mA. Vogel-Sprott and Racinskas (1969) used 3.25 mA and 850 volts, and Lebow, Gelfand, and Dobson (1970) used 100–120 volts (no current reported).

Many authors, however, do not report specific voltage and current level used. Other means were used to determine shock intensity; for example, Mees (1966) used a shock level that the patient reported as uncomfortable but not painful. Mills, Sobell, and Schaefer (1971) adjusted the shock level to 30 per cent above the voltage level the patient found painful, while Heck (1969) and Lang and Melamed (1969) set the shock at a level the experimenters found to be unpleasant. Low levels of shock also have been successfully used. Whaley (personal communication) reported that he successfully treated self-destructive behaviors in retarded children using levels of shock that were only mildly stimulating and definitely not painful to the experi-

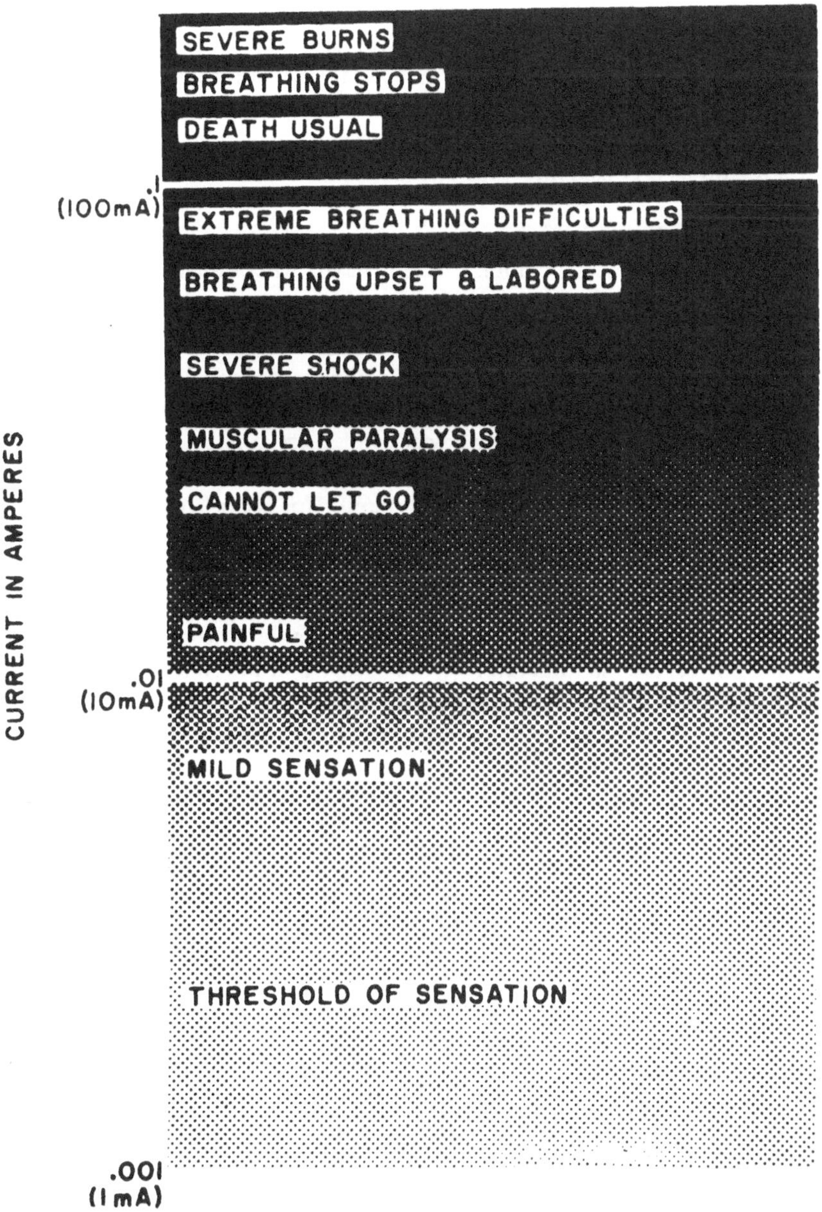

FIGURE 25.2 *Relationship between physical reactions and amperage.*

menter. Wolpe (1969) used low levels of shock which were mildly stimulating and somewhat distracting to treat patients with high levels of anxiety. A number of authors, Kohlenberg (1970), Lovaas and Simmons (1969), Risley (1968), and Tate and Baroff (1966), report that they used cattle prods for shocking human patients. These prods evidently produce a very painful shock. It is not clear what the levels of the voltage and current in these devices are, though Bucher and King (1971) report that the prod they used produced peak currents of about 150–300 mA and peak voltages of 200 to 500 volts. It is obvious that the *average current* and voltage levels in cattle prods is considerably lower than the *peak* levels measured by Bucher and King.

Average voltages and currents in cattle prods probably have not been measured because of the complex output wave form of the cattle prods. Even so, it would seem advisable to measure the voltage and current levels in order to determine the margin of safety of these devices.

Operating and control voltages. Another consideration is how the shocking device is powered. Shocking devices which are connected into a standard 117 V household electrical outlet must be built so that the shocking circuit is electrically isolated from the 117 V input. If it is not sufficiently isolated, there is an extreme danger that unintended and dangerous current levels may be applied to the patient (French, 1972). This problem can be eliminated by using low-voltage battery-powered shockers.

If the shocker is to be connected to a 117 V outlet or to some other source of line power, the manufacturer should certify that the shocker is electrically isolated from the line input and that the device is safe to use with humans. If the manufacturer is unwilling to provide such certification, *do not use the shocking device with humans!*

Some shockers are relay-operated and thus require an external low-voltage power source for actuation, usually either 6, 12 or 24 volts. Some shockers have a built-in low-voltage control power supply. Other shockers require a switch closure to be operated. These shockers are not usually designed for remote control; however, they can usually be easily modified for remote control.

Portability. Battery-operated shockers are usually portable, but there are also larger battery-operated shockers designed for office use only.

Mode of control. Most shockers can be remotely controlled by using an extension cord with a switch attached to it, while others can be remotely controlled *via* a radio transmitter.

Cost. The cost of shockers varies from about $15 for a simple hand-held shocker to about $120 for a simple office shocker. Radio-controlled shockers range in price from about $200 to $400. More complex office shockers vary in price from about $150 to about $2,000. The visual and acoustic shockers mentioned earlier cost about $600 and $300 respectively.

Applications of Shocking Devices

Many kinds of behavioral problems have been treated by using shock as an aversive stimulus. A representative sample of the studies is discussed below.

Wolpe (1965) treated a patient with Demerol addiction by having the patient shock himself whenever he felt an urge to take Demerol. Shock has been used to treat alcoholism: McGuire and Vallance (1964) shocked their patients as they sniffed whiskey; Mills, Sobell, and Schaefer (1971) shocked their patients when they manifested heavy drinking behavior; and Lovibond and Caddy (1970) shocked their patients when blood alcohol levels exceeded .065 per cent.

Autistic behaviors have been treated with shock by Lovaas, Schaffer, and Simmons (1965). Termination of shock was made contingent upon approach behavior by the autistic child; Risley (1968) shocked a child for disruptive and dangerous climbing behaviors.

In treating a patient who was having difficulty keeping his eyes open, Jones (1967) shocked the patient each time his eyelids closed.

Exhibitionism and other sexual deviancies have been treated by Abel, Levis, and Clancy (1970), by McGuire and Vallance (1964), and by Thorpe, Schmidt, Brown, and Castell (1964). McGuire and Vallance shocked patients when they had clear visual images of unacceptable sexual fantasies. Thorpe *et al.* paired shock with words representing the sexually dysfunctional behavior. Feldman (1966) and Rachman and Teasdale (1969) discuss the use of aversive techniques in treating sexual and other disorders.

Pyromania has been treated by Royer, Flynn, and Osadca (1971), who shocked their patient each time he lit paper with matches.

Millard (1966) used shock in treating a case of giggle micturition. He used a small portable device that delivered shock to the patient's back when an electrode in the patient's underwear detected moisture from urination.

Bucher and Fabricatore (1970) taught a patient to control his hallucinations by instructing him to self-administer shock when he heard imaginary voices.

Schwitzgebel (1968) reported that Hilgard and Marquis (1940) developed a shock avoidance procedure for treating a case of hysterical anaesthesia and paralysis in a hand and an arm. Schwitzgebel also reported that Bucher (1967) developed a portable device for treating nail-biting in adults.

McGuire and Vallance (1964) treated a patient with paranoid obsessional thoughts about his wife by having him think about a triggering remark about the wife made by his mother, and having the patient shock himself when he had the thought clearly visualized.

Meyer and Crisp (1964) have treated patients with obesity problems by shocking the patient for inappropriate food approach behaviors and for exceeding dietary limitations.

Solyom and Miller (1967) used an escape paradigm in treating patients with phobias. Ongoing shock was terminated when the experimenter presented the phobic material.

Bucher and King (1971) treated a psychotic child who was destroying electrical appliances (TV, etc.) on a ward by shocking the child as he attempted to play with the forbidden items.

Lebow, Gelfand, and Dobson (1970) treated a patient with respiratory stridor by shocking the patient when the number of stridors exceeded a preselected limit.

White and Taylor (1967) treated rumination by shocking the throat and eye when coughing gestures were observed that had, on past occasions, preceded rumination.

Long and Melamed (1969) have treated a similar case of vomiting by shocking muscle contractions of the abdomen.

Lovaas and Simmons (1969), Corte, Wolfe, and Locke (1971), and Tate and Baroff (1966) have all treated self-destructive behaviors by administering shock upon the occurrence of such behavior and terminating the shock when the behavior stopped.

Smoking has been treated by McGuire and Vallance (1964), who associated the smoking of cigarettes with shock several times a day, and by Powell and Azrin (1968), who developed a cigarette case which shocked the patient when he removed a cigarette from the case.

Daly and Frick (1970) and Daly and Cooper (1967) treated stuttering in patients by punishing stuttering utterances with shock.

Brierly (1967) used shock in treating a case of torticollis. He used a mercury switch attached to a headband which operated a shocker when the patient's head tilted too much.

Barnard, Fleisher, and Steinbock (1966) used shock to cause sphincter relaxation in order to help a patient with urinary retention problems learn to voluntarily control his urination.

Writer's cramp has been treated by McGuire and Vallance (1964) and by Liversedge and Sylvester (1955). In both cases a pen was used to deliver a shock for excessive finger pressure on the pen barrel.

Other Aversive Stimulation Devices

Loud bells, buzzers, and even car horns have been used in the treatment of enuresis. This use is discussed in the section on moisture transducers.

Forester (1971) has used various aversive stimuli such as bright lights, loud sounds, and music in the treatment of some epileptics.

In treating obesity, Kennedy and Foreyt (1971) used an oxygen mask to convey aversive odors from test tubes after the patient had eaten a bit of favorite food.

O'Brien and Azrin (1970) used a bone-conduction tactile stimulator as an aversive stimulus in treating slouching behavior.

Grimaldi and Lichtenstein (1969) used an air blower to blow smoke in the face of patients who were attempting to stop smoking.

TELEMETRY—REMOTE SENSING AND CONTROL DEVICES

Devices that allow remote observation and control permit the therapist to complete many tasks that would otherwise be more difficult or impossible. They have many advantages, but they are rarely used in behavior therapy. Because these devices are not commonly used, this section simply lists those available and their known behavioral uses.

Types of Remote Control Devices

Telemetric devices can be divided into four broad categories: (a) radio-controlled devices; (b) remote communication devices; (c) telephone-controlled devices; and (d) power line transmission devices.

Radio-controlled devices. These devices all utilize a radio transmitter and a radio receiver. The transmitter may be used to actuate a device at some point such as a counter on a student's desk (Coleman, 1970) or as a shocker which delivers a shock to a patient.

More commonly, they are used to transmit information to the experimenter. Schwitzgebel (1968) reports that:

> Winters (1921) and Tursky (1962) attempted to correlate ward behavior of adult schizophrenics and telemetered physiological data; and Schnauss and Rader (1964) devised a portable FM transmitter for voice and physiological monitoring of hospital asthmatic children. Gianascol and Yeager (1964), using scalp electrodes with schizophrenic children, were able to obtain simultaneously telemetric EEG data and film of the patient's behavior. Jacobson, Kales, Lehmann, and Zweizig (1965) observed incidents of sleepwalking and telemetered EEG in a laboratory setting [p. 446].

In a study of cardiac patients who were conditioned to control the occurrence of premature ventricular contractions, Engle (1971) reports that he used telemetry to monitor his patient's heart action during nontraining periods. The data he collected suggest that physiological monitoring during nonconditioning periods may be equally as important in treatment as monitoring during conditioning periods.

The physiological telemetry systems manufactured by the Lafayette Instrument Company and the Stoelting Company are typical of the systems available. Both will operate over ranges of up to 100 yards. Both are lightweight (5 to 6 ounces) FM radio devices. Both can be used to transmit data about such physiological variables as EKG, EEG, EMG, GSR, respiration, body temperature, and physical activity. Both are available as single-channel units as about $1,000, and as multichannel units (two to four channels) from about $1,700 to $3,000. *The Electronics Buyer's Guide* lists about eighty other companies which manufacture telemetric equipment.

Remote communication devices. Remote communication devices either utilize a radio transmitter or an induction loop. The radio units can be used almost anywhere and their transmissions can be picked up by anyone equipped with an FM radio tuned to the proper frequency.

The units utilizing induction loops can only be used in locations where the wire loop can be attached, and thus they are limited to specific areas. Since their transmission is limited to special receivers in the immediate vicinity of the loop, information transmitted over them is less likely to be monitored by unauthorized parties.

At least five short-range communication devices are readily available to the behavior therapists: (a) the bug-in-the-ear (Krapfl, Peter, and Nawas, 1969), manufactured by the Farrell Instrument Company, is available in two models, one utilizing an industion loop and one which is a short-range radio receiver; (b) the Graflex model #3460 headset utilizes an induction loop; with this device, the patient or therapist can receive instruction through a pair of earphones; (c) short-range FM transmitters are available from several radio parts houses and can broadcast through small pocket FM radios; when used with an earplug, these devices are an acceptable substitute for the bug-in-the-ear, though they are not as reliable nor as troublefree; (d) a behind-the-ear hearing aid with a telephone switch on it can be used in connection with an induction loop antenna as a communication device; it is unobtrusive and about equal to the bug-in-the-ear in reliability and sound quality; and (e) simple walkie-talkie devices adapted for use with lapel microphones and earplugs can also be used to provide relatively unobtrusive, two-way communication over short distances.

The cost of the above items varies a great deal. The short range FM transmitter and a small FM radio cost about $35. Two walkie-talkies with microphones and earphones can be obtained for about $100 (these are the only devices that allow two-way communication). The Graflex headset is under $50. The bug-in-the-ear costs from about $600 to $1,000, depending on its capabilities.

Telephone-controlled devices. It is now possible to control devices remotely with a telephone and a special answering device. One such control device is the Teletrol, manufactured by Accu-Sort Systems, Inc., which can be used to turn on devices at a remote location for specific time periods. At $94, this device is relatively inexpensive, considering the more sophisticated custom-tailored answering and control systems available.

Now that devices can be remotely controlled via a telephone, it is within the realm of possibility to contact several such remote stations through use of a small computer and for it to operate devices at each location. If the data at each location have been collected on audio tape in the form suggested by Butterfield, Thomas, and Soberg (1970), it is possible to poll the station and to record and print out the data the computer receives at some central location.

Power line transmission devices. Power line transmission devices consist of a transmitting unit and a receiving unit. The transmission unit is plugged into a standard 117 V wall socket and sends a high frequency electrical signal over the power line to the receiver, which is plugged into a wall socket at some remote location. These devices will work over ranges of up to one mile provided there are no intervening power line transformers. Both RCA and Hearld Electronics Company of Chicago manufacture such devices, which cost about $20.

TRANSDUCERS

Transducers are defined as "devices capable of being actuated by one form or source of energy and of supplying a related energy to other devices, transmissions systems or media . . . It is sometimes implied that the input and output energies shall be of different form" (Van Nostrand, 1958). It is not necessary, however, that the input and output energies be of different forms. They may simply differ in magnitude. The more common transducers are listed below. Some have no presently known behavioral application, but they are listed so the reader will be aware of their existence. Some devices are listed in more than one category, since they can be used for more than one purpose.

Acoustical Input Devices

Acoustical input devices are of two general types. The first type is designed to convert a sound input into an electrical signal which can be amplified so that a listener may hear, observe, or record it. In this case the device is expected to produce an electrical analog of the sound signal. The most commonly used are microphones which are used to pick up sound transmissions through gases and solids. Less commonly used devices include hydrophones which are used to pick up sounds transmitted through liquids, and phonocatheters which are used to pick up sounds inside the bodies of men and animals. Wallace, Brown, Lewis, and Dietz (1959) and Tanenbaum and Kiser (1964) discuss the use of phonocatheters.

The second kind of acoustical input device is designed to measure only certain specified parameters of sound input (such as intensity, duration, or frequency) and to convert this input to an output that is usable by the therapist. This output is commonly used to operate counters which record the number of occurrences of a particular sound, timers which measure the duration of that sound, or chart recorders which record the frequency, magnitude, and duration of that sound. Devices that fall within this second category include sound level meters, audiodermographs, speech rate meters and voice-operated relays.

Microphones. Microphones are classified according to (a) construction, (b) sound acceptance patterns, and (c) impedance. Other factors to be considered in selection should include cost and overload control.

Microphone construction is important because it determines frequency responses, output voltage, and shock resistance.

The frequency response of a microphone plays an important part in how faithful a reproduction of the original sound it allows. Microphones with excellent frequency responses, however, are expensive and their voltage output is relatively low. As a result, one must often compromise on this parameter.

Output voltage is an important factor in that it determines how much external amplification will be needed. With more amplification, there is a greater chance of noise also being amplified or introduced. One type of microphone, the carbon microphone, does not produce any output voltage, so that it requires an outside voltage source for its operation. Still other microphones have built-in amplifiers which increase the output voltage.

Shock resistance is important because many microphones are easily damaged by slight bumps or shocks. Ruggedized microphones are available for situations in which the microphones will be abused. The carbon microphone is among the most rugged. In contrast to other microphones, however, it is quite noisy and it has a poor frequency response.

Microphones come in different sound acceptance patterns. Some are highly directional, that is, they only accept sound coming from a specific direction, while others (omnidirectional types) will respond to sounds arriving at the microphone from any direction. Some are provided with a switch so that they can be used as either directional or omnidirectional microphones. Some directional microphones also have a built-in noise-cancelling feature, which allows them to be used in high-noise environments. In general, the more extraneous noise in the environment, the more directional a microphone should be.

Output impedance is an extremely important factor. If the output impedance of the microphone and the input impedance of the device to which it is hooked do not match, the effective output of the microphone will be severely diminished. Impedance-matching transformers are available for connecting devices which have different impedances.

High-impedance microphones should not be used if the distance from the microphone to the amplifier exceeds about ten feet. This is because it is difficult to eliminate hum pickup where high-impedance circuits are used.

Most microphones do not have any means to control their output voltage, so that when a loud sound impinges on them, they overload. The result is a distorted sound output. A few, however, have a built-in automatic level control (ALC or AVC) that prevents loud sounds from distorting while at the same time it amplifies faint sounds. This feature is very desirable from a therapist's point of view because the resulting sound output is more consistent. Automatic level controls are also sometimes built into tape recorders and amplifiers. When ALC is built into them, it is *not* necessary to use a microphone that has a built-in ALC.

Microphones can cost as little as $5 and as much as several hundred dollars. Michophones costing from $50 to $100 are usually quite acceptable for therapy purposes. Phonocatheters cost from about $80 to $150.

Acoustically controlled devices. Acoustical control devices utilize an ultrasonic sound signal to remotely actuate sound-sensitive relays. Such devices, for example, can be used to actuate counters in a classroom, the points on the counter being used to gain access to reinforcers. BRS/LVE manufactures such a device, costing about $150.

Sound level meters. Sound level meters measure the average intensity of a given frequency band of sounds. Some simply average all sounds in the audio spectrum, others only measure a portion of that spectrum. There are also devices called frequency spectrum analyzers that measure the intensity or magnitude of each frequency component of a sound.

Bostow and Bailey (1969) used sound level meters to measure and modify aggressive and disruptive behavior, while Schmidt and Ulrich (1969) used a sound level meter to measure and modify levels of sound in a classroom. BRS/LVE now manufactures a device similar to that used by Schmidt and Ulrich. Used in monitoring the noise level in a classroom, this device accumulates points at a rate that can be set by the teacher (from one per second to one per 60 seconds). When the noise level in the room rises above a level set by the teacher, the counter resets itself and the class loses points. This device costs about $125.

In general, good sound level meters are expensive, selling for several hundred dollars.

Audiodermographs. Audiodermographs are devices that allow a therapist to determine if a mute or unresponsive patient can hear certain sounds. This device measures a subject's GSR as certain sounds are played into his ear. A GSR response tells the therapist that the subject has heard the sound. Audiodermographs cost about $1,600.

Speech rate meters. Starkweather (1960) designed the speech rate meter which is used to provide an electronic means of counting the number of verbalizations that occur during a given time. It has been used in modifying the verbal behavior of speech-deficient children (Cook and Adams, 1966), and mute schizophrenics (Wilson and Waters, 1966).

Speech rate meters are not known to be commercially available.

Voice-operated relays. Voice-operated relays (VOR) are essentially sound level meters that are designed to operate switches which operate other devices. Simple VORs turn on when the intensity of the sound reaches a certain level and immediately turn off whenever the sound subsides to a point below that level. More sophisticated VORs can be adjusted to turn on only after the sound has been at the trigger level for a certain period of time, and then to remain on for a certain period of time after the sound level has subsided. This permits the VOR to be adjusted to respond, as desired, to sustained sounds, to sound peaks, or to separate sound bursts. VORs have been used to turn on tape recorders when a certain noise level was exceeded (Bostow and Bailey, 1969), to count the occurrence of verbal behavior of certain durations, and to operate reinforcement devices when the sound duration exceeded a preset limit (Sundel, 1969; Butterfield, 1970). VORs cost from about $30 to several hundred dollars depending on their complexity.

Acoustical Output Devices

Acoustical output devices fall into two broad categories: sound reproducing devices and sound producers.

Sound reproducers. Sound reproducers convert an electrical input into a sound that varies in frequency with the frequency of the electrical input. Audio speakers and earphones are the two most common sound reproducers. The major factors to consider in using these devices are frequency response and power handling capacity. To be of use the devices must obviously be able to produce the frequencies of sound the therapist desires to use, and with an unobjectionable distortion. If sound pressure level is important, then the required input voltage to obtain a given sound pressure level at each frequency will have to be determined. For situations requiring constant sound pressure levels, earphones are preferred over speakers, since the relative distance between the subject's eardrum and the sound source remains constant with earphones, whereas the subject can vary his distance from the speaker by simply moving.

In terms of power handling capabilities, the important factor is whether the sound reproducer can produce the desired acoustical output without being damaged.

Sound producers. Sound producers simply manufacture a sound which may or may not have a relation to the frequency of the electrical or mechanical input signal. Common examples of such devices are bells, buzzers, clickers, white noise makers, and the sonalert.

The sonalert is available through radio parts houses for about $15 and will produce either a 2.5 kHz continuous tone or a 2.5 kHz pulsing tone output. The advantage of the sonalert is that it does not introduce electrical noise into other systems such as tape recorders and amplifiers.

A white noise producer that may have some use for behavior therapists is the Sleep Sound which makes a humming noise that can be used to mask other sounds. This device is available from Invento Products Corporation and costs about $20.

A few examples of the uses of acoustical transducers are listed below.

Donner and Gurney (1969), Neil and Howell (1969), Miller and Nawas (1970), Lader and Mathews (1970), Paul and Trimble (1970), and McGlynn (1971) have all used sound reproducers to present relaxation and/or desensitization hierarchies to patients.

Azrin, Jones, Flye (1968), Burke (1969), Brady (1969 and 1971), and May and Hackwood (1968) have all used acoustical devices as distracting stimuli in treating stuttering.

Nathan (1966), Hensen and Rubin (1971), Stumphauzer (1971), and Butterfield (1970) have all used intercommunication devices to talk to their patients while they were in the treatment room.

In studying the desensitization of an anger response, Rimm, DeGroot, Boord, Heiman, and Dillow (1971) used an acoustical signal to calibrate a patient's GSR.

Auditory stimuli have been used as reinforcers by Reynolds and Adams (1953), who used a click as a reinforcer, by Cleary and Packham (1968), who used words as reinforcers, and by Gale (1969), who used tones as reinforcers.

Acoustical devices have been used as discriminative stimuli. Azrin and Powell (1969) trained a patient to take pills at regular intervals by using a pillbox which emitted a loud tone when it was time for the patient to take a pill. When the patient turned the tone off, a pill was delivered into his hand. Schmidt and Ulrich (1969) used a buzzer to signal time periods in the treatment of disruptive classroom behavior. Lomont and Brock (1971) used an acoustical cueing device in studying cognitive factors in systematic desensitization.

Compression, Tension-strain and Torque Transducers

Tension and strain transducers. Tension or strain is a force that tends to stretch or pull two or more connected points apart. The most commonly used strain transducer in behavior therapy is the mercury plethysmograph. The primary use of this device is in monitoring changes in penile volume. As the volume of the penis increases, the mercury column is stretched. This change in length of the column is converted into an electrical signal which is recorded on a polygraph. Examples of this use of the mercury strain gauge are found in Henson and Rubin (1971), Laws and Rubin (1969), and Bancroft (1971). Bancroft (1971) also compares this strain transducer with two other transducers used for measuring penile volume change.

While not actually a tension transducer, the electromyograph does measure muscle tension by measuring the electrical potential of a muscle under tension, so it is included here. Lippold (1967) has a good discussion of electromyography which has been applied to numerous behavioral problems. Examples include the treatment of headaches by Stoyva (1971), the treatment of depression by Rimon, Steinback, and Huhmar (1966), the treatment of torticollis by Cleeland (1971), the measurement of relaxation by Lader and Mathews (1970) and Paul (1969), and the measurement of small muscle movement by Hefferline *et al.* (1960).

Plethysmographs cost between $1,000 and $2,000. If the therapist already has a polygraph, he can purchase a plethysmograph attachment for the polygraph for a few hundred dollars.

Electromyographs, which provide an audio tone that varies with muscle tension, are available for about $100. The more usual electromyographs are part of a standard polygraph and with the polygraph cost from one thousand to several thousand dollars.

Compression transducers. There is no reported use of compression transducers in the behavioral literature reviewed. However, one manufacturer of psychological apparatus, Stoelting, does manufacture a force-sensitive platform that appears to use compression transducers. They report that "the platform is capable of measuring the forces exerted by a subject while performing various types of muscular activity" and that it is also sensitive enough to record the heartbeat in a motionless subject. This platform costs $2,200.

Moisture Sensors and Humidity Transducers

The moisture sensors used in behavior therapy are simple devices. When moisture is present between two electrodes, an electrical circuit is completed. The completion of the circuit operates such devices as bells, lights, buzzers, and counters. The primary use of these devices has been in the treatment of enuresis and encopresis. Three major types of devices are in use (a) bell and sheet devices, (b) toilet training devices, and (c) wet underwear sensors.

Bell and sheet devices. Bell and sheet devices consist of either a rubber pad embedded with electrodes that are covered by a light cotton pad or a quilted pad with electrodes built into it, a moisture sensing transducer, and a bell or horn. The bell and sheet is used in the treatment of nocturnal enuresis. When a child urinates (even a small amount) the moisture from the urination bridges the set of electrodes causing the bell or buzzer to ring. Turner, Young, and Rachman (1970), Peterson, Wright, and Hanlon (1969), and Lovibond (1964) all report on this use of the bell and sheet. The cost of these devices ranges from about $20 to $200. At least one company, the S & L Signal Company, leases them to patients for $6.50 a week.

Toilet training devices. Azrin, Bugle, and O'Brien (1971) have developed a device that can be inserted in a standard toilet seat. This device, which is like a miniature toilet bowl, has electrodes at the bottom of the bowl which sense any moisture (from either feces or urine). When moisture is sensed, an audible alarm is set off. This device is now commercially available from BRS/LVE for about $40.

Others (Millard, 1966; and Crosby, 1950) have used shock instead of an audio alarm to treat enuresis and encopresis. Madsen, Hoffman, Thomas, Korpzak (1969) compare several of the above toilet training techniques.

Movement Sensors and Transducers

There are several distinct types of movement transducers such as (a) accelerometers, (b) vibration indicators, (c) displacement indicators, and (d) velocity indicators. All of the above transducers except vibration sensors come in two types: linear movement transducers and angular movement transducers. Linear movement transducers measure acceleration, displacement, or velocity in a straight line, and are relatively insensitive to motions that are off their measuring axis. Angular movement transducers measure the rotational acceleration, displacement, and velocity of a body. They are insensitive to linear motion when that motion is not in the transducer's plane of rotation. Vibration sensors usually measure small linear movements on one, two, or three axes (two at horizontal right angles to each other and the third at at vertical right angle to the other two). These devices are usually accelerometers containing piezoelectric crystals, although they can also be electromagnetic. Of the above types, no behavioral uses for angular motion transducers, for vibration transducers, or for velocity transducers were found in the literature reviewed.

Accelerometers. Accelerometers measure average acceleration, which is the average change in velocity over a period of time. This change occurs because there is a change in the force applied to an object. An increased force produces a positive acceleration of the object (i.e., an increasing velocity per unit time). A decreased force produces a negative acceleration of the object (sometimes loosely referred to as a deceleration). It is a decreasing velocity per unit time. The primary behavioral use of the accelerometers has been in measuring activity.

Schwitzgebel (1968) reported that Larsen (1940) used a pedometer (which is a rudimentary accelerometer) in the treatment of obesity, and that

Schulmann and Reisman (1959) used modified self-winding wristwatches to measure hyperactivity. Weiss (1971), in a study on the production of gastric ulcers under stress conditions in rats, found that the activity level of a rat was a partial determinant of the size of gastric ulcers produced in the rat. It is possible that similar studies with humans using activity measures would yield similar information.

The Lafayette Instrument Company currently produces a remote indicating activity monitor that allows for the free movement of the subjects. Accelerometers, with their associated equipment, cost from about one to several thousand dollars.

Displacement measuring devices. Displacement is a change in spatial position without regard to the velocity or rate of the change taking place. (Because some displacement measuring devices do utilize chart recorders for recording purposes, the displacement per unit time is often also recorded.) A number of devices have been developed to measure the displacement of a patient or an object. Schwitzgebel (1968) reported that Haring (1968) used a chair to record the duration and frequency of sitting in a chair. Barrett (1962) used a chair to measure body tic activity. Schwitzgebel reported that he developed devices capable of monitoring the geographical location of delinquents. He also reported that Goldman (1961) used wrist-worn ultrasonic speakers to measure body movement.

Borkovec and Craighead (1971) and Levis (1969), in studies of the desensitization of snake phobias, mounted a snake-containing box on a track, and monitored the position of the cart on the track by counting button pushes. (Each button push moved the snake box one foot closer to the subject.)

The ballistocardiograph, a sensitive movement-measuring device originally used for measuring movements of the body that result from beating of the heart, has also been used as an activity monitor. The output of the ballistocardiograph is a complex wave form. Note that this type of output is difficult to interpret.

Another device that measures movement is the body movement chair, which uses either electromagnetic or pneumatic transducers and whose output is recorded on a polygraph. As its name implies, this type of chair measures the position of the subject on a chair as well as the patterning of position shift on the chair.

Several manufacturers produce eye-blink goggles which detect eye blinks. The lid operates a mechanical switch when it closes. By using a similar device, Jones (1967) treated a man who could not keep his eyes open.

Forster (1971) reported that he uses a photoelectric cell mounted on the bridge of the glasses of certain types of epileptics (whose seizures are brought on by movements of objects which cause a fluctuation in the light intensity the subject is receiving) to detect movement that produces fluctuating light situations. The output of the photocell was fed into a hearing aid which produced a loud clicking sound in the patient's ear, and the clicking stimulus served to prevent an epileptic seizure from occurring.

Complex photoelectric devices which can detect eye movement have been used. While these devices have not yet been used by behavior therapists, the use of eye movement to control equipment has been reported in the press. This equipment, developed by the National Aeronautics and Space Administration, could have use in training paralyzed patients to operate a variety of devices.

Finally, capacitance proximity sensors and photoelectric sensors appear to have promise as movement sensors in a closed situation such as a room. In addition to indicating position, they could also be used to activate equipment such as tape recorders when someone entered a room.

The cost of the devices commercially available are as follows: (a) body movement chairs, $150 to $300, (b) ballistocardiographs, $1,000 and up, (c) eye-blink goggles, $100 to $200, (d) eye movement detectors, $3,000 to $6,000, and (e) photoelectric sensors, $100 to $200.

Pressure and Weight Sensors and Transducers

Pressure is the force applied per unit area. Weight is simply the force an object exerts due to gravity.

A commonly measured physiological variable involving pressure is blood pressure. This pressure is usually indirectly measured; that is, a cuff is placed around a finger or an arm. The cuff is then inflated while a transducer records the patient's pulsebeat. This transducer is usually acoustical or photoelectric. The transducer is usually placed just below the cuff (away from the heart). When the pulsebeat has stopped, the cuff pressure is reduced until a beat is recorded again. It is assumed that the pressure in the cuff at the point that the beat resumes is equal to the maximum (or systolic) pressure in the artery. The pressure in the cuff is then allowed to continue to decrease until the pulsebeat is no longer heard. This is assumed to be the minimum (or diastolic) pressure in the artery. The main problem with this method is that it cannot provide continuous blood pressure measurements and, in the cases of some circulatory diseases, it may not accurately reflect the blood pressure in other parts of the body. The alternative method, which requires that a catheter be inserted into an artery, is not often used with humans because of the possibility of infection or other complications.

Although the changes were small, Bensen (1971) conditioned humans to decrease and increase blood pressures by reinforcing the appropriate changes.

Others have used pressure-measuring devices to help patients with a variety of problems. Jones (1956) treated a micturition problem by measuring patients' bladder pressures and then gradually shaping their retention of urine in the bladder. Liversedge and Sylvester (1955) treated writer's cramp. In this case, excessive pressure on the pen barrel caused the patient to receive a shock. Grimaldi and Lichtenstein (1969), in treating smoking problems, used a pressure-sensitive switch on the bottom of an ashtray to detect when the patient put out a cigarette. The activation of the switch turned off a blower which had been blowing smoke in the face of the patient.

Other devices that use pressure transducers are the mercury plethysmograph and the pneumograph, which is used to measure the respiration rate. These last two devices are discussed in the respiration and volume transducer sections of this chapter.

Blood pressure measuring devices cost from about $45 to several hundred dollars, depending on how automated they are. The other devices mentioned in this section must be custom-made.

The weight-sensing devices used in behavior therapy detect the presence or absence of a predetermined weight. Schwitzgebel (1968) reported that Hix (1966) patented a weight-sensitive toilet-training device which automatically produces a musical sound when urination or defecation is accomplished. Weight-sensing mats have also been used to activate tape recorders and other devices when a subject entered a room. These mats cost less than $100.

Respiration Transducers

Respiration transducers measure respiration rate, respiration airflow, or respirator volume. Respiration rate is measures by either a thermistor or a pneumograph. The thermistor, which is placed in the airstream of a nostril, measures the difference of the temperature of the inhaled air and the exhaled air. This temperature fluctuation is recorded on a polygraph which then provides a visual representation of the respiration rate.

The pneumograph uses a tube filled with air. The tube is placed around the chest and as the chest expands and contracts, the pressure inside the tube changes. This pressure change is recorded on a polygraph, giving a visual representation of respiration rate. Examples of its use can be found in Paul (1959), Paul and Trimble (1970), and Burns and Ascough (1971).

Respiration airflow and volume change can be measured. Vachon (1971) discusses the methods and the problems that are encountered in measuring these parameters.

Thermistor respiration monitors cost about $600. Pneumograph monitors cost about $250 (plus a polygraph recorder).

Tactile Transducers or Stimulators

These devices are all output devices. They mechanically stimulate or vibrate the skin. Their reported uses include: treatment of female sexual dysfunction with a hand vibrator by increasing the stimulation of the erogenous areas of the body (verbal report at the Conference on Human Sexuality in Medical Education, 1970), as a distracting stimulus in treating stuttering (Brady,

1969; Azrin, Jones, and Flye, 1968), and as an aversive stimulus to treat patients with poor body posture (O'Brien and Azrin, 1970). Bailey and Meyerson (1969) reported that they used an industrial vibrator attached to a bed as a reinforcer for profoundly retarded children. Similar devices can be attached to chairs and could probably be used also as reinforcers.

The types of vibrators used in the above reports are all commercially available and range in cost from under $15 to about $100.

Temperature Transducers

The thermistor is the main temperature transducer now in use. It measures relative temperature changes rather than absolute temperatures. Thermistors have been used in medicine to measure skin temperature and by both physicians and behavior therapists to measure respiration rate (Burns and Ascough, 1971). Thermistors and their related monitors cost from a few hundred to several thousand dollars.

Volume, Flow, Fluid Level, and Viscosity Transducers

While transducers are available to measure the viscosity of a fluid and the level of a fluid in a container, no behavioral uses have been reported. Flow and volume transducers have been used, however. The most common volume measurement has been the change in penile volume. Among those reporting the use of transducers for this purpose are Bancroft (1966, 1971); Hansen and Rubin (1971); Laws and Rubin (1969); McConaghy (1967, 1970); and Barlow, Leitenberg, and Agras (1970). Bancroft and Barlow *et al.* also evaluate the psychophysiological measures used in the treatment of sexual dysfunction.

Laders and Mathews (1970) use a photoelectric plethysmograph to measure blood flow. Photoplethysmographs can be used to estimate blood flow, pulse rate, and—with a cuff—to measure blood pressure.

Plethysmograph transducers themselves are relatively inexpensive, but the associated monitoring equipment is not. The overall cost of a plethysmographic system is approximately $2,000.

Multiple Use Monitoring Systems

It should be pointed out that often the same monitoring system can be used with a variety of the transducers mentioned in the above sections. The importance of this is that once a monitoring system (usually a multichannel polygraph) has been purchased, the additional transducers can be used with the system at little additional cost. To illustrate the typical costs involved, several transducers without their associated monitoring systems in the Stoelting Company catalogue are as follows: (a) accelerometer, $175; (b) eye-movement transducer, $600; (c) pneumograph, $25; (d) finger plethysmograph, $2.25; and (e) blood pressure transducer, $195.

Still, Movie, and TV Cameras and Projectors

Cameras are used to monitor behavior or to take or record pictures which will later be projected for stimulus presentation purposes.

A discussion of the technical aspects of photography and television is beyond the scope of this chapter. A few of the applications to behavior therapy, however, are described in the following paragraphs. Doran and Holland (1971) used an eye marker camera to record the amount of time a subject looked at programmed tests of differing difficulties. Sanders, Hopkins, and Walker (1969) suggest using a time-lapse camera to take samples of ongoing behavior at remote locations. They report that remotely operated cameras can be used for on-the-scene observation at a cost that is considerably less than the cost of using a live observer. Surratt, Ulrich, and Hawkins (1969) have used a TV camera for remote, relatively unobtrusive observation of classroom behavior.

The most common use of photographic and television devices is for the purpose of stimulus presentation. (This is particularly true in the treatment of phobias.) Examples of this use include Hensen and Rubin (1971), Vodde and Gilner (1971), Miller and Nawas (1970), Neil and Howell (1969), and Solyom and Miller (1965).

Wilson and Walters (1966), Sundel (1968), and Butterfield (1970) have used slides in attempting to reinstate the verbal behavior of mute schizophrenics.

Kellman (1969) has treated shoplifting by using motion pictures of shoplifting and pairing the pictures with aversive consequences.

Pictures have also been used as reinforcers. Representative studies are those by Hewett (1968) with an autistic child, by Greene (1969) with a retarded child, and by Nathan (1966) in a study of communication behavior.

Audio Magnetic Tape Recorders

Tape recorders are used for monitoring, for controlling program devices, and for treatment. However, before we discuss their use, let us first discuss some of the technical aspects of tape recorders.

There are three major types of audio tape recorders commercially available. They are (a) open-reel (sometimes called reel-to-reel), (b) cassette, and (c) cartridge.

Types of Tape Recorders

Open-reel recorders. The open-reel recorder is still the most versatile recorder. Machines using this format offer the longest recording times, the widest selection of tape reels, the widest variety of tape widths, and the widest variety of special-purpose controls.

Cassette recorders. The most convenient tape recorders are recorders utilizing the cassette format. They have limited maximum recording time (60 minutes a side), are available in only two tape widths (¼ inch and ⅛ inch), have only one tape speed (1⅞ IPS), have fewer optional recorder functions, and have a lower frequency response. Even so, for the vast majority of uses in behavior therapy, the cassette recorder is close to an ideal machine.

Cartridge recorders. Cartridge recorders all use endless-loop tape cartridges. The tape used in these cartridges has no end, but consists of a large loop of tape that is wound inside the cartridge. The main advantage of this format is that once started, the tape plays continuously. Once ended, the tape replays or is ready for re-recording. This feature is desirable for applications such as (a) the presentation of a repetitive stimulus (Cleary and Peckham, 1968), and (b) the temporary recording of speech, such as when the therapist would like to be able to review the last hour's session, but does not wish to keep a tape of earlier sessions. An endless-loop tape of the proper capacity would always maintain such a record while automatically erasing earlier conversations on the tape.

The major problem with cartridge machines is that the tape in the cartridge cannot easily be spliced nor can it be rewound. This last problem means that the only way to reach a previously recorded spot on a tape is to play through the whole tape until the desired section of the tape is again reached.

There are several cartridge formats. The most common is the NAB format which is identical to the eight-track cartridge players used in automobile tape players.

Selection Considerations

Tape width. Various tape widths are used on tape recorders. One-quarter-inch tape is the most common width in both reel-to-reel and cartridge machines. Wider widths are sometimes used in multichannel reel-to-reel machines. Cassette machines most normally use ⅛-inch-wide tapes, though some use ¼-inch tape.

Tape length and composition. Tape length determines how much recording time is available for a given reel size. Twelve hundred, 1,800, 2,400, and 3,600 feet, seven-inch reels are available. The length of tape that will fit on one reel is determined by the thickness of the tape which ranges from .5 mil to 1.5 mil. In general, thinner tapes are less durable and require more careful handling. For most purposes, the one-mil tape (1,800 feet on a seven-inch reel, 45 minutes a side on the cassette) seems to be the most satisfactory.

Tapes are made from several different materials. The plastic base is most commonly either acetate or mylar. Mylar-based tapes are stronger and more durable than acetate-based tapes. The magnetic material deposited on the base may be one of several iron oxide formulations or a chromium dioxide (C_rO_2) formulation. Stark (1972) details the advantages and disadvantages of the various formulations.

Some tape formulations have lubricants included in them, others do not. Tapes without lubricants cause rapid head wear and should be avoided. In general, it is wise to avoid inexpensive tapes as they are usually not properly lubricated. They also tend to yield recordings of poor quality.

Tape speed. As a rule of thumb, as the tape speed increases, so does the frequency response of the recorder. This is not to suggest that all low-speed recorders have poor frequency responses. Some high quality low-speed recorders have an excellent frequency response. Generally, however, given two tape recorders of the same quality, the recorder operating at the higher tape speeds will have a better frequency response. The following table (provided by C. H. Stoelting Company) illustrates how the frequency response of a good quality recorder varies with tape speed.

TABLE 25.1 *Frequency responses of tapes*

Tape Speed	*Frequency Response*	*Recording time for one side of an 1,800-foot reel of tape*
15 ips	30 –24000Hz ± 3 db	22½ minutes
7–½ ips	50 –22000Hz ± 3 db	45 minutes
3–¾ ips	50 –18000Hz ± 3 db	1½ hours
1–⅞ ips	70 –11000Hz ± 3 db	3 hours
15/16 ips	70 – 5000Hz ± 3 db	6 hours

As the tape speed increases, more tape is required for a given recording time. Because of this, some recorders allow the operator to select any of several speeds. The tape speeds normally available are listed in the above table, as is the amount of recording time available on an 1800-foot reel of tape at each speed.

The speeds of some tape recorders are regulated very closely (± .25 per cent or .5 per cent total) while others allow a wider variation (± 2.5 per cent or 5 per cent total). For many purposes, a variation of 5 per cent is acceptable. If, however, the recorder is used to operate programmed equipment, or to present stimuli, a 5 per cent variation in tape in an hour's time would cause an error of 180 seconds in the program, while a .5 per cent error would produce a maximum error of only about 18 seconds an hour.

Test tapes for checking the frequency response and the timing error of a tape recorder are commercially available.

Tape head configurations. There are three types of recorder heads: record, playback, and erase. Some tape heads may be a combination of two or more of these types. The record head causes an incoming audio signal to be recorded on the tape. The playback head converts the signal recorded on the tape to an electrical signal which, when played through an amplifier and a speaker, produces an audio output. The erase head destroys or eliminates any signals that are recorded on the tape. The best recorders utilize separate erase, record, and playback heads.

Tape recorder heads are also classified by the number of tracks that they record on the tape. A one-track head will record one channel on the tape. A two-track (sometimes called half-track) head will record one channel on each half of the tape width.

Some recorders can record as many as 16 channels on a one-inch tape. These recorders are, however, not normally used by behavior therapists. Probably the most commonly used head configuration is quarter-track. This configuration allows for the simultaneous recording of four channels or two channels (as is done in stereo recording) or the recording of a single channel at a time until all four tracks on the tape are recorded. Quadraphonic recorders can be used to record one, two, or four tracks at a time. Most stereo tape recorders can be used in the latter two ways.

Tape recording function controls. The functioning of a tape recorder depends upon the proper sequential operation of several mechanical and electronic devices. These functions may be mechanically or electromechanically (solenoid) controlled or controlled by some combination of the two methods. As a general rule, the better-quality machines are solenoid-operated. If a tape recorder is fully solenoid-operated, all its functions (rewind, fast forward, play, record, and stop) can be remotely controlled. Some machines offer remote-control attachments as accessories. From a therapist's point of view, remote control is a very desirable feature as it permits use of an unobtrusively located tape recorder, and, at the same time, the capability for instant recording and playback.

Special features. Some tape recorders offer additional features, including automatic level control, voice actuation, signal sensing, and auto-reverse or continuous reverse.

The automatic level control modifies the incoming signal level so that low level sounds are increased in volume and high intensity sounds are reduced in volume. Because of this feature, both quiet and loud voices tend to be recorded at more acceptable volume levels. This feature is particularly valuable when several speakers are being recorded, as in a conference.

Voice-actuated tape recorders only operate when someone is talking. This feature conserves tape since the tape is not running during long silences. It also allows for the monitoring of conversations without an operator present to turn the recorder on and off.

Auto-reversing or continuous-reversing recorders reverse the tape direction when the end of the tape (in open-reel or cassette machines) is reached. Some recorders will reverse in both the record and playback modes. Others will reverse in the playback mode only. This feature is desirable because both sides of a tape can be used without mechanically reversing the tape on the tape recorder.

Recorders with signal sensing devices built into them are designed to stop if they detect a certain signal on the tape. Some of these recorders utilize an aluminum foil strip for this purpose while others use a high frequency audio signal. Some recorders are also designed to stop and then reverse when a signal is sensed on the tape. Most, however, must be restarted by an operator and, upon restarting, they continue to play in the direction they were playing prior to being stopped by the signal.

Signal sensing is a valuable feature since it allows for the automatic sequential presentation of instructions on a single tape. This mode of presentation has been used in automatic desensitization devices.

Some recorders simply use signal sensing to stop the recorder at the end of the tape and to actuate a buzzer which tells the operator the end of the tape has been reached.

Also available are more sophisticated signal sensing tape recorders which give the operator random access to any section of the tape, but such recorders are very expensive ($2,000 to $4,000).

Compressed speech recorders. Compressed speech recorders utilize rapidly rotating heads. The function of the rotating head is to increase the amount of speech recorded on any given segment of tape. When the tape is played back, the effect of this is to cause the apparent rate of speech to increase without increasing the pitch of the speech. This type of recorder can be used for a variety of therapeutic purposes, such as increasing the playback rate of speech for talking books for the blind or for decreasing the time necessary to review an interview (from perhaps 60 minutes to 30 minutes). Schwitzgebel (1968) cites several uses for both compressed and expanded speech.

These recorders, it should be emphasized, compress the speech as it is being recorded, a real advantage over the tedious older methods of compressing speech which required that little segments of the original tape be cut out and spliced together.

Serviceability and adaptability. Some recorders are designed so that they are easily serviced. They may even have plug-in submodules, including plug-in heads and electronics. Others require dismantling to be serviced. Plug-in heads and electronics are highly desirable since they are the components most likely to fail on a tape recorder. Machines with plug-in heads are also more versatile, as the track configuration can be rapidly changed (e.g., from quarter- to full-track, etc.). Good machines with plug-in heads are expensive since they require careful design and assembly.

Cost. Good open-reel recorders cost from about $400 to several thousand dollars. Good cassette recorders cost from about $200 to $400. Acceptable portable cassette recorders cost from about $100 to $250, and good cartridge machines cost from about $100 to $200.

If a therapist plans to use a recorder several hours a day, he should invest in a quality recorder. If he has only limited use for a recorder, he may find less expensive recorders acceptable.

Application to Behavior Therapy

Tape recorders have been used as monitoring devices by many therapists. For example, Bostow and Bailey (1969) used a tape recorder to monitor noise level in the classroom. Cook and Adams (1966) recorded the verbal output of speech-deficient children. Hensen and Rubin (1971) recorded verbal responses to erotic stimuli. Rubenstein (1966) recorded changes in vocalization patterns under mild stress, and Sundel (1968) recorded the verbal output of his near-mute schizophrenic patients.

Tape recorders have also served as stimulus-presentation devices. Examples are Paul and Trimble (1970) and Lader and Mathews (1970), who used recorders for deep muscle relaxation training; McGlynn (1971), Miller and Nawas (1970), and Donner and Gurney (1969), who used recorders in presenting desensitization hierarchies, Burke (1967), who treated patients with stuttering problems, and Solyom and Miller (1967), who treated phobias.

Tape recorders have also been used as control devices by Butterfield, Thomas, and Soberg (1970), and as digital monitoring devices by Newton and Buczek (1970). BRS/LVE produces an eight-channel tape recorder that can be used as a control device in a manner similar to that described by Butterfield *et al.* The Lehigh Valley recorder costs about $1,800.

Chart Recorders

Chart recorders are used for graphically recording the occurrence of discrete behaviors, changes in physiological responses, and the occurrence of experimental events (such as the delivery of reinforcements, the changing of stimulus conditions, and the delivery of aversive stimulation). The latency and duration of behaviors and events can also be determined from chart recorder records.

Functional Characteristics and Selection Criteria

Functionally, all chart recorders consist of two major assemblies: the chart drive and the recording head with pens.

The purpose of chart drive is to move the chart paper under the recording pens at a uniform speed. The chart drive is thus a timer, as distances on the chart can be directly converted into time. The recording head and pens transform electrical data inputs into a graphic representation of the data by writing on the moving chart. Some recorders have provisions for changing the chart drive speed by the user. Others do not, in which case the chart drive speed must be selected prior to purchasing the recorder. The chart speed should be selected on the basis of the expected response or event rate. The higher the rate, the higher the chart speed needed.

There are two basic kinds of recording heads: (1) analog, where the magnitude of the displacement of the recording pen is proportional to the electrical input, and (2) digital or incremental where any signal above some minimum threshold causes an incremental pen deflection. Analog recorders are most commonly used to record the occurrence of discrete responses and events.

There are three general types of pens used in chart recorders. They are (a) ink pens, (b) hot stylus pens, and (c) scratch type pens.

Most ink pens use liquid ink, though a few now use felt tip pens or ball-point pens. Ball-point pens are best adapted to uses where response input rates are relatively low (lower than about one per second). Felt tip pens wear relatively rapidly, but are also very convenient. Liquid ink pens are most commonly used with polygraph recorders and are the most versatile of the three types of pens. The main problem with these pens is that they can clog, they are messy, and on portable instruments, unless special provisions are included in the instrument, the ink supply may spill.

Hot stylus pens record by burning through a layer on the chart and exposing a different color underlayer. Although the stylus temperature must be adjusted carefully, these pens work well. When response rates are high, these pens produce an uneven line width, so they are best suited to situations where the response input is moderate.

Scratch pens record by scratching through a wax layer on the chart and exposing a different color underlayer. These pens are nearly maintenance-free and in many situations approach the ideal. They tend to skip at high response input rates so they are also best suited to moderate and low response input rates.

A major consideration in pen selection should be chart paper cost and durability. The cost of ink pen chart paper is the lowest and its durability is the greatest. The other two types of charts are more expensive and tend to tolerate repeated examination in handling less well. If the chart records are only to be examined a few times, however, these latter two types of chart paper are quite satisfactory.

Types of Chart Recorders

Cumulative recorders. Most cumulative recorders have two pens, one for recording the occurrence of events (such as a change in stimulus conditions), the other for recording the occurrences of responses and the delivery of reinforcement.

The first, the event pen, is fixed in relation to the chart and simply moves a small distance at a right angle to the chart when it is energized, producing a "pip" on the chart. The second, the response pen, is not fixed, but is designed to move a fixed distance toward the top of the chart each time a response input occurs. When it reaches the top of the chart, it resets by returning to the bottom of the chart where further responses again cause it to move toward the top of the chart. The response pen also records the delivery of reinforcement by making a small "pip" at right angles to the direction of the chart's movement. This recorder then shows the time relationships between stimulus changes, responses, and reinforcements.

Because the graph paper in the recorder is moving at a known speed, the slope of the cumulative response line drawn by the recorder yields a direct estimate of the rate of responding as well.

Event recorders. Event recorders may contain up to about 40 pens. When the recorder is operating and the pens are not energized, they draw straight lines on the chart paper. When a pen is energized, it moves a small distance at right angles to the direction the chart is moving, producing a shift in the position of the line the pen is drawing. Each pen then records the occurrence or nonoccurrence of one event. There are, however, a few event recorders, such as the Lafayette Model 56043, a discrete level recorder, that can code several events on one pen channel. The Lafayette recorder can record up to 35 events with only five pens. Each event pen shifts in larger and larger increments to the right as different event inputs are applied to the recorder input.

The discrete level recorder is quite often useful, but where one or more of the events being monitored by one pen can occur at the same time, it cannot be used since different inputs to the same pen shift the pen different amounts.

Polygraphs. Polygraphs are general-purpose analog recorders. They may contain from one to 16 pens, or channels. In addition, they usually have at least one event marker channel.

The prime use of these recorders is to record physiological data. They can, however, be used to record the occurrence, magnitude, and latency of responses, or to record changes in stimulus conditions.

With proper interconnecting devices these recorders have been used to record EKG, EEG, GSR, or BSR, respiration rates, muscle potential, blood pressure, heart rate, physical activity, penile volume change, body movement, response latency, response magnitude, and response occurrence.

Cost. Chart recorders are expensive. Simple event recorders range in price from about one hundred dollars to several hundred dollars. Surprisingly enough, some of the better event recorders are relatively inexpensive. A notable example is the Simpson ten-Channel Event Recorder available through Allied Electronics at a cost of about $175. Simpson also manufactures miniature strip chart recorders at comparable prices.

Cumulative recorders are available in a variety of models, including student models, laboratory models, and demonstration models. They normally cost from about one hundred to several hundred dollars.

The cost of polygraph recorders varies a great deal, depending upon the number of channels, the response rate of the recorder, its sensitivity, etc., and ranges from several hundred to several thousand dollars.

Uses of Chart Recorders

Event recorders have been used by Thomas, Carter, Gambrill, and Butterfield (1970) to record the occurrence of patient button pushes and the onset and offset of talk by patients, by Gale (1969) to record the occurrence of button pushes, and by Stuart (1970) to record the rate of positive talk.

Cumulative recorders have been used by Cook and Adams (1966) to record speech rate, by Lindsley (1960), Sundel (1968), Butterfield (1970), and Heck (1969) to record lever pull response rates with mental patients, by Nathan (1966) to record the number of foot pushes in a study on feedback delay, and by Lovitt (1968) to study the effects of conjugate reinforcement.

Polygraphs have been used by a great many therapists. Paul (1969, 1970) used a polygraph to monitor heart rate, muscle tension, respiration rate, and GSR in a study of methods to reduce the physiological arousal level of subjects. Lader and Mathews (1970) measured blood flow, pulse rate, muscle tension, and GSR in a study of various relaxation techniques. Hensen and Rubin (1971) and McConaghy (1967) used a polygraph to record changes in penile volume. Benson (1971) monitored blood pressure and respiration in a study of the modification of blood pressure, as did Engel (1971) who was conditioning cardiac arrhythmias.

Source of Apparatus

Some sources of the devices discussed in this chapter are listed below. Other sources can be found in the annual *Science Magazine Guide to Scientific Instruments,* the *Annual Electronic Buyer's Guide* (Published by McGraw-Hill), and in the annual *EEM* (*Electronic Engineers Master,* published by United Technical Publications).*

* Editor's note: In the March 1969 issue of the *American Psychologist* devoted to psychological instrumentation, there is a detailed buyer's guide.

1. Accu-Sort Systems, Inc., 601 Lawn Avenue, Sellersville, Pa. 18960
2. Allied Electronics, 2400 W. Washington Boulevard, Chicago, Ill. 60612
3. Altron Electronics, Box 103, Somerville, New Jersey 08876
4. BRS/LVE, 5301 Holland Drive, Beltsville, Maryland 20705
5. Behavioral Controls, 1506 West Pierce Street, Milwaukee, Wis. 53246
6. Esterline Angus, Box 2400, Indianapolis, Indiana, 46224
7. Farrall Instrument Company, P. O. Box 1037, Grand Island, Nebraska 68801
8. Ralph Gerbrands Company, 8 Beck Road, Arlington, Massachusetts 02174
9. Invento Products Corporation, 39–25 Skillman Avenue, Long Island, N. Y.
10. Lafayette Instrument Company, Box 1279, Lafayette, Indiana, 47902
11. Scientific Prototype, 615 West 131 Street, New York, New York 10027
12. S & L Signal Company, 525 Holly Avenue, Madison, Wisconsin
13. Stoelting Company, 424 North Homan Avenue, Chicago, Illinois 60624

References

Abel, G., Levis, D., and Clancy, J. Aversion therapy applied to taped sequences of deviant behavior and other sexual deviancies: A preliminary paper. *Journal of Behavior Therapy and Experimental Psychiatry,* 1970, *1,* 59–66.

Azrin, N., Bugle, C., and O'Brien, R. Behavioral engineering: Two apparatuses for toilet training retarded children. *Journal of Applied Behavior Analysis,* 1971, *4,* 249–253.

Azrin, J., Jones, R., and Flye, B. A synchronization effect and its application to stuttering by a portable apparatus. *Journal of Applied Behavior Analysis,* 1968, *1,* 283–296.

Azrin, N., and Powell, J. Behavioral engineering: The reduction of smoking behavior by a conditioning apparatus and procedure. *Journal of Applied Behavior Analysis,* 1968, *1,* 193–200.

Azrin, N., and Powell, J. Behavior engineering: The use of response priming to improve prescribed self medication. *Journal of Applied Behavior Analysis,* 1969, *2,* 39–42.

Bailey, J., and Meyerson, L. Vibration as a reinforcer with a profoundly retarded child. *Journal of Applied Behavior Analysis,* 1969, *2,* 135–137.

Bancroft, J. The application of psychophysiological measures to the assessment and modification of sexual behavior. *Behavior Research and Therapy,* 1971, *9,* 119–130.

Bancroft, J., Jones, H., and Pullan, B. A simple transducer for measuring penile erection with comments on its use in the treatment of sexual disorders. *Behavior Research and Therapy,* 1966, *4,* 239–241.

Barlow, D., Becker, R., Leitenberg, H., and Agras, W. A mechanical strain gauge for recording penile circumference change. *Journal of Applied Behavior Analysis,* 1970, *3,* 73–76.

BARNARD, G., FLEISHER, C., and STEINBOCK, R. The treatment of urinary retention by aversive stimulus cessation and assertive training. *Behavior Research and Therapy,* 1966, *4,* 232–236.

BARRETT, B. Reduction in rate of multiple tics by free-operant conditioning methods. *Journal of Nervous and Mental Disease,* 1962, *135,* 187–195.

BENSON, H. Decreased systolic blood pressure with feedback in essential hypertension. Paper presented at the Conference on New Applications of Conditioning to Medical Practice, University of Wisconsin, Madison, November 1971.

BICK, R. Personal communication. December 1971.

BORKOVEC, T. and CRAIGHEAD, W. The comparison of two methods of assessing fear and avoidance behavior. *Behavior Research and Therapy,* 1971, *9,* 285–291.

BOSTOW, D. E., and BAILEY, J. B. Modification of severe disruptive and aggressive behavior using brief time-out and reinforcement procedures. *Journal of Applied Behavior Analysis,* 1969, *2,* 31–37.

BRADY, J. Metronome conditioned speech retraining for stuttering. *Behavior Therapy,* 1971, *2,* 129–150.

BRADY, J., and LIND, D. Experimental analysis of hysterical blindness. *Archives of General Psychiatry,* 1961, *4,* 331–339.

BRADY, J. Studies on the metronome effect on stuttering. *Behavior Research and Therapy,* 1969, *7,* 197–204.

BRIERLY, J. The treatment of hysterical spasmodic torticollis by behavior therapy. *Behavior Research and Therapy,* 1967, *5,* 139–142.

BUCHER, B. A pocket-portable shock device with application to nail biting. *Behavior Research and Therapy,* 1968, *6,* 389–392.

BUCHER, B., and FABRICATORE, J. Use of patient-administered shock to suppress hallucinations. *Behavior Therapy,* 1970, *1,* 383–385.

BUCHER, B., and KING, L. Generalization of punishment effects in the deviant behavior of a psychotic child. *Behavior Therapy,* 1971, *2,* 68–77.

BUCHER, B., and LOVAAS, I. Use of aversive stimulation in behavior modification. In Jones (Ed.), *Miami Symposium on the Predication of Behavior, 1967: Aversive Stimulation.* Coral Gables, Florida: University of Miami Press, 1968.

BURKE, B. Reduced auditory feedback and stuttering. *Behavior Research and Therapy,* 1969, *7,* 303–308.

BURNS, J. M., and ASCOUGH, J. C. A psychophysiological comparison of two approaches to relaxation and anxiety induction. *Behavior Therapy,* 1971, *2,* 170–176.

BUTTERFIELD, W. A further examination of the learning behavior of a group of near-mute schizophrenics. (Ph.D. dissertation, University of Michigan.) Ann Arbor, Michigan: University Microfilms, 1970.

BUTTERFIELD, W., THOMAS, E., and SOBERG, R. A device for simultaneous feedback of verbal signal data. *Behavior Therapy,* 1970, *1,* 395–401.

CLEARY, A., and PACKHAM, A. A touch detecting teaching machine with auditory reinforcement. *Journal of Applied Behavior Analysis,* 1968, *1,* 341–345.

CLEELAND, C. Conditioning and dystonias. Paper presented at Conference on New Applications of Conditioning to Medical Practice, University of Wisconsin, Madison, November 1971.

COLEMAN, R. A conditioning technique applicable to elementary school classrooms. *Journal of Applied Behavior Analysis,* 1970, *3,* 293–297.

COOK, C., and ADAMS, H. Modification of verbal behavior in speech deficient children. *Behavior Research and Therapy,* 1966, *4,* 265–271.

Corte, H., Wolfe, M., and Locke, B. A comparison of procedures for eliminating self-injurious behavior in retarded adolescents. *Journal of Applied Behavior Analysis*, 1971, *4*, 201–213.

Crosby, N. Essential enuresis: Successful treatment based on physiological concepts. *Medical Journal of Australia*, 1950, *2*, 533–543.

Daly, D., and Cooper, E. Rate of stuttering adaptation under two electroshock conditions. *Behavior Research and Therapy*, 1967, *5*, 49–54.

Daly, D., and Frick, J. The effect of punishing stuttering expectations and stuttering utterances: A comparative study. *Behavior Therapy*, 1970, *1*, 228–239.

Donner, L., and Gurney, B. Automated group desensitization for test anxiety. *Behavior Research and Therapy*, 1969, *7*, 1–13.

Doran, J., and Holland, J. Eye movement as a function of response contingencies. *Journal of Applied Behavior Analysis*, 1971, *4*, 12.

Doyle, O. Isolation transformer—friend or foe? *Electronics*, 1971, *44*, 73–74.

Engel, B. Conditioned modification of cardiac arrhythmias. Paper presented at Conference on New Applications of Conditioning to Medical Practice. University of Wisconsin, Madison, November 1971.

Feldman, M. Aversion therapy for sexual deviation: A critical review. *Psychological Bulletin*, 1966, *65*, 65–79.

Feldman, M., and MacCulloch, M. The application of anticipatory avoidance learning to the treatment of homosexuality in theory, technique and preliminary results. *Behavior Research and Therapy*, 1965, *2*, 165–183.

Forster, F. Conditioning treatment of epilepsy. Paper presented at the Conference on New Applications of Conditioning to Medical Practice, University of Wisconsin, Madison, November 1971.

Franks, C., Fried, R., and Ashem, A. An improved apparatus for the aversive conditioning of cigarette smokers. *Behavior Research and Therapy*, 1966, *4*, 301–308.

French, H. Medical electronic equipment and hospital safety. *Popular Electronics Including Electronics World*, January 1972, *33*.

Freund, K. A note on the use of the phallometric method of measuring mild sexual arousal in the male. *Behavior Therapy*, 1971, *2*, 223–228.

Gale, A. "Stimulus Hunger." Individual differences in operant strategy in a button pressing task. *Behavior Research and Therapy*, 1969, *7*, 265–274.

Goldman, J. A look at human measurements in industry. In Salter, (Ed.), *Interdisciplinary clinic on the instrumentation requirements for psychological research*. New York: Fier, 1961.

Greene, R. J., and Hoats, D. L. Reinforcing capabilities of television distortion. *Journal of Applied Behavior Analysis*, 1969, *2*, 139–141.

Grimaldi, K., and Lichtenstein, E. Hot smoky air as an aversive stimulus in the treatment of smoking. *Behavior Research and Therapy*, 1969, *7*, 275–282.

Haring, M. Equipment listings with examples of application. University of Washington: Experimental Education Unit (mimeo), 1968.

Heck, E. A description of some learning characteristics of minimally brain damaged children. (Ph.D. dissertation, University of Michigan.) Ann Arbor, Michigan: University Microfilm, 1969.

Hefferline, R., Keenan, B., Harford, R., and Birch, J. Electronics in Psychology. *Columbia Engineering Quarterly*, March 1960.

Hensen, D. E., and Rubin, H. D. Voluntary control of eroticism. *Journal of Applied Behavior Analysis*, 1971, *4*, 37–44.

Hewett, F. *The Emotionally Disturbed Child in the Classroom*. Boston: Allyn and Bacon, Inc., 1968.

JONES, H. G. (1967) As cited in Kanfer, F., and Phillips, J. *Learning Foundations of Behavior Therapy.* New York: John Wiley, 1970, 345–346.

KELLMAN, A. M. Shoplifting treated by aversion to film. *Behavior Research and Therapy,* 1969, *7,* 125–127.

KENNEDY, W., and FOREYT, J. Treatment of overweight by aversion therapy. *Behavior Research and Therapy,* 1971, *3,* 29–34.

KOHLENBERG, R. J. The punishment of persistent vomiting: A case study. *Journal of Applied Behavior Analysis,* 1970, *3,* 241–245.

KRAPFL, J., PETER, B., and NAWAS, M. Uses of the bug-in-the-ear in the modification of parents' behavior. In R. Rubin and C. Franks (Eds.), *Advances in Behavior Therapy.* New York: Academic Press, 1969.

LADER, M., and MATHEWS, A. Comparison of methods of relaxation in using physiological measures. *Behavior Research and Therapy,* 1970, *8,* 331–337.

LANG, P., and MELAMED, B. Avoidance conditioning therapy of an infant with chronic ruminative vomiting. *Journal of Abnormal Psychology,* 1969, *74,* 1–8.

LAWS, D. R., and RUBIN, J. B. Instructional control of an autonomic sexual response. *Journal of Applied Behavior Analysis,* 1969, *2,* 93–99.

LEBOW, M., GELFAND, S., and DOBSON, W. Aversive conditioning of a phenothiazine induced respiratory stridor. *Behavior Therapy,* 1970, *1,* 222–227.

LEVIS, D. The phobic test apparatus. An objective measure of human avoidance behavior to small objects. *Behavior Research and Therapy,* 1969, *7,* 309–315.

LINDSLEY, O. Characteristics of the behavior of chronic psychotics as revealed by free-operant conditioning methods. *Diseases of the Nervous System* (monograph supplement), 1960, *21,* 1–13.

LINDSLEY, O. A reliable wrist counter for recording behavior rates. *Journal of Applied Behavior Analysis,* 1969, *1,* 77–78.

LIVERSEDGE, L. A., and SYLVESTER, J. Conditioning techniques in the treatment of writer's cramp. *Lancet,* June 1955, 1147–1149.

LIPPOLD, O. Electromyography. In P. H. Venables and I. Martin (Eds.), *A Manual of Psychophysiological Methods.* New York: Wiley, 1967.

LOMONT, J., and BROCK, L. Cognitive factors in systematic desensitization. *Behavior Research and Therapy,* 1971, *9,* 187–195.

LOMONT, J., and EDWARDS, J. The role of relaxation in systematic desensitization. *Behavior Research and Therapy,* 1967, *5,* 11–25.

LOVAAS, O. I., SCHAFFER, B., and SIMMONS, J. Q. Experimental studies in childhood schizophrenia: Building social behaviors in autistic children by use of electric shock. *Journal of Experimental Research Personnel,* 1965, *1,* 99–109.

LOVAAS, O. I., and SIMMONS, J. Q. Manipulations of self-destruction in three retarded children. *Journal of Applied Behavior Analysis,* 1969, *2,* 143–157.

LOVIBOND, S. H. *Conditioning and Enuresis.* New York: Macmillan Company, 1964.

LOVIBOND, S., and CADDY, G. Discriminated aversive control in the moderation of alcoholics' drinking behavior. *Behavior Therapy,* 1970, *1,* 437–444.

LOVITT, T. Relationships of sequential simultaneous preference as assessed by conjugate reinforcement. *Behavior Research and Therapy,* 1968, *6,* 77–83.

MADSEN, C., HOFFMAN, M., THOMAS, D., and KORPZAK, E. Comparisons of toilet training techniques. In D. M. Gelfand (Ed.), *Social Learning in Childhood.* Monterey, Calif.: Brooks-Cole, 1969.

MATTOS, R. A manual counter for recording multiple behavior. *Journal of Applied Behavior Analysis,* 1968, *1,* 130.

MAY, A., and HACKWOOD, A. Some effects of masking and eliminating low frequency feedback on the speech of stammerers. *Behavior Research and Therapy,* 1968, *6,* 219–224.

McCLINTOCK, C. Instrumentation in social psychology. *American Psychologist*, 1969, *24*, 219–224.

McCONAGHY, N. Penile response conditioning and its relationship to aversion therapy in homosexuals. *Behavior Therapy*, 1970, *1*, 213–221.

McCONAGHY, N. Penile volume change to moving pictures of male and female nudes in heterosexual and homosexual males. *Behavior Research and Therapy*, 1967, *5*, 43–48.

McGLYNN, F. Individual vs. standardized hierarchies in the systematic desensitization of snake avoidance. *Behavior Research and Therapy*, 1971, *9*, 1–5.

McGUIRE, R., and VALLANCE, M. Aversion therapy by electric shock: A simple technique. *British Medical Journal*, 1964, *1*, 151–153.

MEES, H. Sadistic fantasies modified by aversive conditioning and substitution: A case study. *Behavior Research and Therapy*, 1966, *4*, 317–320.

MEYER, V., and CRISP, A. Aversion therapy in two cases of obesity. *Behavior Research and Therapy*, 1964, *2*, 143–147.

MILLARD, D. A conditioning treatment for giggle micturition. *Behavior Research and Therapy*, 1966, *4*, 229–231.

MILLER, H., and NAWAS, M. Control of aversive stimulus termination in systematic desensitization. *Behavior Research and Therapy*, 1970, *9*, 57–61.

MILLS, K., SOBELL, M., and SCHAEFER, J. Training social drinking as an alternative to abstinence for alcoholics. *Behavior Therapy*, 1971, *2*, 18–27.

NATHAN, P. Influence of stimulus preference and feedback delay on extinction of operant communication behavior. *Behavior Research and Therapy*, 1966, *4*, 53–58.

NEIL, D., and HOWELL, R. Three modes of hierarchy presentation in systematic desensitization therapy. *Behavior Research and Therapy*, 1969, *7*, 289–294.

NEWTON, D., and BUCZEK, W. Low-cost stereo recorders can adapt to digital data. *Electronics*, 1970, *43*, (14), 90–93.

O'BRIEN, F., and AZRIN, N. H. Behavior engineering: Control of posture by informational feedback. *Journal of Applied Behavior Analysis*, 1970, *3*, 235–240.

PAUL, G. Inhibition of physiological response to stressful imagery by relaxation training and hypnotically suggested relaxation. *Behavior Research and Therapy*, 1969, *7*, 249–256.

PAUL, G., and TRIMBLE, R. Recorded vs. "live" relaxation training and hypnotic suggestion: Comparative effectiveness for reducing physiological arousal and inhibiting stress response. *Behavior Therapy*, 1970, *1*, 285–302.

PETERSON, R., WRIGHT, R., and HANLON, C. The effects of extending the CS-UCS interval on the effectiveness of the conditioning for nocturnal enuresi *Behavior Research and Therapy*, 1969, *7*, 351–358.

Popular Electronics Including Electronics World. How much current is fatal? January 1972, *1*, 31.

POWELL, J., and AZRIN, N. The effects of shock as a punisher for cigarette smoking. *Journal of Applied Behavior Analysis*, 1968, *1*, 64.

RACHMAN, S., and TEASDALE, J. *Aversion Therapy and Behavior Disorders: An Analysis*. Miami: University of Miami Press, 1969.

REYNOLDS, B., and ADAMS, J. A. Motor performance as a function of click reinforcement. *Journal of Experimental Psychology*, 1953, *45*, 315–320.

RIMM, D., DEGROOT, J., BOORD, P., HEIMAN, J., and DILLOW, P. Systematic desensitization of an anger response. *Behavior Research and Therapy*, 1971, *9*, 273–280.

RIMON, R., STEINBACK, A., and HUHMAR, E. Electromyographic findings in depressive patients. *Journal of Psychosomatic Research*, 1966, *10*, 159–170.

RISLEY, R. The effect and side effects of punishing the autistic behaviors of a deviant child. *Journal of Applied Behavior Analysis*, 1968, *1*, 22–25.

ROYER, F., FLYNN, W., and OSADCA, B. Case history: Aversion therapy for fire setting by a deteriorated schizophrenic. *Behavior Therapy*, 1971, *2*, 229–232.

RUBENSTEIN, L. Electro-acoustical measurement of vocal responses to limited stress. *Behavior Research and Therapy*, 1966, *4*, 135–138.

SANDERS, R. M., HOPKINS, G. L., and WALKER, M. B. An inexpensive method for making data records of complex behaviors. *Journal of Applied Behavior Analysis*, 1969, *2*, 221–222.

SCHMIDT, G., and ULRICH, R. Effects of group contingent events upon classroom noise. *Journal of Applied Behavior Analysis*, 1969, *2*, 171–179.

SCHMITT, D., and MARWELL, G. Talking and the disruption of cooperation. *Journal of Applied Behavior Analysis*, 1971, *15*, 405–412.

SCHULMAN, J., and REISMAN, J. An objective measurement of hyperactivity. *American Journal of Mental Deficiency*, 1959, *64*, 455–456.

SCHWITZGEBEL, R. Behavior instrumentation and social technology. *American Psychologist*, 1970, *25*, 491–499.

SCHWITZGEBEL, R. Ethical and legal aspects of behavioral instrumentation. *Behavior Therapy*, 1970, *1*, 498–509.

SCHWITZGEBEL, R. A survey of electromechanical devices for behavior modification. *Psychological Bulletin*, 1968, *70*, 444–459.

SOLYOM, L., and MILLER, S. A differential conditioning procedure as the initial phase of the behavior therapy of homosexuality. *Behavior Research and Therapy*, 1965, *3*, 47–60.

STARK, C. Quieter tape. *Stereo Review*, 1972, *28*, (3), 65–68.

STARKWEATHER, J. A. A speech rate meter for vocal behavior analysis. *Journal of Experimental Analysis and Behavior*, 1960, *3*, 111–114.

STRONG, P. *Biophysical Measurements*. Beaverton, Oregon: Tektronix, Inc., 1970.

STUART, R. B. A cueing device for acceleration of the rate of positive behavior. *Journal of Applied Behavior Analysis*, 1970, *3*, 257–260.

STUMPHAUZER, J. A low cost "bug-in-the-ear" sound system for the modification of therapist, parent and patient behavior. *Behavior Therapy*, 1971, *2*, 249–250.

STOYUA, J. Personal communication. November 1971.

SUNDEL, M. Modification of two operants (verbal and nonverbal) of near-mute schizophrenics using imitation and modeling procedures. (Ph.D. dissertation, University of Michigan.) Ann Arbor, Mich.: University microfilms, 1968.

SURRATT, P. R., ULRICH, R. E., and HAWKINS, R. P. An elementary student as a behavior engineer. *Journal of Applied Behavior Analysis*, 1969, *2*, 85–92.

TANENBAUM, H., and KISER, W. Transurethral phonocatheter recording of the renal arterial pulse. *Circulation*, 1964, *29*.

TATE, B. G., and BAROFF, G. Aversive control of self-injurious behavior in a psychotic boy. *Behavior Research and Therapy*, 1966, *4*, 281–287.

THOMAS, E., CARTER, R., GAMBRILL, E., and BUTTERFIELD, W. A signal system for the assessment and modification of behavior (SAM). *Behavior Therapy*, 1970, *1*, 252–259.

THORPE, J., SCHMIDT, E., BROWN, P., and CASTELL, D. Aversion-relief therapy: A new method for general application. *Behavior Research and Therapy*, 1964, *2*, 71–82.

THORPE, J., SCHMIDT, E., and CASTELL, D. A comparison of positive and negative (aversive) conditioning in the treatment of homosexuality. *Behavior Research and Therapy*, 1963, *1*, 357–362.

TURNER, R., YOUNG, G., and RACHMAN, S. Treatment of nocturnal enuresis by conditioning techniques. *Behavior Research and Therapy*, 1970, *8*, 367–382.

VACHON, L. Feedback modification of respiratory resistance. Paper presented at Conference on New Applications of Conditioning to Medical Practice, University of Wisconsin, Madison, November 1971.

VAN WAGEN, R., MEYERSON, L., KORR, N., and MAHONEY, K. Field trials of a new procedure for toilet training. *Journal of Experimental Child Psychology*, 1969, *8*, 147–159.

VAN WAGEN, R., and MURDOCK, E. A transistorized signal package for toilet training in infants. *Journal of Experimental Child Psychology*, 1966, *3*, 312–314.

VODDE, T. and GILNER, F. H. The effects of exposure to fear stimuli on fear reduction. *Behavior Research and Therapy*, 1971, *9*, 169–175.

VOGEL-SPROTT, M., and RACINSKAS, J. Suppression and recovery of a response in humans as a function of reward and punishment. *Behavior Research and Therapy*, 1969, *7*, 223–231.

WALLACE, J., BROWN, J., LEWIS, D., and DEITZ, W. Intercardiac acoustics. *Journal of the Acoustical Society of America*, 1959, *31*, 712–723.

WEISS, J. Effects of coping behavior in different warning signal conditions on stress pathology in rats. *Journal of Comparative and Physiological Psychology*, 1971, *77*, 1–30.

WHITE, J. C., and TAYLOR, D. Noxious conditioning as a treatment for rumination. *Mental Retardation*, 1967, *5*, 30–33.

WILSON, F., and WALTERS, R. Modification of speech output of near-mute schizophrenics through social learning procedures. *Behavior Research and Therapy*, 1966, *4*, 119–134.

WOLPE, J. Conditioned inhibition of craving in drug addiction: A pilot experiment. *Behavior Research and Therapy*, 1965, *2*, 285–288.

WOLPE, J. *The Practice of Behavior Therapy*. New York: Pergamon Press, 1969.

ZIMMERMAN, J. Visual performance of a functionally blind person. *Behavior Research and Therapy*, 1966, *4*, 119–134.

Name Index

Subject Index